Mexico, NAFTA and the Hardships of Progress

ALSO BY RICHARD KROOTH

with Minoo Moallem

The Middle East: A Geopolitical Study
of the Region in the New Global Era
(McFarland, 1995)

with Boris Vladimirovitz

Quest for Freedom: The Transformation
of Eastern Europe in the 1990s
(McFarland, 1993)

with Hiroshi Fukurai

Common Destiny: Japan and
the United States in the Global Age
(McFarland, 1990)

Mexico, NAFTA and the Hardships of Progress

Historical Patterns and Shifting Methods of Oppression

by RICHARD KROOTH

McFarland & Company, Inc., Publishers
Jefferson, North Carolina, and London

FRANKLIN PIERCE
COLLEGE LIBRARY
RINDGE, N.H. 03461

British Library Cataloguing-in-Publication data are available

Library of Congress Cataloguing-in-Publication Data

Krooth, Richard.
    Mexico, NAFTA and the hardships of progress : historical patterns
and shifting methods of oppression / by Richard Krooth.
      p. cm.
    Includes bibliographical references and index.
    ISBN 0-7864-0097-8 (lib. bdg. : 50# alk. paper)
    1. Mexico—Economic conditions. 2. Mexico—Economic policy.
3. Mexico—Politics and government—1810– 4. Mexico—Commerce.
5. Free trade—North America. I. Title.
HC133.K76 1995
972.08—dc20   95-18733
                                                            CIP

©1995 Richard Krooth. All rights reserved

Manufactured in the United States of America

McFarland & Company, Inc., Publishers
Box 611, Jefferson, North Carolina 28640

Contents

Preface

This study takes a long view of Mexico's history and social struggles rooted in past patterns and contemporary events that together impart alternative paths to the nation's future.

Depredations imposed on New Spain for Iberian prestige and greed set the frame for the nationalist war of reform that made Mexico independent. Even then, ever-renewed efforts by imperial powers to dominate Mexico openly or through indigenous compradors pushed the country towards a popular revolution promising land and freedom. In the two decades following this revolution, however, foreign interests again compromised the nation's independence.

Falling far short of universal land redistribution, Mexico's unsteady return to old ways of subsistence agriculture and degrees of tenant peonage (1910–33) again changed course under the Cárdenas government (1934–40), which financed advanced technologies and enlarged cooperative production focused on national markets. But despite nationalization of foreign petroleum interests and domestic industrial reform, Cárdenas was forced to compromise Mexico's economic independence in the face of the oil cartel's death-hold over markets and Mexico's essential imports of oil drilling and industrial equipment.

During the post–Cárdenas era, the status quo ante was momentarily reestablished over domestic production and social relations. After 1945, however, a decided shift from the old status quo was promoted by a new government's policy stressing "progress" on four fronts: urban hegemony, enrichment of the national oligarchy, appeasement of foreign interests, and reconquest of the agrarian domain by deploying proletarianized laborers for mass production. In these zones of domination, changes consuming a half century were followed by a purported "new order" of democracy that in fact was imposed by the continuous rule of the dominant Institutional Revolutionary party (PRI), which was led by only a few.

And though the PRI sought to build and expand a North American commercial and investment sphere, the new order would probably leave Mexico's millions more impoverished and degraded than ever, the

vii

anguish of their present ensuring future transformations, peaceful or otherwise.

These historic patterns are the focus of this narrative study, which attempts to unscramble the traditional periodization of Mexico's evolution by synthesizing its essential meaning and revealing the processes involved. Conflict, irredentist struggles, revolution, reform, progress, and developments are thus presented in terms of the underlying forces that set them in motion. Rejecting the traditional approach of a comprehensive trajectory of date-lined Mexican sociopolitical events, I have attempted to view the significance of such phenomena as part of a moving picture positing emerging possibilities, some of which have come to pass by the negation of others. And from these retrospective judgments, I have also posited the future in terms of possible alternative courses instead of picking a one-dimensional, mechanistic, and deterministic pathway. Although the actors in this Mexican drama are thus seen as initially confined by inherited social institutions and structures, some among them are forever breaking the bonds that tie— interacting for better or worse, for evil or good, for themselves or others.

Obviously, to make such an analysis requires an interdisciplinary approach.

Through academic research, discussions with knowledgeable colleagues, travels to the scene of events, observations, and interviews, I have attempted to uncover the logic of past and present imperial designs on Mexico, the limits inhering in the quest for independence from foreign powers, the path of accumulation by Mexico's elite at the expense of indigenous peoples, the strivings for revolution, and the ways in which basic changes have been blocked, undermined, or redirected.

I have also attempted to uncover the mechanisms creating Mexico's landed elite and commercial classes that are rooted in backward ways, the pauperization and immiserization of Mexico's great majority, and the emergence of the dictatorship of the Institutional Revolutionary party (PRI) and its ideological concept and inequitable practice of "progress." I have documented the resulting waste of human energy and fiber that continued over more than fifty years, as the PRI timelessly froze the nation's multitudes in penury and degradation. And in my research, I have discovered the arrogance, hubris, and pomposity that mark the efforts of the PRI leaders to secure the position of the nation's elite and its entourage of upwardly mobile middle classes. It is not merely their unjust selling of Mexican labor and resources below their essential value that stirs popular outrage; their shrill propaganda creates false hopes that free trade and an open door to the United States will lift the nation's common people and do them no harm.

Thus I pursued a deeper investigation, attempting to create a systematic sense of connection and continuity between the past, present, and future of Mexico, as well as between Mexico and the United States, Canada, and Europe.

I reasoned that if the precepts of empire have helped institutionalize the extraction of wealth from Mexico, then the liberation that was supposed to promote land redistribution and democracy but was blocked by a national elite, empowered the Mexican oligarchy to impoverish the nation by extracting wealth for itself. In fact, this systemic extraction was institutionalized over more than seven decades, was only temporarily interrupted by the Cárdenas administration, and then was set powerfully against civil society. Oppressive relations of servitude and impoverishment were thus established for well over half the population—conditions which only today are finally being questioned and restructured by communities taking matters into their own hands.

Following this logic and engaging in cooperative work and discussions with others, I developed a working outline of the emerging sociopolitical patterns encompassing the nations of North America and framed the study with essential materials that point to the contours of political economy that make the account a story of best fit, all in an attempt to know the truth and tendencies that have emerged and might shape the future. Some parts of the study thus review essential historical information, other parts concentrate on ideological questions, still others emphasize socioeconomic factors or momentary events that are linked to both the past and a possible North American future conjectured by extrapolating from the known.

Given the broad subject matter, my presentation, analysis, and conclusions will undoubtedly be scrutinized by both Mexican experts and historical determinists. I believe there is no greater reward than a difference of views entering the arena of debate concerning the present struggle for Mexican resources, trade, investments, independence, democracy, and a fair redistribution of the nation's skewed allotment of wealth and power.

In presenting these facts, patterns, and conclusions, of necessity I have relied on the good work of others. A project such as this involves the enterprise, cooperation, assistance, and expertise of many institutions, agencies, and people to bring it to a successful conclusion, and I wish to recognize these contributions.

I gathered information from a variety of queries, discussions, interviews, speeches, press releases, public statements, negotiating documents, reports and publications of many nations, institutions, government agencies, groups, and individuals. The following is a brief list of important sources drawn from Mexico, the United States, Canada, and Western Europe. In the case of authors and reports, citations are listed in the bibliography.

Emphasizing a sociohistorical perspective, I have relied on the empirical methodologies used by my teachers of three decades: University of Wisconsin history professors William Appleman Williams and Harvey Goldberg, both now deceased; Hans H. Gerth, who before his death was professor emeritus in the Sociology Department at the University of Wisconsin; legal and history professor Willard Hirst of the University of Wisconsin Law School; and former Atlanta University political-economics professor W. E. Gordon, a specialist on colonial systems in the Carribean and the Americas.

I have also drawn on the theoretical approaches of my former professors Richard Flacks and Richard Applebaum in the Sociology Department at the University of California, Santa Barbara, and Professor William J. Chambliss in the Sociology Department at George Washington University.

To still others, I am indebted for economic, sociological, and political approaches used by my colleagues Dr. Robert Girling in the Management and Economic Department at Sonoma State University; Professor Sherry Keith of Interdisciplinary Studies at San Francisco State University; Dr. Hiroshi Fukurai of the Board of Studies at the University of California, Santa Cruz; and Professor Paul Stevenson in the Sociology Department at the University of Winnipeg.

For corroboration and exemplary research data, reliance was placed on the Center for U.S.-Mexican Studies at the University of California, San Diego; the Mexican Data Base Project at the University of California, Riverside; the Agriculture and Resource Economics Department headed by Professor Alain de Janvry at the University of California, Berkeley; Emory University professor Robert A. Pastor, President Jimmy Carter's expert adviser on Latin America and the Caribbean.

There were some limits, of course. Given the uncertainties of Mexican census figures, my findings could not rely solely on tortured statistical sources. Nonetheless, the Mexican Data Base Project at the University of California, Riverside, has done a magnificent job of making sense of census sources, and the *Atlas of Mexico* by James B. Pick, Edgar W. Butler, and Elizabeth L. Lanzer is one of the best sources available, one to which I am deeply indebted.

Nor was it possible to rely on Mexico's political parties for an accurate portrayal of the nation's situation, historical or otherwise. Generous aid was offered by successive secretary generals of the PRI, presidential candidates Luis Donaldo Colosio Murrieta and José Francisco Ruiz Massieu. The far-right-wing "dinosaurs" of the party thought both men were jeopardizing social peace by accommodating the reformers' "too-liberal" policies; both were murdered in crimes followed by traditional Mexican political cover-ups.

Those outside the circle of political power in the Democratic Revolutionary party (led by Cuauhtémoc Cárdenas) and the National Action party (led by Diego Fernández de Ceballos) were at best only of modest help; functionaries in both parties were engrossed more in polemics than in giving a factual rendition or synthesis of events. The same was true of the half dozen parties at the extreme left and right of the spectrum, though press reports of the Zapatistas in Chiapas reveal a clearer analysis of Mexican political economy and a program for reform.

For historical information, I drew on the works of dozens of historians and contemporary writers, the most important being Lucas Alámán, David Barkin, Jan Bazant, Barry Carr, Arnaldo Córdova, Lorenzo de Zavala, Blanche B. De Vore, the Earl of Cromer, Edwin Emerson, Jr., Hector Galan, Lewis Hanke, José E. Iturriaga, W.E.H. Lecky, Soledad Loaeza, Nora Lustig, David Mares, Captain Francis McCullagh, Martin Needler, Christina Pacheco, Robert A. Pastor, Raul Alcides Reissner, Steven E. Sanderson, Harley Shaiken, Justo Sierra, Frank Tannenbaum, William Cameron Townsend, Jacob Viner, and Nathaniel and Sylvia Weyl.

For socioeconomic data, I reviewed information from the following Mexican sources: Banco Nacional de Comercio Exterior; the Benjamin Franklin Library in Mexico City, Centuria de Lucha Populares, Universidad Automa Chapingo, Oficina de Asesores de Presidente, Instituto Nacional de Antropología e Historia, Mexican DGEA, Organa de Difusión del Instituto Nacional Indigenista, Museo Nacional de Antropología, Secretaría de Programación y Presupuesto, and the Mexican SINE-SAM. Other sources used include the Economist Intelligence Unit, the Institute of International Studies at the University of Minnesota, the International Monetary Fund, the National Science Foundation, the North American Congress on Latin America, the U.C.L.A. Latin American Center, the U.S. Information Agency, and the Wisconsin Historical Society.

For United States, Mexican, Canadian, and European angles of vision, I reviewed public information and unofficial studies published by *The Economist* (London), the *Financial Times* (London), *Le Monde*, the *Los Angeles Times*, the *New York Times*, Reuters, the *San Francisco Chronicle*, the *Wall Street Journal*, the *Washington Post*, and UPI. Other sources include American University (Washington, D.C.); the Brookings Institution (Washington, D.C.); the Heritage Foundation (Washington, D.C.); the Hoover Institute, Stanford University (Palo Alto, California); Johns Hopkins University, Paul H. Nitze School of Advanced International Studies (Washington, D.C.); KQED in San Francisco; the "McNeil-Lehrer NewsHour"; the National Geographic Society: Library and News Collection, Records Library, Translations Division, Pre-Press Division, and

Maps and Reports (Washington, D.C.); the Woodrow Wilson International Center for Scholars; and the Center for Strategic and International Studies.

Insightful comments, support, encouragement and assistance were offered by social scientist Lester A. Radke, oral historian Ann Baxandall Krooth, and Emeritus Professor Charles Chakerian of Yale and Dr. Lixing Chen, who works with the United Nations on urban studies; the latter two scholars were both research associates in the Sociology Department at the University of California, Berkeley, during 1990–93.

Adjunct professors Garth R. Ashby and Norman Jan Budman of Golden Gate University also offered constructive criticism on many propositions included in this study, as did the following Golden Gate University doctoral and graduate students: Chayadi Anggrelian, Steve L. Black, Alejandra Carrau, Sandra L. Cruze, Fernando de la Torre, James B. Gustat, Adrea Harris, Syed Hassan, Alison L. Hazen, Peter E. Johnson, Nazreen Kadir, George Ming-Hong Lai, Chi-Lin Lee, Victor M. Nondabula, Godwin E. Ona, Jitka Roos, Sigrid M. Schafmann, John Eber Thomas, James E. White, and Chairat Wongjindanon.

Critiques were also made by R. Jason Holmes, Mercedes Gonzálas, Manuel Hernádez, H.R. Gonzáles, and Michael Escobar.

Credits for technical help are due Marge Sauder and other office staff in the Sociology Department at the University of California, Riverside. I also thank the University of California for facilitation and accommodations while the author was a research associate in the Sociology Department at the University of California, Berkeley.

Finally, I greatly appreciate the support, editorial assistance, and suggestions of Karl William Krooth of the University of California, Berkeley, and, of course, McFarland & Company, Inc., Publishers.

With the aid offered by these institutions, scholars, colleagues, and critics, I have attempted to present an historical overview of the search for land redistribution, full employment, social reorganization, equity, and ultimately peace in Mexico. So, needless to say, I alone am accountable for the contents, the facts presented, and the conclusions in this book.

RICHARD KROOTH
Berkeley, California
October 31, 1994

Night
   Not yet over,

Renewed spirits
   Awaken the dawn

Introduction

Just as the West in the nineteenth century was an idealized notion of a way of life and not a circumscribed regional location, so too in our century the idea of progress holds sway in no particular frame or limited geographic realm, but rather depicts a way of life that historically has transfixed both production and social relationships.

Progress has become a mode for powerful nation-states to shape their domestic efforts to resolve material crises and social conundrums—often by shifting their burdens to others and undermining traditional communities, their cultures, and their mores.

The idea of progress is itself a metaphor of a utopian path to improved material well-being. Those seeking economic progress, however, have often blindly focused on accumulation for the wealthy, while neglecting the impoverished millions.

TORMENT AND RESOLUTION

As an ideological belief, progress is prompted by domestic pressures and outside forces. It has become prominent most recently in the socio-political realm by the collapse of bureaucratic centralism in the former Soviet Union and Eastern Europe, which has opened the door to Western pressure to create regimes based on liberal democracy and commercial statism. As a standard of hope, its spatial sway has similarly enlarged with the spread of poverty and desperation in Africa, Latin America, and the Middle East, India, and the unindustrialized nations of Asia.

Progress in thought and policy has also become the glorified byword for the competitive global struggle for markets and trade zones. It is seen as a path to offset the perennial accumulation crises facing leading nation-states; as a way station for reorganizing national economies to shore up deficits in production, budgets, and trade balances; and as a means to shift capital, production, employment, markets, and losses to other nations in order to make them both a shock absorber and a launching pad from which to regenerate flagging accumulation.

The new pressures of progress imposed on Third World nations have led to rural depopulation, urbanization, restructured industry, new low-wage work, controlled inflation, stabilized currencies, and Western-style "democracy." These have bred open economies, opportunities for foreign investment and trade, privatization of state industries and assets, renegotiation of debt with international lending agencies, displacement of government workers by reduced state payrolls, loss of salaried jobs as privatized companies slash work places, and the extension of unemployment, income inequality, poverty, misery, and social unrest.

From internal crises and disaccumulation within leading nations, then, there have emerged foreign policies that promote progress abroad in a search for transnational solutions to domestic malaise, but thereby create the conditions for conflict abroad.

PROGRESS, TARGETS, AND TRADE BLOCS

It is no surprise, then, that in North America the United States is again focusing its own policies for progress beyond its borders, attempting to mobilize resources, to transform the economies and governments of other nations, and to link their mercantile or industrial policies to Washington's. Immediate rewards are offered to the rich of these nations, and jobs and other benefits under new conditions will supposedly trickle down over future decades, raising the living standards of their middle classes and the poor.

Mexico and the rest of the Americas are among the target states selected by the United States and other leading industrial powers to march this path of progress. They are to fulfill the West's desire for exclusive markets, a shared sphere for investments, and access to low-cost labor for manufacturing, material extraction, and temperate, tropical, and semi-tropical agriculture. Extending their domestic economic domain, these industrial nations have assiduously moved to build trade zones, common markets, neomercantile spheres, and other variations of tight-knit commercial blocs similar to those designed in decades past.

The latest spheres are actually expressions of a common malaise involving domestic production of goods that cannot be sold at a profit, uncompetitiveness and the resulting crisis of national accumulation, the inadequacy of new investment in the latest technologies for production, rising unemployment, government fiscal deficits, and trade imbalances. To alleviate these crises in the 1980s and early 1990s, the regionalization of "international" trade—essentially a form of neomercantilism—has been pursued and this tends to segregate global markets into exclusive trade blocs and investment spheres favoring member nations.

Although it is far too early for definitive consequences to emerge, so far these domestic crises have been temporarily "resolved" by pitting the yet-to-be-consolidated European Economic Community against the emergent strategic trade and investment sphere under Japanese influence in East Asia and the planned U.S. commercial sphere in the Americas. Like the spheres of its competitors, the U.S. sphere is being designed to create a member-restricted zone for preferential exchange and managed trade based on market allocations, quantitative quotas, and rules of output origin regardless of the source of capital invested in production.

In a sense, moreover, all three regionalized systems are emerging as strategically offensive and defensive spheres of influence that do not involve colonies or helotries in the classical imperial sense, but are based on distinctive characteristics of exclusive free-trade and investment zones.

As such economic regionalism is supported and limited by cultural differences, reinforcing geographic and ethnic awareness, each sphere will likely succeed only when it is rooted either in a common cultural experience or an inescapable economic symbiosis.

Questions are certain to be raised when one ponders if European culture, which stresses coordinate economic progress, and common strains of Western Christianity, which sustain an almost pious devotion to work and respect for authority, are not two of the main cornerstones of the European Community.

So, too, there are obvious questions whether the United States in the Americas or Japan in East Asia face irreconcilable strains in creating a common economic entity or zone of influence because their cultural beliefs and "civilizing" ways are unique and quite different from those of their neighbors.

There is little doubt that during the 1990s, largely in response to its internal crisis and the emergent European Economic Community and Japanese trading spheres, the United States has determinedly moved to create its own trade and investment bloc in the Americas. Since 1971, the United States has faced intensifying internal and external pressures to export manufactured wares and means of production on a grand scale. High-cost U.S. production yielded high-priced goods which were uncompetitive in both foreign and United States markets, leading to the export of U.S.-owned, guided, and controlled means of production and finance. Yet the American export of parts and machines to operate U.S.-owned factories did not suffice as a sufficient marketing device for surplus consumer goods still produced within the United States. For both these consumer goods and heavy industrial goods, domestic overproduction almost continuously eroded profit margins and built up lobbyist pressures to create an American trade zone.

It is hardly surprising, then, that the United States took initial steps to establish bilateral "free trade" agreements with Israel in 1985 and Canada in 1988. The Canadian-U.S. Free Trade Agreement (CUSFTA) envisioned a giant leap in mutually beneficial commerce—unrestricted regional trade and investments which would build upon the previous century of mutual exchange of investment capital and goods. Although CUSFTA might not immediately enlarge U.S.-Canadian investment or trade exchanges by much, future cooperative trade negotiations might overcome tariff restrictions on agricultural output, textiles, wearing apparel, and steel, with agreed-upon settlement procedures set to resolve conflicts over specific trade questions and rules of output origin.

Nonetheless, as both Canada and Israel had relatively small populations, supplying their needs could not alone provide adequate markets for the vast, perennial surplus of U.S. manufactured goods.

As high-cost U.S. overproduction, a lack of protected markets, failing investment opportunities, and unprofitability beset the American economy over the next six years (1985 to 1991), the restructuring of U.S. production went forward with an eye to establishing a free trade and investment zone linking Mexico, Canada, and the United States.

In the spring of 1991, under the proposed North American Free Trade Agreement (NAFTA), a massive export of U.S. capital equipment and other means of production was planned. The explicit goal was to stem the U.S. profit drain by establishing Yankee plants in Mexico to upgrade Mexican production technologies, thus creating a new sphere of influence and effectively acting as a barrier to multilateral trade.

MIND-SET, NAFTA, AND NEOMERCANTILISM

NAFTA envisions a managed investment and trade zone for members only—a species of neomercantilism in formation, yet to be concretized.

This means that earlier U.S. multilateral free-trade policies have been in part overthrown in favor of a customs union for preferential, bilateral trade.

Under NAFTA, United States, Canadian, Mexican, and other foreign capital will be allowed to move freely to the lowest-cost area for production within the preference zone, yet lower-cost commodity imports will be excluded from nonmember nations.

Past experiment and experience have proved the scheme is economically viable. For almost thirty years, the U.S.-Mexican *maquiladora* border investment program has been in operation. Its genesis lay in the U.S. need for profitable production facilities in a low-wage, unregulated domain. The resulting manufactured commodities were permitted to enter the United States tariff-free, which also sustained Mexico's need for dollar-earning exports by stimulating industrial production and fueling employment.

For Mexicans, this involved massive population migration and relocation near production centers, as well as extended factory dangers, unremitting pollution in expanding, squalid urban ghettoes, and inadequate finance for public infrastructure and facilities in education and health—failings that have led to illiteracy, epidemics, and shortened lives.

Even if such dismal conditions are partially alleviated under NAFTA, all will not be equal in the latest economic "World of Oz," for NAFTA's bilateral arrangements are designed to provide a western hemisphere trade advantage at the expense of excluded nations and organized labor in North America. Relocated U.S. production facilities, already profitably employing Mexican labor at one-tenth the U.S. wage scale, have deserted U.S. workers and left them without jobs, wages, or insurance.

Although jobs would stimulate Mexican imports in a consumer-oriented milieu, Mexico would hardly receive a fair or allocated share of NAFTA's rewards. Mexican-based production will require the massive import of the means to build infrastructure for technical manufacturing, as well as parts and resources, that will run up an unrepayable mercantile deficit. On top of this negative balance will be debts for the massive import of consumer and other goods made in the United States. And without the further inflow of U.S. investment capital as a positive offset balance, moreover, Mexico will be hard pressed to export enough to earn sufficient dollars to buy the necessary means of production.

Few have explained how Mexico could acquire manufacturing facilities to promote its own self-directed industrialization and also provide the required infrastructure for viable production, trade, and the welfare of its increasingly urbanized population. Only a few faint voices echoing the past have whispered the name of the emergent order—neomercantilism.

The new order will also impose its wrath, uprooting a population steeped in rural traditions. NAFTA promises to set off a huge demographic movement of Mexican labor towards foreign-owned factory and urban production zones. This transregional relocation of labor will place added pressure on Mexico's already frail infrastructure and its shortage of housing, fresh water, and sewage facilities and will threaten its environment. Penalties to regulate factory labor abuses or to enforce environmental standards will probably be imposed against individual companies, so that a costly central enforcement bureaucracy will be given authority to issue heavy citations under NAFTA. In practice, however, authoritative restrictions will probably be inadequate or partial at best; penalties will probably not be severe and will not involve trade sanctions that would undercut NAFTA's goals. Faced with massive violations, moreover, the brave army of enforcers will in all likelihood be unable to police the situation adequately and prevent extensive abuses.

The Mexican-based production process will meanwhile probably come full circle: the export of Mexican-produced commodities that promises to employ workers at low living standards is also expected to degrade the natural environment. The balance of trade may steadily improve, but at a heavy cost to human health, safety, and the natural world. In order to build a protective infrastructure which will offset pollution and provide public health facilities to sustain and rehabilitate the population, large state expenditures will be required. But the government clearly lacks these funds and can probably mobilize them only through new foreign loans. At interest rates of 40 percent or more, such foreign borrowing might "extend" Mexico's financial markets, but it would so encumber the state that within a decade Mexico could conceivably become a financial vassal—a clarion sign of neomercantilism reborn.

HALFWAY CRISIS

And what will happen to Mexico if NAFTA's trade and investment zone faces an extended crisis, flags, or fails halfway to consummation?

The Mexican Constitution has already been changed to eliminate thousands of *ejiditario* common lands, potentially sweeping 8 to 25 million people off the land for a one-time stipend raised by the state through bonds bought up largely by foreign investors expecting timely remission of service charges and principal.

A half-urbanized, landless, and unemployed population unable to grow its own food might by the time of a future crisis already have become dependent on those with industrial capital for employment or on the government for welfare. To provide such welfare, moreover, the state might have to sink further into foreign debt and politically conditioned aid, and foreign lending with political strings might impose new depths of austerity and immiserization on Mexico's millions.

What would then happen if, beset by an unremitting fiscal crisis, the already weak Mexican welfare state failed and set off an unprecedented migration to the United States? United States welfare budgets would be overwhelmed and would fall apart, while economically the U.S. government might become a bloated creditor, a patrician state lording it over an indebted, subject nation.

Although the United States might never be able to dominate Mexico's political economy openly, given its cultural traditions and revolutionary heritage, U.S. companies, banks, and the U.S. government might be powerfully positioned to shape Mexico's future.

The financial debacle of late 1994 might only be a beginning.

NAFTA'S NUMERIC LOGIC

A very different picture portrait was being painted in the early 1990s, as the flood tide of official opinion confirmed NAFTA's merit.

The logic of NAFTA benefiting the United States was evident in numerical forecasts, if not in historic terms. For 1992 alone, U.S. exports to Mexico tallied $40.6 billion, yielding a $5.4 billion trade surplus, and they were projected to grow 10 percent a year. The only factors to offset this negative trade balance were inflows of U.S. capital to Mexico. In previous years, this inflow of capital had come in the form of stock portfolio purchases yielding 18–20 percent returns, even higher interest on loans, a booming stock market, and the possibility to exit quickly if crisis threatened or confidence waned. United States investors were decidedly cautious, as less than a third of their pre-NAFTA, mid–1993 investments were locked into new factories and similar fixed assets in Mexico. Yet once NAFTA was approved in the hothouse climate of the August 1994 election of the PRI presidential candidate that reaffirmed Mexican industrial policy favoring unfettered growth, foreign investment capital poured into all major fields, especially electronics manufacturing, construction, and retailing.

Upbeat forecasts for annual Mexican growth rates of 5.4 percent for the decade 1993 to 2003 were based on an estimated $3 billion in annual new foreign investments. One-half of these commitments were for export industries targeted at U.S. markets, while only one-fifth of production sought domestic Mexican sales that would replace U.S.-produced exports. United States exports to Mexico for this decade were also favorably forecast to rise 10 to 15 percent a year in the near term and 7 to 10 percent a year thereafter. Yet, with the onset of the 1995 economic crisis and government austerity program, the domestic market weakened. Exporters diverted billions of dollars worth of Mexican-made goods into world markets, transforming an $18.5 billion 1994 trade deficit into a surplus ranging between an estimated $5.5 billion to $7 billion for 1995.

Benefits for U.S. producers and exporters would likely require the financial backstop of U.S., Canadian, and Mexican taxpayers, who were not directly consulted by NAFTA's framers. The U.S. Congressional Budget Office estimates of reduced U.S. tariff revenues of $2–$3 billion over five years pale by comparison to the total $15–$20 billion to be spent on connecting U.S. highway, bridge, and sewage-treatment infrastructure to facilitate NAFTA commerce. The $1–$2 billion for retraining displaced U.S. workers, an extra $2 billion or more in U.S. agricultural price supports and export financing programs, as well as some $1.5 billion in outlays to prevent drug and other smuggling will be further expenses. These costs can be covered in part by border-crossing fees which will replace tariffs, direct taxes to support the Inter-American Development Bank, or indirect taxes from the United States, Canada, and Mexico to pay interest and repay principal on Inter-American Development Bank loans, Mexican-American International Boundary and Water Commission bridge-building bonds, and NAFTA Development Bank bonds.

The future legerdemain will produce fiscal balance sheets in the red and lush profits for government bond dealers.

MEXICO'S BALANCE SHEET BLEEDS RED

South of the Rio Grande, what benefits and burdens can Mexico expect from NAFTA?

Enlarged U.S. trade and investments were supposed to reward Mexico with employment, social stability, and sustained growth and keep 500,000 extra migrants a year from illegally entering the United States.

This widely publicized figure on illegal immigration is likely to be much larger in fact. In 1993 alone, the Mexican peasantry was being driven off *ejidos* they did not own, but only had the right to farm. The Mexican government offered peasants one-time compensation for their land rights because the small plots of most peasants represented high-cost, inefficient farms. These farms had already been thrown into crises as government farm aid was cut away in the recurrent economic crises of the 1980s and early 1990s. It matters little if a good corn year (*año maicero*) is in store for the small farmer or whether Mexican corn output is "sheltered" for 15 years under NAFTA: cheaper U.S. corn will immediately flood Mexico. Hard-pressed to compete, small corn farmers and many thousands of peasants will be left with few choices but to abandon their land and head for Mexico's overpopulated, crisis-ridden cities.

As only the richest landowners will remain on the land, a reenactment of the historic land-tenure pattern that existed under the dictatorship of Porfirio Díaz is possible. During these earlier times, one percent of the population owned 97 percent of the land; half the land was owned by 835 families and 3,500,000 landless peasants and hapless peons worked for the *haciendas*. Even after the 1910 Revolution, proposed land distribution was repeatedly blocked by vested interests, and by 1930 only 6 to 10 percent of all land had been handed out.

President Lázaro Cárdenas's distribution of 45 million acres of Mexico's 475 million acres (one-third unusable for lack of water) barely began to change the land-tenure balance over the six years from 1934 to 1940. And World War II industrialization with its aftermath then drove more people to the cities for work and put pressure on the government to cease expropriation of large *haciendas* and agricultural enterprises.

Agricultural success remained conditioned on state intervention, too. Provided state credits continued, *haciendas* could produce enough to meet urban and export needs, thus earning foreign exchange. While the poorest land was given to landless *campesinos*, two-thirds of all farms remained less than five hectares (12.5 acres) — too small to produce efficiently, though the state granary paid cash above the domestic market price if one could raise enough to sell.

The poorer farmers shared some $3.5 billion in annual subsidies when the ruling Provisional Revolutionary party (PRI) sought to buy half its votes in the 1970s and early 1980s. Urban populations had withdrawn their support during President López Portillo's unresponsive administration, so the PRI desperately needed the peasant vote. Yet, the government's fiscal crisis led Portillo's successor de la Madrid to limit the program of agricultural incentives and guaranteed corn and dairy prices. There was little doubt that the new set-price system depressed real farm prices one-third and discouraged farmers from bringing their output to the government or to the free market.

Meanwhile, consumer subsidies in the form of low-priced government produce disappeared, and this caused prices for essential foods to rise quickly.

The process came full circle with the transformation of Mexico from a corn-exporting nation to a vegetable-producing exporter and corn-importing country in the 1980s and early 1990s. Tiny farms producing corn at bare subsistence were replaced not by new, middle-sized *haciendas* producing corn, but gigantic *latifundias* which employed landless *campesinos*, peons, and peasants for labor-intensive mass production of fruits and vegetables. Output was being directed both to the domestic market and to the lucrative U.S. market. The traditional crops of corn and beans were being displaced in part. And as wealthy landowners in Mexico's northern reaches grew the new cash crops by drawing on ground water tables, irrigation beds, and seasonal rains, corn was in short supply and had to be imported using the very dollars earned by the export of winter fruits and vegetables.

What will happen as the small agricultural *ejidos* close down and sell their land rights either to the government or to private corporate interests? The government may resell the land to the *latifundias*, and these estates may either grow vegetables with stoop labor or herd cattle with a handful of *rancheros*, thereby displacing each year hundreds of thousands of *campesinos*. Perhaps millions of the remaining peasants will eventually move north as landless agricultural peons or industrial wage workers and conceivably raise their living standards above a diet of imported grains.

If this happens, they will eat bread rather than tortillas and prefer beef and chicken over tamales as a staple. Mexico will thus be forced to enlarge its import of U.S. grain to fatten poultry and livestock—six bushels of imported corn are required to add one pound of animal flesh. As a result Mexico's import debt will increase, raising the cost of living and setting off an inflationary spiral—that in turn will cut bread and beef consumption.

As a sign of change, by 1993 most tortillas sold in Mexico City were made from imported U.S. corn. With a bitter-sweet nostalgia, Mexico's urban poet Homero Aridjis laments, "Corn still connects the Mexicans of today with Mexicans from before the conquest, but when you don't get a good tortilla in a restaurant, it's a very good indication of a deterioration of the quality of life."

A GRAYING CANVAS

As massive deterioration touches most aspects of civil life, Mexico's future remains uncertain. As more and more *campesinos* abandoned the land and fled to the cities in the 1980s and early 1990s, leaving less than a third of Mexicans in the countryside, some observers believed that the export of Mexican produce and manufactures from domestic and foreign-owned properties would probably cover the bill. Yet an inflationary burst from Mexico's increased demand for U.S. grain, technology, and manufactures could also lead to a series of peso devaluations. Devaluations would then make food imports more expensive and place pressure on more desperate Mexican workers to cross the U.S. border in search of work and welfare.

In addition, the flood of poorly educated Latinos entering the United States would depress wages for less-skilled U.S. workers, displacing poor blacks and whites in major U.S. cities. The deluge would also impose new service burdens on local governments, which in turn would lead to higher taxes on already overwrought communities. And Mexican and other immigrants requiring public education and health care would remain disproportionately more unlikely than poor U.S. citizens (with the aid of supporting families) to face successfully the throes of the economic malaise. Immigrants might go on welfare, turn to drug dealing or other crime, or end up in jail, raising the ire and cost of taxpayers burdened with covering public services and law enforcement.

Thus, the enviable financial scenario that was assumed to clearly benefit U.S. traders, grain farmers, and investors may become a dead weight loss for unemployed Mexican workers and negatively affect U.S. taxpaying communities.

SHOCK ABSORBERS AND COMPANY TOWNS

"It's a market for our exports that is growing at three times the rate of any other market in the world," President Clinton ebulliently remarked, as he reaffirmed NAFTA's purposes on 7 May 1993.

Opposition leaders argued that the lucrative export of U.S. technology, investment capital, and grains might step-by-step lead to the gradual imposition of U.S. industrial policy on Mexico, its government, its upper classes, and its working population.

Naysayers screamed the dangers. Production and workers in the United States faced a potential disaster, they asserted, if the trade-and-capital flow arrangement and high levels of immigration from Mexico continued, and these factors could serve to lower U.S. domestic levels of high-tech investments and wages.

By 1993, the flight of U.S. investment capital to Mexico was already undercutting U.S. production and replacing a skein of high-wage manufacturing jobs with low-wage service employment. But such export of the means and relations of production had been going on since at least 1971; relocated production facilities had led to higher profits for transnational corporations and investors, fueling a long-term, general decline in U.S. wage levels and real incomes. And with the added burst of such flight of U.S. production facilities from 1992 to mid–1993, private sector investments in new technologies that formerly might have enhanced U.S. productivity fell to the lowest levels in 30 years—far below Japanese and German rates.

Would NAFTA encourage this investment export trend, put more workers out of jobs in the already devastated Rust Belt and Sun Belt and drive down overall U.S. wage rates? Although workers hesitated to give up their mortgage-impacted homes to move from "Sunset" to "Sunrise" industries, they began taking low-paying service jobs at a fraction of their former salaries. Some of them were also forced to watch helplessly as their former employers relocated to Mexico, where they could lower plant, consumer, and environmental safety levels to Mexican standards and escape mandatory employee health care, social security, and other costly legal requirements.

The precise outcomes of these trends cannot be predicted, but historic precedents remain. The transmigration of U.S. capital has become politically boundless, locating production and securing markets without the need to respect political boundaries of other nations, political parties anywhere, domestic organized labor's needs or demands, or the fulminations of consumer-protection advocates.

Mexico may also pay a weighty price as the shock absorber for past and future losses sustained by transnationals whose home-bases are in the United States. Is it possible that Mexico will be transformed into a giant "company town" where low wages will cut production costs and the living standards for the Mexican working class family will be effectively set by mobilizing the domestic market as a company store and the nation's bank issue as company currency?

In the early 1990s, U.S. transnationals already operated in four venues to recoup their investment outlays and profits in Mexico, which involved production technology, available resources, relative labor costs, and market shares. They concentrated on (1) the original transfer of dollar-denominated cash or equipment to Mexico, (2) the exchange of dollars for pesos to buy materials, purchase inanimate energy, and pay wages in

Mexico, (3) the similar payment for storage, insurance, and transport, and (4) the sale of output for pesos in Mexico, for dollars in the United States, and for other currencies elsewhere.

Without stable exchange rates of dollars for pesos, however, such realization of original investment capital could not take place. To accommodate the U.S. corporate need for fixed exchange rates over the intermediate term, President Salinas thus pushed for a 1993 constitutional amendment to maintain the value of the peso by using an independent central bank (effectively "ruling out" any major devaluation), and he also introduced a longer-term, peso-denominated, sovereign Mexican debt. The former action, Salinas believed, would keep exchange rates in a fixed range; the latter policy, he thought, would make it possible to fund the state debt with long-term foreign capital borrowed at high interest rates that would be repayable in pesos rather than dollars or other hard currencies. Foreign lenders would thus have a strong incentive to maintain currency ratios and preserve the value of their Mexican assets.

Stable exchange rates would also allow U.S.-owned, Mexican-based factories to recover profits in the U.S. market after lowering the cost of Mexican production by linking wage levels to the cost of maintenance of the labor force. Clearly, if the cost of food, housing, transport, and other family needs could be lowered, wages could be minimized to cover these needs, thereby cutting the cost of production. Some political economists thus argued that lowering the costs of the maintenance and reproduction of the working class family would cut the cost of production and allow competitive pricing to widen markets. Thereby, decreased labor costs *vis-à-vis* constant prices would enlarge profits, expediting the recovery of capital invested and the realization of labor's effort representing unremunerated labor time.

Pursuing efforts to lower labor's cost of living, Mexico looked to foreign precedents. In nineteenth-century England, both workers and employers joined the Anti-Corn League (1836–46). Workers wanted lower prices for the wheat used to bake their bread, and employers realized that lower wheat prices would decrease labor's demand for higher wages. Together they forced Parliament to remove the landlords' Corn Law tariff that kept wheat prices high. Following a similar logic, in late nineteenth-century Germany, Friedrich Krupp created a vast company town surrounding his steel works where low-cost worker-housing and company-provided fuel kept wage demands low. The lower production costs allowed Krupp to undersell competitors worldwide. United States steel mill towns also offered workers low-cost company housing and fuel, low-price rations at the company stores, low-interest loans at company-funded banks, and low-cost transport to and from the mill. In his Homestead steel mills,

Andrew Carnegie honed the techniques for keeping wage demands low. He deployed Pinkerton guards to bring in still lower-paid replacements and eliminated skilled workers by introducing the latest technologies. Both measures further cut production costs.

Following the logic of such traditions, in the 1980s and early 1990s, the import of cheap U.S. corn as Mexico's traditional dietary staple helped keep wage demands—and thus production costs—low. Other living costs were also lowered in the hope of stabilizing wages; such cost-cutting measures included housing on company grounds for a few pesos a month, free company bus service from home to the factory, two free meals a day to keep workers reliably on the job, and free company training to master complex equipment.

In order to further lower overall outlays, U.S. manufacturers directing Mexican plants reorganized the production process by using three major innovations: (1) eliminating skilled labor by introducing high-tech, miniaturized manufacturing equipment requiring precision tools, (2) extending production lines deploying the latest technologies and carefully trained, labor-intensive workers, and (3) employing highly skilled technical workers to maintain and repair complicated equipment.

There was also segregation and division of higher-paid male workers in the most modern factories from lower-paid women employed in *maquiladoras* (twin plants) for hand assembly or as machine operators. Although they were designed to save labor costs, the *maquiladoras*' annual worker turnover rate in excess of 20 percent forced companies to constantly retrain workers to operate the latest automated machinery.

Yet the condition of labor remained Mexico's blind spot. By keeping the workers' living costs low to stabilize wages for a workforce surviving on a protein-poor diet and by emphasizing simplified, repetitious, mindless labor to lower the cost of production, labor was degraded so that outlays could be minimized, the production process sped-up, and overall unit costs reduced.

Thus directed toward simplified tasks to enhance capital accumulation, labor effectively created the means for its own further subjugation.

Trade, Culture, and Labor

Distantly removed from the Mexican factory, U.S. politicians offered glib phrases emphasizing the coming NAFTA era of free trade and investment success.

"I think that a major part of our economic future rests with building up strong two-way trade with Latin America, which requires Latin America to resume growth rates at more or less the level they were in the mid–1970s," President-elect Clinton stated on 19 November 1992, as he painted a brave new world picture. "If they were there today, our trade deficit would be about 20 percent lower and our unemployment rate would be lower in America."

Viable production and employment in Latin America would undoubtedly spell more U.S. exports, production, employment, and profits. The United States thus knowingly sought to extend its sphere to bring in Latin America's existing subregional trade blocs and make them accept U.S.-imposed production standards and government fiscal and monetary stability, as well as to restructure regional production. The United States thus sought secure, unfettered capital movement and negotiable, managed trade. And if Latin American nations sought to increase exports to the United States, they had little choice but to accept the terms set by a nation of lobbyists, special interests, and politicians. It is no surprise that they compromised and often groveled in the face of U.S. protection of vulnerable segments of its own domestic market with nontariff and other barriers. There would simply be no "free trade," "fair trade," or "level playing field" in U.S. commercial dealings with Latin nations that were economically less endowed.

Such economic inequalities had their sequel in political and cultural ones. United States transnational industrial policy was framed by the mobilization of vast sums of capital and the deployment of the labor pools of many nations. Past experience again laid the pathway for future designs, as transnational operations centered on trade-and-investment spheres, as well as the global cultural milieu.

During more than three centuries (1500–1830), Western empires spun an "intellectual" web that entangled subject peoples as consideration was given only to social organization and cultural traditions appropriate to pacification and control. Thus mercantilism envisioned a bilateral relationship with "loyal" populations: merchant companies holding crown charters secured their exclusive trading privileges, enjoying the rights of sovereign states in those colonies or territories seized by firepower and brigandage. Such methods opened the door for imposed labor systems based on an unending system of head-taxes, indentured labor, and communities attached to an owner's land (*encomienda*) that jeopardized indigenous traditions and communal labor.

In its maddened search for metallic wealth, then raw materials, exotic foods, and profitable investments, formal colonialism soon imposed an expanding sphere that dissolved communal and cultural loyalties under foreign state direction. Imperious politicians heralded their achievements, loudly proclaiming the true religion and "Dual Mandate," promising "beneficences" for conquered peoples but all the while driving their labor for production.

Even global crises of the 1930s bred a new colonialism, tightening the spheres of economic might that ensured domination from the metropole. Crises also put an end to the hypocritical Dual Mandate's ever-lacking administrative services and led to the appointment of upwardly mobile indigenes as "liberated" managers of plantations, mines, and factories. Spheres of influence nonetheless remained the focus, sustained by what little remained of indigenous communities' cultural traditions and family heritage.

Few of the post–World War II national liberation movements that replaced these colonized spheres with political independent states either sustained earlier indigenous cultural systems or continued traditional forms of production securing economic independence. Rather, neo-colonialism proved a mighty force, mobilizing Western capital and resources available for direct investments, or providing high-cost borrowed funds and controlled foreign exchange. Using superior leverage, Western nations and their transnational corporations denied and delayed the economic emancipation of these nations. And by nominally deferring to their national sovereignties to negotiate ratios of export/import prices, commercial terms, and foreign investments, these new mediums of empire also extracted information and favors from self-important Third World bureaucrats able to shape laws impacting national policies for investments and labor, exchange controls, tax imposts, tariffs, and other restrictions on Western commerce.

Are some aspects of the old spheres of influence, once so adept at manipulating nations and culture, again being reimposed?

In our time, it is clear that the Western powers and Japan have again strategically extended their commercial spheres to independent states, powerfully impacting local cultural traditions and community structures. Indeed, today's major focus in establishing trade zones — ensuring an open door for goods and capital — is designed to ostensibly shape or transparently sidestep the national and cultural milieu. Trade zones are thereby again transforming both community traditions and family life into the main shock absorbers of the latest cyclical crises and social disorders.

The technical world is unrelentingly attacking what little remains of indigenous cultures and nature's sphere that sustains local social structures, attitudes, and behavioral patterns. And the impact of this techno-cratic scrutiny is the signature work of transnational organizations attempting to realign production relations.

Past attempts to make indigenous, cultural group obligations coincide with Western work organizations largely failed, however. And even today, there are powerful cultural restraints on transnationals determining occupations, mobilizing labor, setting work-value goals, and determining labor standards of satisfaction, behavior on the job, output and pay levels, or full participation in socially essential output and awarded social status.

It is possible that family structure and cultural needs can be extended to or made coordinate with the requirements set by transnational organizations mobilizing resources, labor, and production. Still, the symbiotic, cultural, social unit for needed collectivist group tasks often demands conformity of purpose and cooperation that transnational management cannot easily redirect—at least not without corrupting its filial core that ensures group solidarity, security, and labor. The consequences are usually disastrous.

To sidestep the conflict with indigenous groups, today's transnational management largely deals with the nation-state as overseer of social demands and regulations, completely ignoring any direct responsibility for cultural traditions of community, family, and labor. This remains as true for U.S. transnationals now operating in Mexico as it has been for the U.S. government dealing with the centralized Mexican state authorities, but together these entities now look to NAFTA as the framed reference for future transnational operations in the broadest neomercantile setting, at the expense of Mexico's provincial cultural ways, backward production methods, and undeveloped markets.

CULTURAL TRADITIONS AND TRANSNATIONAL BARRIERS

United States transnationals will undoubtedly continue to face Mexican culture as a barrier that molds indigenous groups and national leaders in thinking and in the timing of action.

From a logical point of view, the managers of U.S. transnationals should actively see Mexican culture as an essential unit, lifting themselves to an awareness of the essential beliefs and practices of the indigenous population, their attitudes towards the gifts of mother earth, cyclical time, communal life, and labor.

Yet, for production, the predilection of U.S. management to impose work structures emphasizing competition among individuals has effectively undercut culturally socialized levels of cooperation among Mexican workers. Corporate-directed, technically oriented production has put labor in motion in such a way that the past symbiosis of community, culture, and social labor is shattered. Traditional values are thereby replaced by transnational pressures, putting U.S. industrial policies in direct conflict with preexisting social structures and time-honored cultural traditions of work and community.

Such practices permeate U.S. transnationals striving for policy and operational communications with their own managers and workers at various points on the global compass. In Mexico, these transnationals are attempting to impart the culture-bound meaning of U.S. upper management. Encoded messages and signs that the indigenous manager decodes and interprets without reliance on his own cultural assumptions function to alienate Mexicans from their heritage. Communication barriers are unavoidable, too, since ingrained Mexican culture and symbolism involves more than just thinking different thoughts and generating unique meanings through language and nonverbal communications. Indeed, such nonuniversal means of relaying information are subject to both sender's and receiver's cultural attributions. Miscommunication promotes unfounded perceptions of the other's culture, elicits stereotypical depiction of both heritage and the individual's cultural standpoint, and engenders ethnocentrism that asserts that one culture's way is better than another.

THE FORCE OF TRANSNATIONAL POLICIES

Under pressures of transnational policies, new contours are surfacing in Mexico as well. Lacking cultural awareness and communication, both Mexican government and U.S. transnational policies have forcefully attempted to restructure Mexican production, markets, and the labor force. Yet this centrist management restructuring has often been pursued blindly, neglecting the enormous potentialities of civil society for democracy, decentralized decision making, and cooperative production.

Following traditional practices as guides, such centralized policy and financial controls over decentralized manufacturing had become the pattern of U.S. transnationals after World War II. But contemporary, decentralized alliance networks and partnerships, without direct central office oversight, had sometimes emerged, often becoming more responsive to both local production needs and sales potential and actually taking account of local mores and customs, community and labor beliefs, as well as culturally oriented communications and decision making.

Ignoring such advantages, both U.S. transnationals and the Mexican government meanwhile pursued industrial policies designed to change economic conditions, population needs, and the nature of traditional labor, often with disastrous consequences. Their coordinate policies aimed to transform Mexico's preindustrial culture by driving populations off the land, out of traditional work, and into technically organized production relying on extrinsic, corporatized, occupational functions and pay scales. They refused to heed Mexico's intrinsic community or cultural needs. Instead, by building an infrastructure of roads, bridges, and transport facilities, they changed the spatial location of work, creating new needs for food no longer grown by the increasing number of urban workers, as well as for housing, sewage, and fresh water facilities outside traditional villages. In this way the Mexican government and the U.S. transnationals exacerbated the population's desperation and need for government services and wage work to cover such costs. The traditional cycles of labor by time and function were thereby disrupted, undercutting old cultural ways, work, and beliefs.

Mexico's resulting linkage of urbanization, wage employment, and a hierarchy of new civil requirements merged with state industrial policies favoring rapid industrialization and the liquidation of earlier production modes. Due to pressures from the United States, which sought to shift its crisis of accumulation to other nations, Mexico's industrial policy preparations began in the early 1990s with the denationalization of 900 of some 1,200 state-owned firms; the privatization of the major banks, including the central bank; the encouragement of applications of more than 100 foreign banks and financial institutions to operate in Mexico to encourage unfettered foreign investments in Mexican bonds and production; the massive importations of U.S.-made technologies; an open door to allow U.S. firms to invest freely in Mexico beyond the border areas extending twin-plant *maquiladora* facilities; the change of Article 27 of the constitution to permit the market sale of the old common lands, an action promising to force 8 to 22 million peasants off the land; and the potential explosion of an ongoing three-stage population chain reaction.

The population is already migrating from the land to the cities to moving closer to the newly built factories and growing *latifundias*. As they experience the problems associated with too large a labor supply, which causes periodic unemployment, many Mexicans are emigrating to the United States, thereby increasing the burden on U.S. labor markets, resources, and budgets.

Double-Threat Industrial Policy

Undoubtedly, the switchback trail of such demographic movements will be complicated by the emergence of new trade zones, poverty, and potential endangerment of the natural world.

In the past, trade zone cycles—First World capital exports, Third World production at predesignated technical scales—have been inextricably linked by the industrial policies of member nations. The North American Free Trade Association also anticipates that capital will move to the lowest cost of production for trade within its customs union and that still lower cost production from nonmembers will be excluded.

Periodic crises are an inherent part of the process too. United States investment capital exports to Mexico will make Mexican workers, suppliers, and consumers vulnerable to any U.S. cyclical production moves. Decreases in U.S. investment will cause periodic unemployment and poverty.

To provide security to those impoverished and to manage the new civil needs emerging under these conditions, the Mexican government will be required to impose new taxes and carry new debt. Building a strong tax base and maintaining financial stability will probably allow the Mexican government to build infrastructure and finance social welfare outlays.

Yet a new paradigm expressing U.S.-Mexican relations will then logically emerge. Technical Mexican production will have to produce exports to earn hard currencies, and this production will require the import of new means of production, finished parts, and food for the urban workforce — especially grain substitutes for what was previously grown by a now disinherited peasantry. Such trade alterations would appear as a negative sum in the balance of payments and would have to be offset by added Mexican exports and or direct U.S. investments; the negative trade balance would thus herald the end of Mexico's old agricultural, communal heritage, periodic peso devaluations only momentarily turning the balance positive. The long-term, negative balance would also increase potential dangers through the speedup of labor and abuse of natural and other production resources, as well as potentially toxic imports for production or marketing. The technosphere of production in both the U.S. and Mexico might also jeopardize nature's inheritance through the production of dangerous byproducts — tailings, hydrocarbons, and other effluents that the natural world cannot absorb — creating an environmental disclimax posing a threat to workers, the population at large, and other species.

UNRESOLVED

And thus the turn of events raised more questions than could be resolved in the 1990s.

Labor was in no position to successfully protest its condition of imposed dangers, low wages, long hours, and intense labor. But future jeopardy to transnational corporate operations, technology, and output might arise from an unhappy, unappeased labor force. It is possible that U.S. transnationals will pull for long-term accumulation, rather than short-term quarterly profits. Perhaps they can remain financially secure while offering Mexican labor a fair day's work for a fair day's pay, creating a safe work milieu, and ensuring measures to protect the health of the workforce, the factory, and the community environment.

What, then, does the future hold for Mexican civil society and the nation's prosperity? Will Mexican progress ride on the coattails of U.S. investments and commerce? Will NAFTA largely secure U.S. interests and the Mexican elite at the expense of Mexico's middle class and poor? Or, is there equity in the agreement — not only for Mexico's upper classes, but for the rest of the population? And if there is to be equity, when will its attributes emerge and how will it be awarded, allotted, or distributed?

Although the present offers few ddefinitive answers, in this study these and other significant questions are nonetheless detailed, as tendencies, probable alternatives, and solutions are pondered.

Part I

A Portrait of Mexico Past

Today, as in centuries past, Mexico is a land of fearful millions. With experience and reason, many fear the government and its officials in both high and low places. Others fear to step out of place in a society where places are predesignated by the state, church, and wealthier classes. Still others fear that any move they might take to better their condition and secure themselves economically or socially will be viewed by the government as either dangerous political protest or unacceptable revolutionary activity. Most fear that if they try to challenge the existing order in any way, they and their kin will not survive the fire this time or in the next life.

And yet, despite fear, there are those who protest their dismal condition. They protest despite the fact that even in so-called democratic elections, opposition parties calling attention to irregularities and outright vote fraud are designated by the ruling party and the media it controls as "terrorists" and "antidemocratic" radicals. And those who dare speak or write in the public domain are in constant danger of being crushed by the state and its most powerful supporters.

True, past revolutionary challenges that once broke the rigid facade of lawless order led to constitutional changes; but these legal mandates have never been implemented for lack of an enforcing state structure backed by resources, political power, and military action. Rather, as the mantle of power has been quietly switched from one class of rulers to another, the overwhelming majority of Mexican peasants, workers, and ordinary citizens have won little in the economic and political realm to prop up and sustain their lives. Theirs has been a weighty past of suffering and oppression. There has yet to be a renaissance in thinking or deed in Mexico, and most of its people, who still lack elemental necessities offering the right to life and social liberties, remain mired in poverty, ignorance, and degradation.

For nearly five centuries, old and new elites have held the whip hand over the vast majority of the Mexican people. For it is a fact that from the Spanish Conquest and Inquisition to the revolution of Zapatistas and Villas, incipient northern bourgeoisie and *hacienda* generals reasserted control. Passage of constitutional changes created the illusion that the nation's peasantry had secured plots of common lands and the workers had won rights and security. But such popular benefits were either never secured or not held for long. And as we shall see, the keys locking up the population in ever-renewed bondage have been held fast by their jailers both past and present.

CHAPTER 1

From Inquisition to Independence

The sixteenth-century Inquisition in Spain and Portugal spilled into their American colonies with a level of brutality and racism unknown in Europe.

About the year 800, Christian ideas had filtered into Spain after the body of St. James the Apostle was discovered in Galicia, thereafter named Santiago, that is Sant Iago, short for Sant Jacobus, the Latin form of Saint James. Legends soon flowered around the shrine. Pilgrims crossed the Pyrenees, exchanging the goods and thoughts of Catholic France, and influencing the fierce and intractable Spanish nobles, who formed military orders of priest-knights to conquer for the cross. Thus the Knights of Santiago, Alacántara, and Calatrava devoted their swords to the cross and their bodies to the enjoyment of the fruits of the reconquest of Iberia from the Moors. "We, who are each of us as good as thou, and who together are far more powerful than thou, swear to obey thee if thou dost obey our laws; and if not, not," they swore to the king of Aragon.

Yet the Moors did not willingly relinquish their territories, wealth, or positions. And even the reconquest left industrious and intelligent subjects who were Moors and Jews holding to a variety of religious affiliations and beliefs. Thus the *Mudejares*, who held their own faith while living under Christian rule, were as Moorish in custom as the converted Moors called *Moriscoes*. The *Mozarabes* were Christians who had lived under Moorish rule. And some Jews called *Marranos* had converted, while others remained staunchly orthodox.

INQUISITION

In the battle marking the transition from Moorish to Christian rule, the Jews had remained particularly vulnerable to attack because of their great accumulation of wealth and their elevated social positions under the Moors. About a hundred years before King Ferdinand's final conquest of Granada established Christian authority, Hernando Martínez had roused the Catholics of Seville to attack the Jewish quarter and murder 4,000 people; Martínez himself presided over the massacre. The next year the massacres spread to Valencia, Córdoba, Burgos, Toledo, and Barcelona. Under the anti–Semitic preachings of Saint Vincent Ferrier, Spanish Jews either converted to Christianity, hesitated and were massacred, or remained loyal to Judaism. Seventeen thousand Jews who refused to convert were imprisoned or burned in the single year of 1481. The same scenes were repeated more than once during the fifteenth century, as the traditional hatred of the followers of Judaism intensified, aggravated by the fact that most of the tax-gatherers were Jews.

As Catholic fervor merged with the crusade against the Moors and reached a high point in the Inquisition, even converted Jews were often massacred. Those Jews who had earlier been baptized during the popular fury fled to the Moors in order to escape or practice their rites, only to find the Moors also in retreat, leaving Jews to resist, be captured, and be burnt alive.

What exactly was the logic of the fury, the tortured rationale enveloping Spain and leading to the Inquisition?

In 1469, Isabella of Castile married her cousin Ferdinand of Aragón, uniting the principalities of Spain as well as their forces to finally defeat the Moors on 6 January 1492 and occupy the ancient city of Granada, which for eight centuries had been the capital of the Moors.

Ferdinand's royal treasury had been depleted, however, by the long wars of reconquest of the Moors, and he looked with intense hatred at the Jews, who had amassed great wealth by refraining from combat, confining themselves to business, and favoring the Moors, from whom they had received partiality for hundreds of years. Ferdinand and his clerics thus reasoned that if the Jews did not demonstrate their complete loyalty to the Crown by becoming members of the state Catholic church, it would be an easy step to appropriate their wealth and property for the royal treasury.

Although many thousands of former Jews and Moors had already been converted by force, they were still suspected of apostasy. They were watched closely to see if they were preserving their former religious beliefs, and they were subject to betrayal by those seeking a promised share of the wealth stripped from anyone accused of being disloyal or a religious heretic. Thus in a movement that started on 6 January 1481 and then escalated that year all over Spain, two thousand persons were burned on charges of Judaizing; many of them were persons of importance and wealth whose property went to the royal treasury.[1]

The same year, seventeen thousand were also forced into cruel penance. Civil crimes like open adultery or canon crimes like stealing religious funds brought sentences of hundreds of lashes or a year or two in jail, without fatal prejudice to their children. Converted Jews who continued to worship in the synagogue, converted Muslims who backslid in secret, or others who had turned to Martin Luther or become mystical subversives were stripped of their possessions, repeatedly lashed, and condemned to perpetual solitary imprisonment. Their infamy was kept alive by the sight of their processional Inquisitional robes depicting their disloyalty, which were to hang forever in their local churches. Those heretics who the church could not "rehabilitate" were separated from the church and burned alive. Those who recanted died within the church; first they were garotted and then their bodies were burned. Their bright yellow sackcloth robes of dishonor were decorated with a flaming red cross and hung for more than fifty years after their executions in churches throughout Spain, clearly labeled with their names, proclaiming forever the holy sin of that family. The descendants of the condemned could never hold office in Spain, become priests, serve as officers in the army, collect taxes, or travel overseas.

Thus were Judaic religious practices impaled on the altar of Spain's Dominicans. Suspicion of apostasy followed by punishment was also visited on any "new Christians" who preserved any of the familiar liturgies or practices, such as putting on clean clothes on Saturday; stripping the fat from beef and mutton; killing poultry with a sharp knife, covering the blood, and muttering a few Hebrew words; eating flesh in Lent or blessing their children by the laying on of hands; practicing dietary restrictions and modalities of feast and fasting; mourning for the dead after the ancient manner of washing and wrapping the body and carrying it upon lath to the grave; or even turning the face of one's dying kin to the wall in the throes of death.[2]

Seeing enemies of the church everywhere in the ancient Moorish city of Sevilla, the governor built outside its limits a permanent platform of stone called the *Quemadero*, which was to serve as a burning place. At the four corners were placed large hollow statues of limestone, in which impenitents were placed alive, to be roasted to death by slow heat. The next year in 1482 the Pope himself, horrified by such spectacles, wrote to Ferdinand and Isabella to rebuke them for the vast number being tortured and to revoke the power granted to the sovereigns to nominate any further Inquisitors.

But when Pedro de Arbues, one of the Inquisitors, was assassinated,

Catholic fury broke in full strength, and Jews by the thousands, including *Marranos* as well as *Moriscoes* and traditional Moors, were seized, imprisoned, and tortured.

DEATH WITHOUT END

Both king and clerics believed that the final 1492 victory over the Moors on the January 6 Feast of Epiphany—representing the manifestation of Christ to the Gentiles—was a sign of God approving their attempted forcible conversion of all those who lived in Spain to the true faith of Catholicism. And God's sign that Spain would spread this true faith to the Americas was reified in October the same year when Columbus unlocked the treasures of the New World. Concretizing this double seal of the divine, the Spanish minister of justice, Torquemada, planned and directed the human carnage by which all who differed from the apostolic canon were punished with the fires of this world that they might escape the tortures of the next.

Isabella meanwhile issued a decree of banishment against the Jews, and in three short months all unconverted Jews were obliged under pain of death to abandon Spanish soil. At least 120,000 Jews, perhaps as many as 800,000, thus went into exile, though great numbers avoided banishment by baptism. Although those leaving were permitted to dispose of their goods, they were forbidden to carry either gold or silver from Spain and were thus almost helpless before the rapacity of their persecutors.

As they fled Spain, multitudes also fell into the hands of pirates who swarmed along the coast, plundering all they possessed and reducing them to slavery. Thousands died of famine or plague; others were murdered or tortured with horrible cruelty by African marauders or were cast back by tempestuous storms on the Spanish coast. Women weakened by trauma, driven from luxurious homes among the orange groves of Sevilla or Granada, children fresh from their mothers' arms, the aged, the sick and the infirm—all perished by the thousands.

Some 80,000 took refuge in Portugal, relying on the king's promise of safety. But the hatred of the Spanish pursued them with organized missions of Dominican priests, who lashed the Portuguese into a fury, persuading the king to issue an edict to banish all adult Jews from Portugal after first taking from them their children below age fourteen, who were to be educated as Christians. One historian has recounted the wild paroxysms of despair this persecution caused:

> Piercing shrieks of anguish filled the land. Women were known to fling their children into deep wells, or to tear them from limb to limb, rather than resign them to the Christians. When at last, childless and broken-hearted, they sought to leave the land, they found that the ships had been purposely detained, and the allotted time having expired, they were reduced to slavery, and baptized by force. By the merciful intervention of Rome most of them at last

regained their liberty, but their children were separated from them forever. A great peal of rejoicing filled the Peninsula, and proclaimed that the triumph of the Spanish priests was complete.[3]

With Iberian Christendom victorious, not only were the Jews forced into exodus with their expertise in finance and trade, but after the expulsion of the Moors from Granada, hundreds of thousands of Moors were driven from the countryside, an action that eliminated Spain's best agriculturalists and handicraftsmen. Vast plains were left uninhabited except by *banditti*, while some of the most important trades were paralyzed. And having eliminated so many of its skilled citizens, Catholic fanaticism prepared the next step, blindly undermining Spain's commercial infrastructure and industrial zeal.

IMPOVERISHMENT, MERCANTILISM, AND EMPIRE

After driving out those who made Spain prosperous, Ferdinand and Isabella proceeded to unite their realm by policies that favored foreign conquest and emphasized a powerful ocean armada, monopoly trade, and the extortion of bullion and jewels from the East Indies and the New World. By these policies, the monarchs undermined the old Spanish nobility who had lived by Iberian production and trade.

Spain's self-sufficiency in agriculture was destroyed by the Crown as it issued prohibitions against the lords' enclosures of arable land and reduced their power by encouraging organized migratory herders of merino sheep, whose long strands of wool were sought after in the European world of weaving. Viewing the future in terms of ocean galleons, the king also subsidized large merchant ships, thus ruining the owners of small vessels essential for coastal trade. The Crown's prohibitions on production also created a body of government agents to oversee all methods of work; the incompetence of bureaucratic oversight reduced the output and craftsmanship of weaver and fuller, potter, shoemaker, and armorer. Almost without exception, these unpaid or ill-paid officials elevated their income by bribes and other exactions, either driving producers to secrecy or out of their trades altogether.

So, too, the army of officialdom fixed prices and levied taxes on everything, farming out collections to contractors who imposed a 5 to 10 percent tax every time any article was sold, a tax on the ox sold to the butcher, the hide sold to the tanner, the dressed leather sold to the shoemaker, the shoes sold to the customer. In the words of the famous Scottish economist Adam Smith:

> The famous *Alcavala* of Spain seems to have been established on this principle ... a tax ... upon the sale of every sort of property, whether moveable or immovable; and it is repeated every time the property is sold. ... The levying of this tax requires a multitude of revenue-officers sufficient to guard

the transportation of goods, not only from one province to another, but from one shop to another. It subjects, not only the dealers in some sorts of goods, but those in all sorts, every farmer, every manufacturer, every merchant and shop-keeper, to the continual visits and examination of the tax-gatherers. Through the greater part of a country in which a tax of this kind is established, nothing can be produced for distant sale. The produce of every part of a country must be proportioned to the consumption of the neighborhood. It is to the *Alcavala*, accordingly, that [the author] Ustaritz imputes the ruin of the manufactures of Spain. He might have imputed to it likewise the declension of agriculture, it being imposed not only upon manufactures, but upon the rude produce of the land."[4]

Thus crushed between the regulatory extractions of government agents, tax farmers, and fixed prices on goods, the craftsman received little, experienced a falling standard of living, and was driven from production for sale beyond local markets. And not even merino wool that might have commanded a wide market could be sold afar. Industrial zeal was also undercut by Spanish Catholicity that encouraged social and religious institutions while casting a pall on production. Wealthy monasteries not only occupied many thousands of men and drained a vast amount of wealth from the productive resources of the country, but they created a popular acceptance of poverty and an ascetic habit of mind incompatible with the energy and enthusiasm needed to pursue industry. Industrial success could not long continue to coexist with such religiosity.

As production and trade within Spain plummeted, one way out of the dilemma was empire, encouraged and justified by Catholic doctrine linked to papal mandate. Under Pope Alexander VI's famous bulls of donation of 1493, Spain laid claim to all hitherto unknown lands west of an imaginary line drawn in the mid–Atlantic from north to south, entrusting to the Crown of Castile the Christianization of these lands. All unexplored regions east of that line were assigned to Portugal. And under her own westernmost claim, Spain was obliged to determine Indian nature and capacity before Christianizing, conquering, and enslaving the native peoples.[5]

During the initial Spanish conquest and the search for gold and silver, soldiers and soldier-priests alike recognized that to possess bullion was to possess authority and power.[6] For this mission, Cortés carried the flag of Spain from Mexico's heartland south to Guatemala and from the City of Mexico northerly towards what would later be named California, lured on by the text of the 1510 Spanish novel by Gaci-Ardóñez de Montalvo, *La cergas de esplendian*, that depicted California as a lost island of Amazon women led by Califia, astride horses, both heavily ornamented in gold rings. Mexico eventually became Spain's principal colony for mining gold and silver; it shipped silver from Ocapulco (Acapulco) to Manila in exchange for Oriental wares and china and shipped these wares plus one-fifth of all bullion to the Spanish Crown.[7]

Spanish theological structures also suited the warlike and idle nobility who had replaced the old merchant families of Italy and attached a stigma to labor. These minor nobles sought to impose slavery in Spain's colonies under church leadership, first in 1511, then in 1516 under St. Jerome, who administered West Indies affairs, and thereafter under Las Casas in 1517. In the name of saving thousands of Indians who were perishing in the conquerors' gold and silver mines, Las Casas sought to replace them with African slaves who allegedly were better able to bear the fatigue, as shown by the Portuguese in their own colonies.[8] Later Las Casas repented and opposed Negro slavery "for the same reasons," but as late as 1544 he personally owned several Negro slaves, and there was no concerted opposition to Negro slavery during the sixteenth century.[9]

Meanwhile, Charles V, emperor of Germany and king of Spain, and his counselors attempted to rise above the factional struggle of ecclesiastics, soldiers, colonists and royal officials in America, as well as men of action and thought in Spain, moving to prevent the reemergence of the powerful and turbulent aristocracy recently broken by Ferdinand and Isabella. This action freed the counselors to decide themselves what doctrine should be applied to the American Indians. Borrowing the ancient theory of Aristotle that some men are born to be slaves, Charles V applied it to the Indians from the coasts of Florida to distant Chile,[10] and his son Philip II continued in the same tradition.

NEW SPAIN

Subjugation by arms was Spanish policy from America's colonial beginning. Columbus's second voyage had carried 1,500 armed Spaniards to Hispaniola (the island shared by Haiti and the Dominican Republic), where they enslaved the natives, put them to work in primitive mines, and by 1513 had them producing $1 million worth of gold yearly. Columbus, who described the Arawak Indians who inhabited the Caribbean islands as "a loving people without covetousness," was followed by Spanish *conquistadores*, largely minor noblemen authorized by the Crown to pacify specific regions, to create *encomiendas* out of the subdued zones, and to place each under the absolute control of a single nobleman. Under their oversight of mines and plantations, whole Arawak villages disappeared through slavery, disease, and warfare. And in Hispaniola alone, the native population declined from some 200,000 when Columbus planted the flag in 1492 to a mere 29,000 only 22 years later.[11]

Throughout Spanish America, moreover, the *encomienda* system was designed to enslave native peoples, chaining them to working the land. Miguel de Salamanca, the oldest and most authoritative of the Spanish clerics, described the system as "Indians . . . being allotted for life in order that, working as they are worked, all the profit deriving from their work goes to those who hold them in *encomienda*; wherefore this form of *encomienda* and the manner in which it is executed is contrary to the well-being of the Indian Republic."[12]

As this land tenure and labor system was extended with the empire, larger administrative units, *viceroyalties*, were created; each was under a *viceroy*, who governed with the aid of an *audencia* of appointed officials which served as both legislature and supreme court.[13] And as the monopolies accumulating wealth were under government direction, Spanish *encomenderos* used local Indian chieftains as intermediaries in directing the very goals of society. Thus by 1600, Spanish America was run by 150,000 Europeans who controlled millions of Indians.[14]

Once subjugated, the population was baptized under Spanish rule, though the cleric Las Casas advised the Spanish Crown to first instruct the natives in the ways of God and then baptize them. But even Las Casas reversed the procedure when Indian children in Cuba had been disemboweled by Spanish soldiers; he was willing to baptize them without religious instruction before they died.[15]

The *conquistadores* justified their deeds as furthering just wars waged to compel the Indians to serve God, the king, and themselves. And the ecclesiastics blindly inquired how the natives could be made to change from what they were to what they ought to be.[16]

The answer seemed obvious. Priests acting like soldiers not only brought the Indians into the church but kept them on the land parcelled out in *viceroyalties*; the owner of the land also owned the Indians, while the priests looked after their spiritual lives.

Yet, the resulting relationship was already obfuscated by language in the first Spanish *Gramática* and *los diccionarios*. The colonial designation of "Indians" and the "West Indies" turned on the concept "de indio," not only a lexicographic conception drawn from the designation of the peoples of India, but an ideological proposition marking the relationship of Spanish rule over Indian subjects as the economic base for production, as well as the class and caste categories of colonial society.[17]

Used as an initial colonial device, the term *Indian* was quickly replaced by new terminology describing sixteen caste positions resulting from the conjugal relations of Crown-favored Spaniards, Indians as "natural slaves," and imported black slave laborers from Africa:

1. Español con india=mestizo
2. Mestizo con española=castizo
3. Castizo con española=español
4. Español con negra=mulato
5. Mulato con epañola=morisco
6. Morisco con española=chino
7. Chino con india=salta atrás

8. Salta atrás con mulata=lobo
9. Lobo con china=gíbaro
10. Gíbaro con mulata=albarazado
11. Albarazado con negra=cambujo
12. Cambujo con india=zambaigo
13. Zambaigo con loba=calpamulato
14. Calpamulato con cambuja=tente en el aire
15. Tente en el aire con mulata=no te entiendo
16. No te entiendo con india=torna atrás[18]

This *mestizaje* characterization of the people in the Spanish colonies, which embodied relations of power between pure-blooded Spaniards and all others, framed the thinking of even the most idealistic missionary zealot. In fact, there were two lines of diametrically opposed thinking. One proposed by Juan Ginés Sepúlveda (author of the book *Demócrates segundo o las justas causas de la guerra contra los indios*) called for enslaving the Indians as natural slaves in the tradition of Aristotle. The other proposal was made by Father Bartolomé de Las Casas in his study *Brevísima relación de la destrucción de las indias*, and called for converting the Indians to Catholicism and teaching them the merits of an ascetic life and hard work.

Although some ecclesiastics thought the Spaniards who controlled the Indians would have their welfare in mind, this was rarely the case. Slavery, elaborate mercantile restrictions, and the contest of the great powers exploiting the colonized—these became the unrelenting forces of oppression eventually goading the wretched into successful rebellion in the throes of Spain's decline.

SPAIN IN DECLINE

Spain's Catholicism was seemingly coordinate with, and invulnerable to, commercial supremacy that step by step led to colonial acquisitions, the boundless prospect of wealth, and Charles V's consolidation of the imperial scepter with that of Spain.

Yet empire proved costly to maintain and concentrated not on trade in the products of colonial *encomienda*, but on gold and silver. Although Austria's Charles V, who was pursuing empire, and Spain's Philip II, who was advancing the church, both employed gold to finance war, the metal switched the focus to imperial goals and sped the decline of Spanish industry. And though Charles organized a powerful navy, elevated himself as head of Catholic interests, and humbled French power, Spain's commerce was undermined step by step.

There were other consequences of the concentration of government and adventurers on bullion mines in America besides extensive neglect of manufactures and almost all forms of Spanish industry. The import of vast amounts of gold and silver made it the preferred instrument of exchange, and eventually depreciated its purchasing power. The price of all other articles was thereby raised, which also inflicted burdens on creditors paid in cheapened coin as well as on those living on fixed incomes.

Spain might have imported more manufactures of other nations, too, but under severe penalties the government prohibited the export of specie, so that the exchange of gold for imported goods violated mercantile regulations. These strictures were nonetheless breached, and Spain squandered its treasure from New Spain and Peru on the purchase of commodities and manufactures from Holland, England, and France. As a result, wealth was seen to reside not in prosperous domestic agriculture and industry, but in the output of foreign gold and silver mines. And in operation, as New Spain became Spain's most important colony, the extraction of its gold, silver, and other material resources for export to Spain paralleled the Iberian importation of essential manufactures produced elsewhere.

This preference for gold used to pay for the import of manufactures dovetailed with the Spanish mercantilist policy of limiting commerce with the New World to the single port of Seville to ensure the Crown's overarching supervision. Such central control was itself based on linking Spain's colonial administration with Catholic mandates—Christianizing, slavery, gold, and the Inquisition.

CHRISTIANIZING, SLAVERY, AND GOLD

In attempting to follow the mercantile methods of Holland, Spain had vainly tried to develop commercial monopolies that comprehended three aspects of production and trade that later became successful models for colonization among the maritime states of Europe.

Through Spain's "monopoly of supply," the Spanish American colonists were prohibited from resorting to foreign markets other than Spain's for the supply of their wants. Then by the "monopoly of colonial produce," the colonists were compelled to bring gold, silver, and other valuables which were their chief output to Spain alone. And by the "monopoly of manufacture," they were required to bring their products to Spain in a raw or unmanufactured state, so that Spanish manufacturers might secure for themselves all the advantages arising from their further use or improvement.

But Spain could not carry through its own mercantile scheme because the Crown, looking to Mexico as its most prosperous colony, was largely interested in extracting Mexican bullion as a store of accumulated wealth. The colonies paid for imports with bullion, but the colonial administration in the Americas was based on slavery and peonage, not the creation of a viable market for goods, even if Spain could manufacture them. The export of raw materials other than bullion to Spain was minimal because Spanish manufacturing was repressed. Spanish capital went into religious monasteries and grain production, and Spain paid specie for English fish and manufactures.[19]

Although Spain's Mexican colonization proceeded as if the mercantile system was intact and operating smoothly, Spain's colonial governments were not favorably disposed to agriculture, improvement, and popular well-being. Not only was creative thought and expertise repressed among the indigenous people, but the Spanish-born ruling caste oppressed the Indians and the mixed Spanish-Indian *mestizo* majority, controlled those Spanish who were born in Mexico, *criollos*, and continued to hold fast against both the ideas of the enlightenment and the inroads of other would-be empires in the Americas.[20] And yet, though the Spanish enforced their "propria cultura," the Indian peoples retained their symbolic, ethnic ways. To maintain its domination, Spain thus imposed slavery, the *encomienda*, and peonage as the foundation of the labor system.

THE CONTEST FOR POWER

With Spain still a minor force in the world system, the major powers held sway over oceanic commerce and warfare.

The Netherlands in the mid-sixteenth century was the industrial center of the world; its rich and prosperous burghers viewed as preposterous the efforts of industrially backward Spain to claim a monopoly of trade with the Americas. Both Holland and England insisted on reaping their share of the riches of the New World and organized their navies to scour the seas in search of Spanish galleons to plunder.

The scene was framed by Charles V, king of Spain and emperor of Germany, who joined France in aiding the papal court to obstruct and suppress the progress of religious reformation in Spanish and French dominions.[21] Charles used his elevated authority as head of the Holy Roman Empire to launch religious wars that desolated the Netherlands. Yet in his zealotry, he battled all his neighbors, eventually impoverishing Spain itself. To pay for his religious and mercantile wars, Charles extracted subsidies from the Netherlands, punished rebelling Flemish subjects, annulled the charters of Ghent and destroyed its guilds. The king's religious puissance was also joined to the pope's authority expressed in the Treaty of Tordesillas to forbid any infringement by others on Spain's trading rights in the New World.

This arrogation of global authority was not to last. The discoveries of the Cape of Good Hope passage and of America had made distant commerce exclusively maritime, and both Protestant England and mercantile Holland powerfully contested the power of the Spanish Armada. Spain's persecutions in the Netherlands had produced a successful resistance that established Holland as a well-armed, commercial state.[22] And Spain brought on competitors by its own decimation of indigenous communities in the West Indies that compelled the occupying Spanish administrators to fill their places with slaves brought from Africa, thereby systematizing the slave trade and drawing in the Belgians, the Genoese, the merchants of Venice and Barcelona, the Portuguese, the Dutch and, most dangerous of all, the English. Englishmen the likes of John Hawkins entered the trade in 1562, learned the coasts of several continents, and began accumulating merchant capital for London's financial adventurers.[23]

It is hardly surprising that without gold or silver mines of their own, England, France, and the Netherlands all sought a portion of the stream of precious metals flowing to Spain and Portugal by formulating two basic, if seemingly contradictory, strategies: pillage and manufacturing for trade.

By the first strategy, their interlopers and "seadogs" successfully pillaged Spain's treasure ships while trading with the Spanish colonies. A handful of English merchants and shippers thus sought to "singe the king of Spain's beard," as they liked to boast, by sending out explorers and traders who were also soldiers equipped to simultaneously hold off the Spanish Armada and conquer the trade of native societies.

Spain moved to stop John Hawkins and other Englishmen who sold African slaves directly to the Spanish colonies in America in exchange for hides, ginger, sugar, and pearls produced by native Americans for Spanish settlers. But though the Spanish Crown sought to limit England's competitive acquisition of wealth by such trade with Spain's colonies, would-be English traders responded by employing guns to hijack Spanish bullion in the Americas and on the high seas. Sir Francis Drake thus became the "sea king" of the English Crown, accumulating by pillage of Spanish treasure what English traders could not earn by peaceful commerce.

As northern Europe did not sufficiently enrich itself by this initial scheme, the second ploy of England, France, and Holland was to build up manufactures and commerce at Spain's expense. Convinced that Spain's power rested upon the treasures of the Indies, both England's Thomas Munn and France's Colbert advocated intense manufacturing in order to trade the resulting wares for Spain's precious metals. "Manufactures," Colbert advised, "will produce returns in money, which is the single aim of commerce and the only means of increasing the greatness and power of the State."

Northern European nations still could not regularize trade without sea lanes of their own, though. Spain held military control of the Atlantic easterly passage to and westerly return from the East Indies, and Portugal monopolized the southeast route from the Orient around the horn of Africa and on westward to the Azores. And though the northeast path proved too cold and impracticable for the merchant adventurers of England in 1553, the northwest passage appeared a possible English route to the East Indies unimpeded by Iberian armadas. Frobisher's 1576 voyage in search of this sea lane was followed by one hundred years of similar efforts, which together did little more than open up fur trade for the Hudson Bay Company in 1670, because the channels between Baffin's Bay and the Bering Straits were icebound and impassable for the greater part of the year. Hence Frobisher had no way to find the northern passage from the Atlantic side on the east, and Drake failed to discover a passage from the Pacific side on the west.

Queen Elizabeth meanwhile granted a host of patents to well-connected courtiers like Sir Humphrey Gilbert (1578) and Sir Walter Raleigh (1585) to take possession of "heathen lands not enjoyed by any Christian prince." And England thereby concentrated not on Spanish America, but on Americas northern zone, though no effective occupation was established until a few years before Elizabeth's death in 1603.

Yet once more Drake—the "masterthief of the unknown world"—gave to Queen Elizabeth of England the spoils of brigandage, a tactical, if momentary, means to contest the power of Spain and Portugal.[24]

The Interim Century

Throughout the sixteenth century, then, the main thrust of empire turned on the competitive struggle of nation-states for metallic wealth, which effectively set the standard of well-being of each nation and its population. W.E.H. Lecky, Europe's first major sociologist, has described the importance of gold and silver in this century:

> To state this doctrine in the simplest form, it was believed that all wealth consisted of the precious metals, and that therefore a country was necessarily impoverished by every transaction which diminished its metallic riches, no matter how much it may have added to its other possessions ... and that to the nation which was unable to incline what was termed the "balance of commerce" [to be settled in gold bullion] in its favour, the entire transaction was an evil. It followed also that the importance of native productions was altogether subordinate to that of the export or import of gold.[25]

Although the increased acquisition of gold was the bellwether of national enrichment, nonetheless large quantities of gold and silver came into the hands of only a relatively small coterie in each of the contending European powers. Even Cortés had limited each of his men to 100 gold pieces from Montezuma's fabled treasure of one million gold pieces, reserving the "royal fifth" for Charles V, taking more than a fifth for himself, and giving the rest to his captains and three churchmen.[26]

Thereafter there was much New World bullion in contest. During the period between Europe's discovery of America and the acceleration of England's industrial revolution about 1760, some $1,859 million in gold and $3,594 million in silver were produced in the world, most in Spanish America. And during this time span, the production of bullion rose steadily to eight-and-a-half times what it had been before Columbus's voyage. The major sea powers tried to accumulate bullion in order to pay past bank debts to the Lombards or Fuggers that had been handed down from the Middle Ages, as well as to buy foreign wares and to lay the base for new capitalist industries.

Controlling the major gold mines in the New World, bullion-rich Spain thus remained England's chief prey and enemy. Not only had Spain attempted to lock out the whole of northern Europe from the New World, but the hated Spanish Crown had supported Irish rebellions against English hegemony. Spain had also taken up arms against English traders, torturing and murdering British adventurers in Spanish America.

In its contest with Spain, the English Crown publicly approved the wholesale pillage of her colonies and ships. And to defend herself, England built a navy that was stronger than the Spanish Armada and defeated it in 1588. By 1648, only six decades later, Spain's colonial and foreign commerce had been practically destroyed.[27] And so weakened was Spain's control over her American colonies that their future independence and quest for land seemed certain.

THE FRAME OF SPANISH AMERICAN REVOLTS

In the interim decades, European conflict pressed upon Spain. Charles V, increasingly encumbered in his attempts to maintain the structure of Christendom, was unable to stop the growth of Lutheranism and was compelled to accede in the 1555 Peace of Augsburg to the principle that each prince should decide his own religion and that of his subjects.

Retiring his crown, Charles then bequeathed the diadem of the central European empire to his brother Ferdinand and the crowns of Spain and the Netherlands to his son Philip, thereby simultaneously forwarding nationalist struggles for religious suzerainty, colonies, gold, and sea power.

Philip concentrated on the gold wrung from Mexico and Peru, suppressing both industry and thought in Iberia. Taking up the gauntlet of the Holy Roman Empire, Ferdinand led the Catholic Counter-Reformation, financing the mobilization of Catholic armies against wayward Catholic nations and Protestant revolts on the Continent. Forced to abandon most of Hungary to the Turks, the House of Hapsburg continued to drain Spain's military puissance, sustaining the Thirty Years War that desolated Central Europe.

Spain's land route to France also threatened that country's national existence. And having established and sustained a chain of small empires throughout South America, each governed by the Crown's appointees, Spain maintained its hold only by seeking to exclude all other European powers from the waters of the New World, a policy that brought on the contest with England that ended in the destruction of the Spanish Armada.

For three centuries after the defeat of its Armada, Spain remained a backwater of industrial development, a nation locked in archaic religious thought, a warlike country of diminishing natural resources. After its treasury was bled white by the illustrious "House of Austria," Spain was transferred to the "House of Bourbon," which dragged her into a new conflict with Austria and Italy as well as with England on the sea.

War between Spain and Great Britain, begun 12 December 1804, only worsened the financial strain on Spain and pressured the government to shift the burden to New Spain by issuing decrees for the compulsory sale of real estate to redeem the Crown's mortgages owed by chantries and pious institutions in Spanish America and the Philippines. The proceeds were to go to the Royal Treasury in Madrid to back up the government's failing paper money used to pay for military expenditures.

But the decree threatened the propertied classes in New Spain. Its wealthy had mortgaged portions of their property at 5 percent a year, with the interest payable under their wills to charitable foundations, to endow daughters and sisters entering a nunnery or to endow a chantry to support a chaplain who was duty-bound to say a certain number of masses each year for the soul of the benefactor. When the Spanish Crown then enforced a 40 million peso loan from these endowments, neither the charities nor the property owners had sufficient liquid funds, so the Crown moved to sell at public auction the Mexican elite's landholdings. *Hacendados*, merchants, miners, and town councils hotly protested, sending petitions to the authorities to block the Crown decree and warning them of the consequences.

The government refused to delay, however, and began compulsory redemptions on 6 September 1805, although the authorities were still willing to accept partial payments. Many owners were unable to raise sufficient funds, and this led to the 1807–8 mass auctions of houses, farms, cattle, and businesses. True, the authorities threatening to sell one of an owner's *haciendas* also haggled, reached new agreements, and limited the suffering they imposed. But as the richest landowners were the largest debtors, the landowning elite was estranged by Spain's immediate extraction of 12 million pesos, which amounted to approximately one-fourth of the total landowners' accumulated debt to charities and pious works.

Estrangement also touched the lower clergy once Spain was unable to pay the interest on the investments it had just "redeemed" from the landowners. As a result, Spain impoverished the majority of the Mexican secular clergy—the parish priests and clerics with no fixed benefice—and their vested "rights" converged with those of the landowners, supplying both clergy and *hacendados* with an ideology for seeking freedom through independence from Spain.[28]

Other classes were also pressured to seek land and freedom. The "colonial century" had brought the *encomienda*, as seventeenth-century Spaniards in *Ciudad de México* (Mexico City) institutionalized their control of extensive lands by creating the *hacienda* system. The Indian population, still small in relation to its need for land, retained its communities' common lands (*ejidos*). But as the Indian population tripled in the eighteenth century, new demands for both *ejidos* and *haciendas* were unfulfilled, and the Indians, becoming progressively unable to rely on subsistence agriculture, became more dependent upon commercial relations between themselves as laborers and the estates.

Hierarchical relations powerfully focused the process. As the *haciendas* controlled by an emergent oligarchy in Mexico City prospered, they also ensured a comfortable life to the provincial Spaniards who served as labor-overseers for that elite. And as Indian leaders who were empowered by their position to allot community lands also channeled "excess" Indians to the *haciendas*, they too controlled the fate of those living at the fringes of subsistence. Dependence on wage and subsistence work on the *haciendas* thereby became a way of survival.

Hacienda administrators might periodically refuse to give laboring communities estate pastures and woodlands in exchange for the regular provision of labor, so the flow of willing workers to the estates sometimes stopped. And when weather conditions and epidemic disease crippled Indian production of maize, brought famine near, and cut Indian labor on the *haciendas*, populations pressing harder to harvest from the *ejido* lands did not avoid the subsistence crisis.[29]

IMPERIAL SPAIN

Divisions by class and caste in both Spain and New Spain thus seeded the struggle of owners and peasants for land and wealth. Still the quest of New Spain's peasants for land, which was spurred on by the revolt against Spain, was long delayed; even partial fulfillment was put off for more than two hundred years.

The drive for unburdened land and wealth simmered, appearing just as imperial conflicts raked Europe, Spain was occupied by France, and the New World demanded independence, cutting off Spain's control.

The historic framing was no accident. By the time Napoleon Bonaparte had invaded Spain and placed his brother Joseph upon the throne to enforce his continental blockade against England in the early nineteenth century, both the Spanish people and the colonies in America had organized their revolts. Napoleon judiciously arrested and forced the abdication of Ferdinand VII, who had just succeeded Charles VI and the queen's royal favorite Godoy. The resulting popular uprising in Madrid against the French occupation army submerged Spain in a civil war, at the same time New Spain's war of national liberation was erupting. And as the authority of the Spanish viceroy in New Spain rested on the crown in Spain, with the king in captivity the Spanish colonies refused to recognize the usurper and declared their independence as republics. Eventually only Cuba and the Philippines remained Spanish colonies.[30]

In Spain itself juntas sprang forth in the name of Ferdinand VII, and in far away Mexico City the town council backed the landowners and lower clergy, demanding the end of the hated Spanish redemption and calling for indemnity for damages and restitution to original, preredemption conditions. Even the Spanish viceroy, Iturrigaray, refused to uphold Spanish authority. He joined the Creole party as New Spain's captain general and schemed to retain his past contracts with Mexican silver miners for imported mercury used for amalgamating silver ore, contracts that had allowed him to amass an enormous personal fortune in coin, precious metals, and gems.

Although New Spain's royal officials were still confirmed in their positions, real power rested with Iturrigaray and those professional Creoles who owned *haciendas* and filled civil and ecclesiastical posts. Thus on 9 August, with powerful *hacendados'* backing, the viceroy suspended the forced redemption.

This single act exacerbated the cleavage between Spanish-born importers of goods from Spain and the Creole landowners who, through independence from Spain, sought cheaper manufactures imported from England or other countries. And as New Spain's European-born Spaniards bred to merchant trade were suddenly allied with Spain against colonial landowners and the viceroy, they conspired to mobilize a small military force comprised of 300 poor, foreign-born employees of Spanish shops, who themselves aspired for security under Iberia's regime. Assaulting the viceregal palace, they easily apprehended and imprisoned both the viceroy and Creole independence leaders.[31] But no sooner was a new viceroy appointed than New Spain was launched on a violent revolt.

The logic of Spain's centuries-old legitimate succession had meanwhile been broken, as the Spaniards themselves had undermined such succession and the "Americans" (as the Creoles began to call themselves) moved to restore the line of royal authority by military means. Although they disguised their efforts as a struggle to save New Spain from the atheistic Bonaparte and restore Spain's legitimate King Ferdinand VII, Hidalgo and others secretly sought New Spain's national independence. And though the Creole revolt under Hidalgo was ostensibly to restore Spanish rule and stability, it soon became a class war when the starving poor unable to survive off the failed 1809 crop sacked the *haciendas* of both Spaniards and Creoles, spreading the revolt through the Bajío.

A stone's throw from Spanish-ruled cities were rural populations living in Bajío under conditions only partly of their choosing. As few European-born Spaniards lived outside the militarized capital, Mexico City, Puebla, and Veracruz, the locus of popular revolt was ideally centered in the distant, broad fertile valley of the Bajío. This valley stretched from Querétaro in the east almost as far as Lake Chapala in the west and from the town of León and the village of Dolores in the north to Lake Cuitzeco in the south. Here Indian laborers had been brought in or migrated after the Spaniards introduced the two-crop agriculture of maize, which was grown in the rainy season and sometimes irrigated, and wheat, which was raised in the dry season with irrigated waters of the Lerma River and its tributaries. Questions of unrelenting peasant exploitation and land rights were especially acute in the Intendency of Guanajuato, where most of the Indians lived as town laborers or peons on Creole *haciendas* and small-farm *ranchos* owned by *mestizos*. And even in the Guadalajara region where Indian villages managed to own land, they leased their holdings to nearby *haciendas* for very low rents, with automatic lease renewals opening the way for the eventual appropriation of their lands.

To secure land and resources to plant their own farms would clearly take a revolution. And yet the express need for such an extreme was practically unrecognized because of the cultural integration of the largely *mestizos* Indians with *mestizo rancheros* and Creole owners of *hacienda*. It is not surprising that their consciousness of landlessness or the low-rents paid them was secondary to the rising national feelings of wealthy Creoles, especially those of the cloth, who were in danger of losing their land and stipends. Raising the banner of the black Virgin of Guadalupe as patroness of New Spain that had been adopted decades earlier in 1746, hundreds of clerics were thus mobilized behind the curate Miguel Hidalgo y Costilla.

A NATIONAL ALLIANCE OF SEPARATE INTERESTS

Could there be a national alliance of separate interests pursuing independence against Spain under Hidalgo's banner?

The rich Creole landowners had hired as managers Spanish immigrants who aspired for their own land, cattle, and black or mulatto slaves, and these immigrants had almost as much to lose as the Creoles by Spain's forced redemption loans and her embargo of the *haciendas*. And to these initial allies were added the soldier sons of prosperous Spanish-Basque merchants, soldiers not tied to commerce but aspiring to landowning, who had risen to lead the small colonial militia. These militia officers were then joined by a core of revolutionary clerics determined to imprison the rich Spaniards, to confiscate their property to finance the revolution, to overthrow any opposing authority, and to threaten Spain itself.

Facing both internal revolt in Mexico and the simultaneous French conquest of Spain, in 1810 Spanish rule in Mexico was confronted by *la burguesía* of *criollos* and *mestizos* who sought to establish their own authority. As Spain had weakened under French attack in the spring of 1810, these Mexicans were clearly invested with a new opportunity to seize power, if only they could mobilize a class alliance behind them.

Life in the shadows of Spain must have seemed immutable to those tied to its mercantile and imperial oversight. Colonial loyalists at first had sent the beleaguered Spanish Crown large sums of money, and even the United States had supplied great quantities of flour, foreseeing that a strengthened Spain would weaken French ambitions in America. But Spain repaid the debt in an imperious, compromising way in early 1810 when the junta at Sevilla granted limited, if direct, representation to the South American colonists. "At last you are raised to the dignity of men," the junta mandated. "The times are already past in which, under an unsupportable yoke, you were the victims of absolutism, ambition and ignorance. Bear in mind that in electing your representative to the Spanish *Cortes*, your destiny will no longer depend on kings, ministers or governors, but is in your own hands."

But all was not equal under the regency at Cadiz, for Spain's South American colonists were to have a single representative for every million inhabitants, while in Spain there was one representative for every hundred thousand, even though the greater part of the Iberian peninsula was then under French domination.

Attempting to extend Gallic rule in South America, France had meanwhile moved powerfully to impose its suzerainty; French commissioners arrived there in the spring of 1810 to demand an oath of fealty to King Joseph. The Spanish colonists refused to budge, however. They viewed these colonial agents as hateful "afrancesados" and burst their sought-for imperial bubble by supporting revolutionary movements to throw off the yoke of all of Europe, first in New Spain, then throughout Spanish America.

The exploding Mexican movement immediately deposed Viceroy Don José de Iturrigaray, installing a marshal of the army. Confronted thus and holding fastidiously to its remaining threads of power, the Spanish junta then moved to reassert control by ordering the marshal superseded by the archbishop of Mexico, only to replace him with the regency of Cadiz, which then appointed General Vinegas as new viceroy.[32]

But this shell game of switching Spanish authority in the Americas ended with Napoleon's conquest of Spain, the installation of his brother on the Spanish throne, Spain's financial crisis, which tore at the heart of its empire, and the collapse of the Inquisition in Mexico.

A LESSON NOT LOST

The ease with which Napoleon overturned the government in Spain and its colony was a lesson not lost in Mexico, for accepted doctrine held that on the disappearance of a monarch his sovereignty reverted to the people. Having already been harshly disciplined by the Inquisition for their dangerous opinions as well as for their efforts to set up small industries violating Spain's mercantile laws, Mexico's politically enlightened began a swift revolt.

With Mexican curate Miguel Hidalgo leading the opposition and calling for popular rule, a small band organized among the *criollo* middle and upper classes to struggle against the despised and now disorganized Spanish regime. Opposing Viceroy Vinegas's demand for money to support the Spanish cause, Hidalgo now issued the *Grito de Dolores*, which listed Spain's imperial impositions but did not yet demand Mexico's independence.

The revolt then moved by degrees of awareness. Inexperienced in forming secret societies, the initial *criollo* revolutionaries had been betrayed in 1809. Acting more cautiously, Hidalgo plotted with army officers Ignacio José Allende and Juan de Aldama, and on 16 September 1810 they outmaneuvered the Spanish *gachupines* ruling Mexico. First they seized the local Dolores jail and freed political prisoners, and then from the ramparts of Hidalgo's own church, they called upon the people who were gathering below from the countryside to engage in mass insurrection.

At this point, though, Hidalgo hesitated, going only halfway. He denounced the *gachupines* for plotting to recognize Napoleon's rule over Spain and to turn state and church over to the French, but he also called on patriotic Mexicans and loyal Catholics to raise the banner of the beleaguered Spanish king, Fernando VII, and drive the Spanish traitors out of America.[33]

Although Hidalgo had loosed powerful forces, his own voice was soon muffled in the sudden tidal wave of passions released as an army of Indian and *mestizo* peasants overran plantations, smashed property, and seized corn, cattle, and weapons. Some starving, most undisciplined, the many thousands sacked not only the property of European-born Spaniards, but also that of wealthy Creoles. Moving from plantation to plantation and through towns, the army grew steadily with peons of each liberated plantation, as it raided and looted the homes of the rich, whether they were of Spanish origin or were Mexican-sired *criollos*. Emotions surged as Hidalgo raised high on his lance the banner of the Virgin of Guadalupe. The soldier peasants, seemingly touched by the divine, wept and knelt before the image of the black Virgin Mary, fastening her image to their sombreros. Some 50,000 strong, they moved powerfully across the face of Bajío, entering the silver mining town of Guanajuato and destroying the Spanish garrison, where the focal point of destruction was the Alhóndiga de Granaditas, a large stone building used by the government for the storage of grain.

Having thrown themselves into the first military action they had ever seen, the Indians could not turn back, for the mob pressed on those who went in front, compelling them to advance, trampling on those shot by the defending Spanish garrison even as men from the rear replaced them. The terrified Spaniards meanwhile tried to placate the attackers. Some defenders threw money out the windows, others clamored to surrender, but their pleas were ignored by the Indians. Still others threw themselves at the feet of priests to receive absolution at their last hour. But the maddened multitude pushed on, looting the wealthy, smashing their homes, shops, and mine machinery, assaulting and massacring Spaniards. And the *criollo* revolutionary leaders dared not, could not, stop them.

The race for power having now reached its highest pitch, arms, authority, and followers became the essential ingredients for victory. Hidalgo quickly set up a cannon factory at Guanajuato. Assuming the title of *generalíssimo* of the revolutionary army, he set up a new government at Valladolid, proclaimed his political goal of an elected Mexican congress that would govern in the name of Fernando VII, and attempted to conciliate the upper classes by offering high military and civil posts to several prominent *criollos*.

But this gesture of deference to a future order sat ill on the shoulders of the terrified *criollos*, who wavered in both cities and country in their support of the revolution and finally allied against Hidalgo with the Spanish government and bishops who had once favored reform. As they hastened their retreat to the side of the Spanish viceroy and Archbishop Lizana (who on 11 October had excommunicated Hidalgo from the Catholic church), battle lines firmed under pressures of the army of exploited.

Hidalgo then broadened his appeal by decree on 19 October 1810, abolishing all payments of tribute to landowners, freeing the Indians from slavery, and restoring the Indians' rights to *ejidos*, which represented their historic communal lands:

> By these presents I order the judges and justices of the district of this capital to proceed immediately in the collection of the rents due this day by the lessees of the lands belonging to the Indian communities, the said rents to be entered in the national treasury. The lands shall be turned over to the Indians for their cultivation, and they may not be rented out in the future, for it is my wish that only the Indians in their respective towns shall have use of them. . . .
>
> From the moment that the courageous American nation took up arms to throw off the heavy yoke that oppressed it for three centuries, one of its principal aims has been to extinguish the multitude of taxes that kept it in poverty. Since the critical state of our affairs does not permit the framing of adequate provisions in this respect, because of the need of the kingdom for money to defray the costs of the war, for the present I propose to remedy the most urgent abuses by means of the following declarations. First: All slaveowners shall set their slaves free within ten days, on pain of death for

violation of this article. Second: The payment of tribute by all the castes that used to pay it shall henceforth cease, and no other taxes shall be collected from the Indians. Third: In all judicial business, documents, deeds, and actions, only ordinary paper shall be used, and the use of [official, crown-imprinted] sealed paper is abolished.[34]

When Guadalajara's printing press fell into the hands of rebel headquarters, Hidalgo publicized his edicts, adding that taxes on alcoholic beverages and tobacco were be removed to make them available to the poor.[35]

Yet these were only phrases, not deeds. And a change of fortunes was in the wind, as Hidalgo failed to outflank Spanish generals. His growing army, now 80,000, easily took Monte de las Cruces, but then lost morale and half its numbers when Hidalgo hesitated three days, refusing to march on the Spanish viceroy's stronghold in Mexico City. He turned back when the city populace failed to rise against the authorities and intelligence reported a well-organized army was approaching to protect the capital. Turning his troops towards Querétaro, Hidalgo was then routed by the Spanish force and retreated to rebel-liberated Guadalajara to set up a revolutionary government.

As the lines of military demarcation tightened, brutalities quickly escalated on both sides. The Spanish arbitrarily executed every tenth Indian and *mestizo* in Alhóndiga, while Hidalgo's forces decimated the Spanish population in Guadalajara. Meanwhile, a small Spanish force under Félix María Calleja had persuaded *hacendados* to lend him their employees, guards, and servants to recapture the towns held by the insurgents, and he finally defeated Hidalgo's poorly equipped, undisciplined, and disorganized army near Guadalajara. And after the final defeat of Hidalgo's ragtag army by Calleja's more professional forces, Hidalgo and his followers were captured in flight to the United States.

The lay leaders were executed first, and then Hildago was convicted of heresy, defrocked, and executed by a firing squad. His severed head, with those of three other leaders, hung in four iron cages placed on the corners of the quadrangular Guanajuato grain storage tower, displayed as a warning to his followers during the ensuing decade, remaining there until Mexico secured its independence from Spain in 1821. Here, towards the focal point of the initial revolt of Indians, miners, and Guanajuato's common people, all future Mexican revolutionaries would look back.[36]

So came and went the first revolt in modern Mexico. The revolutionaries took Guanajuato, stormed its granary, butchered its defenders, and appropriated 3 million pesos in coin and silver bars, but they ended in defeat, even as the battle of the great powers for position in Spanish America intensified.

POWER POSITIONING AND THE END OF EMPIRE

Over three centuries, Spain's empire in the Americas had been weakened as it spread its reach beyond its resources and was unable to stop infringements on its colonial holdings by other European powers.

Financial insolvency had also beset the Spanish Crown; from the day Charles V assumed the throne, Spain was reduced from the status of lender to, then paymaster for, and finally dupe of, the illustrious House of Austria.

Austria was caught in its own predicament, as to maintain its empire it depended upon the maintenance of religious unity and thus political solidarity in Europe. With the Reformation jeopardizing its position, Austria looked to Spain as its swordsman of the Counter-Reformation. This role led Charles V's son Philip into an attempt to subjugate the Netherlands and into an attack on England that led to the defeat of his Armada.[37]

With Spain isolated and impoverished, England stepped into its commercial place in Latin America. England's contraband merchant marine carved out a market sphere that undermined Spain's previous attempt to keep others from trading with its colonies.[38] And still later, the 1795–1815 Napoleonic Wars almost completely undermined Spain's political domination in the Americas.

Britain was at first allied to Spain against Napoleon and was thereby limited in openly aiding the insurgents in Spanish America. But once Napoleon was defeated, Britain maneuvered to prevent other European nations from arming Spain to put down the rebellion. British merchants also sold arms to the insurgents, and many British subjects enrolled in Latin America's revolutionary forces.[39] Backing Simón Bolívar's insurgent troops with funds, horses, equipment, and commissaries, Britain pursued its own future sphere in the Americas.[40] And both Britain and her former North American colonies favored the independence of Latin America, the better to permit security and their own access to its commerce and future opportunities.

FREEDOM'S CALL

With Hidaldgo and Bolívar elevated as symbolic beacons of freedom's call, almost all of Spanish America reverberated in revolt.

In Venezuela, Simón Bolívar hoped to establish and spread the republican institutions he had carefully studied in the United States; he refused the Spanish Commission's 18 April 1810 demand for adhesion to the regency in Cádiz. "This power which fluctuates in such manner in Spain and does not secure itself, invites us to establish a Junta of our own and to govern ourselves," the liberator fulminated.

Venezuelans agreed. Replacing Emperan as the Spanish governor of the colony and rejecting him as the president of an independent state, the population in Caracas proclaimed its own junta and without a gunshot refused to recognize the regency of Cádiz, banishing the former Spanish governor to the United States. The pattern was then repeated elsewhere from Buenos Aires to Montevideo, Chile, and Baton Rouge, as the revolutionaries cut off Spain and Portugal from ruling the Americas and, in the political vacuum created, counted on the United States to try to keep France and Britain from replacing Spain.

Unsatisfied with their respective share of the spoils as the Spanish retreated, Britain and France moved to outflank one another, taking territories and negotiating a new partition of the former Spanish-American colonies. Britain thus blockaded Buenos Aires and Montevideo in response to the audacity of the settlers attempting to oust them and also seized the French colonies of Guadeloupe, Isle de Bourbon, Java, and Isle de France. To offset this 1810 loss of French territory and prestige, Napoleon's new prime minister, Fouché, sent a secret agent named Fagan to suggest that if Great Britain would yield Spain to France, France would join in creating out of the Spanish-American colonies an empire for Spain's Ferdinand VII so that Spain in Europe would effectively cease to exist and be relocated to the Americas.[41]

But in Mexico, conservative churchmen, army officers, and officials preferred separation from Spain rather than submission to the liberal constitution imposed on Ferdinand VII by his army in revolt. And Napoleon pursued still broader plans to conquer Spain by arms and replace the Spanish administration throughout the Americas.

THE UNITED STATES RECOILS

Viewing the European powers' aggressive plans for partition of Spanish America, the United States was deeply concerned that some European power, especially England, might establish itself on the geographic doorstep of the United States.

The U.S. position had taken shape during the Napoleonic Wars, which elevated fears that Bonaparte's move to establish an empire in Spanish America would impinge on U.S. sovereignty. France had long sought to create a North American empire that would link Quebec and New Orleans west of the Mississippi River and sweep eastward to squeeze the United States republic back to the Atlantic seaboard. The central question was now whether U.S. naval forces could handle a French presence in Latin America.

After the fortuitous acquisition in 1803 of 875,025 square miles comprising Louisiana for $15 million[42] from Spain's crowned heads, Louis and Anna, Thomas Jefferson noted the ease with which New Orleans could be attacked from Cuba. He was especially concerned about the possibility that a European power might use Havana to cut off all maritime communications and trade between the U.S. gulf ports of the Mississippi River and the eastern states. Jefferson's advocacy of a "Cuba Policy" for the United States was especially designed to avert the danger which Spanish Cuba presented to the security of the United States and thereby to protect against the possibility that a strong naval power might establish itself in Havana.[43]

The policies promoted by Jefferson were solidified during the 16-year wars fought against the Spanish Crown from 1809 to 1825 for the independence of Latin America.[44] The 1812–14 war between Great Britain and the United States also clearly exposed the lack of U.S. defenses in the South. In 1828 the United States declared its policy that Cuba should continue in the hands of Spain, to which it remained loyal,[45] or else declare its independence. If either of these two solutions proved impossible, then for indispensable reasons of national defense, Cuba could be allowed to fall into the hands of no power but the United States. Clearly the United States was thinking of the military danger of an unbridled France or England on its doorstep.

Presidents Jefferson, Madison, and Monroe all maintained this same policy. When Monroe assumed the presidency, he debated this question with Secretary of State John Quincy Adams and the members of his cabinet in the spring of 1823. These discussions led to the formal declaration of this policy, which was to be maintained even if it meant war with Great Britain or any other power which might attempt to occupy Cuba.[46]

The only acceptable occupying power, then, was Spain. Thus the U.S. Cuban policy was essential to U.S. security, as John Quincy Adams informed the Spanish government in a formal communiqué:

> Cuba, almost in sight of our shores, from a multitude of considerations has become an object of transcendent importance to the policy and economic interests of the Union. Its commanding position with reference to the Gulf of Mexico and the West Indies Seas; the character of its population; its situation midwest between our southern coast and the island of Santa Domingo; its sage and capacious harbor of Havana, fronting a long line of our shores destitute of the same advantage; the nature of its products and wants, furnishing the supplies and needing the returns of a commerce immensely profitable and mutually beneficial, give it an importance in the aim of our national interest, with which that of no other foreign territory can be compared, and little inferior to that which binds the different members of the union together.[47]

The same U.S. policy was extended to all of Spanish America on 2 December 1823 by President James Monroe's message to Congress. In this message he established the doctrine that bears his name, declaring that the United States would consider any attempt by European powers to extend their "system to the Western Hemisphere as dangerous to the peace and security of the United States."[48]

The battle of high rhetoric among the great powers had already begun a year earlier in November 1822; the Congress of Verona had been called to consider the feasibility of restoring the Spanish monarchy in Latin America. Because Britain was firmly opposed to this policy and wanted to bring the American continent into its own sphere of influence, it withdrew from the congress. The British prime minister, George Canning, then contacted the U.S. minister, Richard Rush, in March 1823 in hopes of negotiating an agreement for joint action in Latin America. The crux of the Canning proposal was that Britain considered "the recovery of the colonies of Spain to be hopeless, ... the question of recognition of them, as independent states, to be one of time and circumstances." Canning stated that Great Britain was "by no means disposed to throw any impediments in the way of an arrangement between them and the mother country ... [but] could not see any portion of them transferred to any other power, with indifference." Therefore, Canning argued, a declaration by the United States and Britain would be most effective in intimidating "any European power which cherishes other projects, which looks to a forcible enterprise of reducing the colonies to subjugation, on behalf of or in the name of Spain; or which mediates the acquisition of any part of them to itself, by cession or conquest."

England had France in mind. But the United States was unwilling to embrace the proposal, though it also hesitated to recognize and support any of the Latin American republics. Secretary of State Adams thought it was better not "to come in as a duckboat in the wake of the British man-of-war." And President Monroe's seventh annual message to Congress delineated the U.S. position, insisting that "as a principle in which the rights and interests of the United States are involved, that the American continents, by the free and independent condition which they have assumed and maintain, are henceforth not to be considered as subjects for future colonization by any European powers."

This was an ungloved slap in Britain's face, but the upstart United States remained cautious. It was not the policy of the United States to interfere in the wars of Europe, Monroe stated:

> It is only when our rights are invaded or seriously menaced that we resent injuries or make preparations for our defense. With the movements in this hemisphere we are of necessity more immediately connected.

Speaking of the European powers, he asserted:

> [We] should consider any other attempt on their part to extend their system to any portion of this hemisphere as dangerous to our peace and safety. ....
> With the existing colonies or dependencies of any European power we have not interfered and shall not interfere. But with the governments who have declared their independence and maintain it, and whose independence we have, on great consideration and on just principles, acknowledged, we could not view any interposition for the purpose of oppressing them, or controlling in any other manner their destiny, by any European power in any

other light than as the manifestation of an unfriendly disposition towards the United States.

Clearly, the United States worried that the internal concerns and wars in Europe would be extended to the continents of North and South America. Hence, in Monroe's view:

> It was impossible that the allied powers [of Europe] should extend their political system to any portion of either continent without endangering our peaceful happiness; nor can anyone believe that our southern brethen, if left to themselves, would adopt it of their own accord. It is equally impossible, therefore, that we should behold such interposition in any form with indifference. .... It is still policy to the United States to leave other parties to themselves, in the hope that other powers will pursue the same course.[49]

In this context of great power aspirations, the independence that any republics in the Americas won by hard-fought battles would be readily recognized by the United States.

STEPS TO MEXICAN INDEPENDENCE

As the great powers thus positioned themselves to replace Spain from 1810 to 1824, Mexican rebel forces stiffened in opposition, continuing their struggle for independence.

Hidalgo's execution and the viceroy's military pacification of Bajío were major setbacks. But thereafter another brazen priest, José María Morelos, led a reorganized and disciplined revolutionary army from the "hot country" between the Pacific coast and the central plateaus. Prohibiting looting and indiscriminate killing, Morelos declared Mexico's independence from Spain before Ferdinand VII could recover power from Napoleon's armies that were retreating across Europe.

To escape reimposition of the foreign yoke, Morelos organized a September 1813 national congress of provincial representatives and prepared a program, "Sentiments of the Nation," that called for an America free and independent of Spain and all other nations, governments, or monarchies. And the Congress reaffirmed on 6 November that "under the present circumstances in Europe ... dependence on the Spanish throne should be dissolved."

The property of Spaniards was to be confiscated and then carefully administered to finance the war of independence. All Americans were hereafter to be equal; slavery, tribute, and all ethnic distinctions were to be abolished and the property of all Americans was to be respected.

Without harboring any resentment against the church for its past misdeeds, Morelos argued that the Catholic religion was to be the core of solidarity, with its ministers supported by tithes and nature's first fruits. No other religion was to be tolerated. Catholic dogma was to be upheld by the hierarchy of Pope, bishops, and curates through the methods of the hated Inquisition, so that, in Morelos's literary allusion, "every plant which God did not plant should be torn out." The Congress then moved to recognize the Catholic religion alone, prohibiting the use of any other in public or secret, as the Inquisition had also done. The Congress would also use its power to protect the purity of the faith and the preservation of the regular Catholic orders; the legislators celebrated prospective treaties with the Holy See. On the initiative of Morelos, a decree reestablishing the Jesuit Society of Jesus was announced on the same day that independence was declared.

But all came to naught in the next three years. Morelos's forces were decisively defeated at Valladolid in November, and General Calleja's assaults took the territory held by Morelos. The Congress fled to the heart of the hot country to work in isolation from the Morelos forces on a constitution that was published 22 October 1814. The royalist offensive then dispersed the Congress, and the constitution could not be carried out. Like Hidalgo, Morelos was captured, then executed on 22 December 1815.

For the next five years, only a handful of insurgent groups resisted, and so weak was their threat that Calleja was recalled by the Spanish government in 1816. The newly appointed viceroy, Count Apodaca of Venadito, then offered conditional surrender to the remaining rebels. Many accepted; others went into hiding. By 1820, only Vincente Guerrero, aided by a handful of others in the hot country, led a major main force that refused to surrender.

POLITICAL REFORM IN SPAIN AND ITS REPERCUSSIONS IN AMERICA

Army officers in Spain meanwhile sought a new ordering of political power. On 1 January 1820, they proclaimed the liberal constitution that had been approved by the *Cortes* in 1812 but annulled by Ferdinand VII upon his May 1814 return to Spain. No match for the new revolutionary groups, the king was now forced to accept constitutional rule. Anticlerical measures followed in June, including the suppression of the Society of Jesus and certain other religious orders.

With the Spanish clergy under attack and its privileges and property holdings in jeopardy, the leaders of New Spain's ecclesiastical circles across the Atlantic now sought to save their church by supporting Mexican independence. Seeking a bloodless transfer of power, Bishop Antonio Pérez of Puebla, the rector of the University of Mexico, and canon Matías Monteagudo of the metropolitan cathedral allied with the military commander of southern Mexico, Colonel Agustín de Iturbide, who had fought for the Crown and ruthlessly executed insurgent priests without trial during the civil war. Iturbide had earlier retired under viceregal accusation of unscrupulous financial dealings, but because of his military prowess, he was reappointed to an army command by the Spanish viceroy in 1821.

The backdrop for this new alliance was Spain's political transition and the troubles within its richest colony. Completely frustrated in their earlier attempt to maintain New Spain as part of the Spanish Crown, the Mexican clergy and self-styled nobles now wanted independence and a monarchy for Mexico, with the throne occupied by a prince of the ruling house of Spain. These would-be throne nobles also sought to elevate themselves to the position of *grandees*.

The arrival of an April 1820 royal order requiring that everyone swear loyalty to Spain's new liberal constitution initially quieted the clergy and landowners, but it liberated the press to write freely of past oppressions and needed changes. As a new order was clearly in the making, political prisoners were released from the dungeons, and the Inquisition and tribunal of public security were undermined.

Switching military allegiances, General Iturbide now attempted to gain the goodwill and confidence of his former revolutionary adversaries, Vincent Guerrero in the hot country and Nicolás Bravo, who was languishing in a royalist prison. In February 1821, General Iturbide proceeded to issue a *pronunciamiento* containing his "Plan of Iguala," which called for Mexican independence that would join those born in America with Europeans, Africans, and Asians living there under a Spanish Bourbon prince. In a powerful appeal, Iturbide argued that all great countries had once been ruled by other nations, that they had all outgrown their mother countries, and that now Mexico's moment had come to unite as one:

> European Spaniards! Your country is America, for you live here; here you have your beloved wives, your tender children, your *haciendas*, your businesses and other possessions.
> Americans! Who among you can say that you are not of Spanish descent? Behold the sweet chain that unites us; consider the bonds of friendship, interdependence of interest, education, language, and harmony of feelings.
> . . .
> The time has arrived . . . that our union should emancipate America without need of foreign help. At the head of a brave and determined army, I proclaim the Independence of Northern America![50]

The breadth of the appeal was designed to neutralize opposition of Spanish residents by guaranteeing that they would live unmolested possessed of their property to isolate the remaining handful of royalist officers, to unite the nation of landless and landowners, whites, *mestizos*, and Indians under Catholic clergy high and low, and to offer long-sought independence to the insurgents.

Several rebel leaders responded to Iturbide's appeal, and together they forced Viceroy Apodaca to resign. But as King Ferdinand VII still demanded maintenance of the empire and refused to accept the separate crown for Mexico, General Iturbide issued the famous "Three Guarantees"—independence of New Spain from the king, solidarity of Creoles and 50,000 Spaniards all holding the same civil rights, and the preservation of the Catholic church and clergy.

Juan O'Donojú, a Spanish liberal of Irish descent, was dispatched to Mexico as new acting viceroy. He conferred with Iturbide and on 24 August signed the *Manifesto of Iguala* and thus accepted the plan for future independence. This plan called for a constitutional monarchy under Ferdinand VII, or in case of his refusal, another Spanish prince or a prince of any reigning European dynasty. If they all refused to accept, the ruler was to be selected by the Mexican Congress.

POST-INDEPENDENCE TURMOIL

With Spain divided by civil war and too weak to take action, Mexico, Guatemala, and Costa Rica each formally declared their independence by autumn 1823.

In Mexico, internal turmoil roiled the nation almost immediately after independence. Under the banner of the "Three Guarantees," the Mexican army of 50,000 men had powerfully united the guerrilla forces of nationalist General Guerrero with the well-provisioned troops under Iturbide. Together they defeated the 6,000 remaining expeditionary forces of the colonial regime, eliminated the viceregal power, and forced the count of Venadito to resign on 5 July.

After declaring Mexico's independence on 28 September 1823 and ensuring there would be no succession of a Spanish prince, Iturbide selected a governing junta of arch-conservatives that included himself, the canon Monteagudo, the bishop of Puebla, José María Fagoaga of the opulent silver-mining family, several members of the creole nobility and, as negotiator with Spain, the former Spanish viceroy, O'Donojú. The junta then refused to negotiate a settlement with Spain under the Córdoba convention and tried to block fearful Spaniards from repatriating their funds to Spain.

A group of royalists then recoiled and set up defenses in the San Juan Ulúa fortress in front of Veracruz harbor; they planned to rule the sea while awaiting Spanish reinforcements. Two months later, when word finally reached Iberia by sail, the Spanish Parliament declared the Córdoba Agreement null and void.

OBSTACLES TO REHABILITATION

Mexico was now politically independent but faced an economy in ruins and a bankrupt state treasury. Iturbide's government had no way to rehabilitate flooded mines, burned *haciendas*, and razed towns and villages, and it could not meet the soaring expenses involved in supplying the army and repatriating Spanish troops.

When Iturbide followed bad advice from his confidant Alexander von Humboldt and lowered taxes, the fiscal crisis worsened. This crisis was compounded by the junta's failure to raise a loan and Iturbide's desperate attempt to impose a forced loan on cash-laden Spanish import houses in Mexico City.

When many Spanish merchants refused to pay up and made plans to emigrate with their savings, the government imprisoned some as a warning, thereby violating Iturbide's promises made in both the Plan of Iguala and the Córdoba Agreement.

Meanwhile, Iturbide had to deal with the township selection of republican electors who were trying to copy the U.S. Constitution and royalist, Bourbon electors who were trying to copy the Spanish Constitution. He also faced congressional efforts to keep him from occupying the highest seat as president of the legislature. Congress also suspended the forced loan on Spanish merchants, and Bourbonist deputies opposed their arbitrary arrest. Congress instead called for the public auction of Jesuit properties confiscated a half-century earlier. With the treasury now completely empty, Iturbide declared another forced loan—this one on ecclesiastical bodies, thereby deepening the conflict with Rome.

Iturbide now had Spain, the Mexican legislature, and the Holy See set against him, though he still controlled the army and the populace viewed him as liberator. With popular backing, the army garrisons proclaimed Iturbide as Emperor Agustín I on 18 May 1822 and forced Congress to seat him, establishing a representative monarchical system. Iturbide was formally crowned in the Cathedral of Mexico in July,[51] the emperor being promptly recognized by the insurgents Bravo and Guerrero (whom Iturbide had rewarded respectively with the titles of marshal and commander of southern Mexico). But with the legislature under Iturbide's dictatorial control, conspiracies abounded, leading to his imprisonment of 19 deputies and several army officers. Then in October the emperor dissolved the Congress, and the Mexican church, fearing liquidation, rallied to his support.

Confronted by mutual distrust among Mexicans, Rome, and imperial Madrid, Mexico sought new allies to provide national security; in January 1823, Mexico established diplomatic relations with Washington, London, and the Holy See. President Monroe had recognized Mexican independence in March, and the United States sent its special envoy Joel R. Poinsett to negotiate with the new democratic government. He found a self-installed emperor who was about to dissolve the Congress and maintain military rule by keeping his troops well supplied and paid. Iturbide had already raided a convoy carrying 1.2 million pesos from Mexico City to Veracruz bound for Spain. Britain meanwhile was more interested in providing a loan than in supporting Mexican democracy. And Mexican democrats and opposition parties were bridling to revolt.

Then in early December, Antonio López de Santa Anna, the Veracruz military commander, proclaimed a revolution. (Santa Anna was a former royal officer who had fought for the Manifesto of Iguala and then supported the empire.) Accusing Iturbide by letter and proclaiming a Mexican republic at Veracruz, Santa Anna called for the reinstallation of the Congress and the formation of a constitution based on "religion, independence and union," elements which had been the core of the Manifesto of Iguala that the new emperor had violated. As generals Bravo and Guerrero promptly seconded the move (with Guerrero's incisive aside that Mexican independence had not been solely Iturbide's achievement), the way was open for the bulk of the army to support the revolution behind two of Mexico's former liberal deputies to the Spanish Parliament, Ramos Arizpe and Michelena. In checkmate, Iturbide was forced to abdicate on 19 March.

Although independence was only 18 months old, the Manifesto of Iguala was a dead letter and the emperor's reign had lasted only ten months. Santa Anna had outflanked Iturbide, and Congress declared Iturbide a traitor and banished him to Italy with a pension for good behavior.[52]

SHUFFLING THE GLOBAL POWER DECK

Congress then reassembled and appointed a provisional governing triumvirate (the Supreme Executive Power consisting of generals Guadalupe Victoria, Nicolás Bravo, and the turncoat Spaniard Pedro Negrete). The Supreme Executive Power in turn appointed four cabinet members led by conservative Lucas Alamán.

Having established a strong provisional government, Santa Anna had returning ex-emperor Iturbide shot in July 1824 and formally took Mexico out of the Spanish sphere.

The new alignment in Congress meanwhile swung Iturbide's former followers into the republican camp opposed to the Bourbonists, ensuring that no European emperor would follow the defeated Iturbide.

This concretized a global realignment of imperial centrists representing Spain set against anti–Hispanic forces representing the Americas. The opponents did combat under two factions of the secretive organization of freemasonry: the "Scottish Rite" supported by Spain and the "York Rite" supported by the U.S. and America's revolutionists. Associated with the freemasons of the Scottish Rite, Mexico's pro–Hispanic Bourbonists supported a strong, centrist regime, while the anti–Hispanic republicans favored a federation on the U.S. model, supporting provincial interests and regional autonomy. The latter, organized in lodges of the York Rite, followed the ideological beliefs of U.S. freemasons, with the help in 1825 of Poinsett, now the U.S. minister to Mexico in charge of implementing the Monroe Doctrine.

It is not surprising that the struggle of social classes in Mexico powerfully reflected Spanish and U.S. interests. This struggle was mediated by a Mexican state at once centrist and federalist in which the parry and riposte of these classes determined the leverage of provincial interests on central government policies and the relative privileges the state provided to each social class. And for the next three decades, such policies and privileges were skewed towards benefiting the upper and middle classes at the expense of all others.

At the start of October 1924, Congress approved a federal, republican constitution headed up by President Guadalupe Victoria and Vice President Bravo, the second-place candidate, who was still the darling of the old privileged classes and the well-known leader of the Scottish Rite Masons. Upper-class wealth and connections had allied with the larger middle class; these two groups balanced their power in office, but represented only a small proportion of the total population, which was composed mainly of lower-class elements that the middle class feared and with whom it refused to share power.

To maintain its stability, oil the wheels of state, and solve its fiscal crisis, the government then solicited two British loans that put Mexico 32 million pesos into debt to the firms of Goldschmitt and Barclay. Although a low contract price and the usual bankers' deductions netted Mexico only 10 million pesos, this amount was immediately spent on current government expenses and salaries to keep government bureaucrats politically contented and quiet.

But contentment did not last once the York Rite federalists gained the upper hand over the Bourbon centrists during congressional elections in 1826. Now European-born Spaniards in Mexican government positions not only had to fight a rear-guard defense, but also sought succor in Spain's continual refusal to recognize Mexico's independence. In January 1827, arch-conservative Father Arenas was accused of plotting to restore Spanish power in Mexico. The Scottish Rite Masons loudly campaigned against the federalist influence of U.S. minister Poinsett and then resorted to arms under Vice President Bravo.

Bravo's forces were promptly defeated by Guerrero and the vice president was sent into exile. New presidential elections then pitted Guerrero, who was backed by the middle and lower classes, against the war minister and former Iturbide understudy, General Gómez Pedraza, who was supported by the conservative upper classes.

Pedraza won a narrow margin, igniting a revolution against him led by civilian radical journalist Lorenzo Zavala with the backing of the urban lower classes. Crowds sacked and burned both Spanish and Mexican shops in the capital in December 1828.

Constitutional government having collapsed, Guerrero was then "elected" president in January 1829 and took office from President Victoria on 1 April.

If the anti–Hispanic Guerrero and his radical, anti-clerical finance minister Zavala had had their way, the federalist program favoring the common people and the poor over the rich might have been implemented. By Guerrero's decree on 20 March 1829, Spaniards were to be deprived of their posts, social positions, and property and were to be expelled from Mexico.

Although the decree could not be implemented, Zavala moved to shore up the empty treasury, cover the annual state deficit of 3 million pesos, and pay arrears on the two foreign loans. He ordered the final sale of nationalized church property on 1 May 1828 at one-fourth its 1 million pesos value. Taxes on yearly rents and income were to be graduated. On 22 May, Congress approved Zavala's proposal of a 10 percent tax on incomes of the upper classes over 1,000 pesos, a 5 percent tax on yearly rents and incomes of the middle classes between 1,000 and 10,000 pesos, and tax exemption for lower class incomes under 1,000.

Not only did the propertied middle and upper classes recoil in an alliance against Zavala and the Protestant U.S. minister Poinsett, but President Guerrero's position as a nationalist military hero was only maintained by the July Spanish troop invasion near Tampico. Mobilizing his forces at Veracruz, Santa Anna attacked and defeated the invaders, raising his own prestige as liberator. And Guerrero could not defend Zavala, who was forced out on 2 November. This action was followed by the December revolt organized by Vice President Anastasio Bustamente with the supporting of the returning centrist Bravo.

On 1 January 1830, Bustamente assumed power as acting president, forming a cabinet of conservatives and reactionaries led by Alamán as minister of foreign and internal affairs. Thus the brief 1823-27 era of federalist, libertarian government ended with the suppression of the opposition that had expressed the aspirations of the lower social classes. The Bustamente government now sought a new order of economic and financial stability to secure the upper and middle classes.

Hereafter, the mantle of state and its policies could be shifted by class and vested party interests, so whichever force held governing authority from the seat of state would also hold the whip hand over the destiny of all other social interests or classes. The struggle for state power and the exercise of governmental authority would henceforth become the path of class rule in Mexico.

CHAPTER 2

From Empire to
the War of Reform

Independence of Mexico from Spain and the struggle against attempted British, French, and U.S. interpositions led to bitter internal conflict to control the state. The main lines of demarcation placed wealthy conservatives and liberals in one camp and most other social classes in the other. Retaining its puissance, the military caste was unwilling to share its power with civilian politicians, but kept them in office to serve its purposes.

When new conflicts emerged and revolutions threatened from below, the upper classes usually allied with the army and sometimes with the church. But once the danger of popular revolt was swept away, well-heeled, centrist-minded conservatives again did battle with the provincial middle class, each trying to woo the army in order to control the central government and stabilize its rule.

Thus in the first 12 years of its independence, Mexico was for varying periods a monarchy, a constitutional republic, a radical populist regime, an arch-conservative government, and a liberal state. In turn, as each regime failed to produce stability for long, the principal leaders of the army were called upon to bring forward and secure a new order, the short reign of governments being emblematic of Mexico's struggles within.

The main leader holding the pulse of the army between 1834 and 1855 had been Santa Anna, the key figure able to control both liberal and conservative governments. Charismatic, exhibiting a flair for opportunism and frequent changes in allegiances, he was Mexico's leading military leader a dozen times, was president five times, and was sent into exile three, never to return after August 1855. But in these two decades, Santa Anna became the leading actor on the Mexican stage, cast to use his resources of army influence and rhetorical prose to rehabilitate himself each time foreign empires threatened and the nearly equal balance of liberals and conservatives awarded him leveraged control to tip the balance by mobilizing military power.

IMPLOSION

With military forces critical, the démarche from one dictatorial government to another dominated the 1830s and 1840s.

Anastasio Bustamente's reactionary regime, begun 1 January 1830, did not last long. Although the liberal opposition was at first suppressed, stability escaped Bustamente's hold as his ministers tried to industrialize Mexico at popular expense, opening the way for the hot country's revolutionary forces under Guerrero to take up arms against both the government and the propertied classes.

Bustamente's minister of foreign and internal affairs, Alamán, had limited his sights to national independence, seeking to free Mexico from subservience to British financiers and export industries. He momentarily sidestepped foreign bondholder demands for interest payments in arrears by increasing the principal of Mexico's obligations by more than 4 million pesos. Then he set up a state bank that recruited government-connected merchants and financiers like Escandón, Barrón, and Martínez del Río to invest in factory machinery for cotton spinning and weaving and guaranteed them strong protectionist measures prohibiting the import of mechanically woven English cottons.

As these industrialists drew on cotton fields in the state of Veracruz and developed water power to turn the looms, weaving factories soon seeded the landscape as far as the old textile city of Puebla. Even when the state bank eventually failed, an industrial revolution had been launched; fifty textile factories were still supplying Mexicans with cheap cotton cloth more than a decade later.

Despite the benefits of these new industries and government efforts to revitalize mining from its earlier crisis of overexpansion and military and civil disturbances, the countryside was not relieved of rigid land tenure relations and tithes collected by the Catholic church. Bustamente's ministers openly supported the church during 1830–31 and appeased both the Holy See and clerical Spain in an attempt to guarantee property rights and privileges of the Mexican upper orders.

Attempting to secure peasant land holdings, Guerrero then led a powerful revolt in the south. Yet his forces were overwhelmed by General Bravo's well-provisioned army that was defending the nation's propertied interests. Guerrero was executed in the Chilapa on 14 February 1831.

An anticlerical alliance then roiled the nation as the political opposition denounced Guerrero's execution at the hands of church and state. From the silver mining state of Zacatecas, liberal governor Francisco García publicly castigated the government for bowing down to the clerics, knowing that Alamán dared not send the army against his supporters possessed of wealth and armaments. At the behest of Gómez Farías, Governor García's friend and senator from Zacatecas, the disentailment of ecclesiastical property was then advocated by theology professor José María Luis Mora.

Seeking military backing, Farías appealed to General Santa Anna and forced Bustamente to dismiss Alamán and War Minister Facio, both publicly held responsible for Guerrero's execution. With his authority undermined, the president quickly turned to arms to maintain power but his government troops were defeated by Santa Anna's forces.

Farías then took command of the federalist government in Santa Anna's behalf while the Liberator retired to his *hacienda* until Congress elected him president and Farías vice president in March 1833. Next Farías launched an offensive against the church. He removed the *hacendados* civil obligations to pay the church tithes that had most benefited the bishops and canons; stopped the enforcement of monastic vows, thereby freeing both friars and nuns to leave the convent at will; and prohibited the church from transferring any property acquired since independence, thereby disentailing monastic real estate. But Congress assumed neither ownership of church real estate to sell at public auction, nor the power to pass it to church tenants. Rather, the *fueros* of church and army pressured Santa Anna and then convinced him to undermine the liberal reforms made by the previous generation of urban middle-class leaders and ideologists, to repeal most anticlerical decrees, and to allow only the conservative *hacendados* to secure the benefits. They retained the "right" to pay tithes voluntarily.

CONFLICT WITH THE UNITED STATES BREWS IN TEXAS

In January 1835, Santa Anna went still further, stripping Farías of the vice presidency and establishing centrist powers as the nation's protector. In March, he pressured the Congress to amend the 1824 constitution, invaded Zacatecas to depose its liberal governor, and planned a similar invasion of the now-apprehensive Texas province.

Texas had grown by 1835, and most of its people sought self-determination from Mexico. Its authority harked back to the 1821 viceregal government franchise awarded Moses Austin to colonize, to Emperor Iturbide's confirmation of the concession to Moses' son Stephen Austin, and to the Mexican Congress's later ratification of the privilege. But the 1835 Mexican Congress reversed course on 3 October, decreeing that all state governors should hold office only with the approval of the central government and that all state legislatures should cease to function.

Despite Santa Anna's seemingly good intentions towards Mexico's northern neighbor and his dictatorial prowess, the United States had second thoughts about a militarized Mexico on its doorstep in Texas. The United States had hailed Mexico's separation from Spain and Santa Anna's initial annexation of Spanish California. Along with other independent governments in America, Mexico had gained recognition from President Monroe and England's Canning.[1] But now in a momentary, if transparent, ploy to conquer Mexican territory under U.S. tutelage, on 20 December 1835 Texas declared its independence from Mexico. Santa Anna quickly mobilized his armies, hotly blustering to the British and French ministers that U.S. aid to the rebel pirates would lead his marching army beyond Texas to Washington to "place upon its Capitol the Mexican flag!"

Taking up the challenge, the United States openly supported Texas with guns and cannon; 500 soldiers defeated Mexican forces at the battle of Gonzales. The Texans then took Goliad and the Alamo from Mexican forces.[2] Ambitious to defend Mexican sovereignty, Santa Anna raised a force of 8,000 men for his 6–7 March 1836 massacre at Fort Alamo, overwhelming the small garrison of 200 American troops under Colonel Jim Bowie. But on 21 April, Santa Anna's 1,500 men were defeated by 800 Texans under Sam Houston.

Captured, in danger of being shot as a war criminal committing atrocities against Texans, Santa Anna acknowledged the independence of Texas and gained his personal freedom. Although the Mexican people refused to ratify his act, serious hostilities against Texas were thereafter abandoned.[3]

Nonetheless, in the spring of 1837, President Van Buren still opposed congressional interference in the struggle between Texas and Mexico, and Texas as part of Coahuila formally declared its independence.[4] Meanwhile, Yankee settlers in Texas maintained their independence from Mexico, though the U.S. Senate again voted in 1843 against its annexation by a two-thirds majority. Still the Texans' movement was joined by the northern states along the Rio Grande and the independent state of New Mexico was also formed in the spring of 1840.[5]

Despite Santa Anna's defense, Mexico was nonetheless being fractured. Although a centralist constitution was adopted in late 1836 to keep military generals in the presidential seat of power, foreign nations sought to partition what remained of Mexican territory and pick this wealthy plum from the boughs of America's bountiful tree.

COMPETITION TO PARTITION MEXICO

Like the United States and Britain, France also sought a stake in Mexico and Latin America.

The French excuse, though historically absurd, was injuries inflicted on a French pastry shop and a handful of residents during turmoil in Mexico City. Naturally, the French government demanded reparations. It sent a squadron of warships to blockade the Mexican coast and proceeded to bombard San Juan d'Ulloa and Veracruz, parlaying French puissance with a blockade of Buenos Aires when Argentina declared war on France.[6]

Santa Anna, cleverly lying in wait amidst the popular uproar, valiantly marched to Veracruz, capturing both San Juan d'Ulloa and Veracruz and restoring his military reputation as a national hero. He was now minus one leg to prove his mettle, however. Still, not even Santa Anna was able to bring in reinforcements, and President Bustamente was forced to sue for British peace mediation based on paying France a $600,000 indemnity.[7]

England meanwhile fancied keeping France at bay, as each country jockeyed with the United States for a sphere of its own in Mexico. Spain kept its distance to avoid becoming embroiled in a new war. In spring 1836, Spain had formally acknowledged Mexican independence under Santa Anna. Yet, in the face of imperial designs fostered by agents of the competitive powers and classes aligned to them, discontent within Mexico remained rife.

As a result, Mexico City was beset by one "revolution" after another. On 25 July 1840, General Urrea ousted President Bustamente; Santa Anna replaced him as interim president in the summer of 1841 and then unseated him as president. After imposing high taxes on the many, Santa Anna displayed pomp and flourish, burying his own amputated leg with the solemnity of a state funeral, financing theaters and statues of himself, and lavishing rewards on his coterie of favorites. Yet, as the weight of this infrastructure of emoluments cut living standards and swelled popular discontent, the military saw an opportunity to revolt in 1844, ending Santa Anna's three years of dictatorship and exiling the president to Cuba, supposedly for life.

New imperial designs soon ended this exile, however, as Mexico again called on the Liberator to defend its honor. On 1 March 1845, the United States had annexed the republic of Texas; President General Herrera was unable to stop the advance. The great liberal politician Valentín Gómez Farías, exiled in New Orleans, sought to ally his mass following with Santa Anna's supporters in the army to defend Mexico against the United States in case of war and to modernize the nation.

The situation was both dangerous and tense, as the northern states of Mexico continued to assert their independence.[8] As U.S. and Mexican troops clashed on 25 April 1846, Santa Anna and Farías prepared for war with the United States. They based their action on their planned "fusion of the people and the army," proclaimed a new constitution, and assumed dictatorial powers.[9]

The United States was equally adamant to ensure its hemispheric security and extend its southwestern boundaries by military means. On 26 April 1846, Congress had declared war, and a joint resolution of Congress admitted Texas to the Union. General Taylor was positioned in Texas opposite Matamoros on the Rio Grande; troops and ships on both sides fought for terrain. Appropriating $10 million, Congress called for volunteers and enrolled 75,000 men to add to the regular army of 40,000. President Polk explained to Congress on 11 May that Mexico had initiated the war, and he ordered General Taylor's occupying army to seize and hold points on the Rio Grande.

After crossing the river on 18 May 1846 and unfurling the Stars and Stripes on Mexican territory, Taylor took Matamoros, Reinosa, and Camargo. From the moment Mexico formally responded by declaring war on 23 May, one démarche followed another. As the territory of the Rio Grande proceeded to annex the states of Tamaulipas, Coahuila, and Nuevo León, U.S. Col. Philip Kearney also annexed the state of New Mexico as a territory of the United States. Captain John C. Frémont upstaged a Mexican offensive in California by assuming command of American forces. He captured Sonoma on 15 June 1846, sent commodores Sloat and Stockton to take possession of coast towns as far as Los Angeles, and secured Monterey, the capital of California, on 13 August. Frémont placed himself at the head of a provisional government.[10]

Mexican forces finally capitulated at Monterey on 24 September. When the U.S. secretary of war refused to negotiate an armistice, Mexico was forced to reappraise its relative weakness and sue for peace.

Amidst domestic revolt against the plan of Mexico's General Paredes to restore monarchical rule, General Santa Anna, who enjoyed popular support, again took supreme military command and raised a war chest of $6 million. He held back, however, from any military confrontation, awaiting President Polk's attempt to make peace with Mexico under the so-called "Wilmot Proviso" to his $2 million peace plan request. The president split the Congress, though, when he declared that it was "an express and fundamental condition to the acquisition of any territory from Mexico, that neither slavery nor involuntary servitude shall exist therein." On 8 August the Wilmot Proviso was defeated by congressional proslavery forces. The antislavery faction lost its majority in the next Congress,[11] and as a result, hostilities with Mexico continued. The battle escalated in 1847, and U.S. forces completed their conquest of New Mexico and California.

In the heart of Mexico, meanwhile, Santa Anna accepted an armistice with the United States long enough to strengthen his forces, but in ferocious fighting he then lost Chapultepec Castle and Mexico City by 15 September 1847 and was forced to flee to the Gulf of Mexico.[12]

On 2 February 1848, Mexico concluded peace with the United States under the provisional authority of the president of the Mexican Congress. Events followed fast and furious. With slight amendments that both the U.S. Senate and the Mexican Congress ratified, President Polk proclaimed peace on 4 July in a treaty that offered Mexico peace and money for land.

The United States paid Mexico $3 million immediately, another $12 million in three installments, and assumed $3.5 million in debts due U.S. citizens from Mexico. These payments of $18.5 million were made in consideration for the U.S. accessions of 523,802 square miles of Mexican territories, including Texas, Arizona, New Mexico, and California; the price amounted to about $35 per square mile. Under the treaty, U.S. forces were to evacuate other Mexican territory within three months.

Thus the war that had cost the U.S. approximately $25 million and 25,000 men had brought new cotton-growing lands to the Southern planters and future markets to a nation that was quickly industrializing.[13]

To settle the Mexican boundary dispute and avert all danger of future war, a U.S. payment of $10 million for the 44,000-square-mile Marrila Valley, the sliver of land that remained between the Mexican Cession and Mexico proper, was negotiated by James Gadsden in the summer of 1853 at $230 per square mile.[14]

WAR NOT OVER

Although the war was seemingly over, Mexico endured northern invaders, domestic conflict, and discord under imperious U.S. and Spanish pressures.

In the wake of defeat, the loss of territories, and Santa Anna's renewed military dictatorship, the fringes of Mexico were threatened by Apaches and Comanches in the province of Coahuila. A military expedition under Major Walker angled to foster U.S. annexation of Baja California, and this attempt was followed by the failed military adventure of Count Raousset de Bouldon, a Frenchman.

Santa Anna was the whirlwind of the moment. His coup and persecution and repression of all liberals heralded the May 1853 arrest, violent abduction, imprisonment, and exile of Benito Juárez to New Orleans, along with Melchor Ocampo, the great reformer-disciple of Rousseau and Proudhon.

JACOBINS IN POWER

A switch of political terrain in the mid–1850s momentarily brought Mexico's libertarian Jacobins to power with great promises of social transformation.

Once their *Revolution of Ayutla* became a war of reform and then a struggle with an exotic monarchy based on foreign aid, the Jacobins launched the great Mexican Revolution. In the interim, though, a disjointed, switchback trail led from internal military conflict to political disunity, with the patterns being periodically repeated until the foreign invaders solidified national resolve to defeat them militarily once and for all. Herein lay the future of Mexico's libertarian 1850s.

Constituting themselves as natural leaders of the libertarian Jacobins, Ocampo and Juárez, who had both been governors in Mexico's divided land, joined in supporting federalism. With Mata and Ponciano Arriaga, they hammered out an 1855 party program—the *Proclamation of Ayutla*. This proclamation, which became the basis of the Constitution of 1857, called for a new constitution and promised the abolition of personal taxation, of military conscription, and of the feudal system of internal passports restricting the peasants' movement from place to place. It included these goals:

- The complete emancipation of civil power, with the definitive destruction of the power of the church other than in strict spiritual matters through the suppression of the reactionay *fueros* and religious communities and the nationalization of church property
- The linking of liberty and prosperity by promoting internal trade through abolishing the *alcavalas* at each state border or other domestic subdivision
- Freedom of conscience and individual liberties, made effective by judicial review (*Juicio de Amparo*) of all state administrative action.[15]

On the southern military flank of the revolution, General Juan Álvarez meanwhile advanced under the banner of the *Proclamation of Ayutla*. As the Álvarez revolutionaries took Monterrey and insurrection spread throughout the country, Santa Anna raised 1,400 troops, but he soon foresaw defeat, abdicated, and fled to Havana. After his departure, there was a turnover of five presidents in four months and default on the original independence indemnity debt owed to Spain.[16]

The saga of arms had begun with the victorious military junta assembled in Cuernavaca that named General Álvarez provisional president. He established himself with his ministry in Mexico City as the capital and named Juárez secretary of justice and ecclesiastical affairs in his coalition cabinet. Juárez organized the administration of justice under the Juárez Law as the foundation of reform, thereby keeping alive the ideals of the radical *puros* [purists] wing of the Liberal party.

As a revolutionary codex, the Juárez Law was a federal mandate that the individual states could neither modify or change. It also overrode the bishop's efforts to have the Pope make final judgment, as well as the Supreme Court's objection to the framing of organic court law without its consultation. Once set in place, moreover, the Juárez laws of reform became enduring facts, a form of *res adjudicata* against the interests of the clergy, who were epitomized by arch-conservative Father Miranda and the right-wing branch of the army under Santa Anna's favorite corps.

Given these polarities, civil war seemed impending. Yet, among the *puros* representing the Álvarez government, the minister of war, Ignacio Comonfort, wanted peace. He feared that the clergy would convert a political conflict into a religious question, transforming civil strife into a religious war. Juárez also sought to avoid a civil war by the slow, methodical introduction of reforms. Thus, the November 1855 Juárez Law, Article 42, was tactfully applied. It was implemented by suppressing the Special tribunals in commerce, treasury affairs, etc., exempting ecclesiastical courts in their handling of common offenses of members of the clergy (who in turn could reject ecclesiastic trial of penal matters), and exempting military tribunals limited to purely military matters or soldiers involved in mixed military-civilian offenses.

Thus restricted, the clerical-army alliance bided its time, waiting for a weak moment in the *puros* government. When General Álvarez retired, passing the mantle of provisional president to peace-seeking Comonfort in December 1855, the reactionary clergy and generals were emboldened. From Guanajuato to Querétaro, Jalisco, the northern states, and especially church-controlled Puebla, internal revolt threatened. Puebla's Bishop Don Pelagio Antonio de Labastida y Dávalos (who became the future archbishop of Mexico) had already hobbled both aristocrats and commoners with pious exercises of devotion. He exercised considerable control over the lower classes that lived by the charity and protection of the priests. If the church lost power or revenue, these lower orders would have disordinately suffered, a potential that existed throughout the republic except for some coastal towns.

Puebla was also the headquarters of the spokesmen of military and clerical reaction; large groups of the regular army staged a powerful revolt in 1856. Following the lead of the bishops and clergy who sustained them, the Catholic population naturally sought to defend themselves by overturning the government. This time, however, Comonfort struck back ruthlessly, putting down the military insurrection in Puebla, ordering the confiscation of the property of its bishopric, and degrading and humiliating the officers of the permanent army.

The defeated officers then planned revenge, and exiled Bishop Labastida went to Rome to conspire with Pope Pius IX against the Jacobin government. The Pope refused to receive Comonfort's agent of reconciliation, thereby turning him into a resolute enemy of the church. This led to Comonfort's suppression of the "Company of Jesus."

Mexico's upper classes exploded with wrath and then eloquence, claiming that the suppression of religion was the work of the devil. They proposed that the Congress should pass legislation stating: "There shall not be promulgated any law or order that prohibits or impedes the exercise of any religious cult; but since the Roman, Catholic, Apostolic Faith has been the exclusive religion of the Mexican people, the Congress of the Union shall seek to protect it by means of just and prudent laws, providing they do not injure the interests of the people or the rights of national sovereighty."

For the moment, the aristocracy was defeated by the government, however, and popular opinion of both the illiterate class and emergent bourgeoisie backed the new constitution fulfilling the promise of *Ayutla*. Gómez Farías, the founder of the reform government, took an oath of loyalty to the new law on bended knee, hand upon the Bible, and the whole country was summoned to take the same oath. The Church chose war, however, excommunicating all who swore allegiance to the new, libertarian constitution.

Comonfort then decided it would be impossible to govern under the new constitution, with its unitary Congress and the right of incessant intervention of the judiciary. He believed the unimpeded, extraordinary presidential powers he thought necessary would be denied by the Congress, leaving the clergy, the army, and the revolutionary forces free to organize to displace the constituted authorities.

Comonfort's worst fears were confirmed under the 1857 Constitution. Comonfort himself was elected president and, as president of the Supreme Court, Juárez became vice president. Both quickly became pawns in a larger game, for as Comonfort had predicted, the Liberal party majority in Congress rejected his requests for special powers, as well as Juárez's proposed revision of the constitution to provide for religious tolerance. With the wheel of power turning backward, the defeated, but now resurrected, clergy and dissident armed forces mobilized their domestic forces. Reactionary to the core, these forces inched the Liberal government towards conservative solutions. They asserted that the central government was too weak to keep Spanish warships from entering the Gulf because of the murder and robberies of Spanish subjects. War was averted only by English and French mediation. To keep off the Spanish invasion that reactionary leaders like Paredes had requested and Santa Anna had demanded, great sums of money were required—sums the Liberal government lacked in the wake of the small tax on the disentails of land and the transfer of clergy tithes to the Comonfort government.

Church funding would flow again only with the reestablishment of a military dictatorship, the reactionary leaders insisted. And in fact, such funding followed the military revolt in the Mexican interior, which produced a new bloodbath at Puebla in the course of a military victory by General Félix Zuloaga. In November 1857, as the foremost representative of conservative military and clerical groups, Zuloaga announced his support for a Comonfort dictatorship, dismissed Congress, and arrested Juárez. Zuloaga's Plan of Tacubaya repealed the constitution as unsuited to the usages and manners of the country, placed dictatorial powers in Comonfort's hands, and proposed a future constituent assembly whose decisions were to be reviewed *ad referendum* by the people.

Although he was now a fearful Caesar, Comonfort nonetheless refused to adhere to the Plan of Tacubaya, which was supported by the church. He refused to destroy his own alliance of the Council of Conservatives, *moderos* and *puros*, refused to repeal the Juárez Law, refused to do away with the Lerdo Law of disentails of land, and refused to return everything to the church. Moreover, despite Zuloaga's pronouncement of 11 January 1858, Comonfort ordered Juárez released from jail.

The next day, Zuloaga's brigade reversed itself, disavowing Comonfort as president. Comonfort, mobilizing his frail forces to declare the Constitution of 1857 reestablished, quickly lost the ensuing military encounter with the massive army led by General Zuloaga. As the defeated president fled the country, Supreme Court President Juárez replaced Comonfort according to the constitution.[17]

The reactionary Zuloaga provisional government then annulled the laws against the privileged orders of church and army and raised funds by enforced loans and extractions from foreign commerce. This action was opposed by most of the republic, and the most important trading towns and seaports protested and refused to recognize the authority of the central government. The Yucatán also proclaimed its independence, and this led to civil war. Guerrillas organized, terrorizing the provinces of Puebla, Jalisco, and Guanajuato and penetrating into the suburbs of the capital as robberies and military executions became everyday affairs. From the island of St. Thomas, the exiled Santa Anna issued a proclamation demanding a renewal of his power, and Benito Juárez, who was now free, led a new national party at Veracruz.[18]

DOMESTIC SPLITS AND IMPERIAL DESIGNS

With the clerical party now at odds with both Juárez's movement and commercial aspirations of the United States, the United States again became kingmaker.

Fearing a foreign invasion, General Zuloaga quickly resigned in favor of General Miguel Miramón, whose initial presidential decrees rescinded the forced loans of his predecessor and promised indemnities to injured English and French traders. But the United States refused to recognize Miramón, recalled its minister and legation from Mexico City, and sent its new minister to negotiate with Juárez in Veracruz. On 14 December 1856, in return for a financial subsidy of $8 million, the United States received far-reaching commercial concessions from the Juárez regional administration.

Trade routes were to be opened to U.S. commerce over the Isthmus of Tehuantepec, over the Rio Grande from Mazatlan to the Pacific Ocean, and from the Guaymas into Arizona. United States troops were also to be permitted to pursue Indians and guerrillas across the Mexican border, and they were given other rights of intervention as well.[19]

With the foreigners temporarily appeased, both Juárez and Melchor Ocampo now pushed for adoption of the Constitution of 1857, attempting to transform Mexico from a subjugated agrarian nation into a middle-class state.

The central government in Mexico City momentarily remained under President Miramón, but Juárez's popular army under General Jesús González Ortéga soon advanced on the capital, defeating Miramón's army at San Miguelito on 22 December 1860. Miramón quickly fled the country with 600,000 piastres appropriated from the British Consulate in Mexico, and Juárez arrived in Mexico City to restore the liberal constitution.

No sooner had Juárez entered the capital, however, than his regime was thrown into the crossfire of demands by the old estates of wealthy *criollo* landowners, privileged Catholic clerics, and secure government administrators.

Bolstering his position, Juárez relied heavily on United States support. But such favoritism engendered new problems, and the European powers again threatened a new partition of Mexico. Spain, France, and England made an allied landing at Veracruz in 1862 with their warships and troops, demanding redress and indemnity for all past outrages against their interests, as well as the right to establish themselves in three cities—the French in Tehuacán, the Spanish in Orizaba, and the English in Córdoba.

Although its interposition was soon established, the still dissatisfied French Crown sought a defensive Mexican emporium as a counterweight to U.S. regional power. Emperor Louis Napoleon hoped to stop U.S. commercial control of Mexico, the Antilles, and South America by establishing a strong colonial government with the aid of France.

Opposing this imperious imposition, the liberal Mexican Congress unanimously resolved that "Mexico would never more tolerate the least interference in her affairs, and in the establishment of her social and political organization."

Mexico also readied its defenses. Louis Napoleon's message that he was not waging war against Mexico, but against Juárez and his faction favoring the United States, was offset by a declaration that Mexico was not waging war against France, but against that monarch who, "seduced by ambition, wished to conquer a rich land and rule over the destinies of another continent."

The French demands were truly outrageous. Gallic banker Jecker glibly listed excessive Mexican debts in arrears, and Vice Admiral de la

Gravière raised indemnity claims. These claims allegedly necessitated the occupation of the capital to insure reorganization of Mexican affairs. Shocked and outraged, the Spanish and British withdrew from the alliance with France, recalling their forces.[20]

With conquest and war now in the wind, Napoleon III captivated wild French enthusiasm for establishing a Mexican empire, and Empress Eugénie mobilized zealous clerical approbation. Napoleon quickly ordered General Lorencez to march on Mexico City. This action brought President Juárez's sharp 12 April 1862 declaration that regions occupied by France would fall under Mexican military law and all who assisted the French would be viewed as enemies. To resist the threatened French invasion, all able-bodied Mexicans were called to arms, but General Lorencez arrogantly issued a counter-proclamation, warning: "The flag of France has been raised on Mexican soil, and shall not be hauled down. Wise men will welcome it as a friend. Let fools dare to oppose it!"

Invading French forces moved cautiously, though. At first they withdrew to Veracruz, then they advanced to Orizaba to claim their own injured forces that Mexican General Zaragoza planned to treat as prisoners of war. Engaging battle and suffering defeat at Puebla, the French then retreated to Orizaba to await reinforcements from General Forey and orders from Louis Napoleon.

Thus set, the battle lines then fanned out as the French army victoriously moved from Córdoba and Orizaba to Jelapa, Tampico, Tehuacán, and Puebla, where a great battle broke the backbone of Mexican resistance, opening the way for the 5 June 1863 triumphal French entry into Mexico City.[21]

Establishing a provisional government under the triumvirate of the French generals Almonte and Salas with Archbishop Labastida, the French declared a monarchy under Louis Napoleon, revived the nobility as a recognized estate, ceded the province of Sonora to France, suppressed all Mexican newspapers, and confiscated the property of all who had borne arms against France. The French invaders then shot many guerrillas, declaring those still at war outlaws. But this action and other cruelties so unsettled French rule that Louis Napoleon revoked the decree and replaced his hated commissioner Saligny with Montholon.[22]

Seeking a way to avoid the costs of his own conquest, Napoleon then arranged for the puppet emperor Archduke Maximilian of Austria to pay for his exploits (and suffer the deadly consequences). The ostensible purpose was that the French emperor sought to compensate Austria for the loss of her Venetian provinces by cementing a secret alliance with Austria against Prussia. For the support of French troops in Mexico until his government could be established (after which 5,000 French foreign legionnaires with allied contingents of Austrians and Belgians were to remain in

Mexico for six years), Maximilian was to pay the 270 million franc cost of the French expedition in Mexico in annual installments of 25 million, to pay each remaining soldier 1,000 francs per year, and to pay 12 million to French subjects whose interests had been injured in Mexico. For this purpose, Maximilian borrowed some 201.5 million francs, paid 64 million to France as an initial repayment, paid 12 million in indemnities, and gave a large part of the remainder to the financiers of Paris and London negotiating the loan.

But it was no empire Maximilian inherited, for the United States refused recognition. The Mexican population was hostile, and the French general, Bazaine, and Maximilian's court made greedy demands. The 26,000 French troops could not stop the depredations of the Mexican guerrillas, the Austrian auxiliary troops were restive under Marshal Bazaine's authority, and their release from the jurisdiction of French commanders undermined unified military action. Meanwhile, Washington refused to recognize Maximilian, and Juárez's emissary Romero made the most of his opportunities in the U.S. capital.[23]

Still the French forces were decidedly victorious, and on 1 January 1865, President Juárez confessed defeat and appealed to the righteousness of the national cause in Mexico. Only General Porfirio Díaz held out at Oaxaca, and he too soon surrendered to superior French forces. Later, however, he escaped from prison to lead and solidify a growing opposition army. Bazaine proclaimed martial law to check its activity, and Maximilian resorted to force, impressing Mexicans into his army against their will.[24]

The United States lay in wait. As Maximilian's financial resources were quickly running out, the United States seized the advantage by dispatching a large army under General Sherman to the Rio Grande that was ready to cross into Mexico at any moment. Secretary Seward then instructed the U.S. ambassador in Paris to insist on the withdrawal of French forces from Mexico, for which the French government gave ready assurances. On 31 May 1866, Napoleon applied the screws, demanding that Maximilian pay half of the revenue receipts of the ports of Tampico and Veracruz until his debt to France was paid. He announced the withdrawal of the last regiments of the French army by 1 November 1867. The pay of Belgian auxiliaries was also cut in half as they were incorporated with French troops under Marshal Bazaine. When this action caused them to mutiny, their corps was then disbanded. The puppet emperor was thereby stripped of his military shield against an impending Mexican uprising.

Furious, Maximilian threatened to abdicate his throne, and to save it, Empress Charlotte financed her personal mission to plead with Napoleon in France by using $30,000 from emergency funds traditionally held for repair to Mexico City dikes.

Louis Napoleon nonetheless outrightly rejected the empress's plea, and fulminating against Napoleon's common ancestral forbears, she conveniently went insane and never returned to Mexico. In late November 1866, the United States drove the final nail into Emperor Maximilian's heart by pressing France to immediately "desist from the prosecution of armed intervention in Mexico."[25]

As the imperial drama thus played out, with the U.S. Monroe Doctrine leveraging its weight to exclude European powers from the Americas, both Maximilian and Louis Napoleon began their grand march to oblivion. The United States now called the tune for France to play; the French emperor instructed Marshal Bazaine to inform Maximilian that his default of 25 million francs due France released the French government from all obligations under their agreement. Ordered to leave Mexico with his army, Bazaine surrendered French positions directly to Juárez's army.

Maximilian stayed, however, rejecting the solicitous advice of Louis Napoleon's emissaries to abdicate the crown, give up his post, and leave the country with the French troops rather than pursue the vain hope of his Viennese confidant Eloin that Emperor Francis Joseph was on the point of abdication and that a firm stand in Mexico would improve Maximilian's chances for the Austrian throne. There could be, in fact, no firm stand with a dwindling army of 9,000 men and almost no funds with which to face the powerful, advancing Mexican armies. Thus Maximilian was driven back to Querétaro, besieged by Republican troops, and unable to get relief from Mexico City, under the control of General Márquez. Márquez in turn was intercepted and crushingly defeated by militias under Porfirio Díaz; he retreated to the capital, where his forces were quickly demolished by Díaz's troops.

Trapped in Querétaro, the emperor capitulated and consented to enter negotiations for surrender. But his commanders only relinquished the cloister at La Cruz with a feigned defense. As Maximilian's last forces were defeated in full battle, he was captured with his officers. At his 13 June 1867 trial, he was condemned to death as an outlaw taken in arms under his own legal terms set for the fate of *bandero negro*. Exclaiming "Long live Mexico," Maximilian was executed six days later with his generals Miramón and Mejia.

After a few months' siege, Mexico City capitulated to Porfirio Díaz. General Márquez fled the country, President Juárez entered triumphantly, and Maximilian's remains were carried home by Admiral Tegethoff.

The French era having ended, the Porfirio dictatorship was about to begin.

Part II

Return to the Past

Throughout Mexican history, injustice weighs heavily in the grasp for land and wealth, shaping the existential condition and thoughts of the downtrodden.

The hold of the foreigners; the blindness of wealthy, domestic owners to the needs of peons, landless, and workers; the brutalities imposed by their appointed managers, overseers, and purveyors; the grinding poverty of laborers high and low on the scale of work and caste—these remain the age-old ties that draw wealth and pain from Mexico's body and soul.

Herein reside implosive forces—unnumbered schemes for revolution, powerful hopes for freedom to return to an idealized, pre–Columbian past in which laborers were free and peasants worked the land communally without domestic or foreign impositions.

CHAPTER 3

Revolution, Independence, and Imperial Impositions

Momentous events swept Mexico between 1867 and 1910. Napoleon III's Mexican empire had collapsed. United States influence over Mexico had grown steadily under the corrupt Díaz regime, with the two nations signing a 1908 arbitration treaty largely benefiting U.S. investors. Presidents Taft and Díaz had met at the international boundary line to solemnize the mutually beneficial link between Mexico's wealthy favored by Porfirio and U.S. investing corporations with oil and mineral concessions. Revolutionary and oppositional groups had recoiled, however, consolidating their efforts to overthrow the oppressive Díaz dictatorship.

Since Díaz assumed power in 1876, implosive pressures had been building in Mexico. During that time, the old *encomienda* system of landlocked labor had been modified but not yet destroyed, appearing as a neofeudal relationship between great landowners possessed of hundreds of thousands of hectares sowed and reaped by populations of tenants, sharecroppers, peasants, and peons who were hardly more than serfs. In its quest for stability, the Díaz regime had not only supported the great landowners, but granted others vast concessions to enterprises in railroads, mining, production, and trade. Once strengthened and solidified, this class of northern and eastern business interests demanded a political voice and economic influence, but Díaz powerfully opposed this demand. The United States also exerted its influence when oil was discovered near Tampico and Tuxpan.[1] In 1900 a group of American capitalists led by Edward L. Doheny secured a vast concession of 280,000 acres at Hacienda del Tulillo for $325,000 and then added an adjoining 150,000 acres. The first oil gushed forth on 14 May 1901 at Ebano.[2]

All these land, railroad, trade, mining, and petroleum interests aligned and realigned with or against one another, impelled by a promised transformation that was to award land to Mexico's *ejidos* and peasants and the means of a decent life to labor. In effect, there was an upper-class revolution, where the Díaz forces were replaced by those under Madero, then Carranza, and then a succession of presidential reformers.

The Mexican ruling classes thereby switched appointed leaders, and the peasantry and workers provided the grist of battle. Reforms were promised, but as we shall see, there was never a revolutionary transformation in either the rural or urban domains.

Aiming the Overthrow

Aiming to overthrow Díaz, in the northern areas of Mexico great landowners had coalesced politically and created a loose, if effective, alliance with those industrialists, merchants, mine owners, middle classes, and intellectual circles which Díaz had controlled and quieted, ruling them with impunity and excluding them from economic opportunities and political influence.

Well-heeled Mexican investors also believed they had been outflanked by Díaz's repeated concessions to foreign interests to obtain revenue that was no longer provided by the great landed estates and the church.

With the Catholic church long under attack, Mexican politicians and lawyers had conveniently switched the source of their revenues from the church to the foreign heirs of fortunes handed down from past imperial adventures. These heirs were now bent on circumventing and manipulating Mexican law for their own advantage. The Díaz regime and its retinue had conveniently maintained direct liaison with these agents and foreign interests, leaving little place either for Mexican capitalists as an independent, indigenous middle class or for the still small urban labor movement.

As the foreign property holders meanwhile mobilized their respective national diplomatic representatives to secure Díaz-awarded concessions, they spread benefits among a small circle of Mexican politicians, military men, and lawyers. The concessionaires thereby acquired great holdings among land-surveying companies, as well as in railroads, harbors, oil lands, mines, city water systems, and other public utilities. Foreign interests eventually acquired control of 66 percent of the nation's total investment base, with their degree of ownership most concentrated in the north. These interests also owned and controlled the state-subsidized railroads, most large mining operations, the production of electric power, and almost 95 percent of Mexico's banks.

The great landholdings of some oil, mining, and timber companies linked to the railroads and other industries also made them *latifundista* in the eyes of the peasants seeking land reform. To work these estates as well as to operate the tobacco plantations in Oaxaca's Valle Nacional and the coffee plantations in Chiapas, foreign capital mobilized the system of forced labor handed down from feudal society in the *monterías* of Chiapas, Tabasco, and Quintana Roo. Colonial interests also forced the migration of the Yaquis from their native habitat, and in Morelos they destroyed the villages by absorbing native lands to benefit the largely Spanish-owned sugar industry.[3]

Expanding on Spain's feudal system, foreign domination thereby alienated Mexico's resources, linking colonial-style landlordism with raw material extraction and imperial industrialism. Díaz had thus extended special government accommodations benefiting both *hacienda* and foreign extraction and industry in such a way that rapid capitalist development was grafted onto a feudal economic structure, strengthening and reaffirming existing social and racial distinctions. These interests in turn played on the inferiority of the peon as low-paid, semislave labor, thereby utilizing racial superiority for their own ends and fueling notions of the competitive, individualistic survival of the fit.[4]

Social Darwinism, as an ideological import accompanying foreign inroads, reaffirmed itself racially and socially, as well as through the brutal labor system.[5]

As opposition to Díaz grew among peasants, industrialists, and urban labor, however, arrows of protest rained down upon the foreign concessionaires and their Mexican *compradors*. Questioning their legitimacy became a national passion. Was it not Díaz's own high tariff that benefited foreign capital by securing the high-price Mexican consumer market for its products made with cheap Mexican labor? And why were the large mines all owned by American, English, and French interests, managed by foreign residents in Mexico, with head offices in the nations where the capital originated? Were not the railroads also English and American owned, managed by foreign staffs and run by skilled foreign workers?

Clearly, the U.S. and British-Dutch oil and land interests were the first and second ranking interests in Mexico, and the textile mills owned and managed by the French were the third largest investment in Mexico. Foreign capital, management, and technical staffs in public utilities were complete in street cars, electric lights, and water systems. The Spanish, U.S., and English citizens remained the dominant owners of Mexico's best lands. German, French, and Spanish capital also continued to dominate the most important sectors of commerce; the Spanish were active in both wholesale and retail trades. Retail operations in the largest cities remained in the hands of Turks, Armenians, and Chinese; the latter also controlled many restaurants on the railroads.[6]

Imperial by design, the massive foreign presence touched everything essential for Mexico's survival. Mexican manufacturers, small by comparison, suffered continual exclusion from the circle of Díaz's favorites. Emergence of a Mexican middle class was also delayed by concessions to foreign managers and investors.

With Díaz cutting off Mexican commercial, industrial, and middle-class elements from the nation's best opportunities, the northern capitalists seethed, gradually coalesced, and broadened their political base in the hope of securing protective legislation and state controls over foreign investment ownership. Deprived of the special benefits showered on the army and Catholic church, moreover, this emergent northern bourgeoisie sought anticlerical laws to curb the power of the Catholic church over landholdings, other forms of wealth, the government, and the population's personal rights and freedoms.

As this coterie excluded from Díaz's favorites spread their revolutionary outlook among other classes, they formed the base for a unified opposition movement along several fronts. Extending production, employment, and commerce, they found ready allies among those depending on them as employers for wages, as well as among the peasantry seeking to market their output. Employers also discovered allies among other groups fighting to improve their condition in the Díaz-directed economy—small- and middle-sized farmers, hired clerks, ranchmen, and overseers of estates, as well as small commercial entrepreneurs and an educated class of professionals, teachers, and white collar clerks of various levels. Although clearly part of an emergent middle sector, these skilled professional workers were of little or no use in the antiquated, nepotistic, and crisis-ridden system that awarded professional and government jobs to Díaz's favored circle, blocking middle-class economic aspirations and social mobility.

OPPOSITION ON THE MOVE

As these forces began to coalesce, moreover, they moved in tandem against Porfirio's dictatorial machine that suppressed the press, neglected public education for their children, supported church-directed schools, forced military conscription of their young men, and mobilized groups of brutal mercenary soldiers called *rurales* to maintain the regime's lawless order.

In their demands for elementary democracy and broad-based social justice, these classes found still other allies during the crisis of 1905–09, when the northern peasantry railed against oppressive land exactions and the loss of markets. The small urban working class also protested the joblessness that undermined their living standards and the ability to find alternative work. Meanwhile peasants in peonage and debt slavery sought release from the ancient bondage of *encomienda*. Sharecroppers demanded their own land, calling for an end to paying their landlords large shares of their output. Tenants, too, denounced land rents as extortion, and agricultural laborers sought a better life through increased wages and improved conditions in the fields.

From the unemployed in mines and fields to displaced shepherds, cowboys, and muleteers, there was now near desperation to find work as these helpless moved around Mexico, many crossing the U.S. border. Organizing among themselves to seek jobs promising security, fair wages, and safe working conditions, they sought to do away with employer-imposed servitude and debt encumbrance, as well as payments in tokens only redeemable at the employers' company stores.

Nor were these unemployed isolated in the northern area, for in south-central Mexico revolutionary forces had consolidated their own alliances. Here large commercial landowners had taken the peasants' communal lands and small farm holdings, leaving them to barely survive as peons and serfs. These actions fueled the peasant-led and peasant-based revolutionary forces of landless in Morelos and south-central Mexico.

Seventy thousand mountain-based, armed guerrillas followed Zapata's promise of revolutionary transformation and mobilized to fight for their hereditary rights to village and communal lands, as well as for freedom from landlord exploitation and government dictation.

As the revolt broadened, anti–Díaz northern forces brought together a middle-class, liberal army under Venustiano Carranza that was seeking political reforms; a coalition of workers, ranchers, and middle class elements backing troops led by General Alvaro Obregón; and Pancho Villa's 40,000-man cavalry of *banditos*, miners, cowboys and small ranchers, who had been bred to the saddle and could take on federal forces through lightning attacks.

STEELED IN CONFLICT

This far-flung military alliance was tested by conflict; it was ever tenuous, strained by the divergent forces backing its various leaders.

Breaking with the moderate northern generals, Villa soon realigned with Zapata. Yet Villa did not understand or pursue the *Zapatistas*' quest for overall land reform. He eventually awarded his own generals the great estates they seized, thereby empowering them as a new landed elite that would oppose their own landless allies who fought as the lightning cavalry of the revolution.

Although the *Zapatistas* won unquestionable victories in early battle, ambushing invading federal forces, many of those peasants who were guerrillas by night did not survive Díaz's scorched-earth policies that left millions dead, wounded, or in a state of starvation. Those who survived were rootless soldiers under steeled military leaders. After a grueling year of battle leading to the disintegration of Porfirio's regime, in the political foreground of the remaining revolutionary forces stood the head of the liberals, Francisco Madero.

Assuming the revolution's presidency, Madero quickly attempted to disarm the peasantry, while leaving Díaz's bureaucracies, Senate, and army intact. Thus he effectively curtailed the revolution without establishing a governing force that could ensure land reform, economic transformation, or democratic rights. Although the revolutionary forces had clearly won the battle, in its wake there was no social revolution.

IN THE WAKE OF REVOLUTION

From May 1911 to 1917, as the revolution attempted to consolidate its forces under Madero, the principal generals pursued their own versions of what the revolution should bring, refusing Madero's appeal to lay down their arms or begin to implement his plan for limited land distribution.

Madero had initially formed the opposition New Democratic party, had been jailed, and had escaped. In a 5 October 1910 manifesto from self-exile in San Luis Potosí, Texas, he had proclaimed null and void the reelections of President Díaz, Vice President Corral, deputies, and senators, as well as the appointments of magistrates of the Supreme Court. Madero had also announced his assumption of the provisional presidency "with all necessary powers to fight the usurper government of General Díaz until the people should choose its government according to law."

Madero's manifesto not only questioned the prolonged Díaz dictatorship, it also called for a constitution embodying the principle of no reelection of any president. Madero's call to take up arms and overthrow the Díaz regime had become the rallying point for the final victory of Pascual Orozco's capture of Ciudad Juárez on 9 May 1911, which forced the government's conditional surrender and the resignation of Díaz and Corral. As interim president, Madero then called for a general election, and on 7 June 1911 he made a triumphal entrance to Mexico City.

But had Madero now lost sight of the purposes of the revolution involving land and labor and focused on which classes would control and direct affairs?

Land rights had resided at the heart of Madero's Article 3 of the *Plan de San Luis Potosí*, which provided:

> In abuse of the law on public lands, numerous proprietors of small holdings, in their greater part Indians, have been dispossessed of their lands by the rulings of the department of Public Improvements [*Fomento*] or by decisions of the tribunals of the Republic. As it is just to restore to their former owners the lands of which they were dispossessed in such an arbitrary manner, such rulings and decisions are declared subject to revision, and those who have

acquired them in such an immoral manner, or their heirs, will be required to restore them to their former owners, to whom they shall also pay an indemnity for the damages suffered. Solely in case those lands have passed to third persons before the promulgation of this plan shall the former owners receive an indemnity from those in whose favor the dispossession was made.

What this mandate meant concerning village land rights was undoubtedly not the same to Madero, the *hacendados*, Pancho Villa, and Emiliano Zapata. Zapata had been in revolt against the local *hacendados* and the government in 1910 and had endorsed the Plan of San Luis Potosí. He took its meaning as a condemnation of any encroachment or intrusion of village lands by *haciendas*. The plan's key provision explicitly dealt with the usurpation of lands that had been owned by small, mostly Indian proprietors by the Ministry of Development or the tribunals. It required that unjust takings be returned to the former owners and thus redistributed land to the communal Indian *ejidos*.

Yet after the revolution, Madero focused on the restoration to the small land-owning *ranchos*—not the *ejidos* that had lost their land, and not the millions of landless peons. Perhaps Madero also spoke for the northwestern Yaqui Indians who had been dispossessed of their lands, sold as slaves to southeastern tropical planters, and required restitution. But Madero and his coalition of moderates clearly tried to stop the partition of the large estates, to block Zapata's demand for the restoration of village lands, and to prevent a general land redistribution.

Although by late June 1911, some peasants were seizing land in Oaxaca, Puebla, and Morelos, Madero only urged the *hacendados* of those states to alleviate suffering voluntarily, and he sought an evolutionary path to resolve the land and other economic questions. In addition, a national commission of conservatives under Madero and De la Barra reaffirmed Díaz's traditional land-holding arrangements.[7]

Thus was there little land redistribution in the immediate aftermath of the revolution.

The Land Tenure System in 1910

Age-old methods and the *encomienda* had locked up the system of land tenure in 1910.

Rather than investing in irrigation works, technical equipment, and other infrastructure, the *hacendados* had retained an atavistic, feudal outlook. Extracting current revenues from land production, they had mortgaged their *latifundia* to the hilt, and oppressed their peons and tenants to draw added surplus, relying on the Díaz regime for usurpation of village *ejidos* and protection and security of their tenure.

On the *hacendados'* southeastern sisal domains, debt-serfdom predominated alongside an enslaved workforce of northwestern Yaqui Indians.

In the Yucatán and the states bordering the Gulf of Mexico, such slavery and peonage prevailed because there was no labor mobility along a peninsula that had yet to connect its rivers and rail network, let alone link itself to Central Mexico. The terrain of rivers, marshes, lagoons, and tropical rain forests also impeded the land route to the principal port at Veracruz.[8] Apparently the *hacendados* did not know that earlier peoples had built a thriving commerce linking the cities of central Mexico with the north-central Gulf Coast from Tajín and El Pital at the head of navigation upstream on the Nautla River.[9]

By contrast, in central and northern Mexico, the development of railroads, industry, commerce, and mining had loosened the grip of landowners on peons, created a mobile labor force that moved to northern mines and even across the Rio Grande, and led to both urbanization and a rapid growth of the laboring population during the Díaz regime. Those remaining on the land were often still in peonage and were kept under the unbridled power of the *hacendados*.

Estates with resident peons also deployed a seasonal labor reserve of squatters living on the fringes of their domain. They turned these squatters into tenants paying rent with their labor or sharecroppers and kept them under their strict authority by the link of *hacendados*, state governors, and district chiefs. Village peasants and their progeny, who had once owned their own land and lost it to the *hacendados* in the reforms enacted starting from 1856, were now sharecroppers, tenants, and laborers on the very land their ancestors had owned. They believed they had been cheated by the *hacendados*, though titles were often long lost, or vaguely drawn or had even once been sold at low prices to these same *hacendados*.

In the hot country of Morelos, sugar cane cultivation had also pushed local *hacendados* to take over new land in an already overpopulated state, choking small villages with too little land and forcing their inhabitants to work as part-time laborers on *haciendas*.[10] After the Morelos crop failure of 1909, the price of maize skyrocketed, and desperate village peasants of San Miguel Anenecuilco asked Governor Escandón to let them plant on nearby disputed land. When he rented the land to farmers from a neighboring village, the leader of San Miguel Anenecuilco, Emiliano Zapata, called the villagers to arms, and expelled the renters from the fields to sow the maize quickly as the rainy season of 1910 began. By this action, he initiated the Mexican agrarian revolution.[11]

ZAPATA'S *PLAN DE AYALA* VS. GOVERNMENT REFORMS

Zapata's war against the landowners was localized, but it broadened in 1910–11 into a full-fledged civil war in which millions flung down the gauntlet against oppression. Throughout Central Mexico, guerrilla bands sprang forth, harassing the federal army, and aligning with the closest northern commander—Carranza or Villa.[12]

The three revolutionary leaders were bound to different goals, causes, and views of the future, however. Zapata's following was landless, Carranza's included prominent landowners, Villa's ranged from generals in search of estates to hapless *vaqueros* owning nothing more than a stubble-grazing horse, a rifle, and a blanket.

The issues were clearly stated in Zapata's *Plan de Ayala*, which advocated immediate seizure of lands taken from the villages, the expropriation of one-third of the lands held by *hacendados* who did not obstruct the revolution's course, and complete expropriation of lands held by men who "directly or indirectly" opposed the plan.

Where *Zapatistas* controlled areas in Morelos and contiguous states, the peons seized the land from the *hacendados* and worked it as their own, though in contested terrain there was little semblance of peaceful occupation and cultivation.

Most leaders and officers of guerrilla bands were independent farmers, peasants living on small or middle-sized, isolated homesteads, or *rancheros*, however. They were not laborers and some had peons of their own, but they were largely poor and uneducated. In most cases they joined the revolution, modeling the leader of *Los de abajos*, to avenge a personal insult or injustice, not to change society.[13]

Carranza and Villa recruited among the hungry fighting for food, landless peons, peasants and tenants seeking land, and the wronged demanding a redress of grievances. As Huerta had established a military dictatorship to replace the Madero government, Carranza's main war aim was the defeat of Huerta. He recruited landowners as leaders and placed at the head of his entourage a chief of staff from a leading landowning family of San Luis Potosí.[14]

Huerta initially appeared to young, inexperienced radicals as a champion of agrarian reform through his minister of finance Toribio Esquivel Obregón. Obregón surmised that the heavily mortgaged large estates would be willing to sell their family land to the state-financed landless, with the credit backed by guaranteed government bonds. The landowning class would thereby be retired to make more productive investments, and the *haciendas* would be subdivided. But the plan was stillborn as Huerta's military dictatorship, already drowning in debt, borrowed new money from Europe to import arms through Veracruz harbor for transport to Mexico City, where they would be used to hold off the steadily growing military onslaught mobilized by Carranza, Villa, and Zapata.[15]

In the heat of conflict during April 1914, President Wilson landed U.S. forces in Veracruz, clearly favoring the revolutionary movement. Huerta then played his trump card, appearing to Mexicans as a defender of national sovereignty against renewed foreign interveners who were protecting the constitutionalists with supplies and seeking a permanent foothold in the Tampico oil fields and on national territory.

United States troops nonetheless remained half a year, long enough for Carranza to condemn the aggression to maintain his following and long enough to weaken Huerta, compelling him to relinquish power and go into exile in July 1914.[16]

THE CENTRAL ISSUE: AGRARIAN REFORM

The central issue driving the revolution remained agrarian reform, but even Zapata-inspired revolutionary land expropriation had only forced the new Madero government to fund increased agricultural output, not to support land redistribution.

The government program was thus token, weak, and reformist. It issued bonds to finance infrastructure in dams, irrigation systems, wasteland reclamation, and the purchase of private lands at reasonable prices for resale in small plots at least at cost. The National Agrarian Commission of 1912 also recommended the sale of small plots on easy terms; this land was to include reclaimed wasteland, purchased private property, and certain national forest lands.

The government plan rested on the philosophy that land should be made available to those with the resources and ambition to cultivate it profitably. There were to be no gifts, and the government was not to suffer a financial loss from its land program, though it would use a corps of trained agronomists to offer education and aid to the new landowners. The commission thus recommended there would be no help for the destitute, but those with a small sum of capital could pay the balance due over time. There was to be no concentration of large holdings or land speculation permitted.[17]

The government planned to allot *ejidal* holdings to members of communities, and to sell national lands, limiting every individual to the purchase, rental, or lease of no more than two hundred hectares of arable land or five thousand hectares of pasture land. Villages were to be restored possession of *ejidal* lands, and those villages without *ejidos* were to receive sections of any contiguous national land available. Land was also to be awarded to agricultural colonies to encourage small-scale farming in isolated areas.

Redistribution of two million acres of national land to the 60 percent of rural population attached to the *haciendas* was blocked in Chihuahua by the legislature's refusal to grant Governor Abraham González official leave to serve in the federal cabinet and by Pascual Orozco's rebellion. The Plan Orozquista safeguarded private property and provided for indemnification for any expropriation.

In Durango in 1912, only a limited portion of the 70,000 hectares the government announced for sale was sold because Indians remained in their own agricultural communities where land was not available, the available land was not suitable for cultivation, and the *hacendados* would only sell at exorbitant prices to the government for resale.

Elsewhere, too, though Madero announced over twenty million hectares were for sale, little had been sold by the end of 1912. The only small successes were some agrarian colonies serviced by trained agronomists.[18]

Thus the institutional land distribution program under Madero remained largely unfulfilled, while the old system of land tenure remained essentially unchanged.

All came to naught after Madero's murder with U.S. complicity, though a 4 March 1913 plan proposed by a San Luis Potosí school teacher demanded the confiscation of all *haciendas* belonging to Huerta, Porfirio, and Félix Díaz and their supporters, to be divided into lots of 10 hectares for each family. This was clearly a radical agrarian reform that attacked the holding of most *hacendados* in the republic.

THE U.S. LIES IN WAIT

This was a moment of reckoning, too, as U.S. forces had lain in wait. Now they moved Mexican politics to the right as they whipsawed one uncooperative or recalcitrant regime after another.

Madero's public opposition to U.S. business property and concessions prompted President Taft to shift his earlier support, and secretly promote a conspiracy to kill Madero and make Victoriano Huerta president as the cat's-paw who would secure U.S. business interests. But when Woodrow Wilson replaced Taft as U.S. president, Wilson's new policy denied recognition to Huerta's openly despotic government.

The United States meanwhile promoted arms sales to the revolutionary factions it favored, embargoed arms to factions it opposed, threatened to invade, and then extracted concessions by seizing Mexico's main port at Veracruz, the nation's commercial windpipe and main source of foreign revenues. Powerful U.S. backing for General Carranza then made his army the dominant force, and led to the overthrow of Huerta in July 1914, but Carranza withheld the benefits the United States had hoped to gain.

During the following six years, U.S. policy vacillated, helping to keep Mexico's domestic power balance unstable. A deepening split in the goals of the revolutionary armies over proprietary rights to land, labor, and resources ensued as Zapata, Villa, and Obregón made war on Carranza and also betrayed and attempted to assassinate one another.

Until Villa marched into Mexico City in December 1914, and audaciously posed with Zapata in the president's chamber, he had supported and protected U.S. property holdings in Mexico, especially those of the American Smelting Company. As a reward for his efforts, he strongly believed the United States would recognize him as the nation's official leader.

Carranza by contrast had been critical of foreign holdings, had declared himself *Primero Jefe*, and had caused the United States to worry about the security of its citizens' extensive holdings in Mexico. But as the revolutionary alliance of Carranza and Villa disintegrated into postrevolutionary squabbling that led to the momentary defeat of Villa's cavalry by Carranza's machine guns in the spring of 1915, the United States sought to further divide Carranza and Villa in hopes of controlling both.

Conveniently switching its support to Carranza and depicting Villa as a lowly bandit to whom it embargoed arms sales, the United States forced Villa to pay black market prices for guns and ammunition. It was no surprise that Villa charged the United States had signed a secret pact with Carranza, and then he attempted to create a buffer zone to stop a U.S. invasion at Aqua Pietta, only to be upstaged by President Wilson's 5,000 troops that arrived before Villa's ragtag cavalry, dispersing his forces.

Opportunism fed U.S. designs to outflank Carranza, too. Falling into a cleverly set U.S. trap to destroy Villa totally, Carranza was favored with U.S. guns in exchange for inviting U.S. companies to return to Mexico to operate as they had under Díaz. Villa, ever vigilant, then powerfully attacked, killing 16 U.S. workers sent to operate Mexican mines. On 4 March 1916, he made a raid into Colombus, New Mexico, where he killed 17 defenders. Although the U.S. chased Villa's forces back to Mexico and burned his dead horsemen left at the scene, President Wilson seized the offensive, mobilizing a "punitive expedition" of tens of thousands, including the Civil War–era Tenth Cavalry of black soldiers, under General John Pershing and his aide-de-camp, Lieutenant George Patton.

Carranza initially demurred at the incursion but was assured by President Wilson that the purpose was to capture Villa, not to kill him. So into Mexico now proudly rode the last U.S. cavalry, 8,000 strong, backed up by mechanized armed vehicles, 600 trucks and operators, and an air force used for the first time in war. It was forced by Pershing to fly blind without lights at night.

Yet the U.S. logic of superior forces and weaponry was flawed. To feed the uninitiated troops as well as the well-bred cavalry and their overweight horses, the U.S. supply train was enormous and long.

By contrast, Villa's army of peasants, lightning fast in the saddle, with no uniforms, needed little food for themselves, and their lean horses were accustomed to live on stubble. They were, however, dutifully followed by a train of female cooks. Brilliant in tactics, the peasants blocked detection of their desert maneuvers as they took the sun side and ran parallel to Pershings' cumbersome, thirsty forces, which were blinded by the sun in their eyes and were ever more exhausted in the blazing sands. Thus Villa evaded Pershing in north Durango and south Chihauhau, driving the general 125 miles inland to the southern Chihauhau border to make a total invasion route of 410 miles. When the naive troopers asked for Villa's whereabouts, an entire armed pueblo and 200 Mexican troops fired on Pershing's forces.

Retreating with heavy losses, Pershing demanded Mexican reparations and called for a new U.S. invasion by 150,000 national guardsmen in a war of revenge. His demand helped make Villa a Mexican hero and forced Carranza to secure his honor and defenses and insist that U.S. troops withdraw—a measure President Wilson smugly refused.

The U.S.-Mexican war was on, as the Tenth Cavalry picked up their dead and left 24 men as Mexican prisoners. President Wilson called for full-scale war, closed border bridges, and demanded Carranza release the prisoners, as he reluctantly did. When some captured U.S. cavalry riders claimed the Mexicans had severed their trigger fingers, U.S. ire and demands were elevated.[19]

Villa then seized the moment and divided Carranza's forces that were poised to hold off the U.S. invasion; 2,000 Villa guerrillas initially took several towns from Carranza's forces.[20]

As the struggle of Carranza, Villa, and Zapata intensified, however, the latter two allied their forces, and together they expelled Carranza and Obregón from Mexico City. Carranza recoiled, winning some peasant support, and grandly proclaimed the need to dissolve the *latifundia*, form small holdings, and restore lands unjustly taken from villages. His appeal initially appeared in the form of the manifesto "Additions to the Plan of Guadalupe" and then in a corresponding January 1915 decree.[21]

Carranza also reestablished his power base through alliances with organized labor and military victory over Villa. Reentering the capital in the summer of 1914, Carranza established friendly relations with labor leaders. Then in February 1915 he signed a government agreement with the leaders of the anarcho-syndicalist *Casa del Obrero Mundial*, promising laws for the betterment of the working class in exchange for political support.

General Obregón meanwhile reorganized his forces, and using barbed wire and trenches then in fashion in militarized Europe, he routed Villa's hitherto invincible cavalry in April 1915 near Celaya, between Querétaro and Guanajuato. Villa later suffered a decisive defeat in January 1917 when his force of 40,000 was reduced to a few thousand horsemen.

As Villa abandoned the entire north save Chihuahua and Zapata left Mexico City in August 1915 to bolster the revolution in Morelos and parts of neighboring states, Carranza's constitutionalists took control of the rest of the country save parts of the northwest and the sugar cane district south of Mexico City. Gaining U.S. recognition on 19 October 1915, Carranza then appointed his best general, Obregón, as minister of war in March 1916, but he had no fear of another U.S. invasion because President Wilson soon became entangled in the European war.[22]

In fact, during its Mexican campaign the United States had been decisively defeated because its military forces were divided on three fronts—two in Mexico and one in Europe. Pershing never sighted Villa, and exited Mexico on 4 February 1917 to lead his troops to fight in World War I.[23] Carranza had won because he did not oppose the U.S. invasion that diverted Villa's forces.

Villa had also survived, however, because he was able to divide U.S. and Carranza forces, becoming a living legend who was unassailable for his nationalism, populism, bravery, and tenacity. Three years later in 1920, the government awarded Villa, by then a mythic figure, an old *hacienda*. His generals also sequestered estates, enriching themselves at the expense of the peasants they were supposed to liberate.

THE NEW COALITION MAKES LAW

The civil war had left 1,500,000 dead, two-thirds of them civilians who were executed, died from wounds, starved to death, or were overcome by disease. The combatant armies also destroyed the nation's infrastructure for transport, energy, communications, mining, agriculture, and production. In addition, the destruction led to soaring food prices, starvation, and riots, and the condition of both workers and peasants was far worse than before the revolution began.

With initial U.S. backing and with no further significant opposition to his military victory, General Carranza quickly brought his closest followers into a new coalition made up of both old and new class interests, including four major factions:

- Villa's generals now comprising a landed gentry
- The prerevolutionary landowning oligarchy adhering to the new regime to secure their plantation and *hacienda* interests
- The industrialists and commercial classes coalescing as an urban elite
- The aspiring, only partly developed, middle classes.

From these groups, deputies were elected in October 1916; the following month they assembled in Querétaro to draw up a new constitution. Carranza selected the setting to emphasize the similarity between the postrevolutionary situation and the triumph of Juárez over Emperor Maximilian in 1856-57. But there was a difference, as the earlier liberals sought to destroy the power of the church, while the revolutionary intellectuals of 1916 wished to undermine the puissance of the *haciendas*.

This difference played itself out as Carranza attempted to protect the landed estates, submitting his own plan to nominally amend the 1857 Constitution. He recommended no reelection to the posts of president or state governor, and the elimination of the vice presidency so it could not be used for Díaz-style political maneuvering.

Carranza also proposed a few additions to Article 27, which had been used to deprive villages of common lands and which specified that no corporation could own real estate. As the liberals' earlier agrarian reforms had failed and most Indian peasants had not become independent farmers, Carranza recognized the right of villages (but not the church) to own property. He suggested, however, that the banks should be allowed to accept mortgages, thus alienating land.

Belonging to the upper class, however, both Carranza and Obregón were out of sync with the profound social and economic reforms sought by the great majority of young, middle-class revolutionists, deputies, civilians, and army men under Carranza's command. Introducing legislation for deep-seated agrarian reform in Article 27, these deputies provided that property in land was vested originally in the nation, which in turn could transfer it to private persons. Thus the nation could impose restrictions on private property to achieve an equitable distribution of wealth, to break up *latifundia*, foster small and middle-sized farms, create new settlements by endowment of land, and develop agriculture.

Article 27 provided, moreover, that villages lacking enough land to be relatively self-sufficient would receive it from adjoining large properties. All land lost by villages since the 1856 disentailment law (under Lerdo and Juárez) was also to be returned to them, and restitution grants of land thus far made under Carranza's own 1915 decree were thereby confirmed. The communal use of village land was also safeguarded pending the preparation of a law to divide these lands among the users.

The constitution also specified the method of redistribution, favoring middle-class landowners against foreign interests, rather than those in peonage. Article 27, section 1, specified that only Mexican citizens and Mexican companies could own land, except that the government could concede this right to foreigners willing to renounce the protection of their own governments. Domestically, moreover, the federal and state congresses were to issue laws concerning the division of large estates, designating that the owners would break up and sell in easy payments all land in excess of a specified amount. As guarantee of payment, the large estate owners would receive bonds issued as part of a new public debt, and buyers would not be permitted to sell until they had completed their payments to the former owners.[24]

Middle-class buyers could weigh the profitability of such an investment in good or poor land. But landless peasants were outside the market economy, had little if any money, and hoped for free land—not land with a price.

Taking national power, depriving the underclasses of almost all political influence, and limiting land redistribution, the generals thereby effectively realigned their interests, secured the spoils of the civil war, and became part of the new ruling class. Old leaders were either shunted into oblivion or murdered. Zapata was assassinated in 1920, and Villa was assassinated in 1923. Carranza was later overthrown, and still later Obregón was murdered.

INSTITUTIONALIZING REVOLUTIONARY GOALS

From such killing fields, future strife in Mexico would grow from seeds of past rights to land, opposition to foreign interests appropriating the national patrimony (*dominio directo*) in oil and other resources, and the condition of the multitudes.

Constitutionalism was a momentary gesture to idealistic, revolutionary goals—not to apply them, but to institutionalize, limit, and destroy them. To undercut peasant solidarity and disperse the focus of domestic politics concerning land distribution and questions of landlord interests and labor rights, the postrevolutionary constitution immediately shifted political power to the divergent states and their respective governors. And while the unrelenting domestic struggle over land and labor rights roiled the nation, the foreign interests and the imperial oil companies battered the national government, attempting to undercut the constitution and shape the *realpolitik* of Mexico to their liking.

INEFFECTUAL LAND DISTRIBUTION

Repeatedly threatened with betrayal, the Mexican revolution could not and did not fulfill the rights of rural peasants and peons to own and till the land for survival.

The Spanish *encomienda* had awarded the conquerors native labor in servitude with the land itself. As tenure evolved, peons had subsisted in the so-called "plantation community," living and working upon the privately owned *hacienda*, without either municipal or property rights. Most owed rent payable to the owner in kind, labor, or money, and exchanged their labor for pulque, corn, and candles secured at the owner-operated company store (*tienda de raya*).

As the peon held no *fundo legal* in the *hacienda*, the owner could forcibly move him from place to place on the same plantation or oust him from the tract at any time. This made the peon less than a serf, for the traditional serf in Western Europe had held hereditary rights to work the soil in perpetuity, that were recorded in the feudal manor's book of *doomsday*.[25] The plantations absorbed both land and the self-directing life of village communities, reducing the peasants to a state of virtual slavery, destroying their previous community structure, and undermining their traditional moral attitudes.

By the close of the Díaz regime, more than 90 percent of all inhabited village communities were on plantations in the states of Guanajuato, Michoacán, Jalisco, Zacatecas, Nayarit, and Sinaloa. Plantations held fast more than 80 percent of rural communities in Querétero, San Luis Potosí, Coahuila, Aguascalientes, Baja California, Tabasco, Nuevo León, and Chiapas.

Lying outside the immediate surroundings of Mexico City, these states together comprised one-half of the states of the republic, with at least 80 percent of all their rural communities located inside plantations and thus deprived of any local or municipal rights. Throughout Mexico there were nearly 57,000 of these plantation communities, but only 13,000 free villages. The latter had best survived in the mountainous regions surrounding Mexico City, while the plantation communities were more frequently found in less mountainous states. These villages which were not free were reduced to less than one-fifth the size of the free village.

For 400 years villages had been reduced to plantations, and the Díaz regime accelerated this transformation. Focusing on the free village communities in the states surrounding the Valley of Mexico, Díaz planned to change agriculture from a way of life into an efficient production enterprise.[26]

To defend the existence of the surviving village communities, millions had joined in the rural revolution in the states of Morelos, Guerrero, Oaxaca, Puebla, Hidalgo, Tlaxcala, México, and Veracruz. In an attempt to keep this following, General Carranza promised them land, as he was driven to Veracruz by Pancho Villa and Zapata, who were more revolutionary. Yet, though Carranza decreed partial land redistribution on 6 January 1915, as already detailed, this law neither attacked the plantation system nor provided for dismemberment of the large estates.

Carranza's decree applied instead to one of two different types of agrarian communities: those village communities covered by the law that had been partially or completely deprived of their lands, to the misery of their members, and the other half of the rural population not covered by land redistribution, whose inhabitants had been reduced over four centuries to resident plantation peons and laborers.

Even for the villages covered by the law of 1915, restitution was only for land illegally appropriated for which villages could prove title or necessity. This system led to unending legal manipulations, chicanery, bribery, and delay. The law created a National Agrarian Commission with a cumbersome system of committees, each of which was subject to heavy-handed official and unofficial administrative pressures—both honest and dishonest—that delayed execution of the program. And though the law awarded state governors the right to make provisional grants to villages to be later confirmed by the national government, in September 1916 Carranza took this power from the local authorities, bringing land distribution to an absolute standstill.

TOKENISM, PACIFICATION, AND LEGAL FRAMING

Was the agrarian law in effect a token propaganda and pacification program designed to offer the more rebellious communities enough land to keep them quiet for a time?

Clearly, because the victory of the revolution had come from the most vocal and insistent peasant agitation, the countryside writhed with discontented impatience to devour the *haciendas*. Land redistribution was prevented, however, by the law's own authors, who had transformed the popular, unorganized surge into a national movement resting on a legal frame that itself remained unimplemented. Possession and use—not provable legal title—were the basis of the peasants' conception of ownership. But Carranza's law of 1915 had made restitution, with proof of both previous legal title and unjustified deprivation, the basis of the resolution of the land problem, thereby negating the principle of the peasant and Indian/*mestizo* village right to land, and effectively securing the *latifundia*.[27]

The law of 1915, moreover, provided rights only to villages that held political status (*categoría política*), enumerating such villages as *pueblos, rancherías, congregaciones,* and *communidades*. The benefit of the law was thus denied to the majority of Mexican communities with different characterizations, though they had an equal or even a greater population. With state legislatures and courts denying these rights, wide and persistent conflict followed—conflict that was not resolved until April 1927, when the law was broadened to include villages in general, so that all villages with 25 (later 20) agrarian families were qualified to ask for land. The law shifted its basis to land rights as a matter of social policy, rather than rectification of injustice, and excluded resident plantation laborers (*acasillados*)—thereby ensuring an ample labor force for the remaining *haciendas*.

Landowners could also delay land redistribution under the law of 1915 by resorting to court action against all officials trying to allocate land. They even pursued legal review and injunction (*amparo*) to hold up presidential land restitution. It was not until February 1932 that the Mexican Supreme Court refused to prevent land distribution under the *ejido* legislation, which compensated the landowners.[28]

In the interim, the governor of each state was empowered to declare every plantation community a free *municipio* as well as to declare that all *tierras ociosas*—idle lands—could thereafter be tilled by propertyless peons. Yet, without a more thorough revolution against the landlords and their *hacienda* plantation system, these landlords held the power to shape the balance of state politics in their own interests and sidestep the constitutional focus on domestic land redistribution, *latifundia*, and foreign land holdings.

The Constitution of 1917 clearly guaranteed citizen land rights; relevant sections stated:

> (a) No foreign corporation or individual can legally acquire or hold any mines, oil wells, land or other real property in Mexico unless he renounces his citizenship.
> (b) No corporation, either domestic or foreign, can own agricultural, grazing, or other rural lands in Mexico, and if title to such property is already vested in a corporation, provision is made for its acquisition by respective State governments in exchange for state bonds.
> (c) No corporation owning a mine, oil well, factory, or other industrial enterprise can hold or acquire land in excess of its actual immediate requirements, the area to be determined by the Federal or State executive.
> (d) No foreign corporation or individual can, under any condition, hold or acquire ownership to lands or waters within 60 miles of its [national] frontiers or 30 miles from the sea-coast.

Nonetheless, under the constitution's provisions it was difficult, if not impossible, to expropriate land. The law was ignored in most states and barely secured in others. After Carranza was overthrown in December 1920, however, if peasants could not easily prove despoilation, their demands could be converted into a request for land donation.[29]

Although the constitution had clearly awarded state legislatures the power to create free villages out of resident plantation communities, until 1927 the overwhelming influence of the *haciendas* meant few states actually used this power to declare villages a *categoría política*. The small number of villages so designated became part of the municipal structure of the state with municipal ground and an internal legal organization (i.e., they possessed the right to an expropriated domain constituting a *fundo legal*), and they also held agricultural land in communal ownership (i.e., *ejidos*).

FUNDO LEGAL

The idea of a *fundo legal* with specific boundaries had been defined during the Revolution in 1913, with the first agrarian law in Durango providing: "The Government may erect new villages within the State in those places it judges to be convenient by taking 2,000 hectares, part of which land shall be set aside for the *Fundo Legal* of the new village."[30]

The first village proper had been carved out of a hundred hectares of a *hacienda* occupying the area surrounding the railway station at San Gabriel, which functioned as the railway center and marketing community for many surrounding villages. The lands placed under village communal ownership (*ejidos*) were taken from the adjoining plantation of *La Tapona*. The worth of these lands were valued by assessors and backed up by government bonds payable with interest in ten years, so the taking was more a forced sale than expropriation without compensation.

To prevent new grants of *fundo legal*, many landowners cleared the peons from their *haciendas*, destroyed peasant housing, and forcibly scattered their families. Few states blocked such moves, but in Guerrero, Governor Castrejón officially declared in favor of the *fundo legal*, providing that every place inhabited by more than thirty families located on private property was a village with an internal legal organization as part of the municipal structure of the state. Such a village had a right free from all costs to ask and receive for each family resident an area equal to 2,500 square meters of land for a house and the surrounding land upon which it was located and an equal amount of land for streets, a school, a plaza, and a market. The village also had the right to bridge rivers, construct other community facilities, fences, wells, and to plant trees, etc.

This property was to be paid for at its tax valuation plus 10 percent, with payment made for each parcel over a period of 20 years through issue of state bonds. The peasants' property was then inheritable, but could not be alienated or transferred for any reason. If it was abandoned for over a year, then with the previous consent of the governor of the state, it was to pass to another resident in need of a home.[31]

Yet the struggle over land allocation went forward state-by-state, so that in Querétaro, even when the peasantry elected an *agrarista* as governor, the landowners continued to pressure for a return of the *ejidos* taken from them.

Little changed after the revolution, either. By 1921 the great majority of rural villages were still excluded from the benefits of land redistribution; the census revealed the extent of deprivation:

- Overall there were 46,381 resident plantation communities with an average of 84 people and 13,388 agricultural villages with an average of 495 people

- With the law denying resident plantation communities the right to land, over 46,000 out of the possible 60,000 rural communities were thereby excluded.
- As 35,595 communities (both resident plantations and free villages) had fewer than twenty agrarian families, the law excluded another group of landless comprising more than half of the 60,000 rural communities.
- To stop land redistribution in communities of twenty families or more, plantation owners burned peasants' houses, forcibly ejecting them from the estates.

Almost a decade later, fear, discouragement, and ignorance still imbued the peasantry. The National Agrarian Commission estimated that by 30 June 1930, only 8,995 of the 25,854 villages (fewer than 35 percent) with more than twenty agrarian families had made any attempt to take advantage of the legal right to claim land.

The Logic of Land Distribution

What then was the logic and framework of land distribution?

The creation of utopian, isolated communities in the face of technological progress and imperial pressure was rooted in the assumption that the amount of land given to a village ought to be sufficient for each family to maintain its living standard using its existing tools—thus remaining perpetually as backward as when its life was dominated by the plantation.

This might result in thousands of little communities owning their own lands in semicommunal form, tilling them collectively, operating with a high degree of community cooperation, and, with a school in the center, solidifying a unified community acting as the foundation of a democratic government. The small size of the *ejidos* meant, however, that many villages that received them actually resorted to the labor output supplied by neighboring plantations to provide themselves subsistence. And insufficient land distributed to an increasing population also meant that village *ejidos* unable to raise their living standards eventually overflowed their boundaries.[32]

The only way to settle this population overflow in the face of the *haciendas'* powerful resistance to dismemberment was forcible federal expropriation and distribution of small parcels to the Indian villages. Yet the constitution did not provide for federal intervention. Rather, only the states held the clear constitutional right to break up the large *haciendas* by imposing a limit to the area that any one individual could hold, and forcing the sale of the rest. As only a few states applied legislation to break up the large estates by July 1930, enforcement of village land rights had been negligible, and *hacienda* estates of a million hectares had been broken into tiny parcels only in the six states of Guanajuato, Durango, Zacatecas, Michoacán, Tlaxcala, and Nayarit.

Nonetheless, though their influence proved short-lived, peasants in rural villages coalesced in leagues such as *Ligas de Comunidades Agrarias* in the states of Veracruz and San Luis Potosí, electing their own leaders, creating armed militia, and acting as local and national political blocs.[33] Yet they too could not break up the *hacienda* system.

The social contradiction was clear: as land redistribution to the peons and Indian villages remained minimal, only renewed revolution or state expropriation breaking up the large estates could end the system of near slavery. But there was no resumption of the revolution demanding land. And the reformist state program proved impossible to implement because the *hacendados* would never voluntarily break up their own plantations, the government would only force them to do so if full compensation was offered, and there was no political coalition leading the states to take such measures beyond minimal programs.

Although utopians envisioned a future *ejido* system as an historical throwback reestablishing the milieu for cooperative mores antedating the Spanish Conquest—with the rural village retaining some land in a harmonious, communal form, at least for pasture and woodlands—such semicommunal, collective agrarian communities never replaced the plantation tenure system.[34]

Thus there was little change in land holdings from before the revolution:

- In 1910, not only did the plantation system hold the greater part of the nation's lands and contain the vast majority (81 percent) of all populated places within its boundaries, but in most of the states only a fraction of the rural population had any land at all.
- In 1923, thirteen years after the revolution, some 2,682 owners out of a rural population of about 11 million held 50.1 percent of all land. Of these, 115 of the largest owners held nearly a fourth of the nation's private lands, with ownership concentration enlarged because some individuals owned properties in different states.
- With the plantation system most fully developed in the states north and south of the Central Plateau (encompassing Mexico City), once-free Indian villages were destroyed and the population reduced to peonage on the plantations to the following degree: Aguascalientes, 65.8%; Chiapas, 59.7%; Coahuila, 57.8%; Colima, 57.8%; Durango, 66%; Guanajuato, 84.3%; Jalisco, 65.5%; Michoacán, 60.1%; Nayarit, 63.2%; Nuevo León, 60%; Querétero, 64%; San Luis Potosí, 81.8%; Sinaloa, 73.4%; Tamaulipas, 74.6%; and Zacatecas, 76.1%.
- In the states surrounding the Valley of Mexico, by contrast, more Indian villages retained their autonomy, resisting direct controls by the plantation. Thus in Hidalgo, only 20.7% of the rural population lived on plantations; in Morelos 23.7%; in México 16.8%; in Oaxaca

14.5%; in Puebla 20.1%; in Tlaxcala 32.2%; in Veracruz 24%; and in the Federal District 6.9%.[35]

It was not surprising that the forces feeding the revolution could not easily have succeeded outside the Valley of Mexico where the plantation had absorbed most of the lands, though the villages themselves might escape peonage. Yet during the Díaz regime, when the plantations attempted to absorb remaining villages to enforce peonage, self-defense transformed the villagers into leaders of the social revolution.[36]

THE OPPOSITION GROWS: LABOR RIGHTS, LABOR STRUGGLES

The refusal of successive Mexican governments to break up the *haciendas* controlling the agricultural domain had its counterpart in state failure to keep foreign capital from dominating industry, and limiting the expansion of a relatively weak Mexican industrial sector employing a small, if growing, urban working class.

Domestic capitalists had hoped to replace the foreigners lavished with benefits by the Díaz regime, and Mexico's workers had railed at the yoke fixed on forced laborers in the *monterías*, low-wage factory labor in the urban domain, and those employed under foreign-imposed conditions in the mines, on the railroads, and in the leading industries. Lacking a domestic middle class on which to vent its anger, the working class viewed foreign interests through the lens of the feudal-like labor conditions these foreigners had enforced for three decades under Díaz. In Europe, a *petit bourgeois* class opposed feudal landlordism,[37] but in Mexico the absence of a vibrant commercial sector meant opposition to foreign interests would be shouldered jointly by domestic industrialists and the working class.

It was extremely difficult for the population to organize into a viable opposition, however. Labor organizations were still legally forbidden, and conspiracy charges were brought against any attempting to force wages above their "natural level." The *ley fuga*—death—was visited on those attempting to escape prison sentences, forced labor, or impression into the army. As a deadly example, the federal army murdered hundreds of laborers during the 1907 labor protests issuing from the mining region of Cananea and the textile mills of Río Blanca.

During the 1910 revolution, in fact, the frail numerical strength of labor was leveraged its anarchistic and socialist adherents, and expanded by its concentration in the urban domain with its foreign-owned industries dominating political life. Scattered in a few industrial centers, the movement for industrial revolution, socialism, anarchism, and syndicalism had embraced only a fraction of factory labor. Yet the *Casa del Obrero Mundial* made Mexico City the mecca of labor leaders and intellectuals on the cutting edge of social issues, and helped hone the skills of those at the forefront of the revolution.

Postrevolution politics cut its teeth against the liberalism of Madero and the reactionism of Huerta. Yet both suppressed labor, and the *Casa del Obrero Mundial* expelled foreign labor agitators and even used government authority to undercut organized labor and its propaganda machinery. Once President Carranza crossed swords with Villa and Zapata and was driven from Mexico City, however, he was compelled to recruit labor supporters. He signed a virtual treaty with the *Casa del Obrero Mundial* and mobilized workers into "Red Battalions" to fight Villa in return for favors and labor rights to organize behind the lines of fire.

Recognizing the added potential of an alliance against the foreign interests, Carranza then mobilized a constitutional faction to appease labor demands. His secretary of the interior, Rafael Zubáran Capmany, elaborated, signed, and published an April 1915 unofficial labor code that was designated as a *proyecto* rather than a demand for a labor law to be submitted to the Constitutional Convention. Once Carranza had defeated Villa and established himself firmly in power in 1916, he suppressed labor, used Juárez's 1864 law prohibiting public disorder against the workers, and shot strikers as traitors.

Carranza meanwhile appealed to the Constitutional Convention in session to be given the right in Article 73 to pass labor laws for the entire country. Recognizing the shifting political sands, the tiny labor movement understood Carranza's hypocrisy making this appeal while the state was repressing unorganized workers. Yet labor's position throughout the world had been transformed in the wake of World War I by the rising power of workers, the shaping of new labor legislation, the participation of labor in governments, the Russian Revolution, the establishment of the Labor Office at the League of Nations, and the articulation of labor rights expounded in Article 123 of the Mexican Constitution of 1917.

In Mexico labor supported action against the foreign interests and called for the emancipation of Mexico from exogenous tutelage and exploitation. This position appealed powerfully to the committee that brought the completed labor code in Article 123 to the floor of the convention, a body largely composed of lawyers and military men. Among them only Nicolás Cano and Carlos L. Gracidas had had trade union experience. But the chairman of the Committee on the Constitution, General Mujica, shaped the labor code from the Veracruz *proyecto* issued two years earlier, elaborating the basic worthiness of the ideas and institutions new to Mexico (*una verdadera novedad*). These ideas, the preface to the *proyecto* elaborated, were drawn from *paises cultos*, like Holland, Belgium, France, Germany, Switzerland, Spain, Italy, Australia, New Zealand, and some states of the United States. Justice Louis Brandeis, Father John A. Ryan, and Justice Higgins of Australia were listed as sources of inspiration, as were laws presented to the French Parliament by Gaston Doumergue and

M. Viviani in 1910. Not only freeing "man" as the French Revolution earlier boasted, this Constitution Convention sought in script to "free labor."

The state legislatures, Article 123 thus provided, "shall make laws relative to labor with due regard for the needs of each region of the Republic and in conformity with the following principles, and these principles and laws shall govern the labor of skilled and unskilled workmen, employees, domestic servants, and artisans, and in general every contract of labor." Even the lowly agricultural laborer was to receive a minimum wage. And the main constitutional provisions liberated and secured all those who worked to live.

IMPERIAL INTERESTS

Emancipating Mexican labor proved impossible in the face of imperial interests, however. Even before the revolution, foreign investors had sought unmitigated access to Mexico's copper, silver, gold, and oil. For this goal, President Wilson supported U.S. land, mining, and oil companies, as well as banks, in openly backing the military forces of General Carranza, Pancho Villa, and Emilio Zapata. And while the domestic imbroglio over Mexican land reform raged, Britain, France, and the United States intensified their competitive efforts to control Mexico's resources, trade, and financial affairs.

With Britain and the United States the primary contestants, the Mexican Revolution and the new constitution were soon subverted as these two powers made economic war. United States investors played havoc in Mexico's political domain by refusing to pay taxes to the British-backed Mexican government led by Victoriano Huerta, which favored British oil interests, and providing instead subsidies and "credits" for the rival, pro-U.S. faction opposed to the Huerta's federal machine and its army.

United States investors also provided monthly stipends to the military brigands protecting U.S. oil companies from paying these taxes to the Huerta central government, and they loaned great sums to the so-called Constitutionalists mobilized against his regime, while avidly lobbying and campaigning in the United States for military intervention in Mexico.

The foreign investors also kept Mexico from asserting its right to an equal place in seating at the League of Nations by pressuring President Wilson at the peace conference at Versailles after World War I. The U.S. State Department became the avowed partisan of American oil interests in Mexico, demanding that the Mexican Constitution be amended to allow U.S. investors to invest profitably in Mexican oil and other resources.

As the oil lobbies flexed their muscle when the successful Mexican Revolution threatened foreign investments in Mexican petroleum, conflict emerged over Article 27 as the key provision of the new Mexican Constitution of 1917. This article provided that the subterranean rights of Mexico in minerals, fuels, and other resources belonged to the Mexican people.

Mexico's internal struggle meanwhile promised to give the foreign lobbyists an edge, as the deepening domestic struggle pitted both old and new ownership classes against the peasantry and workforce. The *Zapatistas* and peasants' demand for thoroughgoing land reforms was staunchly opposed by the landlords and the hitherto-excluded northern industrialists now backing Carranza. And the anti-imperial opposition took on new strength as the Mexican government attempted to maintain power under the failing hold of the old ruling classes aligned to the British oil companies.

These opposition forces tried, unsuccessfully, to undermine efforts of the United States and its oil companies to shape access to Mexican resources by supporting and manipulating a succession of "revolutionary" constitutionalists. And these constitutionalists soon discovered that so long as foreign influence over Mexico's resources retained a dominant role, a new order of government control and stability was not possible.

OWNERSHIP OF SUBTERRANEAN RESOURCES

Although the British imperial policy and the U.S. Monroe Doctrine were extended to cover Mexican oil resources and attempted to impose limitations on Mexico's sovereignty, revolution and independence raised the historical question of who owned the nation's subterranean lodes.

From the fourteenth century, Spanish kings had issued decrees describing the Crown's ownership rights over subterranean resources. Half a century after the Spanish Conquest, Fray Bernardino de Sahagún described the sea bitumens in New Spain as being "like the pitch of Castile which easily melts ... and on certain and specific days in conformity with the waxing of the moon, it becomes broad and fat like butter."[38] Later, in 1780, Charles III refined the issue of ownership rights by decreeing that coal deposits belonged to the Crown and awarding them by the Crown's concession of its rights to vassal proprietors. The king also empowered others to alienate subterranean rights from the owners of surface land by so-called "denouncement." And looking to New Spain, Charles issued royal mining ordinances in 1783, that declared:

> The mines belong to my royal crown. ... Without separating them from my royal patrimony, I concede them to my vassals in ownership [*propiedad*] and possession, in such manner that they may sell, lease, devise and in any other manner alienate the rights which they hold thereto.... Any person shall have the right to discover and denounce a mine or a vein, not only in common lands, but also on those privately owned, provided he pays to the owner of the land for the surface occupied and for the damage resulting, a compensation fixed by the appraisal of experts.... I also concede permission

to denounce in the manner referred to, not only mines of gold and silver but also . . . all other fossils be they ores or minerals, bitumens or juices of the earth.

Such powers of alienation of subterranean materials in common lands or privately owned surface soil thus cut two ways: the Crown could cede ownership and mining rights to its vassals and any person could discover and mine these materials by denouncing (alienating) the right to them by the owner of the surface land, provided he compensate the landowner for surface occupation and any resulting damage to that surface from mining operations.

Although the king excluded bitumens of coal from his patrimony in 1789 in order to stimulate private mining to advance the royal navy and fulfill other public service requirements, the Napoleonic invasion of Spain led to the passage of a new constitution in 1812 that applied to all parts of the existing kingdom, including Mexico. Yet Mexico's declared independence thereafter clouded the law, leading to uncertainty over whether any person could denounce coal or other deposits against the interest of the surface owner of the land.

Jumping forward a full century, the need for subterranean bitumens enlarged as New England fishermen killed off the last of the sperm whales for oil and the demand for kerosene rose. In 1859, a venture capitalist named Drake had drilled the Western world's first commercial oil well. Eleven years later the lure of Mexican bitumen drew a ship captain into a Boston-financed, short-lived company engaged in shallow drilling and refining in Tuxpan. Celebrated Cecil Rhodes also tried but failed to bring Mexican oil into production as part of his emporium. Although it was wary of imperial adventurers, in 1881 the Mexican Supreme Court ruled that the royal ordinances of 1783 were still in force in Mexico, thus making coal deposits open to denouncement, yet it recognized that the Mexican legislature held the future power to sanction the system of landowners' rights to subterranean minerals.

Thereafter, Mexican statutory legislation in 1883, 1892, and 1909 dealt with subsoil rights acquired by U.S. oil companies by virtue of their ownership of the surface land or by petroleum leases from private Mexican landowners. These laws effectively declared that all petroleum deposits were the "exclusive property" of the owner of the land in which they were located.[39]

Such limited definitions could not survive in the age of industrialization, merchant shipping, and imperial conquest, though. The shift from coal-fired steamers to oil-powered navies and merchant ships set global adventurers afoot, making crude oil a critical strategic mineral and no nation invulnerable to pressure and subterfuge.

Porfirio Díaz provided the missing pieces of the imperial puzzle by initially inducing two of his most eminent *ceintificos, señores* Pimentel and Enrique C. Creel, to invest 200,000 pesos in a failed adventure in oil exploration and drilling, and by thereafter showering favors and concessions on foreign investors. Preferring British promoter Weetman Pearson, Díaz's wife, Doña Carmen, sold her Tehuantepec lands at then staggering prices, alienating pasture and communal fields from disinherited, rebellious villagers, who were butchered by the dictator's armed *rurales*.

Later, Edward L. Doheny's imperial discovery and Díaz's grant of drilling concessions to over 600,000 acres of land was only equaled by the five-year search of Britain's Pearson for the Petrero de Llano well, which was soon to draw daily 15,000 barrels into sumps and storage tanks. But Doheny offset Díaz's favoritism towards Pearson by secretly backing Francisco Madero's liberal revolution, thus setting off the inter-imperial British-American oil war fought with Mexican lives and fiber.

"The Americans even hired bands of Mexican brigands who destroyed Pearson's oilpipes and set his wells on fire," Anton Mohr reported.[40] And indeed Madero set loose his armies to destroy Díaz's concessionary strongholds.

Britain took its pound of Mexican flesh, too, backing General Huerta to murder Madero. It then recognized the usurper and guided Pearson (who had now been made the Home Office's genteel Lord Cowdray) in floating a loan enhancing Huerta's stability. While Doheny openly opposed Huerta with $100,000 in cash and $685,000 in fuel credit to finance Venustiano Carranza's planned revolt, American envoy John Lind inveighed that Huerta was a puppet of Cowdray and Whitehall and Washington's Secretary of State Bryan scolded British envoy Sir William Tyrell, charging: "The Foreign Office had simply handed its Mexican policy over to the oil barons for predatory purposes." To this allegation, Tyrell replied that Bryan himself was "talking just like a Standard Oil man ... pursuing a policy which they have decided on."[41]

As the Mexican Revolution raged for more than a decade, there was no way the United States could establish an unrestricted open door for its investments in Mexican oil or any other resources because these interests intersected with the historic sequence already recounted in Chapter 2.

Because he opposed the system of so-called "concessions" and was dismayed that U.S. interests in Mexico might be permanently in jeopardy, President Wilson in 1914 had refused to recognize the Huerta government. He proceeded to land U.S. troops at Veracruz, and on 20 April 1914 these U.S. forces captured the Customs House—Mexico's commercial hub and its source of revenues linking it with the outside world. They succeeded in forcing Huerta to resign a month later.

Imperial Germany then played its hand, offering to back Huerta in a revanchist Mexican war to seize Texas and California; Admiral von Hintze also extended Huerta military aid against the revolutionary forces in return for a government monopoly over an oil pipeline from the Huasteca oil fields supplying Germany and a promise to cut off oil supplies to the British navy in an expected war.

General Carranza then seized control of the Mexican government, and gained U.S. recognition in October 1915. He proceeded, however, to order registration of all petroleum leases, taxed oil production (reversing Díaz's policy), and hesitated in granting rights to U.S. oil and mineral prospectors.

President Wilson, nonplussed, immediately made plans to secure U.S. oil leases by any means necessary, not excluding brigandage, or even murder.

Carranza was meanwhile unable to stop Pancho Villa from raids across the U.S. border, and this gave the United States an obvious excuse to intervene in Mexican affairs. Responding with arms in March 1916, President Wilson planned General Pershing's punitive expedition into Mexico. As U.S. troops were then mobilized en masse at the border, U.S. investors in Mexican mines, *latifundia*, rubber, and oil wells openly called for war. Although President Wilson held off for another year, on 3 July 1917, Secretary of State Lansing ordered Ambassador Fletcher to stop any threatened oil strike in Tampico. This led to the Tamaulipas governor's arrest of three key labor leaders, the workers' threat of a general strike, and a press campaign to smear the labor movement by claiming that Moscow and the U.S.-based Industrial Workers of the World were planning to blow up the oil wells and establish a Soviet republic.

Recognizing the ever-present danger of U.S. oil interests backing intervention in Mexico to establish a puppet government, the Carranza government desperately searched for allies. Mobilizing its supporters to adopt the new 1917 Constitution with its protective Article 27 designed to safeguard the nation's right to Mexican resources and land, the government persuaded the legislators to make subterranean substances, including coal and oil, the *dominio directo* of the nation, thus denying underground mineral rights to the landowner by virtue of ownership of the land alone. Article 27 specifically provided: "In the Nation is vested the *dominio directo* of all ... petroleum." Its draftsman, who later acted as secretary of industry, elaborated on congressional efforts to regulate all petroleum rights:

> In dealing with products of the subsoil, the constituent Congress desired to be still more specific as regards the rights of the Nation and therefore employed the words *dominio directo* by which it was clearly expressed that in resources of this class the Nation held not only the original and absolute ownership (*propiedad*) but [that] the private ownership (*propiedad privada*) thereof likewise pertains to the Nation.

Domestic and foreign landowners thus had no rights of any degree or nature in the petroleum deposits in any Mexican lands if they had not held rights and performed certain "positive acts" prior to 1 May 1917, the effective date of Article 27 of the constitution. If such "positive acts" had been performed, the petroleum rights acquired then had to fit within the terms of Mexican regulatory laws, which later included making application for "confirmatory concessions" for their exercise after 11 January 1929.

IMPERIAL OIL AND *DOMINIO DIRECTO*

The oil companies fulminated, pressuring Senator Albert B. Fall to hold an austere investigation that recommended that unless Mexico's Constitution Article 27 be rewritten to U.S. specifications, U.S. military occupation and conquest should proceed.

Not only had U.S. petroleum companies railed against any Mexican limitations on their rights to extract and ship Mexico's oil, but large sums of U.S. capital had been invested in Mexican petroleum deposits on the basis of earlier mining laws that the oil companies interpreted as either awarding mineral rights to the owner of the surface land or allowing subterranean resources to be extracted against the interests of the owner of the surface.

Before Mexico had drawn up its new constitutional provisions on oil, Secretary of State Lansing had on 19 January 1916 telegrammed the U.S. consul located near the Carranza government headquarters in Querétaro:

> Department reliably informed *de facto* authorities contemplate issuing a decree providing for the nationalization of petroleum, which, if we are correctly informed, would affect most seriously the interests of numerous American citizens and other foreigners who we have hitherto engaged in business in producing and selling petroleum in Mexico. Point out to General Carranza in unequivocal terms the dangerous situation which might result from the issuance of any decree of a confiscatory character. Request that definitive action be delayed until department shall have had opportunity to examine proposed decree, and mail copy thereof to department.[42]

Although the consul replied on 26 January that General Carranza personally informed him that the government was not contemplating issuing a decree nationalizing the petroleum industry, before the end of the year Carranza had convened the Querétaro Convention, which drafted a new constitution containing Article 27 vesting all subterranean resources in the nation, limited only by Article 14 that the law would not retroactively prejudice any person.

Six months later on 28 June 1917, however, the Mexican minister of foreign affairs advised U.S. ambassador Fletcher that the effect of Article 27 was "nationalization." Then on 18-19 February 1918, using the extraordinary powers granted him by the Mexican Congress, Carranza imposed "certain taxes on the surface of oil lands, as well as on the rents, royalties, and production derived from the exploitation thereof." He also required the holders of petroleum rights to manifest and "denounce" rights to their properties that *dominio directo* invested in the nation, take a denouncement title from the government comparable to a lease-right, and pay royalties on all oil produced.

The U.S. State Department protested "emphatically and solemnly against the petroleum decree, declaring it to be an act of despoliation and confiscation" of "American citizens who have expended large sums of money in securing petroleum lands in Mexico." And the State Department further declared that "the United States cannot acquiesce in any procedure ostensibly or nominally in the form of taxation or the exercise of eminent domain, but really resulting in the confiscation of private property and arbitrary deprivation of vested rights."[43]

The battle raged during the next decade. The State Department not only protested the decree's infringement of U.S. private property rights alleged to have been legitimately acquired, but threatened the Mexican government with potential action "to protect the property of its citizens in Mexico divested or injuriously affected by the decree."[44] Taking the State Department lead, foreign oil companies operating in Mexico then refused to comply with Carranza's decrees calling for the filing of documents showing the basis of their titles by concessions.

Then on 1 August 1919, Carranza's *Circular No. 9* listed the oil companies and individuals that had failed to comply with his decrees and stopped all drilling except under permit from the federal executive, to be based on compliance with Mexico's future congressional regulations under Article 27.

When the companies began to drill without permits, the Mexican government threatened to take over such wells. It sent military forces into the oil fields and stopping drilling on 12 November 1919 and then prohibited further oil extraction from existing wells on 19 November 1919.

Although Carranza granted provisional drilling permits to U.S. oil companies on 20 January 1920, he was nonetheless overthrown by a U.S.-backed movement headed by Huerta, Obregón, and Calles, all of whom were also supported by Mexican socialists and "Red" newspapers seeking complete nationalization of oil.

"The worst enemy of Mexico is Yankee imperialism," declared future president Calles's political paper *El 130*, named for the article number in the Mexican Constitution that led to the persecution of the Catholic church in Mexico.[45]

Nonetheless, to gain U.S. recognition, Provisional President Huerta and President-elect Obregón quickly backtracked, publicly declaring that

Article 27 did not retroactively invalidate foreign property rights secured before the 1917 Constitution was effective.

On the other hand, in 1921 President Obregón hesitated to sign a treaty of amity and commerce safeguarding U.S. rights of property, and relied instead on the August 1921 decisions of the Mexican Supreme Court to issue injunctions (*amparo*) against implementing the 1918 Carranza decrees and also relied on his own agreement with the International Committee of Bankers to resume payments of approximately 22 million pesos annually on Mexico's national debt to foreign bondholders. The latter in turn was funded by the production and export oil tax.[46] U.S. companies would extract Mexican oil and pay Mexican taxes, these taxes would be paid to U.S. bankers, and Obregón would remain president for the moment.

Still, political factions and institutions were clearly out of joint in Mexico—some encouraging, others opposing, U.S. investment and oil rights. Thus despite the new political regime's seeming accommodations, a 1921 Supreme Court of Mexico decision granted an injunction favoring the case of the U.S.-owned Texas Company that ignored the U.S. landowner's *propiedad exclusiva* in subterranean materials covered by the law of 1909. Thus the United States was not satisfied, and Secretary of State Hughes stated on 10 August 1922 that the Mexican Supreme Court "decisions do not ... effectively deal with the rights of American citizens in lands containing petroleum or other subsoil substances where the lands were owned prior to May 1, 1917, but had not been developed or as to which leases or contract rights to prospect for and work petroleum had not been granted before that date." Hughes thus argued that the Supreme Court decisions were "inadequate to protect American rights against a retroactive and confiscatory application of the Mexican Constitution" and that the Mexican government refused to protect such rights in any international treaty that might provide that "confiscation—even if the Constitution decreed it—may not be carried into effect."[47]

Yet in the autumn of 1923, Calles fell into a military and financial condition of dependence on the United States when General Adolfo de la Huerta rebelled against Obregón and Calles; the latter were saved by the United States selling them an enormous supply of arms and ammunition to maintain their position. They literally sold out their country by accepting a supply of eleven aeroplanes, thirty-three machine guns, fifteen thousand Enfield rifles, five million rounds of ammunition, and other military equipment.[48] After another year of discord, in September 1924 the principal foreign oil companies conferred a month with officials of the Mexican government and agreed to a plan approved by both President Obregón and his successor Calles. Under its *Alien Land Law and the Petroleum Law of 1925*, however, the Mexican Congress again limited U.S. citizens' full ownership and use of their properties.

History was then confusingly replayed, with oil center stage. On 27 December 1926, when the principal oil companies refused to "confirm" their rights as required by the law, Mexico refused drilling permits to those companies that had not complied with the law. Drilling permits issued to them before the expiration of the previous year were canceled in 1927. Drilling operations conducted without permits were stopped by military force. When the oil companies filed injunction suits in the Mexican Supreme Court, the judges in the case of the Mexican Petroleum Company of California declared on 17 November 1927 that the company had a perpetual private right which was not forfeited by failure to apply for a permit and the company was constitutionally guaranteed an unlimited time right to apply.

The Mexican Congress then legislated that confirmation of such concessionary rights would be granted "without limitations as to time" in the case of surface owners and "for the term stipulated in the contracts" in the case of rights held under petroleum leases.[49]

According to the Mexican government's new agreement to offer recognition of foreign investors' petroleum rights, these investors had to apply for "confirmatory concessions" on or before 11 January 1929, under penalty of complete forfeiture of all rights. The government's interpretation of the constitution held, however, that a foreign corporation could neither receive nor hold a concession from the government for the exploitation of any petroleum at all. And this was ensured by Congress's "Law Regulating Article 27 of the Constitution in the Branch of Petroleum," for Article 2 repeated the declaration of the constitution that, without exception, the *dominio directo* over petroleum in the subsoil pertained to the nation and "only with the express authorization of the federal executive granted . . . may work required by the petroleum industry be carried out."[50]

It was now not clear if foreign corporations could or could not drill under a presidential concession.

On 27 March 1927, Mexico had already upstaged foreign petroleum demands by purposely imposing absurd regulations. The government reserved to itself the right to determine how much of any given area of land was effectively awarded an "exclusive property" right vested in mineral deposits through, of course, a "positive act" performed prior to 1 May 1917. Thus the government could decide whether a well drilled in one corner of a tract of land created vested rights to oil in the entire tract or only in the comparatively infinitesimal portion occupied in the drilling and operation of the well.[51]

The deeper one went into the labyrinth of legal and administrative *obscuranta*, the more contradictory the contest between Mexican and foreign control of the nation's oil resources became, until it reached mind-boggling absurdity and military solutions seemed appealing for what was clearly an economic and political impasse. "Pressure was ready for use and would be sufficient to set up in Mexico a President ... who would be satisfactory to Mr. Coolidge," one report of the U.S. president's thinking and personal utterances revealed. "General Obregón ... would be elected President of Mexico [Coolidge advised] 'if the elections are peaceful and free from riots and revolution.' But [Coolidge continued] 'if the [U.S.] Government should consent to the exportation of arms to Mexico, it could bring about the *election of any faction*, and such a course would assure the settlement of long-standing disputes with Mexico.'"[52]

LEGAL OBSCURITIES AND FOREIGN OIL RIGHTS

Mexico's own catch-22 was a denial of all foreign oil rights that deprived the nation of foreign exchange to pay its foreign debts. The enabling law to the constitution that the Calles government had passed in 1925 compelled foreign oil companies to confirm their legitimately acquired titles to oil properties in order to exchange such ownership for fifty-year leases. As most of their acquisitions were fraudulently acquired by uprooting and murdering illiterate Indian peasants with bribes to Mexican officials to forge documents and could thus be annulled, the companies sought to shift the focus of inquiry to the reduction of their interests to fifty-year terms. The State Department then used the subterfuge of protesting that the exchange was confiscatory, though Mexican oil fields were being depleted in considerably less than fifty years.

As President Calles then threatened to seize all oil properties, oil production steadily fell, and the oil tax on production and export declined in step. The June 1927 payment on foreign-held government bonds could not be met, and the International Committee of Bankers on Mexico representing European and U.S. bondholders wondered if they would continue to receive payments to add to the 30 million gold dollars they had already collected.[53]

Calles was left with little choice if the International Committee was not to turn thumbs down on future loans or a foreign committee under President Coolidge was to be dissuaded from organizing a call for armed intervention for the sake of oil and land interests, again choking off Mexico's economic windpipe at Veracruz. True, Protestant organizations in the United States successfully opposed such armed intervention, foreseeing it would only benefit the Catholic church.[54] And Thomas W. Lamont of the financial house of Morgan and Co. had already scoured New York, trying unsuccessfully to get money for the Mexican government, until he discovered that Mexico had a considerable deposit in the United States which under Mexican law could be used for government purposes in America such as paying interest on the defaulted bonds — a point conveniently impressed on President Calles's brother Señor Arturo Elías, the Mexican financial agent in New York.

This discovery allowed Lamont to convince the International Committee of Bankers to loan Mexico another $700,000, which was the amount of the Mexican deposit in the United States, on a short-term note with a certificate of deposit against the cash collateral. The committee made further loans of $2,500,000 after President Calles pledged as added collateral future U.S. consular fees and other payments due the Mexican government. It is hardly surprising that Calles was soon to concede all points insisted on by American oil men.[55] And Calles, who had posed as a strong opponent of presidential reelection, then had himself reelected to the presidency in July 1928, mounting a dictatorial throne.[56]

SOCIAL CLASS, FOREIGN INTERESTS, AND CHURCH INFLUENCE

Calles's reelection was soon followed by a field day for foreign investors in Mexico, the Caribbean, and Latin America.

Morgan Bank chief Thomas W. Lamont, directing the study *American Financial Foreign Policy* (1933), indicated that in the Caribbean, "All of the countries are indisputably within the sphere of influence of the United States, financial as well as political, even though the influence is in some cases overtly manifested only at intervals."

The financial sphere of influence included U.S. investments of $2,867,000,000, and as Lamont explained, "A stake of that size, in practice if not in theory, apparently justifies some disregard for the refinements of constitutionality." Control, moreover, was not limited geographically, he declared:

> These territorial acquisitions were not effected in even minor degree for the purpose of protecting or consolidating previously existing American economic interests in the region affected.... What was involved was the protection of our Latin American commitments as a whole, and the preservation of opportunities for further commercial and financial expansion, not primarily a desire to exploit the economic possibilities of the specific regions themselves.

A worldwide banking policy had been developed through the State Department; Lamont described the U.S. policy toward China in these terms:

> The stated purpose of the department was to establish the "Open Door" in China, in financial as well as in commercial matters, and presumably for China's own benefit as well as for that of the American bankers and investing public. Actually, the episode was part of Secretary Knox's "dollar diplomacy," the policy of extending the American financial empire in the more backward regions of the world by aggressive but non-military procedures.[57]

With Catholicism losing its consolidating state influence and the authoritarian Díaz regime replicated and institutionalized by other Mexican presidents in the late 1920s and early 1930s, Dollar Diplomacy attempted to shape Mexico's internal lifeline.

Part III

Looking Forward:
Old Ways, New Means

Though Europe's earlier free trade philosophers contended that advances in technology justified or otherwise accounted for the rise of a superior population of Creoles above the ancient Indians and their cultures, the view forward in the late 1920s and 1930s focused on old communal ways and new tools for production—an ideological lens focused on nationalism, the drive for development, and repelling foreign powers and their influence. Thus the concepts of Mexican nationalism—attempts at industrial reform, opposition to foreign impositions, commercialization, political and economic unification—provided the impetus for a Mexico looking for a transition forward, relying on old ways of cooperative and communal life, while plumbing the technological instruments of the future.

Lacking a safe means of crossing the chasm from rural to urban life, from an agricultural to an industrial society, the nation had already made many attempts at its peril. But the grandiose posturings of post-revolutionary figures who spoke brave words of industrialization rang hollow both in the Mexico of the *hacendados* and the venues of global industry and finance across the border—the former unable to mobilize the means of production for such a technological venture, the latter unwilling to finance its own market competitors.

Ragged from the war of independence, Mexico still relied upon the powerful *caudillos* who tried to balance their domestic and foreign supporters and enemies in conflicting alliances, ensuring that no single opposition force could displace the reigning central government. And though the greatest *caudillo* of the era, Plutarco Calles, and his political inner sanctum held sway for nearly two decades, their grasp far exceeded their reach,

111

falling short of mastering General Lázaro Cárdenas in the 1930s—bringing on a new reign of checkerboard land reforms, partial reformation of the *hacendado* system, attempts at uniting countryside and city, and new efforts at industrialization—all of which confronted the choking effect of the international oil cartel that was tightening its grip on Mexico.

CHAPTER 4

Nationalism, Development, and Foreign Influence in the Late 1920s and the 1930s

Mexico could not at once respect central authority and local controls, national constitutionality and provincial self-determination, *hacendado* rights and peasant land distribution, unfettered industrialization and popular welfare, exports to satisfy foreign markets and sufficient national resources for development and higher standards of living.

The fracturing of these conceptual opposites, which fueled the battle of their political partisans, was accentuated in the late 1920s as silver mined for export was demonetized and oil wells were being exhausted, with foreign companies unwilling to drill new ones. This loss of foreign exchange was exacerbated by the world economic malaise of the 1930s as exports markets fell away, and cash crops like sisal and cotton as well as mineral mining and metallurgy brought Mexico half the income they had previously generated. Although the domestic market for maize and other food crops remained fairly stable, both the area cultivated for export crops and the number of farm hands were reduced one-half from 1930 to 1932, leading the unemployed to demand unused *hacendado* land to grow maize for subsistence.[1]

Yet the economic malaise provided Mexico an opportunity to pursue agrarian reform, to nationalize the subsoil, to hold off foreign impositions, to grant rights for labor, and to assume an elevated importance in the Americas.

CALLES BENDS THE RULES; CÁRDENAS STRUCTURES THEM ANEW

A brilliant political tactician, Plutarco Calles controlled Mexico with the long arm of a *caudillo*, wielding ultimate military power to control the succeeding presidency, hold *hacendados* in line, and promise sufficient land redistribution to keep the agrarian militias in his fold.

With the descent to global depression in the early 1930s, Calles was further emboldened and sustained by the inauguration of President Roosevelt's New Deal in March 1933 and Roosevelt's appointment of Josephus Daniels as his liberal ambassador to Mexico.

The 1933 spring upsurge in the agrarian movement was a rebellion against Calles's earlier efforts to break land distribution, however. He had declared in June 1930 that agrarian reform was a failure and had then reduced land redistribution in the three following years. This further limited the federal labor law of 1931 that had protected the rights of permanent agricultural workers, but excluded resident peons on the *haciendas*.

With peasant discontent and turmoil on the rise, however, in May 1933 Calles called for the resumption of agrarian reform. Knowing the small-sized *ejidos* parcels were inefficient, Calles proposed land distribution to villages and the elimination of at least four-fifths of all peonage by the end of the next presidential term in November 1938. To implement these plans, Calles also proposed that the government force the estate owners to subdivide the remains of their properties, selling them in fractions to enable *ejido* members with too little land to purchase them and become modern farmers as part of the nation's mixed economy.[2]

Yet it appeared Calles's agrarian reform might fail for lack of authority. His power was on the wane once Congress, in April 1933, annulled Obregón's amendment to the constitutional ban on reelection. Portes Gil and other liberal politicians moved to break his remaining hold. But on 1 May, acting on behalf of agrarian leagues of several states, the liberals issued a manifesto calling for resumption of agrarian reform and, to pursue it, urged the nomination of Minister of War General Lázaro Cárdenas as presidential candidate of the official party.

When Cárdenas then resigned from the cabinet and agreed to become a presidential candidate of the PRI, Calles had already altered his stand on agrarian reform, which thus far had been strictly limited to land grants to villages and had not yet awarded centrally located *hacienda* land to their permanent labor force of peons. But as these lands were held alike by the old Díaz oligarchy and the leading generals surrounding Calles, onerous conditions were set for permanent peons to receive such land, which effectively slowed the demise of the *hacienda* system.

Before the close of 1933, however, Congress amended Article 27 of the constitution and approved an Agrarian Code to implement it. Elected in 1934, President Cárdenas then mapped an independent course guiding state action to raise the nation's technical level and improve agricultural output, hoping to thereby enhance the economic well-being of the population.

The Cárdenas regime also confirmed the nation's ownership of subterranean wealth and forced foreign oil companies to live by Mexican law and institutions as concessionaires, not owners. During his liberal administration, the Mexican government controlled the operations of these companies, so that they became supplicants, not rulers of the nation's economic destiny.

"In political terms," wrote a U.S. scholar in 1942, "this means that the State owns and governs, and that both capital and labor must function within its laws or abandon the right to function at all. This principle established by Mexico may henceforth govern the operation of foreign capital throughout the world. It was because the oil companies fully realized this that they fought it so ruthlessly to the bitter end."[3]

The Logic of Nationalism and Labor Control

The logic of Mexican nationalism in the 1930s was linked to concepts of self-sufficiency in both agrarian and industrial production. Such self-sufficiency was initiated by the 1934-40 Cárdenas program for transferring power into the hands of worker and peasant groups while pacifying the wealth-shorn church. This represented a new stage in the program and progress of the Mexican Revolution.

President Lázaro Cárdenas had become the era's principal nationalist proponent in Latin America, using the power of the state to attempt to unify not only regions of the nation, but also social groups, castes, and assorted classes. By covering Mexico with semicollective farms linked to regional industrial systems under government guidance, Cárdenas hoped to industrialize the nation rapidly and enlarge food production through worker and peasant cooperation and control of the means of production and life.

Cárdenas held a pancontinental vision as well. Viewing Mexico as the hub of the Western hemisphere between Tierra del Fuego and Point Barrow, Cárdenas believed that the link of Indio-Latin nations with the Anglo-Saxons to the north would promote continental unity, and he foresaw "a continental coalition with a full consciousness of its destiny and with the noble desire to fulfill it."[4]

Cárdenas realized this broad formulation could not be put into practice, however, unless independent and viable Mexican mining, industrial, financial, and agrarian structures were firmly in place. In order to free Mexico of U.S. economic impositions and to extract concessions from the U.S. investors and government at key moments, moreover, Cárdenas understood the necessity of consolidating his own domestic political power. And the great popular support Cárdenas received after finally dislodging Calles's extensive ties and political influence during 1936–37 was based not only on new class alignments, but on an attempt to improve the condition of the population by building a national market.

Mobilizing new ideological allies and political factions, Cárdenas set the stage to confront both the Mexican upper classes and the foreign interests controlling Mexico's natural resources and exploiting its labor force. He initially did this through an assortment of revolutionary government programs, attempting to bring together the nation's growing population of landless, urbanized workers with the rural peasantry.

Government-expropriated land was thus distributed to landless peasants. Programs were designed to aid rural workers. Other programs were established for farm credits and irrigation projects, sanitation, reforestation, and electrification. Provisions were made for hospitals, asylums, water works, rural schools, and technical institutes. The government promoted cattle-raising and sugar mills, as well as associations of producers, cooperatives, and commissions to regulate prices, living costs, monopolies, and unemployment.

The list of government benefits for the army, the merchant marine, commercial undertakings, and cultural projects reflected a powerful belief in Mexico's independence and self-sufficiency, which would promote the cooperation of different social classes pursuing national consolidation.

The army was thus funded for new equipment, modern barracks, special schools, and boarding schools for the soldiers' children. The merchant marine was supplied with new ships, and the government encouraged commercial and cultural contacts with other nations. To protect the nation from the manipulations of foreign investors, Mexico's rate of monetary exchange was propped up in the midst of the 1930s global economic crisis, while national income was increased.

Such measures and reforms became the hallmark of the Cárdenas era.

LAND REFORM

Land tenure was one of the focal points for reform promised in the 1917 Constitution. As land reform had not much advanced by the time Cárdenas assumed office, he came to power determined to transform the face of Mexican agrarian life.

In the long travail of making such changes, however, there were many deviations in program and gyrations in power. Postrevolutionary peace was followed by initial land reforms under de la Huerta and Calles, then a slowed pace of land distribution, and finally Cárdenas's extensive confiscations of *haciendas* from 1934 to 1940.

When the Revolution's first president, Carranza, was murdered, Adolfo de la Huerta finished his half-year term, securing Pancho Villa's loyalty by signing a conditional surrender, and agreeing to grant Villa a government-purchased 800,000 peso *hacienda* of 80,000 hectares with fifty of his own guards paid by the War Ministry.

After peace was established in the wake of the loss of over one-and-a-half million people and the complete devastation of production, the next president, General Obregón, relied on the support of labor and the peasants to back the army, which momentarily replaced the power of the old ruling classes. He rewarded industrial workers by allowing them to form unions and make successful wage demands, and he appeased the peasantry in central (largely in Morelos) and eastern (mostly in the Yucatán) Mexico.

In Morelos, where the *hacendados* were either in exile or ruined and sugar factories had been burned down, Obregón's agrarian reforms fulfilled the promises of the 1917 Constitution. Breaking up the *haciendas*, offering land to Zapata's soldiers who had saved his life, and boosting his presidency, Obregón gave one-fourth of the total area of the state to the villages and left the *haciendas* with a minor proportion of their land.

In the Yucatán, President Obregón also awarded the peasants one-fifth of the area of the state, binding them more closely to the national government against the autonomous, separatist interests asserted by the local *hacendados*. These *hacendados*, who produced henequen (sisal), were an oligarchy that had converted their rural estates to the new crop, then became entrenched after the Maya victory over the army in the 1848 War of Castes.[5] But Obregón resisted land redistribution in northern Mexico, where Carranza's and Villa's generals had taken *haciendas* for themselves, and Obregón was building his own *hacienda* that came to comprise 3,500 hectares cultivated by 1,500 laborers.

Obregón also limited agrarian reform in order to sidestep any potential U.S. military intervention on behalf of oil companies worried about annulment of concessions and confiscation of properties, as well as American landowners in Chihuahua and Sonora, who opposed land redistribution in these areas of extensive U.S. interests. Overall, though, Obregón directed the distribution of a full one million hectares to the peasantry.[6]

In the 1920s, political stability required further land distribution. Nation-building was in process. Capital was extended into commerce, new industries, and banking. Rapid urbanization also drew and mobilized idle capital to employ the new, inexpensive wage workers. The year 1923 was also the political cutting line for rural support: agrarian reform was stepped up and President Calles distributed 3 million hectares, stemming peasant migration.[7]

After President Calles left office, he became the ex-officio chief, *jefe nato*, of the party and controlled succeeding presidents. He was disconcerted that his successor, Provisional President Portes Gil, had distributed more than 1 million hectares in a single year—1929. Tightly holding onto the reins of power, Calles insisted that his stand-in, President Ortiz Rubio, sharply cut the redistribution of land from 1930 to 1932.

Calles tried to cover this retreat from social action programs by focusing on the efforts of Catholics to dominate social affairs. On 21 December 1931 he called a council of ministers, demanded that cabinet members answer police allegations that they had attended services in honor of the Virgin of Guadalupe, and forced the resignations of the secretary of the interior, the comptroller general, and the attorney general, as well as other distinguished office holders.

In defense, the church renewed its salvos soon after the September 1932 inauguration of Abelardo Rodríguez because the new preident had closed down churches in Mexico City in conformity with the constitution and on 4 November 1933 had sent a draft of the Six Year Plan to the National Revolutionary party (PNR) stating that "primary education must be lay ... not only excluding all religious teachings, but also presenting a scientific and rational treatment" of all other subjects.

In response, Mexican bishops allegedly dictated the Pope's *Encyclical Acerba Animi*, which repeated that Rome did not "accept the Mexican laws concerning worship" and exhorted the faithful "to continue defending the sacrosanct rights of the Church with that generous abnegation of which they have given such noble examples."

In Mexico, this papal call for the faithful to defend the church was viewed as an allusion to the bloody 1926 Cristero rebellion, which had been unreservedly endorsed by the Pope. The *Encyclical*, fulminated President Rodríguez, was a tissue of "falsehoods directed against the nation" that smacked of incitation to civil revolt. "The present Government, which emanates from the Revolution," he warned the clergy, "having among its guiding principles the intellectual liberation of the people and the destruction of fanaticism ... will not tolerate domination by a foreign power."[8]

For the next three years, 1932–35, aspersions and vendetta between church and state left both ideologically wounded and on the edge of violence. State legislatures limited the number of priests and Rodríguez's secretary of agriculture won Calles's and Cárdenas's backing for anticlerical action. Rome's apostolic delegate, Ruíz y Flores, attacked Cárdenas for suggesting that liberty of conscience was a phrase masking "the clerical dictatorship." The delegate demanded that every Catholic organize "with maximum discipline ... to defend his rights," but he neglected to say whether this should be by pen or sword.

"If in the realm of violence, there also let us defend ourselves and our sons," declared Bishop Manrique of Huejutla. "The fathers of families will convert themselves into lions, their homes into fortresses, and every Mexican heart shall be a bulwark of our dignity and freedom."

Although General Calles sent President-elect Cárdenas to President Rodríguez with the demand that the archbishop of Mexico be deported to the United States, the president refused, but then instructed Attorney General Portes Gil to investigate if the Catholic hierarchy was guilty of fomenting insurrection against the government.

As Portes Gil seized incriminating documents and published a bulky, denunciatory report, both the apostolic delegate and the bishop of Huejutla conveniently emigrated to the United States. President Rodríguez decreed 30 October 1934 that the two were subject to arrest if they returned.[9]

CALL OF THE RED SHIRTS

At first, Cárdenas supported and called on others to emulate the revolutionary Red Shirts holding state power in Tabasco under its governor, Garrido Canabal.

Strongly anti–Catholic, Canabal had abolished the various saints' days, replacing them with almost uninterrupted rural fairs, each dedicated to a single agricultural product of the region. His zealous organization against church fanaticism and drunkenness from 1932 to 1934 took the form of propagandistic orations, plays, parodies, even political murders.[10]

Canabal meanwhile ran a state administration centered on his family's monopolization of the best posts in the state apparatus that operated within the network of a more or less revolutionary organization under Canabal's personal control. Under this nepotism, 26 relatives received concessions that in effect involved larceny of public funds.[11]

Canabal also wove a web to snare anyone trying to evade his grasp. He positioned himself at the center of the official *Partido Socialista Radical*, which controlled the Canabal-led Central League of Resistance, which in turn ran 37 trade unions. These unions were subject to Tabasco's Department of Labor which was empowered to rule that the only legal trade unions were those affiliated with the Central League. As the union ruled industry and shipping, boat owners were judiciously advised they could not dock their vessels unless they hired union crews, and employers who failed to register with the official organization were crushed by the state government.[12]

Mass education for production was emphasized. Over one-third of the state budget was devoted to education; teachers were paid better than in any other state and were given free rein to introduce modern educational methods. Physical training and student cultural brigade activity was stressed at open-air schools, vocational institutions, worker night schools, and technical agricultural institutions. Abandoned churches were turned into schools, too, with the development of cooperatives as part of rural school training.

Tabasco land distribution remained limited, though Canabal insisted he sought a Mexico comprised of small, independent peasant proprietors. Only 33 small *ejidos* had been established in Tabasco by 1933. The richest 1.2 percent of the state's landlords still held 45 percent of the total crop land, while by contrast four-fifths of the peasantry with small, self-sufficient farms owned only 13.9 percent of the land.[13]

But this point point did not block Garrido Canabal's appointment as President Cárdenas's secretary of agriculture. Canabal then concentrated his retinue of propagandists in Mexico City, determined to emphasize anticlerical agitation at the expense of agricultural transformation.

With Canabal's organization in the capital extending its sway, his Red Shirts and the Catholics clashed politically. Both sides used propaganda, demonstrations, and arms. One Red Shirt was lynched, five Catholics were killed, and a contingent of seventy-five Red Shirts were detained by the police.

Meanwhile, the right-wing press, the reactionary Federation of University Students, and the fascist Mexican Revolutionary Action's Gold Shirts called for law and order, demanding Canabal's resignation.[14]

As Canabal continued to focus his attack on Catholicism, he rapidly became a political liability to Cárdenas's reforms. He was ousted from the cabinet, and returned to Tabasco, but was ultimately expelled from Mexico. Cárdenas had declared that Canabal was still behind the irresponsible acts of the new head of Tabasco, creating a "duality in administrative control" that was "disastrous for the peace and progress of our people."[15]

NEW SIGNS OF CÁRDENAS UNITY

During the 1935 battle for power, rank and file Red Shirts had openly supported Cárdenas. Giving up their crimson uniforms, most revolutionary youth entered the left wing of the National Revolutionary party, the Mexican Confederation of Labor, and the Communist party. Here they fielded their efforts into teaching, organizing, and political action.

Cárdenas forcefully supported education as the counterweight against Catholic teachings and treachery. When devout peasants murdered 18 school teachers in Ciudad Gonzáles, Guanajuato, chopping one to pieces, and injured 30 other teachers, Cárdenas drove there, gave the instigating priests 24 hours to leave town, and from the church altar told the townspeople that the parties really guilty were "those persons who live in luxury and excite the working class to fight with their brothers. They are the contractors, chiefly owners of *haciendas*, who in order to maintain inhuman systems of exploitation, provoke the spilling of blood and place the entire nation in mourning."[16]

The path to destroying fanaticism was more and better rural schools, Cárdenas proposed. Upgrading primitive agricultural techniques and bringing rural communities out of their isolation would link them to industrial development, and bring to the rural domain modern knowledge and economic reforms. Living conditions and the status of women would also improve.

With such a program, Cárdenas switched focus from Calles's antireligious government campaigns that had exasperated the peasantry and impeded the program of the Revolution. Fostering an armistice with the church, Cárdenas allowed the opening of additional Veracruz churches beyond the one church for every 100,000 inhabitants allowed by the state. Elsewhere measures limiting the number of priests permitted to officiate were also being repealed or blindsided by the government. The Department of Education under Communist influence abandoned its teachings against church and creed, allowing Catholics to organize openly in quasi-political organizations. This actually led to the formation of powerful fascist groups that sought links to the Iberian *Falange* in an effort to resurrect the Spanish Empire under a common reactionary doctrine.[17]

ECONOMIC SEA CHANGE

Mexico's engrossing contest about religion was already being overtaken by an economic sea change affecting the political domain of the early 1930s—a 50 percent fall in the value of export crops like cotton and sisal, as well as silver, oil, and other mining products.

With world markets closing down and widespread rural unemployment, the area devoted to cultivation of export crops was cut by half. The number of farmhands fell a comparable amount, and the *haciendas* abandoned their traditional duty to feed their peons. Calles had recognized the political necessity of quieting the unemployed agrarian workers by freeing them to use idled land for subsistence maize production. A resumption of land reform was thus required. He now argued that though the division of land was economically a failure because of the small-size *ejido* parcels that had been essential to destroy the power of the landlords, land distribution to the villages should nonetheless be continued to wipe out peonage. Thus estate owners should be forced by the government to subdivide their remaining properties and sell them in fractions to enable *ejidos* to turn their meager parcels into modern farms.[18]

But it was too late for partial reform proposals. With the spring 1933 upsurge in the agrarian movement against Calles's continual brake on agrarian change, General Lázaro Cárdenas had become the presidential candidate of the major official party on the platform of resumed land reform on behalf of the agrarian leagues of several states.

Up to this time, such reform was restricted to land grants to villages. The heirs of the Díaz oligarchy still held most of the land, and other landed estates had been appropriated by Carranza's and Villa's "revolutionary" generals. No *hacienda* land had ever been awarded to permanent-resident peons living on the domain, for such a change would have meant the *hacendados'* loss of both centrally located lands and their labor force.

Yet at the National Revolutionary party's 1933 Querétero convention, emerging conflict between the *hacendado* interests protected by Calles and the agrarian leagues supported by Cárdenas was resolved by approval of a Six Year Plan, to be immediately effective, that granted the right of permanent peons to receive land under certain conditions. Congress then amended Article 27 of the constitution and implemented it by approving a 1934 Agrarian Code setting limits on breaking up the estates by future division and sale of sale, so that though peons would not again be completely landless, they would likely remain small-scale, subsistence farmers who were relatively impoverished and uncompetitive in the marketplace.

LEGAL FRAMING OF CONTINUED INEQUALITIES

The legal framing for continued inequalities was critical to the redistribution of tiny land parcels that would temporarily pacify peons and peasantry without adequate credit; to the empowerment of the *hacendados* possessing land and capital, who continued to play the dominating role in the rural domain; and to Mexico's new hierarchical order of landholdings and land rights.

Cárdenas had used his presidential campaign to bring the Six Year Plan to the communities in Mexico's 28 states, traveling 27,609 kilometers throughout Mexico to popularize it. He brought it to life in terms of land, schools, cooperatives, and agricultural credit; its promises became causes worth fighting for and created a groundswell for his election and continued support.

Cárdenas's main themes revolved around the need to distribute national wealth. "That country which does not guarantee all its inhabitants the right to live is not a nation," he proselytized, insisting that the path to change resided with the organization of the people in three social movements: agrarian, cooperative, and educational. "As against the outmoded economic unity of the *hacienda*, we must build the *ejido*; as against the spiritual unity of fanaticism, the modern school must be erected; and as against capitalist industry—surfeited with egoism and bankrupt before all the world—the cooperative of the workers must be established."[19]

As Cárdenas argued for producer-owned organizations to "supplant intermediaries and benefit the working class directly, putting it in possession of the entire value of its labor power," he calculated that profits "should not filter into the hands of speculators and voracious capitalists opposed to carrying out the tasks of the working class, but should be divided among all the human beings taking part in the process of production."

Cárdenas envisioned that consumer cooperatives would gradually shift the balance of economic power from capitalists to workers and would be able to "reduce the cost of merchandise, increase the acquisitive power of wages, fix prices at the lowest level economically possible."[20]

The battle between *ejido* and *hacienda* polarized this process in Cárdenas's developing strategy.

The legal framing of continued inequalities in land tenure was obvious, as all land granted under the agrarian reform had been named *ejido*, giving a new meaning, context, and lack of critical distinction to an old word and concept.

Based on previous practice, the villages could still own the old *ejido*, communal property, and individual peasants could retain private property inherited from their ancestors. But under the new law, government oversight and controls allowed villages to own the new *ejidos* and individuals to receive *ejidal* parcels that were no longer communal lands. The law made it easier for peasants to obtain individuated slivers of insufficient farm land, and the number of land-grants jumped several times between 1933 and 1934.

By contrast, to maintain profitable farming, existing landowners of certain limited areas called "small properties" were freed from nationalization, and their property was excluded from government expropriation for the purpose of making land grants to peons, villages, and population centers. These exclusions covered:

- Buildings of any kind as well as irrigation works
- Landholdings less than 100 hectares in certain cases, less than 150 in others
- Landholdings of seasonal, unirrigated lands less than 200 hectares in certain cases, less than 300 in others
- Plantations of certain tropical products containing less than 300 hectares
- Lands planted with alfalfa and industrially important crops like sisal (entirely exempted under certain conditions)
- Lands devoted to sugar cane on properties with mills that belonged to the owner of the land, up to the number of hectares required to furnish cane for an average level of production.[21]

It was, then, a law filled with loopholes, that used the same name, *ejidos*, for village communal holdings, individual peasant farms, and small plantations.

The law ensured that small-scale, peon agriculture could neither succeed nor complete with the *haciendas* because it stipulated that cultivatable land granted to villages and other population centers should immediately be divided into individual holdings. Although the land area expropriated and the number of applicants determined the size of each parcel, individual

grantees effectively held title through their villages, making them possessors of the land's bounty as usufruct, while being governed by laws that
effectively forced them to individually farm on their own holdings. They
could never sell, mortgage, or lease their lots.

The only common property granted to the villages would be woodland
and pastures, though for crops requiring collective efforts of peasants or
laborers, the law provided that such lands be held and cultivated on a communal basis and that special government banks would organize both production and marketing.

THE NEXT POLITICAL STEPS

Other changes in land holdings followed Cárdenas's election and
assumption of the presidency on 30 November 1934.

Emphasizing the misery of Indian communities, the low wages of the
general population, and the divisions among labor organizations, Cárdenas
called for a populist program of agrarian relief, public works employment,
a united front of labor, and plans for socialist education. His optimism immediately bred divisions by class and caste, state and church.

Cárdenas initially chose the Socialist dictator of Tabasco, Tomas Garrido Canabal, as his minister of agriculture, and Canabal's Red Shirts soon
attacked both Catholic groups and the fascist Gold Shirts.

So too as the government initiated socialist education, strong opposition issued from the clergy and the churches. Already closed in many states,
the church faced a new law forbidding the mailing of religious materials,
requiring imprisonment for priests celebrating mass in a way that violated
laws, and jeopardizing parishioners holding government jobs.

Conflict also cracked the façade of labor unity between Cárdenista
democrats and arch-conservative Callista centrists.

With Cárdenas's support of most labor demands, 1935 had witnessed
642 strikes, with general strikes in Puebla and Veracruz for overtime compensation for past labor as far back as 1906. Two great unions, Morones's
conservative Confederación Regional de Obreros Mexicanos (CROM) and
Lombardo Toledano's radical Mexican Workers' Confederation (Confederación de Trabajadores Mexicanos, or CTM), were also at odds with one
another.[22]

Calles had powerfully attacked the "marathon of radicalism" on 13
June 1935, adding: "To disturb the march of economic construction is not
only ingratitude but treason." And for this purview, Calles was enthusi-
astically supported by the employers' association of 1,150 industrial concerns. "Your courageous and categorical declarations," the association
noted, "indicate clearly that Mexico's real revolutionaries clearly understand the disastrous effects of the unruly passions of political leaders and
labor elements."

With the Callistas and Cárdenistas diametrically at odds, the possibilities for renewed military conflict, even civil war, were obvious.

On 16 June both houses of Congress declared their support of Cárdenas, and the Veracruz revolutionary leader, Adalberto Tejeda, demanded the expulsion of Calles from the country.

As Calles then renewed his critique of labor unrest, Cárdenas expressed confidence in both labor and peasant organizations. He solidified his position by having all his holdover Calles ministers resign in June and by concentrating powerful army contingents in Mexico City.

Attacking Garrido Canabal as a counterrevolutionary, students meanwhile demonstrated in front of his house, while thousands of Catholics paraded in the capital shouting "Long Live Christ King! Down with Calles!"

The next day, a new cabinet was appointed; Garrido Canabal was displaced by General Saturnino Cedillo, a Catholic who had bitterly opposed Calles's efforts to enforce anticlerical laws and introduce secular education in his domain of San Luis Potosí.

Cedillo's appointment also swung the army and conservative and Catholic groups, as well as politicians slighted by Calles. Massive support for Cedillo came from labor, large agrarian groups, the growing left wing within the PNR, and both houses of Congress.

In a reversal of some antichurch regulations, 63 of the 375 churches remaining open in Mexico were in Cedillo's home state.

Fulminating right- and left-wing military movements then confronted Cárdenas head-on in the agricultural domain. Controversy swirled over the question of whether the expropriated *hacienda* land would be divided in small *ejido* parcels or be transferred to collective farms that would also be crowned by the justifying description *ejido*.

As Cedillo enjoyed widespread peasant support for advocating the small *ejidatarios* and had joined the Michoacán governor, Gildardo Magaña, to force Cárdenas to eliminate Calles's influence, once Cedillo became minister of agriculture, he realigned with Magaña to overthrow Cárdenas who, he alleged, had become a Communist who supported collectivized land cooperatives.

Since Cárdenas could not simply dump Minister Cedillo, who was reputed to be a champion of agrarianism, he kept him in the cabinet for two and a half years, while the left wing exposed how Cedillo's machine had murdered over 200 militant agrarians in San Luis Potosí, had crushed trade union organizations, and had repressed the opposition.

Meanwhile, Cárdenas allies attempted to keep Cedillo powerless. Cárdenas appointed Graciano Sánchez leader of the party's official National Peasant Confederation, eliminated Cedillo partisans from controlling posts, and promoted rural collective farms rather than the small peasant parcels Cedillo advocated.

Despite Cedillo's planned insurrection against the government with the financial backing of Gold Shirt leaders, conservative business groups, and Nazi agents, Cárdenas tried pacification, offering Cedillo command of the Michoacán military zone. And to stop his own appointee from organizing a fascist revolt, President Cárdenas mobilized federal troops to take over Cedillo's home state of Michoacán. Even when the insurrection was crushed, the president sent a message urging Cedillo to accept a pension with safe conduct to the United States—a belated gesture as government troops had already tracked him down and killed him.[23]

Cárdenas also sent troops to Tabasco to curtail the Garrido Canabal dictatorship there and to keep Tabasco in the union and reverse the dictator's decrees.

Even the 11 September 1935 battle in the Chamber of Deputies that left two members dead and ended with banishing 17 Callistas from the Chamber, was a step in making the Congress more strongly Cárdenista.

And as Cárdenas increased his power despite Calles's return to Mexico in December 1935, five more Callistas were expelled from the Senate for seditious and subversive activities, four pro–Calles state governors were removed from office by the Senate, and several Cárdenista members of the Chamber of Deputies spoke openly against Calles. Calles's old opponents also called for investigating the sources of his private income and his connection to arms smuggling supporting the Revolution. As well, they wanted to try him for the murder of Lucio Blanco (1922), General Serrano (1927), and President Obregón (1928).[24]

CÁRDENAS: FREE AGENT TO RULE

Having already sidestepped Callistas at the 1933 PNR convention that had agreed on the first Six-Year Plan and having freed himself of former president Calles's political machinery and cabinet members in 1935, Cárdenas then initiated the Six Year Plan, with land grants in 1935 alone almost quadrupling the 680,000 hectares of 1934.[25]

Given Calles's previous puissance and alliances, moreover, it was now politically dangerous for Cárdenas to allow Calles to organize anew against his programs. Pro–Calles labor leader Morones had led his CROM into battle against the pro–Cárdenas Mexican Workers' Confederation (CTM) led by Lombardo Toledano and had then called a general strike which Cárdenas declared unjustified. This led to rioting that was followed by the dynamiting of a train on the Veracruz–Mexico City line that killed 13 and wounded several others.

Blaming Calles and Morones, on 10 April 1936, Cárdenas then had Calles, Morones, and Calles's closest supporters expelled from Mexico to Brownsville, Texas, finally ending the influence of *Jefe Máximo* in Mexican affairs.[26]

Yet political intrigues continued, as Governor Gildardo Magaña attempted to build a nationwide league of small and middle peasants amidst labor union charges that this presidential aspirant's organization was dominated by *hacendados* who escaped agrarian reform by posing as "dirt farmers" through fraudulent land sales to relatives and friends. And to break up the meetings of the Mexican Workers' Confederation (CTM), the Magaña machine deployed police violence and arrested labor organizers.[27]

Intrigue also emerged from within the official National Peasant Confederation, which was the sole representative of the peasantry within the Party of the Mexican Revolution. Regardless of their will, all *ejidatarios* belonged to the confederation, which was run by state and national committees consisting of nonpeasant politicians who determined organizational policies in an autocratic fashion and also wielded enormous influence over local, state, and national elections.

To protect themselves from National Peasant Confederation dictation, the most active local peasants groups turned for consultation to the Mexican Workers' Confederation (CTM), deciding on policies and effecting decisions before informing the National Peasant Confederation. As Cárdenas effectively controlled the National Peasant Confederation and its leader Graciano Sanchez, nonpeasants remained in charge of its 1938 convention that proposed changes in the Agrarian Code and land-distribution procedures and favored a bias for cooperatives and state farms rather than the small-scale *ejidos* the land-hungry peasants often preferred.

True, the convention demanded that the *ejido* become the sole form of agrarian organization, urged that the *hacendados* be left with only as much land as the average *ejidatario*, and opposed special privileges to private landowners. But it also favored collective farming over small parcels and demanded that any land remaining after total expropriation of the landlords be set aside for state farms where all peasants and laborers would have the right to work.[28]

FRAMEWORK FOR REFORM

The political polarization of those favoring individually owned *ejidos* and those seeking collectivized agriculture became the frame for reform as Cárdenas freely filled his cabinet with his own supporters and favored the activities of labor leader Toledano's Mexican Workers' Confederation (CTM).

Replacing Calles's followers in government and party offices, Cárdenas accelerated social reforms, and to keep the Callistas occupied with fruitless intrigue, he allowed the conservative generals and politicians exiled by Obregón and Calles to return.

Planning large-scale land redistribution, Cárdenas then neutralized the church (which was no longer a large landowner) by abolishing the harsh anticlerical regulations. This freed him from their opposition to land reform[29] and allowed him to pursue unhindered state planning and centralization of control over Mexico's agricultural domain.

To establish a legal basis to expropriate private properties, in September 1936 Cárdenas had sent Congress a draft law giving him wide power to expropriate both rural and urban real estate, land, and enterprises. After it was passed and was put into effect a few weeks later, the government moved to back the struggle of peasants for *ejido* land ownership, cooperative commercial farms, and the right of farmhands to minimum wages. Yet, in keeping with his agrarian goals, Cárdenas tried to keep the Marxist-led Mexican Workers' Confederation that had concentrated on organizing urban workers from organizing *hacienda* peons and instead awarded nationalized *hacendados'* land directly to these peasants.[30]

For instance, when the peons of the rich cotton *haciendas* of La Laguna struck for higher wages and benefits at harvest time in 1936, Cárdenas ordered the immediate division of all *haciendas*; most were awarded to peons, though the requirements of irrigation of cotton lands demanded collective, cooperative commercial cultivation with government supervision and credits. Thus land redistribution in itself was usually not sufficient to liberate peons or peasants.

TRADITION, MACHINERY, COLLECTIVIZATION, AND CREDIT

True to their traditional communal structure and way of life, the new cooperative and collective farms fit well with the techniques already in use in Mexico's industrialized and irrigated regions. Yet the *ejidatarios* were largely inexperienced with collectivized agriculture on the scale sought by the Cárdenas government to increase output for the market.

To bring this new structure into existence, moreover, the government had to create agrarian banks to reorganize crop production, to concentrate on crops producing high incomes, to diversify crops, to use the soil for intensive farming, and to shift the agricultural population from the eroded central plateau to the tropical coast lands and irrigated northern zone.

Viewing government credit as the critical factor supporting and financing the variable and fixed costs associated with land redistribution, Cárdenas in 1935 split the old Agrarian Bank into two separate federal banks to support small peasants and *ejidatarios* and lead them along the path towards capital-intensive, collectivist agriculture.

One was the National Bank of Agrarian Credit, which was mandated to loan money to peasants with small and middle-sized holdings, organized in credit societies, and to administer and finance national irrigation districts. A key goal was to determine which crops the peasants planted and how they tended their crops.

The National Bank of Agrarian Credit breached its chartered purpose, though. While it advanced between 11.5 and 19.5 million pesos annually from 1934 to 1938, it concentrated on safe loans during hard economic times, denying credit to drought-ridden peasantry of the central plateau, refusing loans to dozens of small peasant credit societies, and lending landlords 55 percent (6.5 million of 11.8 million pesos) in the case of the "colonists" of the Delicious irrigation district and the private *hacendados* of the Laguna region.

Although a high bank official recognized that the "kulaks and *hacendados*" had repaid capital plus interest equal to 102.3 percent of new loans made in 1938 compared with 57.9 percent in 1937, when the bank curtailed credit operations in Laguna in 1939 to finally concentrate on helping the small peasantry, it was both too little and too late for *ejidos* lacking water, tools, fertilizers, and seeds.[31]

This lack was in part made up by the other federal agency, the new National Bank of Ejidal Credit, the effective planning board for the new collectivized agricultural areas. This bank was committed to advance agricultural credit to the cooperatives in an effort to "organize the different phases of the economy of the *ejido*." The bank loaned money to the *ejidatarios* organized either as credit societies or societies of collective agricultural interests which knit groups of *ejidos* for cooperative use of large land areas, irrigation systems, or interlinked agricultural and industrial enterprises.

It was thereby reasoned that the work-efficiency and capital requirements of large-scale agriculture would be satisfied by three essentials—communal organization, collectivist work, and government credit.

Collectivist work was an obvious goal of the bank's central government plan to use communal organizations in replicating some aspects of *hacienda* production. The bank recognized that by destroying the efficient use of land, labor, tools, and livestock in dividing *haciendas* into small land parcels, the *ejido* became inefficient by comparison with the traditional *hacienda*. Indeed, in 1936 an *ejido* land area that required the deployment of 120 teams of oxen and 22,500 annual work days could have been worked as a *hacienda* using 70 teams and 10,000 work days.[32]

With *ejidatarios* communally organized and collectively worked, 200 million pesos in bank credit covered from 1935 to 1938 the cooperatives' need for variable expenses and long- and short-term fixed outlays. The credit was apportioned thusly:

- Running expenses for cultivation absorbed most of the bank's credits, which lasted 18 months and covered up to 70 percent of the probable value of the crop
- Machinery, fertilizer, and livestock purchased on five-year credits were secured against *ejido* crops, herds, and movable equipment, to be paid off in annual installments

- Permanent improvements for irrigation canals, processing plants, and plantation railroads were financed by long-term advances up to thirty years.[33]

The National Bank of Ejidal Credit also acted as the nation's agricultural planning center, a source of subsidies, a fulcrum to improve farmers' living standards, and a market to buy the output of *ejidatarios*, thereby sidestepping speculators and moneylenders. By drawing up plans for production on the collectives, the bank created a forum to discuss these plans with the peasants for approval and implementation. By repairing irrigation canals, building power plants on collective farms, and buying machinery for the peasants, it made large-scale agriculture not only possible but efficient through instructions in use and repair of machinery. By analyzing soil, experimenting with different varieties of wheat, fighting plant parasites, and battling mule diseases, the bank created the infrastructure for national agricultural security. By organizing consumer cooperatives on the *ejidos* and discouraging alcoholism, it lowered the cost of living and improved the quality of life. By effectively buying, warehousing, and selling the peasants' crops, it established fair market prices that would reward peasant labor without gouging consumers with a middle agent's profit.[34]

In sum, the *ejido* banks not only met the credit needs of these collective farms, they stored and sold the crops of the *ejidatarios*, furnished instructions in agriculture, conducted experiments, and provided other services to the *ejidos*.[35]

Such collectivization was effective; one-third of Mexican *ejidatarios* engaged in more or less collectivized agriculture by 1938.[36] But as resident peons were in many cases unwilling to apply for land, and it proved impossible in this case to bring landless peasants from other regions into La Laguna to apply for the remaining land, local *hacendados* kept the rest.[37]

By contrast, in the Yucatán, government authorities took over technical machinery required to extract fiber from sisal hemp, reasoning that awarding the peasants the land where the only crop harvested was hemp would not have been sufficient to liberate them from exploitation because the hemp would have had to be sold at low prices to the old plantation owners who owned the extraction machinery.[38]

Land redistribution nonetheless cut particularly deep in both the Yucatán and Sonora. In August 1937, collective *ejidos* under government control were established in the Yucatán and markets from the peninsula to the rest of Mexico were connected by the Yucatán-Veracruz railroad.

Then in October 1938, Sonora's upper-class owners—in part U.S. citizens, in part politicians of the Obregón-Calles grouping—watched anxiously as the Cárdenas government divided their fertile, irrigated estates.[39]

WOULD THE *HACENDADOS* LOSE PLACE?

Would the *hacendados* lose their central position in the Mexican order-ing of ownership classes, then?

The *hacendados* had engaged in the real and fictitious sale of their lands to their peons, renters, or sharecroppers, but the government ruled that most *hacendados'* sales were designed to evade the law in order to perpetuate their hold.

Even when the Agrarian Code was obeyed, *hacendados* kept the best land, though this might have been only a very small part of their original property. Still, as they were hated by the peons they had long oppressed, they often risked their lives by living on the domain of any property left them, and if they had no other property, they were economically ruined.

Without land on which to feed their cattle, many *hacendados* went out of business, disrupting national cattle-raising and adding to the disorgani-zation of most traditional agricultural production following the division of estates.[40]

In the face of impending expropriations, *hacendados* also accelerated the absorption of capital by undermining the long-term agricultural useful-ness of their domain through their refusal to invest in the maintenance of barns, fences, tools, machinery, and herds. To also enhance momentary profit-extraction, *hacendados* excessively cut henequen (sisal) plants in the Yucatán, undermining future production. They neglected irrigation canals in La Laguna and, facing expropriation, drove needed work animals into the desert to die.[41]

Chiapas coffee *hacendados* outflanked the short-sighted central government land reform by taking half the government-allotted funds as restitution for hectares expropriated and then using the lands they were allowed to retain to lock out their old peon workers and replace them with still cheaper migratory workers. Not only were the owners thereby funded to raise the efficiency of their remaining lands, but they were empowered to starve peons who no longer received wages and were unable to secure adequate government subsidies to run the newly awarded *ejidos*.

This duality enabled the *hacendados* to continue the past subservience of the coffee plantation peons because there was no unified government ex-propriation scheme covering nearly one-half of Mexico's coffee crop pro-duced in the state of Veracruz and another one-quarter in the cold Chiapas uplands. Chiapas coffee plantations had traditionally employed both migratory Guatemalans and Chamula Indians drawn from primitive maize agriculture by poverty and free liquor the owners distributed to Chiapas villagers. The *hacendados* sent trucks to pick up the inebriated Chamulas, carted them off, and had them sign yearly work contracts. They then locked them into debt servitude through company stores.

As the coffee they produced was one of Mexico's leading export crops, these *hacendados* maximized profits by relying on cheap labor instead of upgrading transportation methods, stopping inefficient coffee chopping, intelligently selecting seeds, and planting bushes farther apart. As a result Mexican coffee yields were only half as large as those in Colombia. And this labor system was continued in the Soconusco zone, where the majority of coffee estates expropriated by the government in 1939 were allowed to keep 750 acres apiece, as well as to retain their tools, dryers, machinery, shelling equipment, and power plants.

Only a limited number of hectares were turned over to the Chamula Indians, so these *ejidatarios* had to rent such machinery on the landlords' terms and ultimately sell them their crops at set prices. And such extortion never stopped; the continued turmoil led decades later to the 1994-95 uprising in Chiapas.[42]

Recognizing the need to undercut the old production relations of *hacendados* and peons, Lombardo Toledano, the head of the Mexican Workers' Confederation, had proposed complete expropriation of plantation fields, tools, and factories, with reorganization of coffee plantations in vast worker-peasant cooperatives. This logical solution was also proposed by the National Peasant Confederation: total confiscation of *haciendas* as the *ejidos* were created, thus removing the landlords' incentive to remain in the rural domain. But this was not done.

Rather, because the planters were awarded 750 acres of land, a shortage of land for the new *ejidatarios* resulted. And by the Agrarian Code, the government payment for expropriated land, crops, fences, barns, and machinery—amounting to about one-half of the total loans of the National Bank of Ejidal Credit—went to the *hacendados*. The other half was left as short-term advances to keep the peasantry alive between planting and harvest, but it was insufficient to supply them with adequate tools, selected seeds, fertilizers, blooded livestock, and machinery.

As soon as the 1939 crops had been harvested, moreover, the plantation owners suspended all work on their plantations. The newly emancipated peasants were now without wages, as well as with too little land, too little money, and no credit to begin the season for coffee cultivation, chopping, and trimming.

Thus at the Mixcum *ejido*, 48 peasant families were awarded only 75 acres of the minimum of 453 they were legally entitled to receive, while the government Ejidal Bank denied them credit on the grounds that their acreage was inadequate for loan repayment.

Nor could the peons peddle backward to the previous productive relations, for the Central Board of Conciliation and Arbitration refused to force the planters to continue field labor, declaring that "The peons of

Soconusco are already *ejidatarios,* and the relationship of worker to employer no longer exists."

Because this decision undercut the landlord/worker contractual relationship, the planters immediately discharged all trade-union members, used their legally retained land as the means for hiring "free workers" at lower wages, and left their unionized peons without work and lacking the means to survive.[43]

The old land tenure system, only partly dismantled, thereby resumed its life with a new, cheaper labor force.

THE STATE OF NATIONAL AGRICULTURE

National agricultural policy had nonetheless uplifted a portion of the peasantry.

With nearly 60 percent of Mexico mountainous, population pressure on the central plateau historically forced peasants to plant corn patches on steep slopes incapable of yielding an agricultural surplus beyond subsistence. Given traditional farming methods, by the early 1930s only 11.8 percent of Mexico's land was arable compared with 47 percent of the land in British India, 44 percent in Germany and Italy, and 19 percent in the United States, according to Director Manuel Mesa of the National Bank of Agricultural Credit.

Agriculture remained in a sorry state of technological backwardness, too. The monoculture of corn on 66 percent of cultivated land brought on plant diseases and parasites. Failure to rotate crops and use fertilizers resulted in a tremendous waste of land resources. Hectare yields on corn, beans, and wheat were among the worst of the planet, and grain output per acre was half that of the United States. And with landlords holding arable land in abeyance while the bulk of the peasantry was located on poorer lands, only about one-third of Mexico's arable land was harvested during the years 1925 to 1933.

Fifteen years (1915–30) of the post–Revolution's spurious agricultural reform had left the landed aristocracy firmly entrenched in undisputed mastery of the nation's soil. In 1930, Mexico's 13,444 *hacendados* each owned more than 2,500 acres of land, monopolizing 83.4 percent of the total privately owned agricultural land and leaving the remainder for 600,000 small and middle-sized peasant holdings. Some 668,000 *ejidatarios* owned less than a tenth as much land as the *latifundists,* and with some 2,332,000 landless peons, Mexico's polarity of landed and landless populations was worse than that of any other Latin American country.[44]

The Cárdenas victory notwithstanding, restrictions in the 1934 Agrarian Code also prevented the availability of sufficient arable land to satisfy the needs of the landless peons. Although the code entitled each *ejidatario* to four hectares of well-watered land or eight hectares of semiarid crop land, the 3,500,000 *ejidatarios* and landless peasants could have received 25,900,000 hectares of arable land only through the expropriation of all private land holdings as well as the use of every acre of potentially arable soil in the country. But as the *hacendados* were permitted to retain 300 hectares of semiarid crop land or 150 hectares of irrigated land, in the face of the 18 percent increase in the population from 1930 to 1938—a million persons born every three years—the landless would at best receive less than two acres per peasant, just enough for subsistence farming. Each increase in the rural population, moreover, meant additional capital had to be applied to limited, arable land, just to maintain already wretched living standards.[45]

With the rural surplus population already far short on capital equipment and credit, the Six Year Plan that proposed "quantitative and qualitative" increases in the population made no sense in its demand that the government encourage: "a displacement of population from the cities to the country," as well as the repatriation of U.S.-bound Mexican emigrants and their colonization in Mexican agriculture at public expense "as highly productive investments."[46]

CÁRDENAS UNDERSTOOD, YET COMPROMISED

Given the class-riven battle of *hacendados* and peasants, Cárdenas clearly understood that the battle against land feudalism would be won only when the peasantry held the land necessary to maintain life and possessed the tools, government subsidies, and credits to elevate labor efficiency and production. He thus emphasized the birth of collectivist agriculture in Laguna:

> In the past, groups of peasants were given worthless parcels of land without tools, equipment, credit or organization. This was indeed meager fruit after the great sacrifices made. The *ejido*, so conceived, would have resulted only in disillusionment and in giving the landlords yet another excuse to reduce to a still more wretched level wages that are already wretched enough. . . .
> But the nation's conception of the *ejido* had been entirely different. . . . The *ejido* shoulders a double responsibility—as a social system, it must free the peasant from the exploitation to which he was subject under both the feudal and the [*hacendados'*] individualistic regimes; and as a mode of agricultural production, it must yield enough to furnish the nation with its food requirements.[47]

Despite the needs and shortcomings of the *ejidatarios*, an end to land redistribution was in sight by 1938, as intense opposition to Cárdenas's nationalizations of land, industry, and foreign petroleum rights hobbled his domestic political effectiveness and laid the ground for possible uprisings led by dispossessed landlords, dissatisfied manufacturers, and unappeased foreign oil companies able to finance dissident movements.

To attain national unity and secure his presidency, Cárdenas now moved to dilute his social reforms and slow land redistribution. He continued to support the training of *ejidatarios* in the newly created agricultural schools, and guided their efforts to organize through associations and unions to arbitrate *ejidal* disputes, obtain credit, and deal with government bureaucrats. But land redistribution was sharply scaled back, so that whereas some 3.6 million hectares had been distributed in 1936 and over 5 million hectares in 1937, distributions then fell to around 3 million in 1938, 1.75 million in 1939, and 1.7 million in 1940.

To protect landowners from further peasant demands, the Cárdenas government then opened the Office of Small Property in May 1938 and issued the landowners certificates of exemption from expropriation.[48] Cárdenas thus left office after six years with a half-hearted, compromised program that effectively appeased the *haciendas*, secured their remaining holdings, and maintained production in cash crops.

Nonetheless, Cárdenas's land redistribution had made a significant historic mark. In the first four years of his presidency, Cárdenas awarded 15,478,000 hectares, giving *ejidos* to 813,000 peasants—almost twice the figures for the previous 20 years of agrarian reform. On 1 January 1939, 1,606,000 *ejidatarios* held 23,600,000 hectares of agricultural land. Cárdenas land grants averaged 47 acres of mostly irrigated soil, compared with those of previous administrations of 25 acres per peasant, of which only 8 acres were arable.[49]

Cárdenas had momentarily changed the face of the rural domain. The redistribution of land during his six-year presidency totaled 17.9 million hectares, amounting to almost one-half of the *hacendados*' arable land.

Although by the close of 1938, only 19 percent of the plowed fields, pastures, and woodlands of Mexico had been turned over to the peasants after two and a half decades of revolution and reform, nonetheless the *ejidatarios* held 23,609,000 hectares of agricultural land, and peasants with small and middle-sized holdings held 20,000,000 hectares. The *hacendados*, on the other hand, held 87,000,000 hectares.[50] As a numerical majority, then, the *ejidatarios* still owned less agricultural land than the *hacendados*.

Cárdenas's plan for collectivist agriculture had been designed to maintain Mexico's productive base. Land was distributed as both individual and collective *ejidos*, but collective work was encouraged through the sharing of both agricultural equipment and access to water. Sometimes individual *ejidal* plots were merged into larger agricultural units worked collectively; these units shared profits on the basis of labor on the collective. Other times, individual *ejidos* shared the use of expensive agricultural equipment. Both individual and collectivized *ejidos* also shared water rights, and sometimes they shared harvesting and marketing. All had some access to the National Bank of Ejidal Credit's supervision and credit guiding their operations or administrative methods.

Yet the redistribution of too little land to too many people with too little capital led to a severe decline in Mexican domestic food production of its two major subsistence crops, corn and beans. Between 1934 and 1937, corn harvests shrank 5.4 percent, bean harvests 21.1 percent.

But cash crop increases from 7 to 61 percent came in barley, wheat, rice, potato, henequen, coffee, cotton, sugar cane, and bananas. And between 1932 and 1936, Mexico's coffee sales to the world more than doubled, with the United States taking 69 percent and Germany 26 percent.[51]

These crops were the output of *hacienda* and *latifundias* that had sidestepped expropriation, used peon labor, and profited handsomely.

CHAPTER 5

Nationalism and Industrial Reform in the 1930s

From 1934 to 1940 the redistribution and socialization of land as the means of life was supplemented by nationalization of a sizable part of the nation's public services and natural resources.[1] Although such nationalization heralded Mexico's possible industrialization, this future turned on new sources of accumulation, extensive capital investments, employer and state relations with labor, and relationships between various factions and segments of the work force and peasantry.

As Mexico could only deploy the material resources it already possessed, there were obvious limits to the Cárdenas government battle to nationalize and industrialize at home. The industrial complex of Monterrey was at best a miniature of Pittsburgh; its tiny coterie of Spanish and Creole bankers and industrialists controlled the iron and steel works, the furniture factories, and the breweries. Organized in an employers' association maintaining the open-shop to stop unionization, this oligarchy also opposed any form of nationalization and clandestinely aligned itself with National Revolutionary party machine leader Emilio Portes Gil to consolidate a centrist power bloc between the remnants of Calles supporters opposing labor and the Cárdenas left wing supporting it.

When the Monterrey clique organized its workers in massive demonstrations in late 1935 to "support" Cárdenas if he bridled the strike movement and opposed the government's arbitration tribunals in making awards against the employers, the Cárdenas response focused on two interrelated spheres: support for labor against all employers to raise Mexican living standards and the takeover of means of production controlled by both Mexican and foreign interests.

STAGES OF PRODUCTION

It was clear to Cárdenas that the earlier inroads of imperial interests under Porfirio Díaz had given Mexico a specialized technical apparatus.

Extractive processes supplying foreign heavy industries required rail networks, mechanized mines, and oil drilling facilities that demanded substantial investments by comparison with the capital placed in a handful of Mexican cotton and spinning mills scattered in an ocean of small family workshops and cottage weaving centers using handmade wooden looms. Cottage industries were at best able to supply the nation's self-contained villages, feudal *haciendas*, and the undeveloped domestic market.

Yet in the following three decades, the switch of imperial enterprises into the production of consumer wares changed the social structure in the larger Mexican cities. British and U.S. capital was increasingly directed toward the establishment and control of public utilities, automobile assembly plants, rayon factories, and cement mills. These industries were fueled by an enlarging Latin American market that helped destroy Mexican craft artisans as an uncompetitive class while drawing the output and labor of the nation into the vortex of a growing market economy. In turn, the enlarging consumer goods industry paved the way for the import of essential equipment and the development of Mexico's own future potential machine industries.

This process did not proceed smoothly or successfully, however. Following an anti-imperialist strategy from 1934 to 1938, the Cárdenas regime began to concentrate on nationalization of foreign assets, and this led to U.S. interdiction of its own exported technology and replaceable machine parts, which effectively showed Mexican industrialization.

The contradiction was self-fulfilling, too, because Mexico could not at once stir the psyche of its masses to a raffish hatred of the old imperial interests and simultaneously hope to attract new foreign investments and essential trade. Revolutionary economic nationalism also could not of itself stimulate manufacturing and extend the market without an infusion of large capital investments and skills that Mexico's self-serving middle classes lacked and the *extrajeros* would not risk.[2]

The lucrative imperial sector of Mexican industry covering large-scale investments in mining, metallurgy, machine shops, and the oil industry still employed 76,000 workers by the mid–1930s. Supplementing the technical developments made in this pre-industrial, imperial sector, Mexico's first stage of industrialization was largely based on imported technologies that supplied the equipment needed by the manufacturers of consumer textiles, clothing, and food products. Thus factories were still small by 1935; those averaging 30 workers produced goods worth 10,000 pesos annually, but employed a mere 215,000 workers of the total 16,500,000 population.[3]

If the imperial sectors and the domestic sectors in Monterrey and the sugar-refining states could be nationalized, Cárdenas reasoned that Mexico could command oil, mineral, railroad, shipping, and manufacturing revenues. Yet even nationalization of these sectors would not suffice to initiate an economic revolution unless labor gained a modicum of self-determined control and direction over these means of infrastructure, extraction, and production.

THE POSITION OF LABOR

For several decades labor had continually weakened its power as its own organized factions did battle with one another under the guidance of dominant politicans.

Although the Regional Confederation of Mexican Labor (CROM) had initially organized the work force, its support by the Calles presidency had led the leadership into corrupt practices and graft. The CROM had also come under the control of Luis Morones's self-appointed "action group" that diverted attention from its control with virulent anti–Communist propaganda.

Recognizing CROM's weaknesses, Cárdenas favored Vincente Lombardo Toledano's pro-populist Mexican Workers' Confederation (CTM). When Calles revolted in 1935, weakening CROM's position, Cárdenas drew Lombardo's CTM into a unified working-class movement opposed to Calles, the Gold Shirts, and other reemergent reactionary forces linked to European fascism.

The basic units of the CTM were the big industrial unions in the railroads, mines, powerhouses, oil fields, printing shops, and sugar fields. To these were added a conservative wing of bureaucratically run shop unions organized by regional federations in Mexico City and Puebla. State labor federations of small-factory and craft unions comprised another wing, as did large groups of agricultural workers and *ejidatarios*, small artisans, self-employed professionals, intellectual workers, and the powerful teachers' union.

As the CTM did battle with the CROM and the Mexican Labor Department engineered a split within CROM, the internecine conflicts led repeatedly to embattled workers being caught in senseless slaughter. In addition, the smaller, right-wing General Confederation of Workers (CGT) and the labor organizations fostered by ambitious stage governors further weakened trade unions, though Lombardo's CTM finally achieved partial unity of action with regional CROM, CGT groups, and the Federation of Government Workers.

Such cooperation backed Cárdenas efforts to secure an elevated standard of living for labor by forcing implementation of the 1931 Labor Code. With Mexican law now requiring that all industrial employers enter written labor contracts with trade unions, labor gained control over management on questions of the eight-hour day, regulated female and child labor, the closed shop, the check-off of union dues, limits on closing factories, dismissals only for cause, prohibition on blacklisting, and secured compensation for sickness and accidents.

As strikes for such causes supported by the government increased annually (70 from 1931 to 1934, 642 in 1935, 674 in 1936, and 833 in 1937), both the courts and government arbitration boards sided with labor as the "weaker side" against capital. Once declaring a strike legal, the government prevented the employer use of nonunion workers, kept the enterprise sealed off, and made the employer liable for wages during the period of conflict, except for disagreements over economic matters based on the employer's actual capacity to pay. Even under Cárdenas, however, the labor boards broke strikes that disorganized national economic activities.[4]

Cárdenas also put the Monterrey industrialists on notice that favoritism to the weaker side in the class struggle was supported by revolutionary law, so that strikes by labor against low wages and exploitation were viewed as efforts to improve their living standards and benefit the nation. Warning of the danger of civil war should the employers organize themselves into "a political band," Cárdenas boldly advised: "If the employers become weary of the social struggle, let them turn over their factories to the Government or the workers."[5]

Yet it was not against these Monterrey industrialists, but against the exploitive sugar *haciendas* that Cárdenas initially moved. Expropriation began after the United Sugar Company, the largest producer in the country at Los Mochis, suspended all medical services for labor. As the takeovers spread, the National Bank of Ejidal Credit advised peasants to purchase *hacienda* refineries and establish collectives of workers and peasants, the outstanding example being the Rafael Picazo Ejidal Agricultural-Industrial Collective Society purchased from the Jiquílpan *hacienda* of Guaracha. Profits of the operations were managed by peasants exercising maximum self-discipline for continuous operations.

There were nonetheless conflicts when the Mexican Workers' Confederation (CTM) tried to control agricultural processing plants to the exclusion of the local representative of the National Bank of Ejidal Credit, who incited the peasantry in the state of Veracruz. Although the mill-collective controlled by the workers paid cash advances for the peasants' crop, the peasants had stopped cane deliveries, blockaded the plant, and covered the roads with barbed wire. They were only stopped by the CTM threat of a nationwide general strike unless the peasants let the workers' cooperative operate unmolested and shared year-end dividends between both workers and peasants.[6]

In Morelos, with the government providing the capital, a new administrative coalition arranged for profit distribution to workers and peasants. The United States sold the technology to reconvert to sugar refining, after the postrevolutionary switch to small-scale corn planting by individual peasants.[7]

These measures of the moment then broadened into a national effort to promote cooperative labor controls.

THE ROLE OF THE BROADENED NATIONAL REVOLUTIONARY PARTY

Despite the individual victories for labor, Mexico remained unindustrialized. Even for the production of consumer goods and basic foodstuffs, Cárdenas relied heavily on using government influence from 1934 to 1938. Once his 1938-39 nationalization program butted heads with the foreign oil concessionaires able to inflict incalculable harm on Mexico, however, the next year he toned down his nationalism.

The production of machines as the second stage of industrialization was also postponed to the future, and it was clearly questionable if independent Mexican industrialization was possible without machine-making industries.

With little place for upward mobility in the rest of society, the army and bureaucracy of state had meanwhile provided places for those not possessed of estates or industries. Thus the National Revolutionary party that became Cárdenas's mainspring for power was based on a widened alliance of bureaucrats, labor, peasants, popular organizations, and the army.[8]

EXPROPRIATION

As the Federal Labor Law of 1931 made no provision for the nationalization of private enterprise, in September 1936 Cárdenas sent Congress his draft law awarding him wide powers to expropriate private properties and enterprises.

Six months later, in June 1937, the National Railways were nationalized, completing the policy begun by Limantour 30 years before. The next year Cárdenas awarded the rails to a workers' cooperative by government intervention to ensure labor's self-management, and he completed the distribution of 40 million acres by land grants to the peasants reliant on the rails for potential markets.

Using the Bank of Mexico as his money tree, Cárdenas then pumped lucre into government projects: a new dam for the peasants in the La Laguna cotton district, farm equipment for collective *ejidos*, and a giant modern sugar factory to process output from the entire state of Morelos. In early 1938 this factory was turned over to a cooperative of mill operatives and peasants. By the expropriation of the modern factory of sugar magnate Aaron Sáenz in 1939 (itself financed in 1930 by Sáenz's loan from the Bank of Mexico), a similar cooperative was organized.[9]

As these carte blanche asset expropriations were immensely popular, yet often blindly carried out, questions were raised about whether Mexico was enhancing either production or industrialization.

COSTS OF PRODUCTION AND REPRODUCTION

The Cárdenas regime was soon forced to assess the central relationship between the cost of Mexican manufacturing, the level of wages to sustain the workers and their families, and the pricing of consumer products to ensure a return of invested production capital. It was obvious to Cárdenas that, if the cost of living could be lowered, the cost of production and thus market prices could also be lowered.

As government policy favored the workforce and the need to assure a reasonable return for cooperatives and investors, it focused attention on preventing the extortion of surplus by the army of middle agents that stood between producers and consumers. The government accomplished both by fixing minimum wages on the cost side of the ledger and controlling middle-agent pricing on the sales side.

The 1931 Labor Code had provided that commissions be established in each geographic zone to fix minimum wages in relation to living costs and prevailing living standards. But by 1933 this had been done in less than a tenth of the nation's 2,247 municipalities, and living standards were not materially improved under Cárdenas's minimum wage program because government inspectors did not enforce the law and employers habitually paid less than the statutory minimum.

Yet without wage increases, workers' living standards were cut by rapid increases in prices charged by middlemen. Between 1934 and 1938, the percentage of the retail value of meat taken by the railroads, the slaughterhouses, the bulk buyers, and the wholesalers increased from 3.8 to 25.6 percent for beef cattle and from 19.8 to 40.9 percent for sheep.

To combat such middleman price gouging, an alliance between employers and workers soon emerged under government guidance. Enormous demonstrations against profiteering pushed the government to establish regulatory commissions in various cities to fix maximum prices, with labor and business representatives cooperating to prevent exorbitant increases in the cost of tortillas, charcoal, medicines, and other necessities.

The dual logic was clear. Employers wanting to cut costs by holding down wage demands and strikes were in favor of pacifying labor by lowering the cost of food purchased by the workforce, while workers seeking a higher standard of living also favored eliminating the exploitative middlemen who made up a growing segment of the middle class.

Understanding the need to undercut the agents of inflation, in 1938 the government set up the nonprofit Regulatory Committee of the Subsistence Market to buy and sell huge quantities of essential crops directly from the peasants and sell them through controlled distribution channels.

Although the committee attemptd to reward efficient food processors and merchants, the Regulatory Committee raised farm prices and reduced food costs to retail consumers by preventing middlemen from taking unreasonable profits and preventing speculators from cornering grain supplies.

Offering preferential treatment to the poorest agricultural zones, the committee often bought the entire crop of *ejidal* regions. It crushed a "corner" on the rice market by purchasing the entire Sonora crop. To offset extensive crop failures and threatened price rises in 1938, the committee imported large quantities of wheat from the United States. It cut retail prices one-third in marketing 65 percent of Mexico City's total consumption of beans. By marketing its products through 4,000 retail stores in Mexico City, the committee made it impossible for independent middlemen and retailers to sell food to the public at higher prices.

After operating for about a year and a half, the Regulatory Committee had checked the rise in retail food prices and increased the peasants' income by selling more than 8 million pesos worth of wheat, corn, beans, rice, and meat through retail channels in half of Mexico's cities. It thereby secured peasant incomes, shielded the workers' real wages, and protected the industrialists' profits.[10]

If the middle agents who had oppressed workers and employers were more or less squeezed, it foretold a possible future of cooperative agriculture involving collective farm production, nationalized rail transport, worker-controlled processing plants, and retail cooperative distribution. Such a government central plan would not only limit the power of the middle agents to raise prices, but would probably eliminate them altogether.

But by the end of the Cárdenas regime, the middlemen remained. Despite their price increases, though, enlarged Mexican production fueled employment and a temporary labor shortage, leading to higher real wages. As Mexican industry expanded rapidly during the first half of the Cárdenas administration, total employment surged in key industries from 39,915 in 1936 (first quarter) to 45,448 in 1937 (third quarter), although it fell slightly in the 1938 petroleum crisis. And between 1936 and 1938, real quarterly earnings for industrial workers in the Mexican City area rose about 14 percent, despite the 1938 increases in wholesale prices of 48.7 percent for consumer goods and 53.9 percent for food.[11]

Without unbridled middlemen, better pay for the "slave" of capitalist industries was clearly possible.

THE SLAVE OF CAPITAL

State police powers both liberated labor and kept it the charge of capital during the Cárdenas era.

The government promised labor an enlarged sphere in the direction of nationalized and cooperative industries requiring uninterrupted production, but the workers found themselves as the human engine of production needing adequate wages and amenities. If labor did not comply with the government's interpretation of the need for continuous production and compulsory arbitration, however, state police powers could be mobilized against it. On the other hand, if the government declared a work stoppage legal, labor could rely on the police powers of the state to force the employers to bargain.

Was the state predominantly a workers' government or a capitalist one then? The Cárdenas government developed a plan that favored labor over capital, but directed both workers and peasants how they would organize and where they would work. Cárdenas believed that, at least in the field of oil nationalized by the government, workers' acts of sabotage could not be tolerated, and he told the convention of Mexican Oil Workers Union on 1 July 1939 that its position "cannot be that of fighting against the State, which, in this case, is neither a capitalist unit nor a profit organization, for an improvement in the conditions of oil production will necessarily be reflected in larger incomes for the workers and for the people as a whole."[12]

This imposed formulation was based on state resources being mobilized as the investment fount of nationalized industries and the cooperatives' source of credit and access to instruments of labor. Almost all Mexican cooperative assets and periodic losses were financially bootstrapped by the government by means of printing press currency, state debt, or the shifting of the burden of taxes to those with wealth, from whom resources could also be appropriated in other ways.

There were limits, however, to the amount the state could burden domestic and foreign interests that were able to withhold new capital investments, so Cárdenas slowed the expropriation of domestic and foreign assets from 1939 to 1940 and reduced government subsidies to the worker and peasant cooperatives.[13]

Labor's entrapment from 1934 to 1940 took place in this larger frame of initial empowerment and later weakness.

War on the European horizon nonetheless kept labor in the Cárdenas fold. As the CTM had broadened into a political organization defending the Cárdenas revolutionary program, it powerfully opposed the rise of domestic and foreign reaction and fascism, particularly the Italian invasion of Ethiopia and Franco's use of Moorish troops to attack republican Spain. Thus the trade union of arsenal workers labored without pay on munitions for loyalist Spain, and the government admitted thousands of republican refugees, whom the CTM provided with union jobs. The Spanish republican government also funded its own bank in Mexico with a March 1939 gold shipment worth 300 million pesos for financing revolutionary action against the Franco regime and for the exclusive use of refugee settlements to set up new industries and deploy trained Spanish farmers to introduce vineyards and olive groves, thereby raising the technological level of Mexico's economy.[14]

In other areas, too, Mexican labor held compromised economic and political power at best and remained leery of the federal government's lack of control over capital and industry. Corporative controls over labor still pitted unions against employers. And fearing both federal and state government administrations could shift to the political right in future, workers refused to abrogate their trade-union rights.

CHAPTER 6

Nationalization
and Imperial Oil

When Cárdenas attacked foreign holdings in Mexico in the name of "economic emancipation," it proved risky to the nation's further industrialization.

Nationalization of the oil industry might initially award Mexico a modicum of energy self-sufficiency and export-earned foreign exchange. But if foreign oil markets shut down and imperial petroleum companies cut off the sale of replaceable parts and capital equipment needed to continue operations and further industrialize, there might be little work in the oil industry, or any other, for that matter.

The alternative for the Cárdenas government would have been simply to retain oversight and remain the policeman securing the foreign interests. "All that is Mexican about the big industry that is developing in our land is the fact that our resources and man-power are utilized, and that a revolutionary government watches over it, seeking to eliminate unfair practices," said President Cárdenas, as he pointed to the government monitoring of profit extractions by the oil investors and other foreign investors.

Cárdenas understood that so long as foreign control of Mexico's resources and its industrial and technical spheres continued, he and succeeding presidents would be subject to the external strictures regulating the pace and type of investments in advanced production and employment, as well as the degree to which labor could earn a living wage and assert its power.

Dangers and Benefits of National Expropriation

National expropriation nonetheless posed both dangers and benefits. In one sense, taking over the foreign-owned, pre-industrial oil sector would limit the pressures Britain and the United States could thrust on the Mexican economy. Mexico was still largely a peasant nation whose population resided in remote villages and engaged in quasi-barter of goods, relatively undisturbed by fluctuations in industrial prices charged in the urban domain or by the rate of exchange between pesos and dollars or sterling.

In a global sense, though, Mexico was highly vulnerable to a boycott of its oil exports by the petroleum cartel. Starting in the spring of 1937, raw material prices had plummeted, making it increasingly costly to import essential machinery for food production, highway construction, and worker-operated factories. Domestic investment capital was also blindsided by panic-stricken landlords and businessmen who liquidated operations, refused to make new investments, and sent their capital abroad, effectively drawing on the dollar reserves held by the Bank of Mexico and threatening to devalue the peso vis-à-vis the dollar.

On the other hand, Cárdenas envisioned that Mexico's emancipation could depend upon control of its resources to maximize their output for domestic use and to export them to earn foreign exchange to finance machine imports.

As Congress's Six Year Plan was vague regarding the methods of stimulation, regulation, and aid to raise oil production based on the likely existence of still unknown reserves, Cárdenas promoted the semiofficial oil company Petróleos de Mexico S.A. for competitive production and marketing in 1935. He further empowered it to compete with the private oil companies and, in 1937, gave it rights to absorb expired foreign oil leases and concessions as well as to regulate domestic and export markets.

Regulation was critical because the foreign companies, fearing that their concessions would be restricted or abolished, reduced their new investments, cutting Mexican production from 193 million barrels in 1921 to 33 million barrels in 1932. Seeking a way to enlarge production, Cárdenas in 1937 awarded a concession for the mammoth Poza Rica field discovered in 1930 to the British-owned Aguila Oil Company. The company in turn agreed to invest £5 million in production and pipeline construction, spudded in new wells, and increased daily production to 200,000 barrels, awarding the government both added taxes and 35 percent in royalties to help finance its Six Year Plan.

Although Cárdenas also assured the foreign oil companies as late as 15 March 1937 that there would be no expropriation, central to his scheme was the 1937 Law of Expropriation, which empowered the government to take over private property as long as it paid for its value within ten years. This law had already legalized the seizure of machinery and other equipment as well as lands on mere proof that expropriation was for the general welfare of the community. So-called private property was thereby placed within the reach of the government, and in this realm, the authority of the people was wielded through the person of Cárdenas. Thus empowered, the government began nationalization on an unprecedented scale.

Having already expropriated properties valued at more than $10 million from U.S. citizens from 1927 to 1937, Mexico reached a high-water mark the next year in 1938 when it expropriated the means of oil production.[1] The contest for these facilities had come to a head on 18 December 1937 when Mexico's Conciliation and Arbitration Tribunal ruled that foreign-owned oil companies had to increase wages by one-third and improve the workers' overtime rates, vacation time, pension, and welfare system. Although the companies had appealed, the Mexican Supreme Court upheld the board's award.

But the oil companies refused to comply, arguing that the total increase would in reality amount to about 100 percent, an amount they declared both extravagant and impossible to pay. Mexican officials answered that they could easily pay twice as much,[2] and the government-appointed committee headed by eminent Mexican economist Dr. Jesús Silva Herzog assembled the following facts:

- Between 1934 and June 1937, the cost of the typical food basket for a working-class family in the oil zones increased 89 percent and this caused a 16 to 22 percent fall in real wages, the brunt affecting the lowest paid group
- The foreign-owned oil companies' rate of Mexican profit averaged 16.2 percent on nonamortized invested capital by comparison with the less than 2 percent average for domestic U.S. companies in 1933–34
- Mexican oil workers were being driven to work faster despite having the use of less fixed capital per worker, and produced more than three times as much as U.S. oil workers but earned only a fraction of their wages
- There was a disparity between the 8.64 pesos investment per barrel of Mexican oil produced and the 48.12 pesos invested in the United States.
- The companies also charged 193.4 percent more for gasoline in the Mexican market than abroad, thereby acting as an obstacle to the economic development of Mexico

The committee concluded that the oil industry should increase its 1936 payrolls by 26 million pesos, awarding labor half its indicated profits.[3]

The corporations announced they were "sorry for Mexico" but insisted they also had no "intention of abiding by the stipulations of Section XXI, Article 123 of the Mexican Constitution"—a clause that would have cost them 100 million pesos by providing that if an employer refused to obey a court arbitration award, the workers had the right to cancel the collective labor contract and receive three months' dismissal wages.

Labor agitation in the oil fields immediately intensified, and Cárdenas then issued his famous 18 March 1938 expropriation decree, which was followed by appeals from U.S. and British companies to their own governments for protection. Following orders from a government commission of three trade union leaders and four officials, the workers immediately took charge of operations through local trade union committees and maintained uninterrupted production. They brought engineers, refinery managers, cashiers, and paymasters into the union as a condition of work and, following the labor tribunal verdict, they required that every foreign technician train a Mexican helper to replace him in three years.[4]

The Mexican foreign minister, Eduardo Hay, stated that the Cárdenas administration policy of placing the land and resources in the hands of those who worked them could not be "halted by the impossibility of paying immediately the value of the properties belonging to a small number of foreigners who seek only a lucrative end." He also said that this policy applied to Mexicans whose properties had been expropriated.[5]

After heavy words of condemnation, the U.S. government then conceded the right of Mexico to expropriate, though the price remained in question. Mexican experts placed it at $10 million.[6] As a follow-up in 1938, both governments agreed that each side would appoint a commission to determine the value of the expropriated property, with the Mexican government agreeing to make a $1 million initial payment by May 1939.

The battle was still far from over, though. Bristling with indignation that Mexico should dare nationalize their interests, the oil companies forced the devaluation of the peso and pressured the U.S. government to discontinue silver purchases from Mexican mines, which in fact were 85 to 90 percent owned by U.S. nationals and gave the Mexican government 10 percent of its total taxation income.

The U.S. secretary of the treasury, Henry Morgenthau, had promptly announced the discontinuance of U.S. silver purchases for April 1938. But when Cárdenas responded by pressuring the silver producers to cooperate with his government to market silver in other world markets, the U.S. silver bloc in Congress lobbied the U.S. government to continue purchases on the New York market.

Although silver thereafter commanded a lower price than before the Mexican expropriation of oil, Mexican production of silver remained viable (2,069 metric tons in 1920, 3,272 in 1930, and 2,570 in 1940).[7]

In keeping with tradition, the foreign oil companies still considered themselves a state within a state because they had made loans to the Mexican government and dealt with it on "equal" terms. But now their interests directly clashed with those of the government as Cárdenas dared to expropriate their holdings and turn their administration over to Mexican oil workers, a policy that evoked the reaction of two imperial powers.

EMPIRES ON A TACTICAL REACH

The United States moved along a tactical reach, using an assortment of inducements and threats. Some zealots of the U.S. press attacked the Mexican "Communists," bringing forth a tide of nationalist Mexican passion from the archbishop of Mexico, middle-class housewives, and peasant women vying to offer their gold jewelry to the national treasury.[8]

Great Britain concurrently tried protecting British Shell and oil magnate Sir Henri Deterding's *Compañía Mexicana de Petróleo El Aguila* as concessionaire of Poza Rica, by far the best Mexican oil field, which produced between 62 and 75 percent of Mexican oil and possessed vast, untouched reserves in comparison with the semidepleted fields held by the U.S. Standard Oil and Sinclair companies in the north. The favored British fields produced light petroleum that was richer in gasoline and appropriate for refining to supply the strategic needs of the British navy.[9] And Aguila also had sidestepped Mexican corporate income tax collectors by transferring assets to its affiliated Canadian company, which bought Aguila's entire crude oil production at two-thirds the market price, stripping the Mexican subsidiary of taxable profit.[10]

There were limits of Aguila's extortions, though. By the spring of 1938, war was threatening between the German-Italian axis and the liberal democratic states, and Britain foresaw an oil crisis once Italian destroyers and submarines undercut Mediterranean oil shipments from Mesopotamia and the Far East. Mexico's Poza Rica fields selling oil at half the price charged by U.S. companies were crucial to Britain. Britain also feared the loss of Mexican oil under the Neutrality Act that permitted nonaligned states to sell strategic raw materials to any buyer for cash.[11]

Although the British government did not openly question the right of Mexico to expropriate, it demanded immediate and adequate payment in cash. Doubting Mexico's ability to pay pounds sterling, the British government reminded Mexico of unpaid British claims of $300,000 and professed to believe that "public interest" was not served by expropriation, that Mexico's real motive was a "political desire to acquire for Mexico in permanence the advantage of ownership and control of the oilfields." Hence, Great Britain refused to consider any solution to the problem except the return of the properties to the company.[12]

When Britain asked for full, immediate payment of the war debt Mexico owed, Mexico paid $82,000 on 13 May 1938, caustically retorting that "even powerful states . . . cannot pride themselves on punctual payments of all their pecuniary obligations."[13]

As the British government continued to point out that Mexico could not pay her entire foreign debt, making her credit worthless, England demanded another $361,737 for four-months arrears on indemnities due British subjects for damages they had suffered during the armed strife of the Revolution more than two decades earlier, a trivial sum that amounted to one one-thousandth of the debt England still owed to the United States. This was a transparent demand to undercut Mexican nationalization, and the insulting tone of the British notes led Cárdenas to break diplomatic relations with Great Britain and recall the Mexican minister from London.

Appealing the expropriation decree to the Mexican courts, Great Britain then refused to await their decision and demanded the immediate return of the properties to the company to secure English stockholders from losses during prolonged court proceedings, despite the company's incorporation under Mexican law and its contract with the Mexican government not to call on its own government for protection.[14]

And so the accounting battle raged. Mexico thereafter paid not only skinflint England, but also made payments to the United States, France, and Italy as indemnities due their citizens for losses following the 1910 Revolution.[15]

EL PRESIDENTE PERSEVERES

Despite foreign pressure and a threatening fiscal crisis that might have led to Mexico cutting its programs, to popular dismay, and even to Cárdenas's overthrow, *el Presidente* persevered against a thinly veiled threat of U.S. invasion and absurd British demands. He seriously planned to burn down every oil derrick, dynamite every well, and blow to bits every tank and refinery.

Dumbfounded, the United States stopped insisting on ownership rights and Secretary of State Cordell Hull made a 26 March 1938 demand for immediate payment for oil rights and expropriated land at their "present effective value."

Cárdenas played his trump card: certainly he was willing to confer with the oil companies about both property valuation and terms of payment, but any payment was for "the irrevocable expropriation of their properties."

Hull replied weakly on 30 March 1938 that the only condition the United States insisted upon was property indemnity; the companies demanded $450 million based on estimated future productivity. It was an imperious demand that Mexico refused out of hand.

With a threatening European war likely to embroil the United States, President Roosevelt on 1 April 1938 then moved the question, stating the indemnity basis to be actual investment minus profits taken.

Cárdenas immediately agreed, calling for a 100 million pesos internal loan to pay off the expropriation debt. Peasant women handed their chickens and livestock to collection agents, ladies gave their jewelry, politicians their gains. Although the 27 March 1938 Congress provided for the immediate debt floatation of 50 million pesos, the loan could not be fully raised. Pledges were solicited, and with Mexican reserves almost exhausted and the peso facing devaluation, there was no way to pay for foreign assets by converting pesos into dollars and pounds sterling.[16]

With Mexico clearly lacking the immediate ability to pay, the oil companies still demanded $400 million or more, thus "verifying" the companies' right to retain their holdings. Finally the companies refused to evaluate their properties at all in an effort to keep their governments in the fray.

THE EMPORIUM CALLS OUT ITS TROOPS

Moving offensively, the oil companies then backed General Saturnino Cedillo and his private army of peasants under a mercenary German general, mobilizing foreign finances and German and Italian planes.

Cárdenas gave not a centimeter, fulminating that the population was "rallying to defend the interests of the Fatherland which have been menaced by the arrogant attitude of the petroleum trusts." Cárdenas went on the offensive, too, railing in San Luis Potosí that plans for rebellion by thousands of peasants could be attributed to General Cedillo. To undermine him, Cárdenas offered pardons to Cedillo-recruited peasants under arms if they surrendered to the federal outposts; he allowed them to keep their guns and to receive farm plows and mules. As more and more peasants accepted the offer, Cedillo was isolated with a handful of followers, and died in a final battle with federal forces.

OIL TRUST INTRANSIGENCE

The oil trust still did not relent, and it shut Mexico out of traditional international markets. Gulf Oil, Standard, and Shell embargoed shipping to the United States and England, prevented Mexico from getting oil tankers, attached Mexican oil entering European ports as property of the expropriated oil companies, and tied up the vessels of independent shippers for weeks during court hearings.

Although the courts invariably upheld Mexico's right to the oil, the delay and loss of profits momentarily cut off marketing in Europe, leaving Latin America as the only possible immediate Mexican outlet.[17]

Using a secondary boycott, the oil companies then blocked U.S. exports of critical equipment to Mexico. The Ohio Steel Foundry Company denied refinery tubing to the Mexican Petroleum Administration; the Worthington Pump and Machinery Corporation refused $10,977 in pumps and parts; the Aluminum Company of America and four other concerns withheld $19,000 in fractionating towers; and Babcock and Wilcox denied $21,000 in caldrons. Although U.S. heavy industry was in the doldrums, about a dozen other large concerns rejected similar Mexican orders.[18]

Not to be undone, Cárdenas called out his own troops of oil salesmen to barter with Germany, Italy, and Japan, a move that threatened the predominant share that U.S. corporations already held. "The three chief sources of supply for the Italian Navy are the Standard Oil Company of New Jersey, the Shell Oil [of Britain] and ourselves," stated President R.B. Kahle of the Eastern States Petroleum Company. "Mexico and Eastern sell only 10 per cent of the oil bought by the fascist powers. The remainder is sold by the highly respectable American and British companies. . . . The only difference is that Standard refines its oil in Aruba, the Shell in Curaçao, while we refine ours in the United States."[19]

In June 1938, the Cárdenas administration defensively appointed William Rhodes Davis as European sales agent for Mexican oil and strengthened Mexican marketing by providing that 60 percent of the price of oil could be paid for in goods, with the balance in cash. Davis arranged sales of Mexican oil at cut-rate prices to Germany. In return for $17 million worth of crude oil, Mexico then received German heavy machinery and equipment. And while U.S. businessmen complained that the oil industry's war against Mexico was costing U.S. machinery concerns millions in sales, Mexican oil was being exchanged for Italian tankers, German rayon, and newsprint. The gauge of Mexican refinery production was also being geared to German machinery, with follow-up and parts replacement orders likely to total several times the value of the original purchases.[20] It is not surprising then that throughout 1938-39, certain members of the British Parliament continued to urge the resumption of diplomatic relations with Mexico, though the government demanded the return of oil properties before such relations could be reinitiated.

Mexico was meanwhile producing more oil, as previous interest and dividend payments to London, New York, and the Hague were now on hand and available for Mexican drilling operations, refinery modernization, and wages. As production was extended, wages were increased and health facilities and workers' housing built. As the pesos was depreciated, boosting petroleum exports and revenues 36 percent, nearly constant domestic costs remitted profits without the need to dump abroad at lower prices.

As foreign markets were found, 1938 exports reached 60 percent of the 1937 level; by July 1939 Mexico was exporting all the oil it could produce, with Brazil taking one-quarter on a cash basis.[21] Thus Mexico had out-maneuvered the U.S.-British boycott and taken charge of its own oil industry.

Is This an Outline of a Future American Common Market?

As the oil fields had already been turned over to a government corporation, *Petróleos Mexicanos*, administered largely by inefficient former trade-union officials who were at first unable to increase their workers' wages, Mexico was pressed to sell its oil to Latin America. As a result, it quickly revived its missions and embassies in Cuba, Central America, Brazil, and Chile.

With a fiscal crisis meanwhile looming in the wake of his revolutionary programs and the possibility that the newly floated state debt for land expropriation might be repudiated, Cárdenas also attempted to attract new foreign capital by launching a campaign advocating self-determination of each nation as the foundation of a future American security zone. On 5 June 1938 he called for "Union within each country representing internal peace and the cooperation of its inhabitants and insuring its political independence and economic autonomy; Union of all the nations of America in the face of whatever common danger the future may hold in store; Union that is free, spontaneous, and strong on behalf of peace and democracy in the world."

With war appearing ever more likely on the European horizon and Cárdenas openly sympathizing with the Loyalist Republicans in Spain to the chagrin of conservative investors, Cárdenas sought a way out of Mexico's fight with the oil companies, which was threatening to isolate Mexico economically. He thus spoke of ending exploitation in the same breath as ending warfare, linking the two in a circle of mutual welfare between nations. Nonintervention, inviolability of territory, and peaceful cooperation, he insisted, would stimulate national industrialization for the production of regional products, extend lines of communication, and end tariff wars.

It was a political formula for a future common market, but it was imprecise because Cárdenas wanted to make the Western oil companies give up their revanchist polemics and the United States put down its guard.

Mexico was willing, Cárdenas said, to pay for its legal right to expropriate oil properties for the welfare of the Mexican public. When he announced that Mexico would give oil-sales preference to the democratic countries at the onset of the European war if Great Britain cooperated, the British position weakened.

The opposition in Parliament began to accuse the British government of upholding a policy towards Mexico which had led to great shipments of oil to Germany and Italy. In truth, Sir Henri Deterding himself was one of several who financed Hitler's road to power; his Shell interests were heavily engaged in selling petroleum to Germany. The same was true for California oil companies that shipped 30 million barrels of oil to Japan in 1938—twice Mexico's total petroleum exports to all countries (Mexico shipped the Japanese a mere 233,000 barrels).[22]

With German agents busily negotiating in Mexico, the British government soon moved into combat with a diplomatic corps. This dovetailed with U.S. pressure for a settlement of the oil controversy in the light of the 2 December 1939 Mexican Supreme Court decision that affirmed Cárdenas's expropriation of oil properties and provided as long as ten years to pay the companies, with compensation due only for capital invested for production plus the tax value of the land.

Despite the companies' protest, Sinclair Oil settled in 1940 for payment of $8,500,000 for their holdings. Then in December, Cárdenas's successor, Avila Camacho, agreed to negotiate with the United States over oil expropriation. In 1941-42, appointed experts valued the holdings of the remaining U.S. oil companies at $23,995,991 and recommended that one-third of that amount be paid in five equal annual installments, payments Mexico timely met.

There was British public pressure to settle, and the price of English-owned El Aguila stock was momentarily on the rise. Nonetheless, it took until August 1947 for the Mexican government finally to agree to pay the company $81,250,000 in U.S. currency plus ten years' interest. The company was released from unpaid Mexican taxes and private debts.[23]

Thus did Mexico free itself of unrelenting foreign pressure. With England guaranteed a final payoff and the U.S. State Department unable to use the coercion of suspended silver purchases or to organize an oil boycott to bring Mexico to its economic knees, the onset of World War II brought Mexico a growing foreign demand for its petroleum, zinc, copper, and henequen.

With Mexico's economic independence momentarily secured, future social movements would be called on to keep politicians from narrow nationalism, isolationism, autarchic illusions, military ambitions, and from ever again selling the nation to foreign interests.

CHAPTER 7

A Historic Breakthrough

Cárdenas brought Mexico through the halfway house of state-promoted cooperative labor that lay somewhere between neofeudal relations and a viable industrial system and extended future market.

Attempting to keep the forces of capitalism from controlling Mexico's political realm, Cárdenas limited their expansive operations by developing new forms of worker control and collective agricultural organizations. He openly used the state to organize trade unions, to guide the struggle of classes and, through schools and training centers, to promote the concepts of democracy and cooperative labor, civil liberties, and the integrity of different cultures. He turned the banking system into a political body mobilizing funds from various classes and using them to direct and forward cooperative enterprises. He created a giant government purchasing organization to regulate the trade in foodstuffs, guarantee the peasants a minimum price for their output, establish a retail price ceiling for food, and limit middlemen to reasonable profits for their efficiency, while curtailing them from gouging consumers.

Cárdenas was in the process of turning the state into an instrument for national reconstruction to employ half the idle and underemployed population, to feed them through land cooperatives employing the other half of the population, and to narrow the field of private capital by controlling or nationalizing business and landlord means of production, profits, and liquid assets. Such mobilization of Mexico's resources might have fueled national development, brought the country into a regulated market, and put it on the road to a mixed economy—partly state-run, partly privately directed.

A FINE SOLILOQUY

A historic turnabout had also been made in Mexico's past subservient relations with foreign powers. Cárdenas insisted on the logic of Mexican oversight of foreign interests, to be followed throughout the Americas: control of foreign interests should reward domestic labor efficiency to elevate the lot of humankind. On a mission to Cuba, Cárdenas explained his philosophy:

> Let us encourage investors who identify themselves with the progress of our people. Let us uproot prejudices fomented by selfish interests against the social reforms that have been instituted by our several nations. ... Let us endeavor to bring back to our people a confidence of their own destinies and their sacred right to govern themselves without foreign interference. Let us instill in the conscience of our laborers the need for self-discipline of greater efficiency in their work, and of a stronger sense of responsibility in their service to the collectivity. Thus, in a Union of all peoples of this continent, let us ensure for our democracies true peace and progress.[1]

It was a fine soliloquy on independence and self-sufficiency, but the foreigners were not easily quieted or controlled. In June 1938 the U.S. State Department had presented the Washington-based Mexican ambassador a $10 million-plus bill for land-indemnity claims that had accumulated since 1927. As the oil companies continued on their simultaneous offensive, and as both Italy and Germany vied for Latin American friendship and trade, the United States momentarily imperiled its historic advantage in Latin American economic affairs.

Six months later, realizing its *faux-fuyant* in the race for Latin American oil, commerce, and security, the United States changed course, calling for inter–American unity and providing millions of dollars of credit for Latin American domestic needs and military preparedness against the emerging Axis powers.

Cárdenas then sought to ease tensions between Washington and Mexico that had escalated in August-September 1938 by promising indemnities for U.S. agrarian claims. He still attempted to overcome oil company demands by refusing to pay the debts all at once, however, thereby preventing Mexican insolvency and maintaining his own political legitimacy at home.

With compromise in the air (an overall settlement was signed 19 November 1941), Cárdenas conceded to the claims of U.S. landowners, called on Mexican citizens who had lost land to surrender their rights to remuneration, and used 1.5 percent of the Mexican budget to pay out old claims stemming back to the Revolution.

Thus did the president and leaders of the ruling party turn to a more moderate policy.

GOVERNMENT DECREES AND LABOR VALUE

Cárdenas believed that his government's decrees and proselytizing would be followed by a groundswell of worker-peasant effort to enlarge Mexico's self-sufficient output that would enable the country to break loose of the foreign headlock. "Every laborer with an opportunity to produce who does not throw all his effort and capacity into his work or who gives himself over to vice or parasitic practices, is evading his responsibility," Cárdenas fulminated. "He is a traitor to his class and an enemy of Mexico's revindication movement."[2]

Such expressions usually touched only those who were already convinced, however, and fueling such workers' élan in the employ of still-viable foreign concerns would likely bolster profits, not living standards.

Cárdenas's personal subscription to labor theory went further, too; he argued that the socialistic school "teaches that work is the source of wealth and well-being, and not the curse of servitude, that productive effort ennobles, and that the castes and races predestined to the privilege of happiness at the expense of enslaved groups simply do not exist."[3]

An inherent contradiction beset this doctrine in the 1930s, though, for it was not possible to set up workers' control over an industrial structure that had yet to be built.

THE NOT-SO-INVISIBLE HAND

Capital, technology, and a skilled labor force were obviously essential for Mexican industrialization. Industry itself was linked to access to raw materials, a viable labor force, and expanding markets. And industrialization and commercialization were dependent on national unification under a centralized state and a coordinated government program.

Yet the middle class was cut out of the reformation that was designing workers' control of industry, land, and means of transport. Government price-controls lessened the profit potential of the middlemen, while Cárdenas government expropriations excluded Mexican business from the management of the national railways and the oil industry.

As the advantages were shifted to the workers and peasants, the middle class moved from neutrality to hostility towards the Cárdenas program, became a threat to its policies, and encouraged future presidential candidates to stress protection of small agricultural properties and opposition to further advances in worker control.[4]

In truth, though he was reluctant to admit the implications of his attitude, Cárdenas relied heavily not on labor and peasant control of the means of production and life, but on the import of U.S. technology, its mobilization to upgrade Mexican output efficiency,[5] and the transitional draw of income from the United States by selling mineral and petroleum resources and promoting migratory, *bracero* labor.

Cárdenas pointed to the commercial advantages the United States would net from such a trade-off, arguing convincingly:

> It is detrimental to the United States for her neighbors to be weak and poor. It would be to her advantage to help them bring their standard of living up to a par with what is considered decent in the United States. To attain this goal we have to be industrialized. We cannot get very far promoting small arts and crafts.... Machinery is sorely needed for factories, and the United States could help us this way. An agreement should be made, for instance, that for every thousand *braceros* Mexico sends to the United States to help in the harvest there, a certain number of tractors will be shipped to Mexico to make up for the loss of man power.[6]

Cárdenas also sought to unify the nation by building means of transport and upgrading its people by centrally directed bureaucratic relocation of the population as well as its education to socialist principles. By 1937, Cárdenas was already planning to move Mexico's surplus agricultural population from "overpopulated areas where there is insufficient land for cultivation, and move them to new zones ... rich areas, especially along the coasts, that have not been developed as much as could be desired." He argued that such steps would integrate the excess rural population into "the general economic life of the nation."

"To make this colonization possible," Cárdenas explained, "the Federal Government will continue to spend large sums in the construction of roads and railroads to these areas for economic and social purposes as well as in sanitation projects to improve the factors that make for health so that the population may be more wisely distributed and new sources of production be developed."[7]

On 20 November 1938, Cárdenas also called for rectification of the nation's work force by bringing home U.S.-based Mexicans to work on fertilized and irrigated lands, opening new lines of communication to government-designated, isolated regions, installing modern processing mills for peasants' output, and electrifying plants to be owned by users. Cooperative labor was to be promoted by state credit grants, and returning Mexicans were either to be sent to government-assisted settlements or returned to work in industries in their native regions.

Such reorganization of resources and the spatial relocation of populations were to be an inherent component of two other Cárdenas plans as well:

- The reforestation of vast areas constantly being stripped of trees, endangering Mexican forests
- The transformation of indigenous Indian means of production to link them to the nation's commercial sphere, making them part of a system of routine selling of goods, minerals, other resources and products of commercial lands and forests

Medical programs were also designed to send young doctors and nurses to the outlying regions where disease reigned.

Financial support for elementary education was seen as essential to build a literate, industrial population as well. In 1910 there were 12,000 elementary schools with 20,000 teachers for 848,000 pupils; by 1930 the number of schools was down to 11,000, but there were 28,000 teachers and 1,300,000 pupils. By 1940 the number of schools had more than doubled to 24,000, and there were 40,000 teachers and 2,114,000 pupils.[8]

MEXICO'S LARGELY RURAL AND AGRICULTURAL CHARACTER

Despite all these programs, Mexico remained a rural, largely agricultural nation that was linked by an expanding network of highways and railroads for internal commerce.

During the Calles, Portes Gil, and Ortiz Rubio administrations there had been 695 kilometers of highways in 1925 and 1,426 kilometers in 1930, but by the end of Cárdenas's presidential term in 1940, there were 9,929 kilometers—more than a sixfold increase.[9] Before Cárdenas, there were 2,262 millions of ton-kilometers of freight transported by rail in 1921 and 4,041 millions in 1930, but at the end of his term there were 5,810, an increase of 44 percent.[10]

What was transported was largely raw materials and foods to the growing population that was also increasingly urbanized. Census figures recorded 5,200,000 Mexicans in 1793, 12,632,000 in 1895, 13,607,000 in 1900, 16,533,000 in 1930 and 19,654,000 in 1940.[11]

As this twentieth-century surge in population growth drew sustenance from the rural domain, production of maize for self-sufficiency and domestic markets increased between 1930 and 1940 (1,377,000 and 1,640,000 metric tons respectively), as did beans (83,000 and 97,000 metric tons respectively). Wheat (370,000 metric tons in 1930, 464,000 metric tons in 1940) and rice (75,000 metric tons in 1930 and 108,000 metric tons in 1940) became increasingly important.[12] The production of sugar cane and refined sugar for export surged[13]:

	1900	1910	1920	1930	1940
Cane	1,267,000	2,503,000	2,873,000*	3,293,000	4,973,000
Sugar	75,000	148,000	118,000	216,000	2,944,000

*Figure is for 1925.

For industry, transport, and urban life, electrical power was essential. Some 20,000 kilowatts had represented capacity limits of power plants in 1900, but the amount rose steadily to 110,000 in 1910, 120,000 in 1920, 510,000 in 1930, and 681,000 in 1940. Actual power generated in millions of kilowatt hours leaped from a mere 56 in 1900 to 308 in 1910, 336 in 1920, 1,464 in 1930, and 2,529 in 1940.[14]

As the textile industry expanded, cotton production jumped from the relatively constant range of 34,000 metric tons in 1907, 32,000 in 1920, and 38,000 in 1930 to 65,000 metric tons in 1940.[15]

Effective industrialization and commercialization depended, however, on access to substantial financial and technical resources which, despite significant increases, Mexico sorely lacked. From the end of the Revolution until two years after Cárdenas left office, bank credits had gone up almost threefold (720 million pesos in 1911, but 2,024 million in 1942).[16] But as these did not suffice, printing press money became Cárdenas's way of financing cooperative projects. Money in circulation rose from 310 million pesos in 1911 and 316 million in 1931 to 1,060 million in 1940.[17] Meanwhile, the peso was depreciated more than 160 percent against the dollar, standing at 2.01 pesos per $1 in 1910, 2.65 pesos per $1 in 1931, and 5.19 pesos per $1 in 1939.[18]

Clearly, Mexican bank credits and printing press money would not buy foreign equipment payable in dollars or other hard currencies. This pressured Cárdenas to solicit foreign investors actively by promises of exemption from taxation.

Other domestic projects were linked to eliminating graft in Mexico and spending funds where people would be most helped, while keeping taxes low and blocking new foreign debt that might bring interference.

COMMERCIALIZATION AND UNIFICATION

Mexican commercialization had historically been centered around the major cities and the port of Veracruz, which was linked to foreign commerce. Determined to widen that sphere to encompass the entire nation, Cárdenas sought to bring both *mestizos* and native peoples into a common marketplace. He could draw upon their resources through construction of a road network leading to both rural and urban markets, but it was doubtful if he could carry out a program to stop the Indians from being exploited as peon labor and unjustly taxed.

True, laws to allow indigenes duty-free import of equipment and supplies were passed to stimulate new community enterprises able to produce for markets. And education of one million Indians to the Spanish language and another million to rely on Spanish rather than their native languages was designed to require two steps: initial education in Indian tongues to desseminate knowledge in order to then bring them into the common frame of communicating in Spanish.[19]

The government also combatted traditional practices that sapped the labor force and absorbed workers' earnings. To stop the almost universal daily inebriation of the male population, Cárdenas sought to build programs to combat the loss of lives and energy wasted by alcoholism and drunkenness linked to religious festivals and political campaigns. From marriage rites and religious functions, which demanded rum-drinking that often led to habit and addiction, to the absorption of peasant resources for liquor supplies, Cárdenas sought to apply state laws for enforced tolerance limits. Yet he realized that though the government might demand prohibition, laws to prohibit liquor sales in labor centers would be evaded wherever local sentiment ruled otherwise. Moral prescriptions did not and would not work, he discovered, unless the local population believed in the justice of the government's plan. And it remained problematic if central government planning could impact any moral realm in Mexico.

Unification of the nation also required substantial government outlays and elevated political pressure designed to control and pacify domestic and foreign opposition forces.

State controls and oversight of agricultural reform efforts involved loans to buy farm equipment and support for the *ejidos* and collective farms then making up less than 10 percent of all *ejido* farmers.

Real unification required extending infrastructure. By constructing highways that connected settlements to the outside world, Cárdenas sought to bring the Indian peoples into the marketplace. To transform Mexico, the central government financed railroads linking central and eastern Mexico, unified the Yucatán with a network of roads and drilled wells there for fresh water, and opened a national market for Yucatán chicle production used for making chewing gum.

Cárdenas built a desert road from Sonora to Baja California to Tijuana in Alta California, and he also enlarged agricultural production by redistributing *Los Angeles Times* magnate Harry Chandler's land to Mexican peasants and taking over the Colorado River delta to irrigate Mexican farm land. His plan of colonizing Baja ran into powerful opposition from British, Dutch, and U.S. oil companies, however.

"Pacification by justice" was another program designed to subdue periodic Yaqui armed revolts. New government treaties with the Yaqui nation were designed to offset the taking of Yaqui land by Mexican settlers after 1740. The government restored 880,000 acres to the Yaqui for them to plant and harvest and gave the Yaqui title to 50 percent of the water stored on the upper Yaqui River by the Angostura Dam. With this water and land, Yaqui wheat production jumped in four years from 40 tons to 5,000 tons annually.[20]

In an effort to raise urban production, labor too was finally regulated under Cárdenas programs for unity of its two battling factions, the CROM and CTM. The government had the right, with court oversight, to arrest and transport anyone guilty of internecine murder to Mexico's penal island within 48 hours of apprehension.

OIL CARTEL DEATH-HOLD FORCES CÁRDENAS TO BACKPEDAL

Unsatisfied still, the oil cartel strengthened its death-hold on the Mexican economy.

It boycotted Mexican oil, curtailed Mexican production by discouraging U.S. manufacturers from selling replacement parts for expropriated refinery tools for drilling, and blocked the sale of tetraethyl that gave Mexican-refined gasoline proper performance by eliminating engine "knock."

The oil companies also frightened tourists away from visiting Mexico; discouraged new U.S. investment capital; forced devaluation of the peso, thereby preventing Mexico from being able to pay for imported U.S. manufactures; blocked Mexican construction programs by discouraging U.S. manufacturers from exporting trucks, graders, and other equipment; and successfully lobbied the U.S. government to import large quantities of Venezuelan and Dutch-held oil owned by Standard and Shell, thereby reducing Mexican oil exports by 45 percent in the six months following expropriation.[21]

How would Mexico cope with such pressures to secure a modicum of economic self-determination and control over foreign capital?

Backpedaling and equivocating on 1 September 1939, Cárdenas called on the Mexican Congress to stimulate new capital investment:

> The Federal Government is desirous of offering to home and foreign capital interested in investing in industrialization of Mexico such advantages and exemptions as are compatible with our laws and social requirements of our Government to insure a situation of equity and justice to capital soundly invested for industrial purposes. To help such capital and the laborers that it employs, I submitted to Congress a project calling for exemption from taxation for new industries that may be established.[22]

This was still not the full concession the oil companies sought, however, as they fought to retain their holdings or failing that to receive complete compensation.

Part IV

From the Status Quo Ante to the Policy of Progress

As the military conflict in Europe, Asia, and the Pacific escalated from 1940 to 1945, directly affecting the Americas, the United States attempted to draw Canada, Latin American, and Mexico into its defensive posture.

Labor throughout Latin America took alarm, holding two great congresses in Mexico City in an effort to build its strength, unifying trade unionism, and oppose the menace of fascism. At the Latin American Trade Union convention, the Latin American Federation of Labor was formed to contribute to "the unity of the workers of the world in a single proletarian army" to fight for popular civil liberties and the rights of trade unions.

When Mexico's Lombardo Toledano was elected president of the new federation, he sought to solidify the international organization of labor to struggle economically against world wide corporate alliances.

Later, at the Mexican Workers' Confederation (CTM) world congress, Cárdenas expressed fears that the concentration of wealth and capitalism would lead to civil and imperialist wars and racialist theories. He called for a Pan-American "alliance to guarantee complete national sovereignty and assure a peace sufficiently lasting to permit development and progress."[1]

Mexico meanwhile provided sanctuary for defeated radicals and revolutionaries throughout Latin America. It built an ideological base opposing feudal serfdom and plantation bondage and supported calls for improved living standards made by people shackled by primitive techniques, ignorance, and social inequality.

Official political rhetoric about the equality of states and the need to ally against fascist aggression was also calculated to build solidarity for the term of the war. Yet after the war ended, the old relations of domination

165

and servitude were reestablished. This was particularly evident in the ways in which the United States reverted to its old maneuvers to keep Mexico in its sphere of influence.

POST-CÁRDENAS REVERSIONS

Although Cárdenas had sought to institutionalize controls by rectification of government administration, and renovation and transformation of the economic and social structure,[2] his successors reversed most of his policies.

When Cárdenas was followed to the presidency by his less liberal secretary of war, Manuel Avila Camacho, on 12 September 1940, a new era of influence by the Catholic church, the United States, and domestic capital immediately began.

The new president immediately announced himself a Catholic "believer," and Archbishop Luis María Martínez hoped for greater "freedom of conscience and religious peace." Now that Mexico's antireligious laws were no longer enforced, the clergy strongly supported the Avila administration's effort to help the Allied was effort. Fascist priests were removed from important posts, and Article 3 of the Constitution was amended to change the requirement of "socialistic education" to an emphasis on nationalism, justice, and democracy.[3]

Although the political Left also extended its cultural sway under Comintern policies promoted by Lombardo Toledano, its main influence was supporting Mexican cooperation with the Allies in entering the war against Germany in 1942 and helping to guard the U.S. southern flank against espionage or attack. The Left also acted as a counterweight against the political Right led by the *Sinarquistas*, who were linked to Nazi intrigue, clerical reaction against Protestantism, and aspirations to establish a fascist state.

The *Sinarquistas* opposed cooperation with the U.S. war effort, charged that Foreign Minister Ezequiel Padilla was a tool subservient to Washington, and tried without success to get the Mexican government to recognize Franco's fascist regime in Spain.[4]

WARTIME UNITY

During the war, Avila Camacho's so-called government of national unity was backed by all five living ex-presidents. Its domestic middle-of-the-road programs quieted popular demands, and its foreign policies ensured Mexico's subservience to the United States.

President Roosevelt's so-called Good Neighbor Policy provided cover for Mexico's swing to the political middle that lasted during the wartime cooperative venture. Production of food was secured by government subsidies, workers were insured through a new social security system, and free public school education was extended.

As the United States loaned capital to Mexico and sent technicians to raise production levels, shortages nonetheless sent prices up faster than wages, and the government was unable to enforce fixed prices it set on essential goods. It meanwhile attempted to raise production by slowing down the pace of land distribution and giving assurances to remaining landlords that there would be no nationalization, by giving the *ejidatarios* the option to till their land individually or communally, and by instituting government programs promoting mechanization, experimental stations, and technical and auxiliary aid to agriculture, irrigation, and conservation.

The government meanwhile met and quieted working-class demands. Social security was extended by law in 1943 (and amended in 1947 and 1949). It was financed by employer and employee contributions insuring employees and their dependents medical services and cash payments for illness, accident, invalidism, and old age and included death benefits.

Exhorting literate Mexicans to teach at least one person to read, the 1944 Federal Literacy Law empowered federal and local officials to reward those who complied, punish laggards, and eventually offer salaries to teachers in literacy centers. Opposed by the church, which was seeking religious education, and the *Sinarquistas*, the program actually languished for lack of reading materials, the diversion of literacy education by the exigencies of poverty, and the difficulty of making progress in rural regions where only Indian languages were spoken.[5]

The unremitting presence of Mexican poverty, inadequate food supplies, and potential social turmoil in the midst of European fascist influence put the United States on alert that Mexico was the critical link in maintaining U.S. security along the lines described in the Monroe Doctrine a century earlier.[6]

It is hardly surprising then that in 1942 the United States and Mexico signed a reciprocal agreement. The United States provided Mexico with equipment, raw materials, and food; armed Mexican military forces; and gained unlimited entrance rights to defend its territory. Mexico supplied industrial metals (copper, lead, zinc), crude oil, cotton, grains and sugar cane.

The United States was determined to stop inflationary prices for its exports by stabilizing the Mexican peso vis-à-vis the dollar, and it funded the government budget for domestic reforms by purchasing up to six million ounces monthly of newly mined Mexican silver at thirty-five cents an ounce.

United States defenses were also bolstered by agreements for reciprocal use of air bases that favored overwhelming U.S. air forces, U.S. warships were given the run of Mexican ports, and U.S. troops and planes were allowed to cross Mexican territory. With Mexico authorized to purchase lend-lease war equipment, close cooperation protected the long U.S.-Mexican exposed coast line.[7]

POSTWAR STRESS

But after the war, the recurrent theme of "nonintervention" did not always correspond to deeds.

At the 1945 Inter-American Conference on Problems of War and Peace in Mexico City, delegates restated the principles of nonintervention offered in the Declaration of Mexico: "Each State is free and sovereign, and no State may intervene in the internal or external affairs of another." International law was to guide "the rule of conduct for all States" that are considered "juridically equal."

As there was no way to enforce such international law, however, a military shield was necessary. Hence the United States again used its 1824 Monroe Doctrine as the founding principle, with Mexico and other Latin American nations as its coguardians. The conference participants recognized the need for cooperation against outside aggression in the Act of Chapultepec signed at the same time.

And, as will be detailed in later chapters, once more in pursuit of progress, the economic components of Monroe's Doctrine were put in place.

CHAPTER 8

Mexico's Historic Transformation

Struggling for its autonomy, attempting to survive under domination and pressures from more powerful nations, Mexico throughout its history has been deprived of its unrequited labor and surplus wealth, its resources and its freedom. But foreign oversight, investments, production policies, and trade prescriptions also required an infrastructure of willing servants, *compradors*, and middle agents, whose rewards in accumulated wealth defined Mexico's upper classes. After the Spanish Conquest, British and U.S. threats and an attempted French empire left their *imprimatur* on the racial complexion of the population and the composition and alliances of class and caste. The United States attempted to impose its structured sphere in Mexico and Latin America by touting the Monroe Doctrine, which was designed to keep Europeans out of the Americas. In the early twentieth century, this policy was built upon, elaborated, and changed in context, leaving an indelible mark on the face and heritage of Mexico's people.

LOOKING BACKWARDS

Turmoil following the Mexican Revolution in 1910 had led President Wilson to apply the Monroe Doctrine to secure a regime that would look favorably on U.S. investment goals and commercial interests. General Carranza seemed likely to fit the bill; he was powerfully positioned as a military man and advocated friendly Mexican ties to the United States.

Openly supporting Carranza as the next Mexican president, Wilson covertly planned to oust pro–British General Huerta and hold Pancho Villa's revolutionary forces at bay. Secretary of State Bryan cabled the U.S. diplomatic corps in Mexico on 24 November 1913: "The present policy of

169

the Government of the United States is to isolate General Huerta entirely, to cut him off from foreign sympathy and aid and from domestic credit, whether moral or material, and to force him out. . . . If General Huerta does not retire by force of circumstances, it will become the duty of the United States to use less peaceful means to put him out."[1]

By following a course to keep European nations from intervening in Central and South America, Wilson demonstrated a boldness of action that had precedent in President Theodore Roosevelt's 1905 seizure of Latin American custom treasuries to settle U.S. claims. "Chronic wrongdoing," Roosevelt insisted, "may in America, as elsewhere, ultimately require intervention by some civilized nation, and in the Western Hemisphere the adherence of the United States to the Monroe Doctrine may force the United States, however reluctantly, in flagrant cases of such wrongdoing or impotence, to the exercise of an international police power."

These earlier gunboat ploys and "big stick" policies were then practically repudiated by the 1928 Clark Memorandum and the Pan-American multilateralization of the Monroe Doctrine within the context of U.S.-inspired Dollar Diplomacy. This new policy was employed to minimize European commercial interests by encouraging U.S. investments in Latin nations. President Taft described it as "substituting dollars for bullets."

Throughout the 1930s and 1940s, the Monroe Doctrine reappeared as a U.S.-fostered Pan-Americanism; it was tightened and solidified during World War II. In 1933 Franklin D. Roosevelt had propounded its outline in the Good Neighbor Policy towards Latin America, and with the threat of expanding European fascism in 1936, Roosevelt gravely warned: "Non-American states seeking to commit acts of aggression against us will find a hemisphere wholly prepared to consult together for our mutual safety and our mutual good." Continuing the Monroe Doctrine after World War II, President Truman outlined its essence in his 1945 Navy Day speech. The U.S. Senate ratified 72 to 1, the 1947 Inter-American Treaty of Mutual Assistance (Rio Pact). It also passed the Vandenberg Resolution calling for the United States to support regional treaties in the Americas and providing for collective action by all signatory nations against an armed attack on any American nation from any quarter. This in effect "multilateralized" the Monroe Doctrine.[2] Then from the late 1950s, the United States attempted to foist its own domestic prescriptions for expanded investments, trade, and price stability on Mexico and the rest of Latin America.

During this period, U.S. domestic economic lore and foreign policy were inseparable, if not indistinguishable. Domestic programs for controlling inflation had called for state oversight of government deficits, prices, and wage rates, "to restrain public and private spending so as to keep demand from rising faster than the nation's capacity to produce" and to build up that production capacity by eliminating "unnecessary demands by government on the private sector of the economy; adoption of tax policies that promote savings and investment; avoidance of artificial restrictions on output by government, business, and labor; and improvements in the mobility of resources."[3]

And looking to the mobility of U.S. resources abroad, the United States sought to impose such standards—and austerities—on others.

ECONOMIC STAGNATION AND IMPORTING FOREIGN CAPITAL

As the United States pressed Mexico to adopt its policies, the Mexican government took the U.S. syllogism as a universal prescription to solve its own problems of supplementing sparse domestic savings (that remained after bouts of capital sent abroad) and inadequate domestic investments by encouraging the import of foreign capital.

To stimulate production, employment, and a consumer base expanding the domestic market, the new government of President López Mateos moved to stop the unbridled export of Mexican capital by the very rich, which resulted in a lack of domestic savings for investment.

"An accelerated rate of investment is needed to reach higher levels of employment and production," Mario Ramón Beteta, manager of the Banco de México, explained in 1965, adding that "since Mexico adheres to a non-inflationary policy, resources from abroad constitute a very important contribution and augment attainable goals in domestic savings. Thus, the first thing to be said is that Mexico does want foreign investment.

The door again opened as retiring President Mateos reaffirmed: "Foreign investors [can] obtain reasonable profits and are free, if they so desire, to export both profits and the amortization of their capital." And at that time, there were no Mexican exchange restrictions to stop them.[4]

Still, foreign investors remained cautious as to where and how they invested during the rest of the sixties.

The disparities of Mexico's rich and poor meanwhile became more polarized. This was a logical outcome of luxury consumption, financial speculation, and capital-flight by the Mexican upper classes; caution taken by foreign investors; and the uncertainty that the government could continue to disperse oil wealth to subsidize wealth accumulation at the expense of the population. Together these elements caused massive stagnation, unemployment, poverty, and degradation.

"The direct beneficiary was the so-called middle-class 'revolutionary' who, holding power, botched the nation's speculative finances. The ensuing collapse profoundly and fundamentally undermined development. In 1970, some 42 percent of the economically active population had monthly incomes less than 500 pesos (though the minimum daily salary was 24.51 pesos, or 735 pesos a month), while a mere 2 percent of the population received 5,000 pesos or more," documented researchers for the Centro De Investigacionnes Historicas Agrarias in the early 1970s.[5]

And as the wealthy with political influence grew richer at the expense of the lower classes, the desperate quest for new sources of wealth intensified.

THE IMPACT OF FOREIGN PRESSURES

Foreign lenders and investors meanwhile held calculations and operated under pressures of their own; those in the United States were not prepared to be outflanked by impoverished neighbor governments to the south.

After the economic crisis in North America of the mid–1960s that culminated in the 1971 U.S. devaluation of the dollar that cut off the exchange of foreign-held dollars for U.S. gold, the United States had recoiled. It attempted to stimulate its exports, its production, and its employment, and it encouraged foreign investors to enter almost all aspects of its economy. But the domestic crisis also fueled capital investments abroad by investors withdrawing from expensive, loss-ridden production in the United States for relatively higher returns elsewhere.

This had an immediate effect on countries locked into the U.S. marketplace and investment sphere. As the third largest U.S. trade partner, the entire Mexican economy was reoriented towards exchange with "El Norte." Foreign corporate lenders that for decades had impoverished Mexico would soon be transformed into "domestic" investors demanding that "nonproductive" government outlays be curtailed, infrastructure be improved, and foreign private investments once more be allowed in key industries and banking.

In the face of these demands, the hegemony of Mexico's Institutional Revolutionary party (PRI) put up little political resistance, even as a public gesture to a wary nation of peasants and workers. As pressures mounted in 1975, newly elected President López Portillo openly allied with foreign interests searching security and higher returns than were available in their own crisis-ridden economies. And under such arrangements, international loan restrictions placed on Mexico were to be overturned by the new government's economic recovery plan.

Thus, following a long line of earlier promises of recovery by Mexican presidents, the logic of foreign stabilization programs promised to cut in three directions:

1. Devaluation of the peso vis-à-vis foreign currencies, thereby cheapening exports of Mexican goods and allowing foreign investors to set up or buy out Mexican production facilities inexpensively and hire a relatively inexpensive labor force

2. Limitations on borrowing abroad to finance government operations
3. A necessary reduction in spending on social services designed to upgrade the condition of the population

Mexico had meanwhile built a negative balance of payments that was seemingly covered after 1974 by exporting newly discovered, high-priced oil reserves. But popular demands for social welfare, outflanked by the schemes of Mexico's wealthy classes, led to vast state spending programs to subsidize production and other projects that generated a gigantic government deficit that was then financed by heavy borrowing abroad.

Then in 1976, President Portillo captured the imagination of corporations north of the border through a "deflationary" exchange agreement with the International Monetary Fund (IMF): $1 billion in aid was to be followed by Mexican austerity in public expenditures, a wage freeze, and Western prescriptions to keep any pay increases below the rate of inflation, thereby ensuring declining living standards for the great majority.

In his efforts to achieve these goals, Portillo was supported by the middle and upper classes seeking to gain under the new financial legerdemain. With access to a larger proportional share of the nation's income than their place in the total population would logically justify, they saw an opportunity to ride on the coattails of the foreign interests. Foreign-induced economic stimulation, they reasoned, would fortify them to repatriate investments and savings they had earlier placed abroad for reinvestment in Mexico. Their own expanded investments in Mexico also promised them lavish returns in the short-run, but they did not foresee the roller-coaster economy that would emerge over the next two decades.

The government also made the mistake of assuming that cuts in social services would somehow be fiscally different than government increments in subsidies for industry and outlays on building an infrastructure for commercial activities. International Monetary Fund loans could be spent on such infrastructure, but the Mexican debt and the state's annual interest payments would thereby rise. While such payments put the state budget in a perennial deficit position, the stimulation to industry and trade elevated incomes of the middle and upper classes, giving them the wherewithal to improve their living standards, to make new investments in production and commercial activities, to hire more workers, fueling migration to the cities, and to employ a new "class" of small traders and a domestic servant class, mainly women. Especially in the Federal District, one study discerned a predominant tendency for the greatest immigration to be women rather than men; a predominance that explained the high proportion of domestic workers.[6]

With the promised foreign financial prop in the 1970s and early 1980s, state social services were thus undermined and Mexico's wealthiest classes got richer, enjoyed more services rendered by the poor, and again exported vast sums of capital seeking security in foreign banks and financial institutions.

THE BILL COMES HOME

The bill came home in late 1981 and early 1982, as the growing internal fiscal deficit could not be funded and the negative external balance of payments led the peso into a free fall to one-fourth its previous purchasing power. To cover accumulated costs and debts, new foreign borrowing then drove up the debt from 30 percent of Mexico's total domestic output in 1981 to 63 percent in 1983, interest on the 1982 transitional debt amounting to one-half of all Mexican export revenue.

With this debt largely denominated in U.S. dollars and held by U.S. investors, Mexico's taxpayers and workers were bled heavily on the collections side but left high and dry when it came to social services. This was in part due to the International Monetary Fund that was repeatedly tapped for loans from 1982 to 1985 and imposed its austerity programs requiring a fiscal cut in social services and a monetary policy of tight money. When these failed to rectify budgets or stimulate production in the wake of the new balance of payments crisis of mid–1985, Mexico moved powerfully to denationalize its industries and sell them off by opening the door to foreign investors, importing capital, technologies, and goods.

The financial bombshell first exploded at the end of López Portillo's presidency in 1982, as he accused the same upper classes he had deployed government policy to subsidize and aid. In his 1 September address on the state of the nation, he charged: "A group of Mexicans, led, counseled, and aided by the private banks, has taken more money out of the country than all the empires that have exploited us since the beginning of our history. . . . We cannot stand with our arms crossed while they tear out our entrails."[7]

Such public grandstanding was cleverly designed to save Portillo's reputation and to try to legitimize his exploitive regime in the public domain. For indeed, the banks had cooperated with Portillo's own government, following its policies and prescriptions and acting within its bureaucratic channels. Their role also followed earlier governments' policies, mediating Mexican wealth accumulation that favored foreign investments, stability, wage controls, and the fight against inflation—components that effectively lowered living standards for the working population, while elevating them for the middle and especially the upper classes.

Foreign investors had meanwhile been actively encouraged by the *maquiladora* assembly plant program that began in the mid–1960s and was enlarged as a series of peso devaluations in the 1980s widened the wage gap between Mexican and U.S. labor. By the end of 1990 there were about

2,000 *maquilas* that employed half a million workers comprising about 20 percent of the total Mexican manufacturing work force.[8] By 1995 3,200 *maquilas* were U.S.-owned.

Appeals for foreign investments brought forth not only more *maquilas* along the U.S.-Mexican border, but the growth of populations on both sides.

Agressive and often avaricious employment policies at first kept wages low, labor risks high, and pollution massive, as the condition of production and urbanization jeopardized both the natural environment and the population's health. Expert Robert A. Pastor had documented this problem:

> The new industrialization overtaxes a thin infrastructure and generated numerous health hazards stemming from improper or inadequate waste treatment of air or water pollution. The National Wildlife Federation identified the border pollution issue as its highest priority in U.S.-Mexican environmental relations, and the data support that conclusion. At Nuevo Laredo-Laredo, 25 million gallons of raw sewage flow into the Rio Grande every day. Contamination levels are 1,650 times greater than those considered safe for recreational use. In San Elizario, Texas, where a shared aquifer has been contaminated, 35 percent of the children contract hepatitis A by age eight, and 90 percent of adults have had it by the age of thirty-five. Numerous reports confirm the multitude of health and environmental problems in the region.[9]

TRADE, DEBT, AND INDUSTRIALIZATION

How had Mexico reached the dual depths of financial servitude and human degradation?

Clearly the quarter century from 1950 to 1974 had offered breathing space for Mexico to erect trade barriers blocking out competitive goods, to fuel rapid industrialization, to secure a respectable 3 to 4 percent annual per capita growth rate that outran the nation's 3 percent annual inflation.

But such industrialization was sustained by imported technologies, as Mexico constructed rudimentary machines at best, and these imported means of production eventually drove the nation's balance of payments deep into the red.

It superficially appeared that Mexico could pay for its post–1974 negative balance by exporting newly discovered high-priced oil reserves. But new demands for popular social spending and business subsidies drilled a hole in the government's fiscal bucket—only refilled by heavy borrowing abroad.

These programs dovetailed with imports of foreign technologies as part of nationalist efforts to restructure Mexican industries begun in earnest under President de la Madrid in mid–1985. By systematically changing laws, transforming economic institutions, and developing new national priorities, his government brought in massive sums of foreign capital and imposed the austerity programs demanded by the World Bank and International Monetary Fund.[10]

Restructuring was then consolidated by President Salinas de Gortari from 1988 to 1994, ensuring that centralized government would sell off state-owned industries to reduce the government's role in the economy. The door was also opened for foreign investments and imported foreign capital. It was expected that production would rise sharply and be secured by the state, that Mexican exports would soon become competitive, and that trade with the United States would expand. As a result, more Mexican peasants would be forced and drawn from the land into the urban domain to swell the growing oversupply of labor being employed at low wages.

PROGRAMS, AUSTERITY, AND PROTEST

As these forces converged, Mexico steadily lifted trade and investment barriers to foreigners.

With PRI-union complicty, privatized national industries laid off thousands of workers with inadequate severance pay. The government extended the free-trade zone along the U.S.-Mexican border. Congress changed Article 27 of the constitution to allow the free sale of once-inalienable communal lands. The government raised university tuition, promoted privatized education, and infringed on the land rights of, and public assistance for, small-scale farmers who were forced out by the quickened outreach of the tourist industry, which earned foreign exchange.

The results were disastrous for the population. The *maquilas* presented dangers to both labor and the environment. Real wages fell approximately 60 percent from the start of 1982 to January 1993. Low agricultural prices depressed the rural economy, forcing thousands to seek refuge in already overcrowded city slums or to cross into the United States. And the government thumbed its nose at upward mobility for the younger generation, promoting instead education biased toward the upper classes.

As the impoverished resisted, their movement rocked Mexico City. Students protested the loss of educational opportunities. Barrio committees galvanized urban resistance, independent labor unions entered bastions of PRI support, and peasant coalitions challenged the PRI's withdrawal of support for small agricultural producers.

These protests in turn led to government repression and extensive violations of human rights—interrogations, torture, "disappearances" of activists. Repression then led to the defensive formation of more than fifty rural and local human rights groups, the most important being the Mexican Commission for the Defense and Promotion of Human Rights under the directorship of Mariclaire Acosta, whose mission was to stop the abuse and repression of Mexico's displaced and impoverished.

"Right now the government is ... reaffirming its authoritarian tendency; society ... is reaffirming its democratic tendencies," Acosta emphasized in early 1993. Given "the interconnected relationship between the [leadership of the] unions, the PRI, the police, and the attorney general," he said, human rights work was very difficult. "The same thing happens with land disputes in the countryside. .... If there is a conflict over land, the landowners hire gunmen to kill the peasant leaders. Generally, local land reform officials support the landowners, and the attorney general ends up protecting the gunmen."

Ruling Mexico for over fifty years with the world's most sophisticated mix of patronage, co-optation, and repression, the PRI was notorious in other ways, too. It engaged in election fraud, quieting most opponents, though not Cuauhtemoc Cárdenas, the leader of the Democratic Revolutionary party, who may have been the real winner of the 1988 presidential election.[11]

THE CHURCH-STATE ALLIANCE REAPPEARS

The controlling hand of the nation's past still weighed heavily on the present in constructing a new social order. Even if fair elections could be had, Mexico's millions would remain locked in place, in part because of the control and exploitation wielded jointly by church and state.

The repressive methods of the church/state alliance kept reappearing throughout Mexico's history, and this alliance resurrected in the early 1990s.

From the sixteenth century Spanish Conquest and Inquisition to the revocation of the vast power of the Catholic church by the severing of Mexico's ties to the Holy See from 1856 to 1861, the question of church ideological and material domination had seized the nation. The dictator Por- firio Díaz had reinstated some church prerogatives, and even after his overthrow in the 1910 Revolution, Pope and Holy See surreptitiously maintained surveillance over the Mexican church, exchanging temporary and lower-echelon envoys.

Despite laws prohibiting any extension of its powers, in practice the church accumulated vast holdings of property, conducted religious education, and sent its priests and nuns into the streets in their clerical dress to proselytize and influence the population and government. From peasants to government officials, Catholic rituals seeped into everyday life, becoming part of the educational apparatus as parochial schools proliferated, inbuing the many with Catholic beliefs and liturgy.

Not satisfied that 97 percent of Mexicans identified themselves as Roman Catholic, the church sought an overwhelming hold on popular awareness. In the early 1990s, the *papal nuncio* saw a political opening in the government yearning for enhanced central controls, and he pressured the state authorities to reestablish full ties with the Vatican, to again allow the church to own property without restriction, to permit religious education in the public schools that comprised 95 percent of all Mexican educational institutions, and to allow the *nuncio* to compete for public consciousness by operating radio and television stations.

Seeking the advantages of church backing for its own programs leveraged on popular compliance to ascetic prescriptions for work and tranquility, the government of President Carlos Salinas de Gortari proposed changes that had been taken away after the 1910 Revolution. Quickly approved by the conservative PRI-controlled congress in July 1992, the Salinas measures awarded the church clearly defined legal status as well as the right to own property and to conduct religious education. Mexico was thus thrown back to the mid-nineteenth century.

With the legal path cleared of impediments, the church immediately mobilized its resources. Its priests and nuns again openly proselytized in public in clerical dress, and the church again pressed the population into its catechism, called on Catholics to cherish the family and strictly observe the traditional acts of faith, and loudly complained that the government itself lay in a bed of immorality, abusing its power by carring on AIDS education, distributing contraceptive devices, and encouraging sexual promiscuity.

Had church and state again allied pursuing a new *acto de fe*, empowered to centrally direct the nation's destiny, impose narrow, skewed solutions, and ride roughshod over popular rights? In one sense, Catholic asceticism joined to state policies to reorganize the economy and control work and tranquility held potential for a throwback to the days of the Díaz dictatorship. In his time, the despot Díaz had undermined democratic rights, empowered the church, raided the nation's wealth, invited foreign interests to exploit resources, directed industry, built railroads with peonage labor, and everywhere ravaged the peasantry and meagerly paid workforce. Almost eight decades later, the new Salinas government drew powerfully on these precedents, rewriting Mexican history texts for the public schools to emphasize Mexico's development and modernization under Díaz. It regimented the workforce, attacked the revolutionary changes in land-tenure brought on by Mexican folk hero Emiliano Zapata, and proceeded to change landholding laws to return the soil to *hacienda* and corporate *latifundia*.

THE NEW ORDER OF NATIONALIST PRIORITIES: RESTRUCTURING PRODUCTION AND NEOMERCANTILISM

Thus emerged the Mexican government's frame for a new order of national priorities that would promote domestic reorganization of essential infrastructure and upgrade the conditions, means, and relations of production through tightened economic ties with the United States.

Pressures in both nations had converged, moreover, to batter down the remaining economic and social barriers structured by the politics of the U.S.-Mexican border. North of the Rio Grande, U.S. industrial decay, unemployment, failing infrastructures, rising immigration of unskilled cheap workers, and lawlessness had increased both the cost of production and government-financed social services and education. Relatively higher U.S. wages had also sent thousands of U.S. companies to Mexico, which led to U.S.-inspired investments and employment, an explosive growth of Mexico's northern and middle regions, a vast migration from south to north, and hitherto unknown levels of wage employment and urbanization. All this was accompanied by crime, corruption, and drug smuggling within Mexico and across the northern border.

Industrial policy from the United States also bred restructuring of production and the renewal of neomercantilism. Striving for a policy to shore up its own triple-threat deficit in government accounts, national debt, and foreign trade, the United States quieted domestic conflict and discord by shifting a portion of the burdens to the Mexican population, and this widened the cleavage between Mexico's upper and lower classes. As the United States imposed its industrial solutions on Mexico, what appeared to be the latter's revolutionary reorganization of its economy was in fact transformation directed from Washington and Wall Street, Detroit and the Silicon Valley.

How, though, could the United States swing its deficits south of the border?

Facing their own inefficiencies in domestic industrial production using outdated technologies, industrial managers reasoned that U.S. technological renewal would displace old skilled tasks, introduce new functions performed by specialized labor, and lead to a fall in overall wage outlays while increasing the average wage of those still at work. Such a highly skilled labor elite would function with better pay and also act as a permanent wedge separating themselves from the industrially displaced, unemployed, underemployed, and low-wage workers in the expanding service industries.

United States production could then concentrate on both high-tech machines and competitive manufactures emerging from the Cyclops of its own Third Industrial Revolution. This would be made possible in part by Mexican industry's transformation into an ancillary production center for lower-level, technical manufactures flowing from its *hornos* of the first and second industrial revolutions. These products would be targeted for export to the United States or third markets and would facilitate a two-way neomercantile relation.

A new division of labor was thus envisioned. Elevating its own techno-logical production at home, the United States concentrated on the output of the most up-to-date means of production which could then be exported to Mexico, redesigning its industrial structure and thereby changing the skill level of both the U.S. and Mexican workforce. And in its restructuring of Mexican industry, the United States concentrated Mexican manufac-tures of consumer goods and machine tools into certain areas, promoting urbanization and labor migration within Mexico and changing the food, water, housing, sewage, medical, and other needs of Mexico's population impacted in the urban domain. The United States thereby extended the commercial system that delivered the means of life in an exchange economy based on access to money, thus making both wage and salaried work a necessity for urban family survival.

The future was clear, too, because once such needs for essentials and labor were transformed, an industrial workforce would be more malleable to direction by both foreign and Mexican managers. Yet this draw of workers to industry would also mean a periodically unemployed flotsam that would generally be in excess of employer demands and thus in need of government social services that, due to fiscal shortages, did not yet and might never exist.

Without doubt, more Mexicans would be employed at wages, acting as the power source for producing Mexican goods for export markets, and, as consumers, they would constitute an extended domestic market. Initial trade imbalances would turn positive in the short term with devaluations fueling a Mexican surge in cheap exports, yet probably become perennial deficits as Mexico became an importer of high-priced machinery and in-dustrial component materials and an exporter of more and more lower-priced manufactures and raw materials to offset imports.

Mexico's restructuring of its system of production and mercantile rela-tions would thereby net a long run trade surplus for the United States that would be offset by foreign loans and the export of U.S. direct investment capital to Mexico.

It is not hard to picture the role of U.S. corporate investors in restruc-turing the Mexican economy in the mid–1990s and building their own in-dustrial base in Mexico. These corporations would import machines, other technologies, industrial supplies, and managerial expertise. They would try to control the lion's share of factories in Mexico and would lobby vigor-ously for a wider free trade zone without tariffs or other barriers between Mexico, the United States, Canada, and the rest of the Americas and Caribbean. They would try to extend their Mexican domain by shifting towards investments in banking, shipping, insurance, storage, and com-mercial services. And they would try to ensure that the upper classes in

Mexico cooperated by seeing to it that they shared in the benefits of the reorganization of both the economy and the state.

In fact, these objectives were being initiated by the Mexican government's reorientation of economic life under presidents de la Madrid and Salinas de Gortari from 1982 to 1994. During these 12 years, the state provided subsidies to industry, continued to sell the nation's resources to cover its deficits and pay foreign loans with interest, and devalued the peso, stimulating commodity exports produced with inexpensive Mexican labor and thereby also cheapening the cost of new foreign investments placed in Mexico. The government also cut social services, eliminated barriers to imports of more foreign goods and investment capital, denationalized Mexican means of production and banking, impoverished Mexican labor as real wages plummeted, and proposed and ultimately negotiated a free-trade treaty with the United States and Canada to create stability that would ensure the import of foreign technology, capital, grain, and manufactures.

The plan to bring Mexico into a wider commercial sphere for the unhindered movement of goods, capital, technology — and possibly labor — was being implemented.

THE NORTHERN DUMPING GROUND

Stimulating Mexican output, employment, and commerce also dovetailed with the logic of using Mexico as a dumping ground for polluting U.S. and Canadian industries.

The U.S. government sought to aid U.S. companies seeking to lower costs by investing in Mexico. Knowing that weak enforcement of Mexican environmental laws offered U.S. corporations a competitive advantage over higher-cost firms saddled with more stringent enforcement by U.S. environmental regulators, the U.S. administration chose not to address adequately the growing tension between environmental and trade issues in negotiating the North American Free Trade Agreement (NAFTA).

Mexican officials rationalized that the resulting enlargement of production, wealth accumulation, and new government tax revenues would award the nation funds to monitor and enforce its environmental laws. But regardless of any provisions in the agreement to prevent local officials from weakening environmental rules to attract new U.S. capital to operate factories, comparable rules in the United States, Canada, and Mexico, even though passed, would still not be uniformly enforced, while disputed questions would probably be decided by international negotiators effectively permitting greater pollution levels in Mexico. In addition, neither the U.S. administration nor the Mexican government had allocated sufficient budgetary resources to clean up industrial pollution along the 2,000-mile U.S.-Mexican border, where U.S. companies continued to build twin plants on both sides. The producers on the Mexican side used dangerous raw chemicals and other toxic substances without restrictions, exceeding U.S. safety standards in exposing both workers and the environment, and they also lacked modern sewage and waste treatment systems.

Further U.S. investments in Mexico would likely spell additional pollution, too, and burdened by a gigantic foreign debt that the United States used as a lever to extract Mexican concessions, the Mexican government had to either wink at the weakened provisions covering environmental standards or prepare the internal framework for a new expansion of large-scale, environmentally safe production.

How Mexico's Upper Classes Accumulate Wealth

On its side, Mexico pursued NAFTA with biases favoring its wealthiest citizens.

Past extractions from the state budget, natural resources, bank funds, international loan balances, and foreign exchange accounts had advanced the aggrandizement of wealth by Mexico's upper classes, impoverishing the nation and its underclasses. As a continuum, the Salinas government encouraged foreign investment capital to stimulate manufacturing for export as the basis to earn foreign exchange to pay for both expensive imports and past debts.

The future for accumulation was heralded by a global banking network holding the Mexican debt and negotiating high interest rates and substantial fees. Foreign and domestic industrialists also planned lucrative returns on Mexican production. Importers of technology and consumer goods looked for profitable margins, and consumers with means had access to luxury goods and other items Mexico did not produce.

The underlying source of this wealth accumulation and access to imports was the unheralded mortgaged labor of the Mexican peasantry and the various segments of the working class. But their exploitation and immiserization remained unrecorded in the grand drama of government expenditures outrunning revenues, the state sale of oil and other natural resources to cover fiscal and trade deficits, the nationalization and later denationalization of corporate banks, the government control of foreign exchange, and ever-new appeals to foreign lenders and investors to again risk new capital to pay off or prop up old bad loans and initiate production in developing the nation.

Accumulation by the upper classes was actually a function of several convergent factors that together elaborated the parasitic absorption of revenues from the nation: (1) exorbitant interest rates on treasury borrowed funds, (2) the government tax on land and labor, (3) high rents on tenant farms and real property, (4) the low price paid peasants for their produce and workers for their effort, and (5) the high market price demanded for everything else.

The state acted as medium, able to control living standards by compressing both peasantry and workers between the bureaucratic enforcement of low farm prices and low wages on one side and, on the other, the regime of high interest charges, taxes, rent, and prices. And control by the PRI ruling party as the basis of government policy became the formulated way in which the upper classes ruled the nation and drained the population of its labor and wealth.

Government policy was usually expressed through statistical expressions of good or evil. Eager to reflect the beneficial ways in which revenues were spent, conservative-minded government bureaucrats ensured that most expenditures supported an infrastructure accommodating the banking, commercial, and industrial purposes of investors and financiers. Popular demands for social services were politically reaffirmed, but cautious government finance ministers generally found it impossible to finance these services sufficiently in their deficit-ridden budgetary calculations. And thus the need for state austerity in social expenditures accompanied dire predictions about the consequent raiding of revenues. The next revenue source after the state budget absorbed billions in oil revenues would be the capital of the banks; then the state would have to resort to promises to foreign lenders for repayment from future oil revenues. Still later, U.S. short-term financial investor loans to Mexican industries would be necessary, thereafter foreign investors' *maquilas* and their extension under the North American Free Trade Agreement would help provide revenue, and renewed devaluations and foreign loans would keep Mexico both solvent and politically compliant.[12]

THE NEW SCALE OF WEALTH-TAKING

The Mexican population was clearly being confronted by a new scale of wealth-taking and profit absorption; foreign interests and the nation's elite were supporting an industrial policy under the centralized, dictatorial state that passed itself off as a democracy.

By the early 1990s, such *democrátia-burguesa* (bourgeois democracy) was being depicted by the government as the culmination of earlier popular struggles for liberty, land, bread, equity, and social freedoms. But under the PRI's authority over both executive and the bicameral congress, the government's priorities were clearly directed towards initial economic change that awarded skewed benefits favoring the rich; only later were promised democratic institutions to appear.[13]

This further confounded the status of Mexico's past accomplishments. Initially, the independence secured in the Constitution of 1810 had proclaimed the liberty and equality of all, abolishing the caste system affecting 16 distinct groups. *Criollos* and *mestizos* had assumed power as "la burguesía." Yet the communal territory of the native peoples had already been appropriated by the church and landlords or sold to foreign capital interests. So the constitutional declaration of all as juridically equal was not able to concede that the "indios" had a special, proprietary right to the land—once more making them unequal before the very law that had declared them equals.[14]

Short of a new revolution redistributing the land and equalizing wealth accumulations, almost one hundred and eighty years later the chasm in Mexican wealth and poverty remained vast and seemingly unbridgeable. Yet the upper classes and agents of government, viewing the revolution as complete, sought to depopulate the land and further skew the distribution of wealth.[15]

Even the revolutionary art of the great muralists was mobilized in the name of commercial progress at Mexico's international trade center—the Polyforum Cultural Siqueiros. In "The March of Humanity Until the Stage of the Democratic-bourgeois Revolution," the Center's curator Manuel Suárez y Suárez interpreted the stages of Mexico's brutal history as depicted by the murals of the famous Communist artist Siqueiros. Suárez y Suárez viewed them as the apogee of the quest for freedom and democracy.[16]

The core of such democracy was now seen linked to state-stimulated, domestic industrialization and foreign investments, with the showcase of such investments viewed as the development and reorganization of the two largest production centers, Monterrey and Mexico City. Branching from the urban domain, billions of dollars and trillions of pesos were to be invested in preparation for the unhindered movement of goods, capital and, eventually, labor between Mexico and the United States.

THE NEW ORDER AND COMMERCIAL SPHERE

With class distinctions and skewed rewards shockingly apparent, the new order would not emerge painlessly, though the 1990s would continue the reorganization and thorough transformation of Mexican society.

The historic conjuncture of the Mexican upper classes seeking new sources of revenue with the need of U.S. manufacturers, lenders, and investors for markets, resources, and inexpensive labor had led to the formation of a free-trade area for members only. Mexico had reached its outer limits. The government budgetary deficit could not be rectified by the sale of oil and other state-owned resources and assets. And Mexico could no longer borrow on future oil revenues and trade. The foreign trade account was also in deficit, as imports of high-price technologies and manufactures exceeded low-price Mexican exports. And Mexican manufactured goods were not yet competitive on world markets, while oil and raw material prices had fallen.

True enough, the accelerated sale of oil and other raw materials and resources might create a positive trade balance if world market prices ever recovered. The sale of industrial assets and denationalized banks to foreign investors could also offset the existing negative balance of trade, though that too would not provide a long-term financial boost. Periodic peso devaluations would cheapen exports in the short term. But only the unhindered movement of all material resources, capital, and future populations might reverse the long-term negative commercial account held with the other half of North America. This would have to be based, however, on a free-trade pact for members only and a future common market for the unfettered movement of goods, capital *and* labor with the United States and, to a lesser degree, Canada.

The United States was also in need of free trade with Mexico and an open door for investments there. As still-unpaid U.S. traders, lenders, and investors searched for a means to recoup the debts Mexico already owed and would incur beyond its ability to pay during the rest of the twentieth century, the obvious means was to facilitate the employment of its relatively cheap labor, the sale of its low-priced manufactures, and the use of its resources, arable land, mines, and factories. "The only things Mexico can offer the NAFTA are cheap labor, raw materials, manufactured goods with low aggregate value, such as [those made in the] *maquilas*, and capital," Cuauhtemoc Cárdenas explained in July 1993. "Mexico will continue to contribute capital in two ways: payment on our debt and investment abroad. As a consequence, NAFTA could mean greater concessions in political and economic decisions: not only to expand economic sectors now open to the international market, but also to open sectors such as oil and fundamental services."[17] These sources of revenue could be both facilitated and accelerated if there were no barriers to the free flow of goods, technology, know-how, investments, and labor. The United States thus pressured the Mexican government to negotiate the North American Free Trade Agreement that was finally signed in 1992 and approved by the Congress in December 1993.

Beyond NAFTA, the United States sought to extend the open door for investments and trade preferences to all the American states, to restructure and spatially relocate U.S. capital and trade for member nations at the expense of nonmembers. Just as NAFTA was designed to restructure production and alter trade patterns by linking Mexican, Canadian, and U.S. industrial policy, a grand alliance of the 11 American states would forward the continental division of labor, trade, and wealth.

Thus the United States sought a preferential trade zone that would liquidate earlier preferential agreements, replace them with a Caribbean and continental free-trade agreement from Anchorage to Tierra del Fuego, manage trade between member nations, and focus 90 percent of all increased exports on Mexico and Brazil.

Nothing less than a U.S. sphere of influence was envisioned.

CHAPTER 9

The Policy of Progress
I: The Lost Half-Century, 1940–94

The quest for freedom and technical progress are the two standard bearers of Mexican history that have brought the nation both independence and subjugation.

After the sixteenth century conquest of Indian Mexico, the country later succumbed to master nations and classes that switched the mantle of domination. This pattern was finally reversed by independence, attempted reform, and revolution. But only five centuries later in the Cárdenas era was any semblance of economic independence achieved, with a program to ensure justice for the Indian population. And even this beginning was overturned at the hands of the United States and Mexico's own upper classes, who were pursuing material benefits for themselves in the name of progress.

As Mexico suffered reconquest from an oligarchy within and powerful interests abroad, not even its vast oil resources could economically free it of the hold of its overarching northern neighbor. "El Norte" dominated significant portions of Mexico's production, labor force, and commerce. In the name of progress beholden to scientific knowledge, technological advance, industrial development, and oil extraction, Mexico and its 90 million people were further uprooted from the rural domain. The traditional beliefs, mores, and cultures of 10 million Indians were nearly decimated and their lives were further impoverished in innumerable ways. With the rest of the nation's 80 million workers, they were either suspended as a superfluous force between country and city or in part proletarianized, in part immiserizated, at the hands of Mexico's already wealthy classes and the foreign interests seeking to accumulate without end.

PROGRESS: URBAN HEGEMONY, NATIONAL
OLIGARCHY, AND FOREIGN INFLUENCE

Progreso, adelanto, marcha—these are the words historically fixed in the minds and tracts of Mexico's leaders as a road map to the future. Progress by equitable deeds, protection for the natural world, and the accretion of benefits for Mexico's peoples were elevated standards, that were articulated most clearly in the Cárdenas era.

But in the name of anointed progress, Mexico and its people were significantly degraded in the following half-century. This was partly due to the lucrative alliances Mexico's upper classes made with the foreign interests to extract the nation's subterranean resources. But it was also the result of dubious government measures promising advances in the economic realm, measures that imposed extreme environmental stress and mass privation, impoverishing most Mexicans and reducing their station in life. The great majority were forced onto a treadmill that led from landlessness and idleness to urbanization; to harder work and lower real wages for some; to human redundancy, unused labor, and uselessness for others; and, for most, to new forms of immiserization in both rural and urban domains.

Progress Mexican style had thus placed the nation in the throes of urban hegemony; the rural flow of surplus populations was partly absorbed in filling the empty spaces of the first industrial revolution. As this rural labor flow grew, however, and as new technologies simplifying manufacturing functions displaced a portion of the old industrial workforce, those jobless and desperate to work at ever-lower wages threatened to displace union labor, thereby weakening demands for higher real wages and job security.

In its urban employed and unemployed wings and in the rural domain, labor became and remained a captive of Mexico's national oligarchy, which in turn controlled land and capital, the major parties, the state, its civil and military infrastructure and departments, its bureaucracies and their link to unionized labor and rural organizations.

Thus controlled, labor had few opportunities for independent expression or action. Urban populations could not return to the land as owners, but only as an army of landless in renewed peonage. City workers, idle and displaced, could vie to work as day laborers at an ever-lower scale, but as they too were forced below subsistence, the quest for a decent life drove them into desperation, semilegal trade, crime, and attempts to cross the U.S. border for work, higher wages, and security. Even in the United States, though, their labor was mediated by degrees of bondage—their hue and features marked them for discrimination, the lowest pay available, and the harshest working conditions.[1]

True, their captivity in the U.S. at the hands of employers extracting maximum work at minimum wages was often a step above their lowly place in Mexico. Yet in both domains they created a vast source of wealth for those for whom they labored.

How Mexico Was Lost to Already Wealthy Classes

Progress Mexican style had another side, too.

The consolidation of Mexico's ownership and political power centers had been speeded by the post–1940 federal administrations of look-alike presidents emerging from the Institutional Revolutionary Party (PRI). With the national bourgeoisie in solid control of the PRI, the party remained at the political center shaping the programs of successive governments. Each administration supported the dominant economic forces linked to the foreign interests and urged the nation to lift itself, to progress economically. "Progress" became the post–World War II byword for Mexico's zealous state programs that supported technical production and attempted to reach beyond the nation's neocolonial position as a raw material and oil supplier to foreign interests and beyond its own first-stage industrial revolution.

Mexico was still unable to manufacture the critical technology that would fuel such growth in first stage manufacturing of consumer goods like textiles and second stage processing of steel and oil refining, however. The country remained highly dependent on the United States for capital goods and other manufactures. Some 80 percent of Mexican imports were machinery, chemicals, or semiprocessed manufactures produced in the United States. And as Mexico became the leading U.S. customer in Latin America, ranking sixth among all nations buying U.S.-made goods, it found itself unable to cover its rising machine and manufacturing import bill by the simple export of Mexican raw materials that suffered declining prices in the two decade period 1968-88.[2]

As Mexico's negative balance of trade was generated along this two-way street, Mexico became more dependent on the United States than the latter was on Mexico. Mexico sent 69 percent of its exports to the United States and bought 64 percent of all its imported goods from U.S. sources; the far larger U.S. economy exported to Mexico only 5 percent of its total exports in 1981.[3] To pay its perennial negative trade balance, Mexico had then borrowed abroad, increasing the government debt to both U.S. and international banking agencies.

This pattern momentarily changed between 1981 and 1983 because of an emergent global oil glut in 1981 that led to a sharp drop in petroleum prices. Mexico's shortfall in foreign exchange earnings led to devaluation, and the consequent domestic economic crash in autumn 1982 caused a sharp drop in Mexican imports and a decline of net capital inflow that undercut the financing of its current account deficit. To pay interest on accumulated debt, Mexico had to increase exports beyond imports to earn dollars.

As the United States still accounted for about two-thirds of Mexico's trade, the trade balance switch from a 1981-83 Mexican deficit of $3.8 billion to a surplus of $13.8 billion meant the United States owed Mexico the balance.[4] What appeared to be the liberation of the Mexican trade balance from foreign controls, then, was in reality a mark of the nation's deeper focus on domestic production for export to meet standards set abroad.

This not only allowed Mexico to pay the service charges on its international loans, but to reduce the loan balance itself, thereby bolstering its self-image as an independent nation. Yet even this proved to be a momentary illusion fostered by the government's program for economic progress.

PROGRESS AND THE ROLE OF GOVERNMENT

Mexico's domestic expansion had been continually bootstrapped by the government policy of keeping the peso stable vis-à-vis the dollar and subsidizing industry, which led to a rapid rise in production and work for the urban populations.

As the center of industry and commerce, the urban domain drew people off the land. In the thirty years from 1940 to 1970, the population had enlarged more than two-and-a-half times from 20 million to over 50 million. In 1940, 65 percent of the population lived in the countryside, but less than 50 percent remained there in 1970. By the 1970s, more than half of all Mexicans lived in urban centers of more than 2,500 inhabitants and worked in industry, commercial and financial fields, as well as in transport, communications, and services.[5]

Imposing social tranquility, the government had meanwhile fueled economic expansion by various protective measures as well as through generous state subsidies taking the form of low taxes on domestic and foreign-owned production facilities, profits, and interest income.

Government programs that supposedly provided a nationalist shield against foreign manufactures were more posturing than real, though. During the 1950s, the government imposed high tariffs and licensing on certain imports in order to stimulate the growth of Mexican manufacturers supported by their foreign partners. Domestic licensing that restricted competition also gave larger companies an advantage, and investment of domestic and foreign capital was further enlarged by tax exemptions, rebate of duties on imported manufacturing machinery and materials, low-interest credit to entrepreneurs, and the government-bank (*Nacional Financiera*) guarantees of low-cost foreign loans channeled into private business.[6]

Other government programs openly aided the ventures of the upper classes. While state-produced electricity and oil and state-owned transport and communication services were sold at low prices to the industrial sector, government officials offered tax relief to those at the higher reach. Under the mid–1970s tax reforms, three-quarters of Mexico's upper class paid no taxes at all, and the aspiring salaried middle classes shouldered the brunt. Government deficiencies in revenue were made up by a 44-fold rise in borrowing abroad ($1.8 billion in the 1960s, but $80 billion by 1982), which had already become the main prop of economic growth by the late 1960s.[7]

As the state pursued a strategy of awarding the greatest benefits of economic growth to the business classes investing capital, the latter were able to hold wages below rising living costs, take profits for reinvestment, and expand their industrial base, eventually extending employment and the production of goods to be sold to a wider reach of consumers.

THE MAIN BENEFICIARIES OF PROGRESS

The main beneficiaries of the first wave of technological production emerged as both agriculture and industry expanded their output over the thirty years 1940–70. Those reaching working age fueled Mexico's steady economic growth, which averaged almost 6.5 percent a year. The second wave of technically advanced production from 1971 to 1995 made the urban domain the core of accumulation by those possessed of capital, proletarianized more than half the population, and brought Mexico to the doorstep of producing the machines that would initiate its second industrial revolution.

Yet in both periods, the benefits of expansion did not go to labor, as wages were frozen, prices rose, and the government emphasized outlays for the infrastructure it considered essential for efficient production, marketing, and private accumulation. This left little budgetary resources for public welfare and service, which together amounted to less than 15 percent throughout the 1940s and 1950s and only 13 percent in 1980.[8]

The logic of extended industrialization fulfilled itself most completely in the two great metropolises, Monterrey and Mexico City, where concentrated, private capital in *Sociedad Anonima Constituida* (SACV) constituting 61 percent of the nation's total empowered finance and big business to shape the economies and policies of the states of Nuevo León, México, and the Federal District. In the economic upsurge, Monterrey corporations raised Nuevo León's share of the nation's corporate value from about 20 percent (7.080 billion pesos out of the nation's 35.477 billion) in 1980 to 38 percent (31.277 billion pesos out of the nation's 81.634 billion pesos) in 1985. Reflecting Mexico City's relative corporate share, the Federal District (11.141 billion of 35.477 billion in 1980, but 6.990 of 81.634 billion in 1985) and the state of México (1.312 billion in 1980 and 11.354 billion in 1985) together accounted for 35 percent of the nation's total corporate value in 1980, but only 22 percent in 1985.[9]

As Monterrey changed places with Mexico City as the command center in consolidating national corporate matters, future politics would see the sharply changing politics and the weakening of the Institutional Revolutionary party (PRI), the strong influence of the Monterrey-centered National Action party (PAN), the merging programmatic lines of both these parties in advocating unfettered foreign investments and free trade with the United States, and the weakening opposition of the left-of-center party of the Democratic Revolution (PRD).[10] Both the PRI and the PAN would probably be driven further to the center to advocate the consolidation of the national economy, full employment of the population, and uplifting of the destitute. Such "proletarianization" of the vast majority was designed to place Mexico in the front ranks of Latin America's first-stage industrial revolution.

Beginning in 1945, for the next 50 years Mexico had progressed to the point where the great industrial employers were positioned to absorb three flows of surplus wealth: one from government subsidies and state-financed infrastructure, a second from the difference between wages paid and the value of goods the workers created, and the third from the difference between the value of these goods and the higher prices charged consumers. As the employed workforce constituted the primary consuming class in Mexico's internal market, the overlapping relations of production and consumption meant the benefits taken by the employers determined the size of the fund for real wages, setting the workers' long-term downward mobility.

It is not surprising that industrial profits rose rapidly, increasing the income disparity between rich and poor in little more than two decades, with the richest 5 percent receiving incomes 22 times those of the poorest 10 percent in 1958, but 50 times greater by 1980 and an estimated 150 times greater by 1994.[11]

As the economy had expanded and the commercial sphere became the fulcrum for upscale living standards, the classes making up the upper 60 percent of the population became the main beneficiaries of the increased flow of income. While the bottom 20 percent of the population lost standing in their share of national income between 1950 and 1977, the next 20 percent of the population was able to tread water and retain their small share, and the upper 5 percent lost a small proportion of the annual flow of nation income, but not their accumulated wealth.

Wrenching poverty continued for the lower 40 percent of the Mexican population for the entire 50-year period 1945 to 1994.[12] And even for the economically active population age 12 or over, monthly incomes below subsistence were the lot of most of those living in the southern states. While the economically active Federal District, Baja California, Baja California Sur, Nuevo León, and the northern regions bordering the enlarging dollar-based economy had proportionally fewer lower-income populations, ranking after the Yucatán, the nation's poorest people with the highest proportion of dismal incomes were found in the five-state zone of Puebla,

Tlaxcala, Veracruz, Hidalgo, and San Luis Potosí. And the west, south, and southwest also held many other states of low-income populations.

Using monthly incomes of less than 1,081 pesos as the poverty line in 1980 (compared with 6,610 pesos as a moderate monthly income), the proportion of low-income populations to those economically active was 21.13 percent in the Yucatán, 18.42 percent in Hidalgo, 15.28 percent in Puebla, 13.41 percent in Oaxaca, 12.79 percent in Tlaxcala, 12.66 percent in Veracruz, 12.65 percent in San Luis Potosí, 11.54 in Guerrero, 11.13 percent in Michoacán, 10.81 percent in Chiapas, 10.22 percent in Campeche, 10.08 percent in Guanajuato, 9.95 in Zacatecas, 9.11 percent in Morelos, 9.06 in Querétaro, 8.80 percent in Quintana Roo, 8.74 percent in Durango, 8.72 percent in Tabasco, and 8.63 percent in Nayarit; there were lesser percentages for the other states.

As expected, the largest centers of manufacturing and commerce held fewer impoverished citizens and more people with high incomes in 1980. The Federal District had 3.20 percent with monthly incomes of less than 1,081 pesos, but 15.01 percent with monthly incomes above 12,110 pesos; and Nuevo León, with Monterrey as its economic core, had 4.55 percent with monthly incomes of less than 1,081 pesos, but 11.91 percent with monthly incomes above 12,110 pesos. So too were there relatively few impoverished people in the manufacturing and trade centers in the northern border states like Baja California, where 4.2 percent had low monthly incomes of less than 1,081 pesos, but 12.95 percent had monthly incomes above 12,110 pesos.[13]

At a higher level, those with monthly incomes over 50,400 pesos (604,800 annually) in 1980 and 162,150 pesos (1,945,800 annually) in 1994 comprised a mere 5 percent of the population.[14] Among the superrich were the members of the Mexican Congress, each earning over $84,000 a year—some 26,400,000 old pesos (1993) or 26,400 new pesos (1994). Their votes to sustain the existing division of social incomes could be counted on by both the PRI and PAN.

FOREIGN TIES EXTEND THE TECHNOSPHERE

Mexico's upper classes also leveraged their accumulation by steadily tightening their ties with U.S. and other foreign interests investing in production and extending the technical sphere of output, communications, and services.

Again, government policies mediated the balance between outright foreign controls and state guidance, setting the limits and sectors where foreign capital operated. Although the state public service sector was technically off limits to direct foreign investments, the government granted concessions in both the state-owned oil industry and petrochemical processing. The Mexican executive branch also determined the categorization that foreign companies fell into when it came to distinguishing the areas of unrestricted foreign investment fields from so-called exclusive Mexican ownership sectors (i.e., communications, automotive transport services, and gas distribution) and from the 49 percent limits set on foreign ownership (i.e., agriculture and livestock raising, mining, basic chemical, fertilizer and insecticide production, processing food and soft drinks, domestic transport, insurance, and media).

With exemptions from restrictions on foreign investment subject to diplomatic political pressures, threats of foreign withdrawals of old and new investments, and open payoffs, Mexico's legal regulations were easily sidestepped. Some U.S. corporations disguised their interests by appearing to be minority shareholders or kept control by manipulations and by engaging Mexican front men lending their names for a fee (*prestanombre*). Other firms like Ford, General Motors, General Electric, Admiral, and Monsanto simply retained 100 percent ownership of their Mexican subsidiaries.

Once they gained Mexican approval for their investment operations, moreover, U.S. corporations were eligible for exemption from Mexican taxes and import duties. These inducements led to a steady rise in foreign investments over the period 1950 to 1980. These investments rose 500 percent (to $2,822 million) from 1950 to 1970, then another 70 percent in 1979-80. By 1992, the earnings of foreign-owned *maquiladoras* were $18.6 billion, over one-half of the $36.1 billion earnings from all Mexican manufacturing.[15]

As happened in the era of Porfirio Díaz, foreign firms again came to dominate the most dynamic sectors of the Mexican economy, with larger plants, greater capital intensive investments vis-à-vis labor, higher wages, and higher rates of labor productivity. The framework for foreign dominance was based on the fact that two-thirds of Mexico's non-*maquiladora* manufacturing earnings came from only three sectors—vehicles, machinery and equipment, and chemicals—where 98 percent of all 1992 enterprises were small and medium-sized companies, employing up to 250 people, yet often lacking capital and technology to withstand foreign competition for long. And the foreign competition in Mexico was both keen and intensifying:

- Four-fifths of all foreign-owned companies operating in Mexico from 1980 to 1994 were U.S., with 70–80 percent of all direct foreign investment coming from the United States.
- Foreign companies produced 35–50 percent of Mexico's total industrial output and held 45–50 percent of the share capital of the 300 largest firms
- Eighty percent of all technology employed in Mexico came from foreign locations, mostly from the United States

- As a door opener to allow U.S. entrance, almost all credit to government or private Mexican borrowers came from U.S. banks.

Trade liberalization itself spoke to the leverage of U.S. companies. Imports of manufactures soared, reaching $48.2 billion in 1992 compared with $38.2 billion in 1991 and $10.8 billion in 1987. And if the *maquilas'* 1992 number of $23.9 billion in imports is included, imports of manufactures accounted for 38 percent of all Mexican 1992 imports and accounted for $11.8 billion or 23.6 percent of 1991 imports.[16]

Increasingly, then, imports benefited the *maquilas* manufacturing for reexport.

Compradors and Class Society

These foreign inroads were not only consolidated by the Mexican elite that has directed state policy since 1940, but also produced inequities between the Mexican upper classes and the great majority, as well as between U.S. and Mexican workers.

In the 1980s, per capita U.S. wealth and income remained seven times that of Mexico, creating an economic incentive for Mexican workers to migrate; one of every five sought employment in the United States at least part of the year. By 1994, U.S. wages for comparable Mexican labor tasks were ten to fourteen times greater.

These polarities were widened as Mexico turned towards petroleum as its key export to pay for imports, interest payments on the accumulated debt, and repayment of old and new loan principal.

Nor Could an Open Door Free Mexico

Nor could an open door for foreign investments free Mexico from relatively lower wages or the need to remit higher profit returns on foreign capital.

Where production and profits would appear was largely based on the locale of investment. Traditionally, U.S. investors had kept the most highly sophisticated technologies for producing manufactured goods at home and sent Mexico yesterday's less-advanced machinery.

After World War II, U.S. investment strategies initially locked Mexico into a narrow range of imported technologies that displaced labor, creating joblessness, and then required the purchase on foreign credit of expensive oil extracting and refining equipment. This made Mexico's giant petroleum reserves less profitable in times of falling oil prices.

Such Mexican technological progress both displaced labor and bred a debt balance that drew Mexico into the U.S. sphere of influence and kept her there. As Mexico opened the door to the foreigners importing and deploying standard gauge production technologies, Mexico's import debt enlarged, but the new equipment did not require a corresponding rise in employment.

Requiring less labor, the cybernetically equipped employers added the jobless to Mexico's existing urban labor reserve and rural labor surplus. The potential for labor conflicts were reduced because the reserve of jobless workers empowered employers to cut wage levels and living standards of those on the job—effects that were enforced by government labor controls and became the source of rising profits. Only the elite state sector unions were able to negotiate higher wages directly with the government, though over time inflation wiped out their gains as well.

Nor would discoveries of vast oil reserves make Mexico independent of the hold of U.S. producers of petroleum-extracting technologies and managers of global oil markets. True, as one oil find followed another along the Gulf of Mexico coasts of Campeche, Tabasco, Veracruz, Chiapas, and Tamaulipas, the old Petróleos Mexicanos (Pemex) set up by Cárdenas in 1938 was no longer faced with dwindling reserves and low world market prices that, from 1950 through the early 1970s, had kept it from costly oil exploration and the upgrading of its plant, equipment, and delivery facilities. But temporarily dependent on importing refined gas and oil to meet domestic requirements in the 1970s, Mexico was in the crossfire of U.S., British, and Dutch petroleum companies keeping Pemex from rehabilitating itself to achieve Mexican self-sufficiency in refined products and export markets. Given this sorry state of subservience to foreign interests, could Mexico then secure itself economically by increasing or by reducing the production of its new oil discoveries?

The surprising response during the 1976–82 López Portillo administration was that by purposely slowing the exploitation of the new oil reserves, domestic inflation would be prevented by limiting the infusion of foreign currencies earned by exporting crude oil. Portillo also proposed the use of oil revenues to buy technologies for oil refining and production; the decentralization of industry from the largest cities to the peripheral regions; the provision of incentives to investors in the form of tax credits, rebates, and discounts on public utility services; the building of the industrial sector for the production of petrochemicals, steel, machines, and other production equipment; and thereby the export of refined petroleum, processed goods, and manufactures to earn dollars and other foreign exchange. Thus were Cárdenas's anointed programs reinstated in part.

Portillo's planned second stage of industrialization was based on cheap Mexican labor in manufacturing and would build an infrastructure for self-sufficiency, expand employment and income, create a domestic market, and give Mexican manufacturers an advantage over competitors using high-cost labor.

Yet the entire plan rested on initial crude oil exports sufficient to earn the dollars required to import the three-quarters of all technical equipment Mexico used for large-scale oil production. As U.S. companies produced most of this equipment, as well as provided service contracts for required technical knowledge and skills, the rising cost of these imports required Pemex to mobilize the needed foreign exchange. But as the price of Pemex imported capital goods rose faster than the price of other manufactures imports—and twice as fast as the global value of exported crude oil—the nation's debt rose, inflation raked the domestic economy, and more than half the population saw price rises outrun their incomes.

The opportunity for employment also fell away as more capital was invested by the state in petroleum facilities that proportionally needed less labor than other industries in which the government might have invested. The state plan favored capital-intensive industries and subsidized cheap oil to other industries, leading them to prefer investment in machine-intensive rather than labor-intensive operations. The resulting surge in petroleum production set off a chain reaction of dredging, destruction, and degradation of fertile land; the contamination of rivers and estuaries along the Gulf Coast; population flight and ruined rural peasant and fishing economies; and destruction of the ecological balances of the region.

From the best of plans came still deeper demographic disaster. The invading Pemex personnel and foreign technicians, equipment salesmen, and unskilled labor looking for work in oil installations and industrial ports put the old communities and their ethos under attack. Shantytowns beset by crime, graft, and prostitution suddenly appeared, in miniature replicating the level of extortions by both Pemex bureaucrats and the oil workers' union officials.

Under pressure of this invading entourage, coastal and inland indigenous communities of the Gulf region received little protection from the Instituto Nacional Indiginista that was originally created by legislation to secure their land and rights. In the state of Veracruz alone, the Huasteco, Totonaco, Tepehua, Nahua, Ixcateco, and Popoloca communities saw their internal social structures teeter and often disintegrate. The same pressures reverberated in the oil zones among Tabasco's Chontal and still unnamed or unrecognized communities in Campeche and Tamaulipas.[17]

Although President José Lopéz Portillo spoke reverentially of the great inheritance of, and need to revindicate, Mexico's ethnic and cultural origins, his call for emancipation of indigenes from poverty, subjugation and marginalization rang hollow in the oil fields.[18]

By 1980 there were 12,802 petroleum and mining workers in the region: 7,832 in Veracruz, 4,678 in Tabasco, and 292 in Campeche. In Veracruz over two-thirds of all workers in the region were concentrated in a single zone in the north containing major oil production facilities and a large port, with a nearly contiguous zone covering several southeastern *municipios* as well as most *municipios* in Tabasco and Campeche. Indeed, the draw of petroleum (and some mining) workers to *municipios* in the oil regions of Veracruz, Tabasco, and Campeche was so concentrated that in 1986 alone the region accounted for 95 percent of Mexico's production of 913 million barrels of crude and 77 percent of its output of 33.5 billion cubic meters of natural gas.[19]

The death warrant of indigenous farming and fishing communities was sealed by the bureaucrats running both Pemex and the oil workers' union. Acting as the middle agents for the state, Pemex bureaucrats paid generously for land expropriated from wealthy ranchers and plantation owners, but only a pittance for land taken from powerless peasants. These bureaucrats also bought off oil workers' subservience for twice the wages received by other industrial workers. Pemex administrators received kick-back payments from foreign companies raising the price of Pemex-imported oil machinery, and they negotiated with private companies contracting for oil at low prices, quietly providing gratuities to the bureaucrats. The leaders and bosses of the *Sindicato de Trabajadores Petróleos de la República Mexicana* (STPRM) also appropriated significant benefits for themselves as they enforced the closed shop, and they sold jobs on a regular basis to both skilled and unskilled willing to pay for weekly, monthly, or longer employment. They joined Pemex bureaucrats in staffing the boards of private companies receiving Pemex's cheap-oil contracts and readily took bribes from foreign firms selling Pemex their high-priced technological equipment—equipment that required fewer operating workers than equipment that might have been installed in other industrial enterprises employing Mexico's jobless.

These connecting links, unforeseen by Portillo and his advisers, were emblematic of Mexico's subservient position to U.S. machine workers supplying its industries, oil workers' subservience to the Mexican elite, and the Indian communities' subservience to everyone else.

Just to deal with its foreign account, Mexico was forced to raise oil production by sixfold from 1970 to 1982, then leveling in the mid–1980s, and rising from 2.5 million to 2.6 million barrels a day between 1987 and 1992. As the world's fifth-largest producer of oil, with the seventh-largest reserve base, and 45.6 percent of the western hemisphere's reserves, proven crude resources underground were an estimated 65.05 billion barrels at the close of 1993, by comparison with 54.9 billion barrels at the close of 1986, and only 6.3 billion barrels discovered at the end of 1976. And Mexico remained dependent on the United States to sell more than three-quarters of its petroleum (1978–79, 80 percent; 1980, 77 percent; 1994, an estimated 82 percent) and to sell by pipeline over 99 percent of its natural gas reserves totaling 2.15 trillion cubic meters in 1986—16 percent of the total in the western hemisphere.[20]

To pay for the rising price of imported food and manufactures and to meet interest payments on the growing external debt, the government increasingly relied on the sale of petroleum for one-third of its revenue. And it is no surprise that until NAFTA, Mexican exports were increasingly composed of hydrocarbons (1976, 16 percent; 1979, 40 percent; 1980, 65 percent; 1981, 75 percent; 1991, an estimated 76 percent). By 1992, Mexico exported 88 million tons of oil, which made up nearly 30 percent of the federal government's budgetary receipts and over a quarter of non-*maquiladora* merchandise exports.[21]

Yet the economic web President José Lopéz Portillo and his predecessors spun was entrapping Mexico. Domestic resources were now being misdirected away from the population's needs, and especially from the physical and educational needs of Indian communities. Of the 5.2 million natives in 1980, 23 percent spoke no Spanish, and of 56 native tongues, Nahuatl predominated (26.7 percent), followed by Maya (12.9 percent), Zapoteca (8.2 percent), Mixteco (6.2 percent), Otomi (5.9 percent), and Triqui (4.1 percent).[22]

Although activity in the oil region had displaced native peoples from their communities, the population speaking indigenous languages had risen over eight decades in Veracruz (196,466 in 1900, 634,208 in 1980), Tabasco (14,292 in 1900, 56,519 in 1980), Campeche (35,977 in 1900, 77,090 in 1980), and Tamaulipas (0 in 1900, but 29,458 in 1980).[23]

Social conditions for Indian communities were dismal throughout Mexico. Some 87.4 percent of all Mexicans over 14 years old could read, but only 59 percent of Indians could read. People over 14 with an education past the sixth grade comprised 42.5 percent of all Mexicans, but only 12.3 percent of the Indian population had this much education.[24] Clearly, this was not the base for material knowledge that was needed for national unification, industrial transformation, and social equity.

It was also not a path that would improve living standards for Mexico's indigenes, or the great majority. Nationwide, households with more than two rooms comprised 66.6 percent; the figure was only 38.2 percent for Indians. For all Mexico, 7.8 percent of households were without any one of the three major utilities of electricity, running water, and sewer connections, but 25.5 percent of Indian homes fell in this category. Nationally, 20.6 percent of households had no connection to running water, but the figure was 47.9 percent for Indians. And 36.4 percent of Mexican households had no sewer connection, while 72.2 percent of Indian households had none.

With sewage running on the streets, cholera and other deadly diseases continued to rake the Gulf states; even in 1994, government health warning signs directed people—if they could read—to drink no water, only bottled drinks or alcoholic beverages.[25] Given these backward and dangerous conditions, would Mexico's governing classes change the situation in the near future?

In January 1992, the Mexican legislature's approval of the nation's first constitutional amendment, which recognized the nation's pluralism and acknowledged the right of Indians to their own culture and language, was largely too ambiguous and too late to recover rights long lost. Even after Chiapas exploded on 31 December 1993, President Salinas did not press for immediate changes, but only for a national commission to hold hearings and propose legislation that was not considered until after the August 1994 national election.

Without political power, without a place or influence in state legislatures and governors' mansions, with too little land to survive, without literacy, education, decent housing, running water, sewer facilities, and electricity, indigenous Indians were a nearly forgotten people, able to raise issues only by mobilized protests and arms. And these actions might just bring brutal repression from the *rurales* and army instead of forcing the government to build passable roads enabling the marketing of corn, beans, and coffee; to erect nearby hospitals medically equipped and staffed with real doctors; to build schools instructing in one or more of 56 native languages; and to construct electricity and telephone lines connecting native peoples with the rest of the nation.

And even if these issues were addressed, there would remain the central matter of land redistribution to reverse the nation's continued system of peonage, servitude, and desperate poverty.

CHAPTER 10

The Policy of Progress

II: Reconquest and Proletarianization of the Land

Since the Spanish Conquest of Mexico, the scales of hunger and survival—set and maintained through the struggles of social classes and reenforced through established institutions—have usually been weighted without benevolence and equity for the nation's indigenous peoples.

There was, and still is, no certainty of egalitarian distribution of the means of life. As contemporary levels of Mexican consumption have come to turn on purchasing power defined by property, revenue, and income, some four out of ten Mexicans have remained impoverished and malnourished, having received a declining share of the nation's food supply from 1950 through 1993, while the middle and upper classes have expanded their share of both wealth and access to the nation's bounty.

In the 1950s, state policy pivoted on pacifying the population by providing a certain minimal level of consumption. Food was kept within the means of the urban workforce through state regulation of staple prices that modulated wage demands that would otherwise have driven up the cost of production, reduced the competitiveness of Mexican goods, and cut profits. State price-and-wage controls effectively created a fund for real-wage maintenance at the expense of the staple food growers, however, forcing these growers to cut unprofitable staple production. This in turn created a food shortage, extended the black market in high-price foods, and further immiserized populations living at the margins of both the rural and urban domain.

Rural depopulation and urban idleness extended the margins of poverty, too. The removal of half the population from the rural to the urban domain required that those still on the land feed themselves as well as those in the cities, a dilemma engrossing the nation and its government.

RECONQUEST OF THE AGRARIAN DOMAIN

The reconquest of Mexico's agrarian domain that began under the Cárdenas administration was stopped sharply in 1940, then reversed, momentarily rehabilitated, and finally undermined with a new proletarianization on the land.

In the late 1930s, Cárdenas had speedily expropriated and distributed highly productive *hacienda* land before the opposition could consolidate. *El Presidente* foresaw the success of collectivized agriculture under various schemes for individual or joined *ejidos* with shared use of irrigation facilities and machinery to maintain the previous organizational advantages of collective work.

Yet the post–Cárdenas era witnessed both internal disintegration and external destruction of the institutions sustaining land reform. As *ejidal* structures were still relatively unstable and remained unable to surmount the dominant *hacienda* and market apparatus that enclosed their operations, they remained vulnerable to hostile outside pressures. Particularly in the Laguna region, communal *ejidos* had too little water, faced too many remaining *haciendas* (legally retaining 150 hectares with essential structures, water rights, and roads that the fractionated *ejidos* lacked, but required), and fought among themselves, as now there were too many claimants eligible for too little land. Some 18,000 traditional peasants were forced to divide the land with 10,000 seasonal laborers and another 10,000 former "migrants" who had been hired by the *haciendas* to break the peasants' general strike before land reform had begun.

While the *haciendas* retained the most fertile land with capital equipment and irrigation systems to maintain output levels, and also made phantom sales to relatives and name-lenders (*prestanombres*) to reassemble neo-*latifundias*, the peasants received small plots that often lacked adequate water rights and equipment for continuity in production. *Hacendados* selling land also used the proceeds to buy more production machinery and to diversify into commercial and credit fields providing essential fertilizers, seed, equipment, and usurious loans to the *ejidatarios*.

When these *hacendados* replaced land labor with machines to enlarge their production for a wider market, the *ejidos* could not compete. They usually maintained their collective labor force on the same land, relying for efficiency in collective use of machines, marketing cooperatives, and insurance and credit societies.

As the emergent collective *ejidos*, which remained relatively small by comparison with the *haciendas*, became increasingly market oriented, moreover, they became increasingly dependent on government funds that were meanwhile being withdrawn under *hacendado* pressures.

And as the *hacendados* were themselves strengthened in the rural domain, they were transformed into agricultural and commercial capitalists largely dependent on the national market, unifying their interests with capitalist groups operating from the urban centers.

NOT A MALTHUSIAN DILEMMA: THE SYMBIOTIC OLIGARCHY AND THE INTERNATIONAL CONTEXT OF CAPITALIST AGRICULTURE

Mexico's agricultural domain was being shaped by a symbiotic oligarchy: the pressures arose from its *hacendados* and corporate agribusinesses that were operating in an international context and the successive governments that were vulnerable to domestic and foreign pressures.

The dominant role of Mexico's national bourgeoisie had been strengthened as a result of the World War II government alliance of business, labor, and *hacendado* organizations. As the raw material supply line to the United States had been extended with labor foregoing the right to strike, the government had won *hacendados* support by slowing land expropriation and distribution. The Cárdenas distribution had averaged 2.9 million hectares a year, but the 1940–45 Camacho administration only distributed slightly more than one-half million hectares per year. There was practically no distribution under the 1946-52 Alemán administration that revised the constitution's Article 27 to legalize further land acquisition by each *hacendado*.

With these changes emphasizing commercialization of agriculture, industrialization, low wages, and rapid accumulation, the land itself was game for rapid capitalization. Successive governments from 1940 to 1960 favored concentration of land by the neo-*latifundias*, which were aided by massive state spending on infrastructure to make their operations profitable. Successive PRI-controlled governments also shifted their agricultural spending to favor the *hacendados*, made ever-smaller distributions of ever-poorer land to the peasants, and put pressure on the collective farms to partition their holdings, thereby dispersing their competitive production potential and undermining their solidarity to organize and wield political influence.

From government irrigation and farm research projects to providing state credit, capitalist *hacendados* were favored over *ejidatarios*, which were often left to wither without adequate irrigation and government assistance. Without water, their small holdings on the central mesa were dangerously jeopardized in some years, relatively unproductive in others. And without credit they were forced to borrow at usurious rates from private banks, moneylenders, and ever-present U.S. corporations. So, too, without mechanical equipment, chemical fertilizers, hybrid seed, and planting knowledge for wheat and cotton, they remained subsistence farmers or worse, unable to compete at the low prices set by the large commercial farms using upscale machinery, chemical fertilizers, and other so-called "green revolution" techniques. Eventually millions of peasants were forced to send their sons to the cities to find wage work, to otherwise break up their families, or to abandon their farms.

This movement of a portion of the peasant population to the urban domain in search of work also accelerated the fall of agricultural output of traditional staples making up the Mexican diet. But rather than the hyperbolic Malthusian dilemma—the geometric growth of the population disastrously facing the arithmetic expansion of the food supply—from 1970 to 1981 the population grew only arithmetically (though a substantial 3.4 percent), while production of staple foods for human consumption increased nominally or slowed.

Logically, there should have been no food shortage at all, as Mexico's total agricultural land harvested scaled upward, nearly doubling from 8,600,000 hectares in 1950 to 10,514,000 in 1955, 12,152,000 in 1960, 14,785,000 in 1965, 14,975,000 in 1970, 15,157,000 in 1975 and 16,825,000 in 1980. For corn alone there were 6,694,267 hectares in 1975 production, but 7,420,623 in 1983. In beans the cultivated area rose from 1,752,632 hectares in 1975 to 1,996,408 hectares in 1983.[1]

Yet although there was more land in crops, the food deficit was largely due to three conditions that together functioned as an apparatus for symbiotic, oligarchic control. Some of the best land was held in abeyance by the regrouped *latifundias*; the small farmers lacked, and were deprived of, sufficient capital and irrigated water to rise above subsistence agriculture; and under the pressure of domestic and foreign agribusinesses, the government-supported *hacendados* shifted from corn and traditional crops to sorghum for animal feed, and fruits, vegetables, and other cash crops as market-oriented priorities.

There were both expansive and limiting aspects to this production shift from traditional crops, in which two time periods marked the path.

PERIOD ONE: FOOD EXPORTS, DOMESTIC DEFICIENCIES

On the expansive side, Mexico had long since blocked small peasant advances in staple food output for the domestic market.

With powerful government backing, advances in large-scale agricultural production techniques in the mid–1960s had fueled output, leading to the export of substantial quantities of corn, wheat, and other cash crop staples. The government not only provided extensive state investments in irrigation facilities favoring the large growers, but favored them for public and private bank lending when channeling the means for mass production towards their operations. From improved seed strains to fertilizers and pesticides, output was maximized regardless of the effect of herbicides and chemicals on their workers. And from state insurance against investment hazards to the use of state police powers and juridical controls over their workers, the new *latifundias* were assured of both profits and secured tranquility.

As the government also subsidized the *latifundias* to export to the United States as a prop to Mexico's balance of payments, Mexican state policy was bent under the weight of the very agro-investors the state promoted, and this policy ultimately created a domestic staple food deficiency by disorganizing, undermining, and restructuring the use of land for producing traditional crops such as corn and beans.

The politically pliable Mexican government quickly advanced such destruction in the 1970s. Denying food producers access to state-financed resources, the government agency CONASUPO established a food-pricing system that steadily degraded the living conditions of farmers producing dietary staples.[2] As inflation raged, the farmers' market prices were meanwhile kept relatively stable under CONASUPO's constant guaranteed corn prices, so that real prices declined one-third in the decade 1963–72.[3] Despite inflation, guaranteed prices for wheat were also kept constant from 1955 to 1972, as were bean prices from 1961 to 1973.[4]

Nonetheless, beginning in 1970, the failure of government policies that favored large growers, but barely improved the lot of *campesinos*, already necessitated substantial corn imports. Agribusinesses operating in U.S. grain fields with high-tech equipment, chemical fertilizers, and U.S. government subsidies were ready and moved powerfully to dump their surpluses. Jumping at export opportunities that were changing the face of Mexican agriculture and consumption and undercutting Mexico's self-sufficiency, they firmed the pattern set by Mexico's initial 1973 net corn imports of 1,113,595 tons. By the close of the 1970s, Mexico was facing a major agricultural crisis. From 1973 through 1980, net corn imports totaled 14,216,671 tons—almost 335 pounds of corn for every man, woman and child in Mexico. And in 1980 alone, Mexico imported 4,186,643 tons, over 25 percent of the nation's domestic corn consumption.

Ejidatarios, small farmers, and peasants unable to compete with lower-priced U.S. corn were pressured from within the family to give up staple production for the market, turn to the *haciendas*, towns, and cities for wage work, and buy imported corn, wheat, and beans to supplement subsistence farming.

As U.S. agribusinesses producing and marketing wheat and beans seized Mexican markets, wheat imports eventually became a partial dietary substitute for tortillas and other products made from Mexican corn. From 1971 to 1980, there was only one year (1976) when Mexico did not import wheat; the cumulative import totaled 5,321,442 tons, about 125 pounds for every Mexican.

By contrast, in the ten years from 1970 to 1980, bean production and exports remained strong, exports cumulatively totaling 234,971 tons. Yet sporadic bean imports were more than twice as large, totaling 589,603 tons; imports of 440,928 tons in the single year of 1980 far exceeded exports for the entire period.[5]

In less than a decade and a half, Mexico's *latifundias* had switched priorities from price-controlled staple crops feeding its population to cash crops supplying both the U.S. and domestic buyers at unregulated market prices.

Land planted in corn dropped from over 50 percent of all agricultural land in the 1960s to around 40 percent at the end of the 1970s. And as the area planted to corn dropped from a 1966 high of 8.3 million hectares to a low in 1979 of 5.6 million hectares, the land put in sorghum soared from 118 hectares to 1.6 million hectares in 1980.[6]

Thus grain lands harvested for human consumption momentarily went into an almost steady free-fall from 11.1 percent of all planted soil in 1950 to 9.5 percent in 1960, 7.8 percent in 1970, and 6.7 percent in 1980.

Those grain lands planted for animal consumption comparably scaled upward: zero in 1950, 1 percent in 1960, 6.1 percent in 1970, but 10.7 percent in 1980. And the land harvest of fruits and vegetables enlarged from 5.8 percent of all agricultural land in 1970 to 7.8 percent in 1979 and 6.7 percent in 1980.[7] The latter were mostly sold across the northern border at first, but were later also marketed at home.

Staple production of essential beans and oleaginous (oil-producing) crops was relatively steady, however. Bean crops retained their relative hold on total land production (10.9 percent in 1960, varying thereafter, but 10.5 percent in 1980), as did oleaginous staples (5.1 percent in 1960 and 6.7 percent in 1980).

So there was an initial threefold transformation of Mexican agriculture from small-scale to large-scale agriculture, from emphasis on the mass production of corn to producing animal feed, and from stress on staple production to cash-crop fruits and vegetables for the U.S. and Mexican markets.

Transnational forces initially shaped this agricultural switch from feeding Mexico's people adequate staples to producing export crops sustaining U.S. demand so that Mexico could earn dollars. By the 1970s, U.S. capital places in Mexican agriculture already concentrated on the cash-market output of fruit, winter vegetables, and cattle fed with Mexican-grown feed. From transnational corporations selling technological equipment, supplying factories in the field, food processors, and packers, to distributors channeling standardized Mexican food exports to assured U.S. markets, the path for mass marketing was already being paved.[8]

As this U.S. invasion progressed in the early 1980s, about one-fifth of Mexican agricultural land was in the hold of foreign agribusinesses that operated in the northwest. These businesses carefully followed marketing conditions and possibilities by shifting production to favored crops, and they maintained long-term contracts with food-processors and distributors, limited only by their experience with alternative crops and the obligations on long-term bank loans.[9]

As mass agricultural production displaced smaller farms and introduced efficiencies of scale in the northwestern border states between 1970 and 1980, both the numbers and percentages of Mexicans working in agriculture fell:

- In Baja California, over 42 percent (10,246 of 24,180) of economically active Mexicans had held agricultural occupations in 1900, 60 percent (11,704 of 19,568) in 1930, 45 percent (34,567 of 77,424) in 1950, 22 percent (49,440 of 221,779) in 1970, and 9 percent (38,245 of 403,279) in 1980. Between 1970 and 1980 the number in agriculture fell over one-fifth.
- In Coahuila, over 37 percent (58,149 of 155,617) of economically active Mexicans had held agricultural occupations in 1900, 60 percent (82,587 of 137,979) in 1930, 48 percent (109,839 of 226,769) in 1950, 30 percent (85,760 of 283,351) in 1970, and 15 percent (74,384 of 483,898) in 1980. Between 1970 and 1980 the number in agriculture fell almost 13 percent.
- In Chihuahua, over 63 percent (78,818 of 124,385) of economically active Mexicans had held agricultural occupations in 1900, 68 percent (102,413 of 149,794) in 1930, 53 percent (141,920 of 264,016) in 1950, 36 percent (151,498 of 416,852) in 1970, and 20 percent (134,070 of 664,707) in 1980. Between 1970 and 1980 the number in agriculture fell 11 percent.
- In Nueva León, over 38 percent (54,098 of 140,746) of economically active Mexicans had held agricultural occupations in 1900, 68 percent (102,413 of 149,794) in 1930, 41 percent (97,680 of 239,558) in 1950, 8 percent (85,149 of 1,060,279) in 1970, and 8 percent (67,034 of 803,764) in 1980. Between 1970 and 1980 the number in agriculture fell over 20 percent.[10]

PERIOD TWO: SUPPLYING DOMESTIC AND FOREIGN MARKETS

There was not an increase in the number of agricultural workers on the northwestern *latifundias* during the two decades 1970–94. Instead, dirt cheap Mexican laborers working on well-irrigated land in an ideal climate were being driven to enlarge production of cash crops for enlarged domestic consumption and an almost barrier-free export. The shift of land, labor, and capital into such export-oriented agriculture turned the state into a prop for the foreign interests, turned the old peasants into peons, and changed the land into an output bastion destined to dry up the water table, divert water from human consumption, and destroy the soil with chemical fertilizers.

Both export and domestic markets accounted for fruits, vegetables, plants, and flowers that made up about 30 percent of the value of all agricultural production. Industrial (largely export) crops of coffee, cocoa, sugar, and tobacco contributed another 10–15 percent.[11] The balance of 55–60 percent of the value of agricultural output went into supplying the domestic market.

Export markets more than doubled for fresh vegetables (from $269 million in 1988 to $551 million in 1992) and fresh fruits (from $144 million in 1988 to $331 million in 1992). Tomato exports waffled ($243 million in 1988, $428 million in 1990, $202 million in 1992). Exports of both cotton ($113 million in 1988, but $31 million in 1992) and coffee ($435 million in 1988, but $258 million in 1992) weakened. Land devoted to these exports continued to squeeze land in grain production relative to growing domestic requirements.

During the 1980s and early 1990s, agribusinesses and the government had also watched rapid urbanization expand the market for domestic staples and fresh fruit and vegetables. To supply the urban domain, maize production rose sharply (from 11.7 million tons in 1986 to 15 million tons in 1991), while the earlier emphasis on cattle-feed production of sorghum scaled up very slowly (from 4.8 million tons to 5.1 million tons).

In this time frame, there was a fall in production of both wheat (4.8 million tons to 3.6 million tons) and beans (1.08 million tons to .8 million tons).[12] The overall picture for other agriculture in the early 1990s was a small decline in the production of livestock, forestry, and fishing (a growth of 1.1 percent in 1990-91; a decline of 1.5 percent in 1991-92).

Despite the growth of maize output as the main staple of the Mexican diet, the fall in other food production combined with the increase of the 1994 population to nearly 92 million, with 27 million in Mexico City alone, left Mexico unable to feed itself. Imports of maize, wheat, sorghum, and barley rose; although there were variations for each product from year to year, the total import value continually scaled upward as seen below.

Food Imports ($ million)[13]

Imports	1988	1989	1990	1991	1992
Sorghum	138	322	331	362	542
Soya	336	326	217	348	512

Imports	1988	1989	1990	1991	1992
Oil-bearing seeds & fruits	138	149	152	229	220
Maize	394	441	435	178	183
Wheat	137	70	46	67	163
Total*	1,397	1,747	1,830	1,830	2,379

Includes forestry products.

Payment for these growing food imports was a problem because agricultural exports did not always keep up: $1,399 exports, $1,397 imports in 1988; $1,461 exports, $1,747 imports in 1989; $1,721 exports, $1,830 imports in 1990; $1,877 exports, $1,663 imports in 1991; and $1,715 exports, $2,379 imports in 1992.[14]

CHANGING THE FACE OF MEXICAN CONSUMPTION: FOOD DEFICITS, IMPORTS, AND A CHANGE OF DIET

The logic of demography meanwhile set its mark on the Mexican economy and its agricultural domain. As Mexican staple food production for human consumption initially fell relative to population growth and urbanized multitudes were unable to feed themselves, other foods originally designed for the U.S. market also found their way into the Mexican market. During both the 1980s and early 1990s, the slowly enlarging real incomes of some sections of the urban middle class enabled them to adopt a new dietary balance, dovetailing with, and partaking of, the enlarged output of crops serving the U.S. market.

This class had itself enlarged on the heels of the shift from rural to urban Mexico. And as the crisis-ridden peasant population deserting agriculture made their way to the cities, they also extended the labor reserve, the market, and the housing and health crises. Then to control and process this new urban population, the ranks of higher-paid bureaucrats inhabiting the maze of government agencies and the so-called service industries had to be expanded.

These forces were together placed on the stage of history. Agricultural labor declined from 70 percent of the national total in 1930 to 39 percent in 1970, 30 percent in 1980 (as much as 37 percent if one excludes respondents not specifying their industry in the 1980 census), and an estimated 25 percent in 1993. But meanwhile, the overall labor force surged at a compound rate of 3.3 percent per year from 1940 to 1990. And from these ranks, those who entered the unnumbered tiers of government—or marched to the tune of middling spheres as merchants and agents serving the thousands of personal tasks the population required—together rose in number from 4 percent of the employed in 1930 to 20 percent in 1970, 18 percent in 1980 (again excluding respondents not specifying their industry in the 1980 census),[15] and an estimated 22 percent in 1993.

Centered in the urban domain, these wage, salary, and service workers were quickly drawn into the fetishes of the market for both traditional staples and the latest in manufactured and packaged foods, opening the door to both domestic and foreign producers.

STRUCTURAL AND STATE ASPECTS OF THE
SHIFT IN AGRICULTURAL PRODUCTION

Fearing the nation was losing its ability to feed itself, many Mexican leaders insisted there had been a disastrous structural switch in Mexican agriculture turning on misdirected state policies for dealing with both the domestic and U.S. markets.

The turn to beef, pork, and poultry had meant, for example, that land would be planted in sorghum to feed steers and pigs, and when Mexican sorghum was in short supply, animals and poultry would be sustained on imported sorghum, chemical feed, and corn. As both growers and transnational organizations meanwhile tried to shape corresponding policies of the critical state agency (CONASUPO) to their needs, the latter subsidized the production of animal feed at the expense of staples. Thus CONASUPO concentrated its resources on two corresponding operations:

- In the 1970s, CONASUPO encouraged the Mexican production of sorghum by a dual pricing policy that allowed sorghum prices to rise while corn prices were kept low. CONASUPO also covered the sorghum-production costs of raw materials, transport, and distribution, thereby promoting the shift from land planted in staples to land in sorghum.
- Whenever the Mexican production of animal feed fell short of need, forcing up the price paid for imported sorghum and other animal feed, CONASUPO paid the importers the difference between the imported and domestic price.[16]

As the state monitored the process and subsidized the shift in these alternating agricultural and import policies, it transformed the face of Mexican production, distribution, and trade.

RECONQUEST OF THE AGRICULTURAL DOMAIN

Mexico's traditional cash crop exports had been cotton, coffee, sugar, henequen, and tobacco. To these 1970s export markets, Mexico added garbanzo beans, sesame, cacao, and bitter lemons—all important parts of the traditional Mexican diet. Crops distributed domestically and exported also included watermelons (from which Mexicans made the drink *sandia*), cantaloupes (also consumed domestically as a major fruit), and tomatoes (the basis for many cooked meals).

Agricultural Exports in the 1970s

| | 1970–1974 | | 1975–1979 | |
	Avg. annual crop (tons)	% exported	Avg. annual crop (tons)	% exported
bitter lemons	409,000	26	438,500	44
cantaloupes	194,900	45	260,800	37
coffee	203,700	55	217,500	67
cotton	410,400	51	311,900	54
garbanzo beans	211,200	17	220,100	28
henequen	148,000	58	112,200	36
sesame	171,700	7	117,700	32
tobacco	68,300	24	217,500	27
tomatoes	1,055,400	33	1,152,800	35
watermelons	288,700	22	406,800	19

Source: DGEA, "Consumos aparentes de productos agrícolas 1925–1980," Econotecnia agrícola 5, no. 9 (1981).

As both domestic and foreign markets variously expanded or contracted for these agricultural products in the 1970s, the large cash-crop growers placed increasing reliance on the foreign market for sesame, garbanzo beans, and lemons. In addition to this fast-growing reliance on the foreign market, there was a smaller, yet increasing reliance by coffee, tobacco, cotton, and tomato producers on foreign (largely U.S.) buyers. As a proportion of total output, reliance on the foreign market actually declined for growers of henequen, cantaloupes, and watermelons. In the case of henequen and sugar, restrictive U.S. lobbies slowed the rise in export markets. But with Mexico's substantial increase in watermelon and cantaloupe production, the volume of these exports actually enlarged, as the increased dollar earnings enticed further production for the U.S. market.[17]

During the 1980s and early 1990s, an even greater market realignment took place that increased staple production directed to Mexico's poor without jeopardizing the favored position ranchers, agribusinesses, and the Mexican middle classes had established in the 1970s. This government policy was built on the logic that enlarged agricultural output could support the entire population without altering the nation's class composition.

Using Cárdenas's 1934–38 land-use plan as his model, President López Portillo had wanted the traditional peasant producers of corn and beans to be the backbone for state-assisted production, without weakening those agribusinesses, U.S. grain exporters, and food-processors that had relied on Mexico's low-quality food standards and the government free-trade policy to guarantee high returns.

Launching the March 1980 *Sistema Alimentario Mexicano* (SAM), the Portillo administration thus designed a six-year central plan for Mexican self-sufficient production of basic foods, mobilizing state resources to subsidize increased output for wider distribution to upgrade the diet of the undernourished one-third of the population.

By improving roads, education facilities, and local health care, the government encouraged the rural destitute to reclaim their 2 million hectares in rain-irrigated lands abandoned from 1965 to 1976. Forcing ranchers to concentrate their herding operations to release land for cultivation and forcing owners to put their idle lands (*tierras ociosas*) in production under the January 1981 *Ley de Fomento Agropecuario*'s threat of expropriation and redistribution, Portillo's SAM also offered small-scale producers access to credit, irrigation, storage and distribution facilities, price-discounted seeds (75 percent off market prices), fertilizers and insecticides (30 percent reduced), as well as reduced crop insurance rates (66 percent). SAM also released peasants from the cost-price squeeze by raising the 1980 guaranteed price for corn (20 percent) and beans (36 percent) and assuring the peasants an income even for a failed harvest under a government-shared risk scheme.[18]

To meet its goal of self-sufficiency in food production that would ensure both the rural and urban poor a level of subsistence, the government encouraged a model basic diet (*canasta básica*) that turned on peasant production for self-sufficiency and a domestic market supplied from state-run stores subsidizing the urban impoverished and setting low prices on staples. Corn and beans, then wheat and rice, were the prime staples encouraged by SAM policies and resources. The government backed the production of improved seeds for a fivefold increase in corn output and a sevenfold increase in bean output between 1979 and 1982; it also guaranteed that corn prices were raised 126 percent and guaranteed bean prices by 190 percent. With government banking credits and insured cropland respectively increasing planted hectares, there was a phenomenal rise in both land use and output: 140 percent and 204 percent for corn and 220 percent and 134 percent for beans. Corn-planted lands alone increased from 5,600,000 hectares to 8,200,900 hectares between 1979 and 1981, corn output rising 75 percent, bean output 129 percent.[19]

Although the goal was to uplift the nation's underclasses, the redirection of staple production hardly affected domestic production of meat, vegetables, and fruits marketed in the urban domain. As SAM encouraged an enlarged output of livestock products, only the food-processors felt the heat of SAM policies that concentrated on staple foods and tried to prevent the import and production of foods that had low protein value or that posed potential nutritional hazards.

THE DRIVING FORCE

As Mexico's population increased more rapidly than domestic food production, the annual food deficit could only be filled by imports paid with foreign exchange earned by oil, manufactures, and food exports.

The driving force was the rising population of Mexico's urbanized industrial sphere, where the long-term advance of the first industrial revolution concentrating on the manufacture of consumer goods had employed millions who purchased all sorts of goods and services, thus extending the market for products and services emerging from the spheres of commerce, industry, finance, and agriculture.

Not only did the enlarged workforce require housing, public water, sewers, schools, and hospitals—extending the urban domain skyward and onto former farmland—but the growing populace also required all sorts of goods, manufactures, and foods brought from ever-greater distances. This led to a vast expansion of the class of middle-agent merchants, lenders, and insurers, and also led to an expanded labor force to build and maintain the growing urban domain with its infrastructure of public works, government roads, means of transport and storage, and communications systems.

These sectors comprising the enlarged middle class had climbed the income ladder as the largest cities became the focus of wealth accumulation from the expanding economy during the 1970s. Making up the central two-fifths of the population, they received a growing share of national income, their larger monetary and real incomes enabling them to purchase many new products and foods that were already being produced for export to the United States in the 1970s. True, their relative income standing was still small by comparison to the revenue flow awarded Mexico's wealthiest 20 percent and minuscule compared to the top 5 percent, but the latter's share was proportionally shrinking as a direct consequence of the forces extending manufacturing in the urban domain, as well as the corresponding rise in the industrial and commercial workforce and the market.[20]

FROM TRADITIONAL STAPLES TO MEXICO'S NEW URBAN "NEEDS"

These changes in production, urbanization, wage work, commerce, and income distribution obviously affected large-scale agricultural production that came to rely on domestic as well as foreign markets.

For more than two decades, the government's agricultural policies had been a disaster. Staple crop production was unprofitable under government price controls, and alternative crops profitably produced for export reduced the domestic food supply required. Clearly imports had to make up the difference.

But what if new government policies ensured that Mexico's total agricultural output enlarged to meet both domestic and export markets? What would be the consequences if a switch in the types of foods and fibers grown enabled Mexico to supply both export and internal markets and any periodic shortfall in traditional staples was handled by imports?

Obviously a segment of the increased production of traditional and alternative crops would be distributed at home along a skewed line of those subsidized by the government and able to buy. But the success of export-import scenarios required that the old government fetters on agricultural trade would have to be shorn away. The government would also have to maneuver to prevent domestic shortages in traditional foods and other foods that were becoming part of the urban diet. And this program would have to be designed to cover markets for the production of both beef and fresh foods.

As the *rancheros* had relied on both domestic and foreign markets, the government positioned itself to ensure that the Mexican beef market was supplied before export markets were filled; a state export quota was set in the late 1970s on the feedlots operating in the northern states. By the early 1990s, the livestock industry experienced inadequate investments, consequent lack of intensive production techniques, high feed costs, fixed prices, drought, and a 1991 drop in domestic demand for red meat that caused a .5 percent drop in total output. This was offset in part by milk production, cutting the import of powdered milk from 287,990 tons in 1990 to 58,000 tons in 1991.[21]

Hitherto, as beef production had risen, the share exported dropped from 12 percent in 1978 to 4 percent in 1979, and 5 percent in 1980.[22] Yet the export of beef remained viable, rising in value from $349 million in 1990 to $358 million in 1991.[23]

In the name of self-sufficiency, moreover, in 1992 the Salinas government tightened control on livestock product imports and eliminated controls on cattle and sheep raising; this was especially important for sheep flocks because they had fallen in number from 30 million to 5–6 million in 30 years.[24]

These policies followed earlier government negative interventions, for despite export opportunities, until the early 1980s U.S. barriers on fresh food imports and corresponding Mexican government restraints on growers had blocked the expansion of Mexican exports.[25]

To cover fiscal and balance of payments deficits, the Mexico government also made the export of manufactures and oil top priorities to earn foreign exchange. The rising scale of output demanded new wage workers and stimulated expanding commerce that in turn supplied the domestic market and fueled new rounds of production. The enlarged urban workforce commanded revenues that they spent largely on staple foods, so that any increase in agriculture to supply export markets would have to take into account domestic needs and food imports and consider government policy, the pressures of transnational commerce and industry, and the regrouped *latifundias*.

These forces coalesced during the 1980s and early 1990s as the largest growers strove to accumulate by expanding their operations and extending their markets, leveraging their activities by influence at the higher reaches of the U.S. and Mexican governments. As these farm organizations mobilized capital, were absorbed by even larger corporations, and extended their market sphere through contracts with transcontinental and transnational distributors, the distributors created a treadmill for exports, often providing credit, farm machinery, and packaging facilities in return for a guaranteed share of each crop. Because marginal profits of these corporate agribusinesses depended upon volume output to lower unit costs, these distributors logically sought greater market sway in both Mexico and the United States. And though it proved difficult to sell the latest processed and packaged food varieties—especially meats and poultry—to Mexico's impoverished classes comprising 40 percent of the population, the middle and upper classes striving for an elevated life style were easily subdued by availability and advertising that redefined their needs.[26] But the inflationary spiral of 1994-95 led the middle sector to cut back such "luxuries."

Surplus Populations on the Move

Adding to the population exodus from small-scale agriculture, the populations driven from the oil regions and the rural domain to towns and cities ultimately concentrated in the larger urban centers, with poverty and idleness then pressuring millions to emigrate to the United States.

State policies demanding progress that favored Mexico's wealthier classes in the spheres of finance, agriculture, manufacturing, commerce, and shipping upgraded a middle sector of professionals, bureaucrats, and middle agents, but further impoverished the rest of the population, leaving some fifty million in a state of destitution—landless, idle, hungry, and desperate.

The glossing over of this immiserized multitude with statistics showing elevated growth in the gross national product or rising average annual incomes or output provided illusory screens for the failure to distribute the nation's bounty equitably. For the Mexican peoples lived and consumed not on averages, but only on what each could eke out and secure.

The situation of the lower classes was worsened by the accumulation policies of the government that favored Mexico's wealthy through the low-price privatization sales of 875 of 1155 government-owned companies between 1982 and 1991; the sharp reduction of taxes on the wealthy, with pressure on the middle classes to cover most taxes collected; the reduction of government expenditures on welfare programs; the control over labor and labor union payoffs; the regimentation of the state bureaucracy to these goals; and the so-called free-trade agreement with the United States to stimulate production for export to earn dollars.

At the close of the 1980s, the GNP growth had run between 3 and 4 percent for three years, and annual inflation was under 20 percent and going down.[27] In the next four years, the pattern continued.[28]

The gross figures were looking better, but the population was faring worst, setting off an exodus that became a tidal wave of surplus peoples crossing into the United States.

Part V

From the Old Status Quo to a New Order

Three theories of international commerce are again afloat in the economic world: free trade, fair world trade, and regional trade.

Free trade, Adam Smith–style, is both utopian and still nowhere to be found. It posits that barrier-free trade allows each country and region to specialize in those products its workers and farmers make and grow most efficiently and at the lowest cost among nations, thereby increasing global economic output and stimulating maximum world commerce.[1]

Fair world trade is less than unregulated global trade. It encompasses those nations and areas committed to fair commercial exchange and again allows each country and region among the fair traders to specialize in those products its workers and farmers make most efficiently and at the lowest planetary cost. Again, this increases global economic output and stimulates maximum world commerce. Such trade might be possible if major in-dustrialized and agricultural nations gave up their tariff protection measures and other trade barriers and eliminated their production and ex-port subsidies.[2]

Regional trade is a cut below free world trade, as such commerce is based on "free-trade" areas, customs unions, and "preferential trade" among a limited group of nations or zones, tending to divert more existing trade carried on with others to and among partners than they create in new trade with others—thus looking inward to trade among group members.[3]

Past experience reflects some limitations on the success of regional trade and customs unions. Regional trade blocs were the nationalist response and consequence—not the genesis—of the depressions in the 1880s and 1930s. But opinions differ as to whether these blocs worsened

217

the economic nightmare. One school argues that the retreat from multilateral commerce to tight-knit empire and trading blocs excluded the trade of others, closing off home markets while attempting to dump surplus goods on world markets, a policy that actually forced global trade to fall.[4] Another school argues that though the U.S. Smoot-Hawley Tariff Act of 1930 raised tariffs on all imports, other nations created spheres of influence by drawing an economic circle around their neighbors, dominions, or former colonial possessions in order to lower tariffs on trade between custom union members and thus maintain their markets.[5]

The United States followed suit as well. Trapped by its own trade policy that caused U.S. exports to plummet from 15.6 percent of world exports in 1929 to 10.3 percent in 1933, American exporters successfully lobbied for the Regional Trade Agreement Act of 1934, under which the Roosevelt administration negotiated trade pacts with France and ten Latin American countries, recapturing some of the lost markets.[6] In this fashion, the United States tried to compete by establishing zones of bilateral economic influence like those of France, England, and the other leading powers.[7]

Today these three frames of commerce are again being renewed by the uncertain future of the new World Trade Organization (WTO) set up by GATT and attempts to create new customs unions.[8] And in the Americas, the North American Free Trade Association is emerging as the most significant commercial zone ever established on the continent.[9]

But the negotiation of a free-trade arrangement between Mexico, the United States, and Canada does not in itself mobilize pressures to pursue a higher level of economic integration in the form of a customs union, unified common market or comprehensive economic union. For NAFTA envisions a free-trade area, not the creation of a supranational policy center to direct national economies. By focusing on preferential trade between its members that increases members' growth rates, NAFTA seeks a quantitative increase in trade that will dovetail with enlarged international trade. And NAFTA might become a building bloc for a western hemisphere free trade area (envisioned by the Enterprise for the Americas Initiative) that would cover all of Central and Latin America.

Possibly NAFTA might erode the trade preferences under the U.S.-Caribbean Basin Initiative and Canada's Preferential Trade Scheme for the Commonwealth Caribbean; but these trade preferences and micromarkets might also become part of the western hemisphere free trade area.

One theorist formulates that the three lowest levels of economic integration—a free-trade area, a customs union, and a common market— may logically be superseded by two higher stages of integration at an elevated political policy level through economic union and complete economic integration as a single economy.[10] And pure economic theorists similarly emphasize the distinction between (1) integration battering down discriminatory and restrictive barriers on the free movement of goods and factors of production between nations, and (2) agreed political policies and economic objectives promoting market integration through the development of common policies and institutions.[11] But political science reveals that rather than a lockstep historical progression from one stage to another, nationalist pressures and pitfalls often delay or block such integrative steps.[12]

Both the stage and sequence turn on the creation of a political foundation for such agreements. And in North America, the free-trade agreement would have to accord with the political demands and needs of corporations, affected workers, labor unions, environmentalists, farmers, and others. Common standards for any trilateral agreement would have to appease these groups. And in step with U.S. and Canadian standards of democracy, labor rights, and environmental safety set at a higher level than those in Mexico, a NAFTA-imposed elevation of Mexico's standards would require explicit trade-agreement provisions, enforcement of such standards, and a financial and technological fund for assistance to raise Mexico to U.S. standards.

Yet the limited nature of NAFTA as a pure free-trade agreement would have to be extended to cover such social, labor, and environmental issues in a way that would ensure that the Mexican Constitution would guarantee popular and labor rights. There would also have to be a mechanism for raising a large pool of financial resources to protect the three nations' common environment. As such an agreement would be inherently unequal, Mexico might well see the United States and Canada as the political enforcers of such legalities as well as the reluctant donors of governmental revenues to upgrade Mexico's conditions essential for both production and human existence. Other inequalities would also prevail. For U.S.-Canadian pressures to create an open door for their capital investments in Mexico would be only partly restricted by the Mexican government and would not necessarily be followed by an open door for Mexican workers to take up residence, work, and prosper in the United States or Canada.[13]

Thus the NAFTA pact would be more than a free-trade agreement, less than a comprehensive common market for goods, and far short of a customs union or economic union allowing the free movement of capital and labor. Rather, NAFTA would approximate a sphere of influence emphasizing unequal relations between its member nations; the United States and Canada would establish the strongest link in terms of trade and investment based on financial and industrial puissance, empowering them to satellize Mexico individually and jointly and guide its destiny.

THE CANADIAN-U.S. LINK

As two former British colonies, the United States and Canada established the initial link in a free-trade zone that became the fulcrum for the subsequent free-trade agreement with Mexico.

Although the 13 North American colonies had broken free of Britain in 1783, a strong British presence had dominated the Canadian economy until the end of World War II. The United States then displaced Britain as dominant owner of Canadian natural resources. This situation lasted until the early 1970s, when Prime Minister Trudeau and important provincial leaders, seeking to regain control of Canada's future, passed and implemented the Foreign Investment Review Act, curbed U.S. ownership in Canada, and pursued numerous cultural and other measures to foster a separate Canadian identity.

As the U.S.-Canadian bilateral trade link had strengthened, however, stimulation to mutual industrial production was backed by both national governments and the interlocks of national and transnational banks, industries, and commercial corporations. By the time the Mulroney government took office in 1984, free trade with the United States had become a top priority.

The pressures for mutual economic development had meanwhile put the environment at risk as greater production feeding free-trade consumption also increased the use and burning of nonrenewable sources of energy, causing air, water, and other forms of pollution. "The health of bilateral [U.S.-Canadian] relations, of diplomatic relations ... is much more dependent on binational balance, and is not directly related to environmental deterioration," John E. Carroll wrote. "Free trade and economic integration, while containing potential to put the environment at risk, lend themselves to reduction of damage to diplomacy, to bilateral relations between these two northern neighbors."[14]

By making transborder pollution and acid-causing emissions a diplomatic issue, the underlying dangers to the ecosystem of both nations was minimized, obfuscating earlier conflicts that had culminated in a struggle over environmental issues. In the U.S.-Canadian disagreement in the 1970s, the United States had faulted Canada for its environmental position. With only 27 million people, Canada had initially viewed its large land mass and extensive resources as part of an inexhaustible frontier territory to be used as required, and had relied on the diluting capacity of the natural world to absorb pollutants. By contrast, when the United States looked to its 200 plus million population and overburdened ecosystems, it saw a need to control the sources of pollution regardless of the air, water, and natural environment's capacity to absorb more destructive effluents and emissions. United States environmentalists were able to use courts to force the government into compliance. During most of the 1970s, Canada's large-scale, mostly energy-related developments along its southern border with the United States became a development corridor that the United States feared threatened northern U.S. environments such as the Boundary Water Canoe area in Minnesota, Flathead Lake in Montana, Lake Champlain in

Vermont and New York, and other highly polluted U.S. areas already over-burdening the environment.

Then in 1978 the acid rain debate excoriated the United States as the polluter threatening Canada's natural ecosystem and economy.

Yet there was no way to keep political expediency for bilateral free trade from relegating this environmental protection issue to the background. Both nations pursued enlarged production, employment, and the use of energy sources to stimulate output, consumption, trade, and profits. Few indeed heard the utopian prescriptions calling for a modulation of these economic goals and the consequent reduction in demand for natural and energy resources.[15]

And, with the bilateral U.S.-Canadian agreement in force, the United States moved to establish a bilateral link with Mexico.

NAFTA FOR MEMBERS ONLY

With the end of the old British Commonwealth trade preferences and the advent of the European Economic Community's discriminatory trade against outsiders, the European Economic Community created a trade bloc that was for members only, but linked less-industrialized nations from Africa and Asia by the Youndé Agreement and the Lomé Convention.

Japan and Asia's newly industrialized economies sought to tie their economic dealings through several trade, investment, and political blocs to draw in the rest of Asia in a members-only trade and investment zone.

Meanwhile, the United States sought its own bilateral free trade pacts in the Americas and elsewhere. NAFTA was thus envisioned as a free-trade area for members only, to eliminate tariff and nontariff barriers, using rules of origin covering the materials and output of major industries. And such bilateral, managed trade might possibly become the model for the expanded creation of a continental trade bloc in the Americas.

CHAPTER 11

Domestic Reorganization and the Emergent Zone of Influence

The creation of the largest trading bloc in the world was at stake. The timing was also precise. At a historic interregnum in both the United States and Mexico, the simultaneous disintegration of economic relations and social tranquility led towards political efforts to create a North American trade bloc and eventual sphere of influence.

Mexico held hopes to industrialize, but had yet to universalize its material base, to draw the great majority to the urban domain of wage-paying industries, to mechanize agriculture and do away with the millions of small peasants and *ejiditarios*, to extend a nationwide infrastructure for transportation and communications, to upgrade the population's standard of existence, and to transform its 92 millions into a body of consumers dependent on the market. Yet, as Mexico switched course to become a secondary industrial power, sweeping people off the land into cheap-labor manufacturing, these people could no longer raise their own food or provide for their own necessities. Because workers required wages high enough to purchase these needs and a workday length that would allow them adequate time to rebuild their energies for the next day of labor, the political context of once dirt-cheap labor would change in the overpopulated urban domain.

Meanwhile north of the Rio Grande, the United States had suffered an acute, increasingly intense accumulation crisis since 1971.

As its competitive industrial base had slipped and traditional heavy industry deserted millions of unskilled, high-paid workers, the export of capital and equipment and the relocation of production and its essential relations with a foreign workforce spread the blight of U.S. unemployment. The effects were experienced by industries supplying materials and wholesalers who serviced these industries; commercial outlets that relied on a market of blue-color families; community-based builders, realtors, employees, and teachers whose salaries were paid by tax-collecting local governments; and an army of unemployed dependent on government welfare and services. To fill the profit, wage, income, and tax-collection vacuum, for more than two decades government went ever-deeper into debt, borrowing the funds no longer generated from the nation's eroding tax base, extending the disaccumulation process from production relations to the social sphere once sustained by governments.

State Industrial Policy to Sidestep Crisis

The government's way out of the crisis was the development of an "industrial policy" to redirect the global flow of revenues, thus creating new channels for commercial income and new forms of employment to reverse industrial disaccumulation; to encourage the export of capital employing earlier modes of industrial labor; to import industrial goods that had previously been exported; and to shift the U.S. workforce to new, higher-paid, more technical tasks at one pole and, at the other, unskilled, low-wage service jobs. Thus had the United States switched from being a nation of industrial workers and farmers to an economy that employed low-paid service workers and better-paid, high-tech labor. Industrial policy was shifted to technical calculations, and domestic geographic frontiers were extended to locations abroad.

Government economic theorists immediately looked to "global competition" as a just rationale for shifting domestic production towards cybernetic advances, making greater technological investments for continuous processing using highly trained and skilled labor, thereby displacing a large segment of the unskilled. Capital's overall relations with the workforce itself would thus be changed. The old relations with the unskilled were then to be transferred to dealing with labor in the foreign domain, where manufacturers in turn would import new and old U.S.-made machinery designed for labor-intensive input. As U.S. production of this exported equipment would employ more highly skilled workers than those Mexican or other foreign workers who would use them, the latter's output of consumer wares for home sales and export to U.S. consumers would maximize production and extend markets, as well as allow Mexico to pay for its imports of the technical base for its industrial revolution. In this fashion, posited state industrial policymakers, Mexico was to become an integral component in the U.S. sphere of economic influence in the Americas.

Pursuing such a division of global labor, state industrial policy hinged on U.S. "competitiveness."

"I've used competitiveness as a synonym for productivity growth," said director Van Doorn Ooms of the Committee for Economic Development in discussing these new U.S. relations of technical domestic investment and skilled labor.

"Competitiveness means the ability to achieve trade equilibrium with a high level of wages," according to director William Baumol of the C.V. Starr Center for Applied Economics at New York University.

Professor Paul Krugman of M.I.T. argued that it was not simply a matter of outflanking competitors by such transformation in U.S. technical production and labor relations; he believes that the battle to secure markets and spheres in global trade at the expense of other nations will inevitably lead to conflict, and could lead to a trade war.[1]

Such economic emancipation of the United States might involve impositions on others and increase their unwitting or unwilling transfer of surplus wealth to the United States, reenforcing their political autocracies and compromising their democracies.

AVOIDING TRADE WARFARE AT A PRICE

To avoid trade warfare, the initial try at reversing U.S. disaccumulation and excess production was to pursue free trade with Israel, then with Canada.

Having signed a 1988 free-trade pact with Canada, by 1992 the United States had already digested the Canadian economy by absorbing billions in surplus wealth, so much so that a change of political guards in 1993 ousted the Conservatives, brought in the Liberals, and raised the hackles of the isolationists bent on self-sufficiency, who worried that the U.S. farmers would use the future NAFTA to cut off Canada's exports of wheat and peanut butter.

Mexico was next on the U.S. agenda for exporting infrastructure and means of production, attempting to create a sphere of influence that was facetiously portrayed as an exercise in free-trade tariff cuts in the "national interest" and equalizing environmental and labor standards. Like the imperiums fastened on Mexico in the past, however, it was a mirrored illusion of the crisis within the United States.

The raid on Mexican resources, wealth, and labor had followed a terrain marked by so many heady adventurers before: the early conquistadors, the viceroyalties, the *encomiendas*, and *haciendas*; the recurrent imperial interpositions, and oligarchies culminating with the Díaz regime; the postrevolutionary generals, and the changing mantle of ruling presidents, cabinets, and legislatures facing off with foreign interests led by oil magnates and Western bankers. At all these points of periodic interaction, extractions were carried forward until resources were exhausted or momentary popular resistance broke the lawless order with its façade of governing authority.

By way of historic relief, the Cárdenas regime had promised a longer rein based on social justice, economic equity, national development, and a break in the imperial system impoverishing Mexico. To accomplish these objectives, however, Cárdenas sought to unify the nation economically, politically, and socially. Although such efforts were a bare outline of national consolidation to come, he built an initial economic highway that the domestic oligarchy and foreign interests would later use to their own advantage. And from 1940 when populist President Cárdenas left office, the rights of the population and the working class were continuously placed under attack, while the conservative, political status quo was reestablished under a domestic oligarchy aligning and balancing the power wielded by the *haciendas*, the bankers, manufacturing class, and commercial interests.

Forces for Mexican Reform

This coterie of power was to remain undisturbed until it was initially contested in 1968 by the middle-class and student movement. Then, with the brutal suppression of *los niños* by the police state, authority of the government was increasingly questioned by many segments of Mexican society, but given its overwhelming controls, it was rarely openly contested.

From the end of World War II to the early 1990s, Mexican economic growth had become a metaphor for the impoverishment of the country's multitude, the creation of an almost secure middle class that acted as a buffer against social change, and the enrichment of an elite largely of European extraction.

Rather than being simply a medium to negotiate and implement this alignment of classes, the central government enforced it, even if it appeared to be a cumbersome monolith beset by bureaucratic replication of functions. The bureaucracy was hampered by unending hierarchies of self-important directors of this or that detail lacking significance in itself, and it was beset by an authoritarian air of officialdom that empowered aficionados to speak of their seeming immutable and unbending implementation of policy. Bureaucrats implemented strategies based on some vague national plan designed, approved, and amended by innumerable agencies of state.[2]

Such bureaucratic, centralized state authoritarianism allegedly held no class biases. At heart though, it was a child of Mexico's wealthy elite, of their PRI that had held power over five decades. By controlling an electoral system beset by bought votes, lost ballots, and computer fraud, the election of presidents and hand-picked successors was as certain as was the maintenance of the balance of power in the federal legislature, its imposition of economic "stabilization" programs, and the implementation of austerity policies fueling unemployment and cutting social services.[3] So long as the people's resistance could be localized and channeled into party "opposition," military power could be minimized, both in size and political influence.[4] Conflict over the allocation of wealth and poverty could thus be confined to a political arena where the party of wealth ruled the presidency and the national parliament.

Although labor militancy reemerged in the 1970s, it was not until the 1980s that organized labor openly reasserted itself, trying to protect real wages in the face of state income policies and hyperinflation. And before the Salinas government began its reforms in 1989, living standards had fallen for over a decade and the annual inflation rate had reached a ten-year high point of 159.2 percent.

Poverty was rampant in both cities and countryside, too. The peso had weakened. Foreign bankers and the International Monetary Fund were worried that Mexico could not pay service charges on its $80 billion foreign debt and might never repay the debt itself. And these *extrajeros* demanded repayment in Mexican goods, foreign exchange, and share holdings in banks, business enterprises, and land.

To generate output, employ its population, and pay its debt, Mexico was being forced to reform its domestic economy to raise production for export, elevate wages, open the door to barrier-free trade, and encourage unfettered foreign investments. By 1993 there were over 2,000 U.S. subsidiaries operating in Mexico that employed over 600,000 workers and freely exported their output to the United States. This economic invasion was to be capped by the North American Free Trade Agreement that over 15 years was intended to create a single $7 trillion-a-year market covering 360 million consumers in Canada, the United States, and Mexico.

With 70 percent of all Mexican imports coming from the United States, with U.S. exports tripling after Mexico slashed tariffs in 1986 to enable the U.S. delivery of technology and machinery that transformed a $5.4 billion U.S. trade deficit into a $5.7 billion surplus, NAFTA promised to create a sphere of influence that would keep Japan and Western Europe at a trade and investment disadvantage unless they too invested in Mexico to employ cheap labor to produce goods for tariff-free export to the United States and Canada.[5]

The drawbacks of NAFTA for Mexico would include the depopulation of the rural domain, the ruin of small-scale agriculture, the transformation of the rural peasantry into landless charges—their own self-enemies as consumers of U.S. corn and processed foods—and the proletarianization of the population in the service of both domestic and foreign capital. It was the latter step that was heralded by economists as the quintessential element of industrialization and accumulation to liberate the nation.

But in fact, the ability to mass produce was brought on by the privatization of the major instruments of labor, the centralization of control over both production and political life, and the relative impoverishment of those who worked for their keep. These millions would one day appear as consumers in a mass society bred to industry and urban existence, thereby losing the certainty of overseeing their destiny in the morrow. Their situation would be made all the worse by the lack of democracy, the absence of equity on the political terrain of campaigns and votes, and the cheap shots presidents Salinas and Clinton fired in their 1993 assertions that, should NAFTA fail to pass the U.S. Congress, trade and investment partners in Europe and Asia would fill the gap, seeking their own bilateral free trade agreements with Latin America.

MEXICO'S DOMESTIC REORGANIZATION AND THE OPPOSITION

The need to fasten added revenues on the bony spine of Mexico's impoverished economy at the expense of traditional economic and cultural ways was obvious in the 1980s and 1990s. Traditional rites and barriers of festivals and rituals such as the *Matanza* slaughter of goats the Spaniards brought to the New World would succumb to the modernity of government transport, sales, and income taxes on operations, as well as bribes to health inspectors and highway police.[6] The ancient Nahuatl language of the Aztecs and other Indian peoples of central Mexico, the many tongues of the indigenous of the Yucatán and the hot country would finally give way to commercial Spanish and words of Spanglish.[7]

In the 1970s, 1980s, and early 1990s, the nation's resources had again been raided to give state subsidies to the wealthy and their Institutional Revolutionary party. The state and PRI-controlled unions had enforced wage and price controls to extract added surplus, whipsawing peasants, workers, and the underclasses, who were pushed and punished to the limits of their endurance.

State subsidies to the powerful vastly exceeded government revenues by 1982; the fiscal crisis was resolved by cutting social welfare, wages, and public services. As government benefits to labor fell, though, the PRI's hold on the working class was somewhat weakened, but it was maintained in part by opening PRI-controlled unions to the changes demanded by its rank-and-file for greater participation in shaping both union and state policies. Nonetheless, almost every PRI union concession was initially refused, only to be made grudgingly in the face of labor's militant opposition.

Radical factions within PRI-controlled unions had fought to change union policies, elect a new leadership, and raise economic and political issues concerning labor's subservient position under employer and state domination. The main opposition during the 1970s was mobilized by the *Sindicato de Trabajadores Electricistas de la República Mexicana* (STERM) to defend its workers' interests against the official electricians' union, which was both affiliated to the Mexican Workers' Confederation (CTM) and under the thumb of the PRI-controlled Federal Electricity Commission. The labor opposition initially raised the issue of subsidized energy provided by the government to privately owned industry, so that total revenues collected were too small to pay electrical workers their due in fair wages.

As a way to sidestep the radical faction, the PRI's Federal Electricity Commission then pressured STERM to join with the official union in a single body called the *Sindicato Unico de Trabajadores Electricistas de la República Mexicana* (SUTERM), knowing the merger would eventually fail and allow conservative union leaders to purge STERM leaders from office. Fighting for reinstatement, the opposition then created the *Tendencia Democrática* within the official union, gained support from other unions, and established a 1973 coalition with other workers in education, steel, railroads, petroleum, communications, and distilling.

As its influence spread to other unions, moreover, insurgencies appeared in the major industries that led to a 1975 coalition of unions that gathered, exchanged views, and issued what became known as the "Guadalajara Declaration." This declaration made three basic demands: (1) state control of collectivized agriculture, foreign assets, and foreign trade, (2) union democracy and worker planning of the state sector of the economy, and (3) defense of "revolutionary" educational rights, real wages, subsidized housing, public services, and social security.[8]

The old union leadership and the state authorities naturally viewed the opposition within these unions as an unwanted pressure group seeking wider democratic participation for members, and threatening continued PRI hegemony. Recoiling against the new syndicalism, the Echeverría administration moved powerfully to purge the opposition leaders from their unions and jobs in government-run industries.

The opposition now found itself largely isolated and almost defenseless in the context of the limited, predefined sphere of union affairs because it had gone beyond economic issues and moved too fast in assuming political tasks without cultivating allies on the Left or building its own political party.[9] Not only was its syndicalist movement a frail foundation to contest the PRI-controlled unions, but the old unionized labor elite viewed the upstarts pursuing political change as going beyond earlier union concentration on pure economic goals. As the job positions and state social security of the union rank-and-file in the advanced sectors of the economy had been secure and these workers would risk losing neither, they became the foundation for keeping the union movement in the PRI fold.

Yet in the course of the rapidly failing economy during the 1980s, rank-and-file sinecures and needs were continually put in jeopardy. Unable to ignore the pressure from below, the elite unions in both government industries and the private sphere began to take up the refrain of the old militant electrical workers that government subsidies to large industry and its owners were undercutting relative wages and living standards.

As the union bureaucracies were forced to take up these demands, moreover, the CTM leadership was pressured to give up its traditional role of imposing PRI wage policies on labor and to make demands for a new division of the value of labor's output, as well as for union participation in shaping PRI policy. Thereafter the old state wage controls of the 1970s were contested by labor's demands to maintain real wages against inflation, to regulate prices, to redistribute wealth through tax impositions, to restructure the economic apparatus to protect jobs, to retain control over nationalized industry and banking, to oversee the economy, and to curtail the impositions of foreign capital.

Unionized workers not only sought a more secure place in the economic system, then, but they viewed their quest as a fount of a viable, wage system that would also sustain the future domestic market.[10]

LOOKING TO THE 1990S

There were two limitations on labor's formulation, however. The PRI government held short-term plans to reorganize the economy to reward domestic capital and long-term plans to import foreign technology accommodating foreign investors and commercial interests.

So long as the unions were too weak to contest the PRI's power, the government would stimulate the economy by lavishing rewards on financial investors and the owners of great means of production, land, and services. Thus the PRI foresaw that in the 1990s, banks and industries would be completely denationalized, domestic investments stimulated, real wages cut, production for export increased, profits secured, nominal poverty subsidies increased, foreign exchange reserves enlarged, the foreign debt reduced, and North American investors encouraged. All this would reorganize Mexico by social class, stimulating the accumulation of wealth and imposing degrees of impoverishment if not servitude.

Steps in these directions were begun by the Salinas government from 1989 to 1994 as it followed a policy of austerity that aided the rich at the expense of the population at large. These government measures improved the rate of economic growth from 2.5 to 4.4 percent a year, cut government spending, slashed annual inflation to about 11 percent, raised foreign exchange reserves to $18.3 billion, started an antipoverty, community-participation program worth $2.3 billion annually, called for a floating exchange rate effectively devaluing the peso vis-à-vis the dollar, and announced a new wage and price agreement with labor unions and major employers that covered the varying value of the peso.[11]

The overall formulation was purposefully skewed in the direction of wealth accumulation, the centralization of economic controls, urban industrialization, and depopulation of the countryside to recruit future wage workers. And this restructuring of Mexican society was centered on tightened economic ties with the United States.

TIGHTENING ECONOMIC TIES IN NORTH AMERICA

United States economic influence over Mexico proceeded by degrees of pressure and rewards during the postwar period. Led by the *maquiladora* program, this sphere allowed U.S. firms to produce with cheap Mexican labor that was both exploited and unprotected from industrial hazards. As the *maquilas* exported almost duty-free (excepting the value added by cheap Mexican labor) to the United States, consumers in the United States had access to competitive goods that U.S. workers often no longer produced. This accelerated the export of U.S. investment capital in the form of means of production as well as the export of U.S.-made components, and enhanced the import of consumer goods and manufactured parts; the balance of payments reflected the process.

The extension of the U.S. sphere through the accelerated export of instruments for production also laid the foundation for the proposed North American Free Trade Agreement, which formally concentrated on trade relations rather than on foreign investments. In fact, extended foreign investments were the bedrock of NAFTA, as the free-trade sphere meant U.S. investments in production using inexpensive, unprotected Mexican labor would gain access to a wide market both within Mexico and across the Mexican-U.S. border. The vision of a vast, integrated economy would place U.S. transnational production and marketing organizations in a prime position against all competitors, Mexican or otherwise. Once in place, moreover, U.S. investments would exert strong influence on Mexican political and social life, so that what began as a trade agreement would eventually be transformed into a sphere of control.

True, the language of NAFTA concentrated largely on trade relations, and the U.S.-controlled World Bank extolled the prospective advantages of NAFTA for the United States, emphasizing that the *maquiladora* industries along the U.S.-Mexican border had provided an expanding free-trade zone that was followed by Mexico's reduction of trade barriers from 1986 to 1993 that covered 80 percent of Mexican production.

In the same period, average U.S. tariffs on Mexican goods were 4 percent, so that U.S. output in Mexican-based plants also reaped a wider market.

Meanwhile, from 1976 to 1992, U.S. exports to Mexico nearly tripled from $15 billion to $41 billion—largely from transfers of plant and equipment, not from any substantial increase in consumer purchases. These exports generated some 350,000 U.S. jobs, adding up a total of 600,000 U.S. jobs in 48 states supporting exports to Mexico.

The resulting transformation of the 1987 U.S. trade deficit with Mexico of $5.9 billion into a 1992 surplus of $4.7 billion was viewed by optimists as a sign of NAFTA's potential to generate 150,000 to 200,000 additional U.S. jobs and by pessimists as what could be the first stage of runaway U.S. factories taking away 500,000 to 5 million jobs.[12]

The crux of the NAFTA relationship was not just trade patterns locking Mexico into U.S. markets, then, but the degree to which U.S. transnational investments would invade the Mexican economy, gaining a foothold that would fuel the cross-border movement of capital equipment, finance capital, labor, materials, energy, and ideology.

"It is known inside your circle of White House and corporate allies that companies are pursuing an informal moratorium on announced relocations of factories to Mexico until after the Nafta vote in Congress," Ralph Nader wrote President Clinton in the first week of November 1993, indicating that a similar moratorium had been observed by companies operating plants in Canada before the decisive 1988 vote on the Canadian-U.S. Free Trade Agreement, which was followed "by a rush of shutdowns and relocations" because it was cheaper for Canadian and U.S. companies to operate their plants in the United States.[13]

Republicans in Congress privately made league with the transnationals and President Clinton's political elite, despite opposition from organized labor and ordinary working people facing potential wage contraction, job losses and reduced standards of health and safety.

In the days leading to the NAFTA vote in Congress, political fights erupted all along the brittle battle line. The president feared that the 20 or so meetings he had held with corporate leaders invited to the White House had armed billionaire NAFTA-opposed Ross Perot and his allies to "characterize this Administration as representing the elite and corporate interests, and ... [the] opposition as representing the working people." Perot fulminated that nearly 6 million U.S. jobs were being put in jeopardy.

"No one has shown how a wealthy country can grow wealthier and create more jobs unless there is global economic growth through trade," Clinton countered in his address to businessmen, foreseeing he was about to be stripped of leverage to persuade Japan and other competitors to open their markets further. "There is simply no evidence that you can do it any other way. If we don't do this with our closest neighbor, it's going to be hard for us to have the credibility to make the case for the world."[14]

But U.S. workers and their unions feared that once U.S. production operations took root in cheapened Mexican soil and other foreign *milieu,* comparatively higher costs of operations in the United States would lead other companies to move under Commerce Department guidance. In 1991 the U.S. Commerce Department had encouraged more than a dozen firms to enter the Caribbean with the promise of saving wages and undercutting higher U.S. health and safety standards.[15] Under NAFTA, GATT, and other economic trade alliances, competitor nations might also complain that higher U.S. health and safety standards acted as barriers to free trade, keeping their products out of U.S. markets. Thus they might pressure the United States to either waive the standards or pay perpetual damages to the offended country for the loss of sales in the United States. Under NAFTA, low-wage Mexican goods and less restrictive health and safety standards might thereby invade the United States.

"The new trade agreements are invading internal sovereignties," Ralph Nader wrote, adding that even a threat of movement to Mexico by a U.S. company could generate pressure to lower U.S. wages.[16]

Thereby the mobility of U.S. capital would outflank and soften the resistance of the relatively expensive, immobile U.S. labor force.

Officials at the World Bank made light of this projected future. S. Shahid Husain, vice president for Latin America and the Caribbean, argued that the Mexican economy was only one-twentieth the size of the U.S. economy, that it would thus not drastically change the way the giant U.S. economic machine would operate, and that crucial business decisions would be based upon not only wage differences, but also higher U.S. productivity (six times that of Mexico in 1993), the skill of the workforce, access to high-quality transport and other infrastructure, proximity to markets and new technology sources, and a reliable governmental and judicial system.

"The image of droves of U.S. corporations heading to Mexico just doesn't make sense when these other considerations are taken into account," Husain concluded. He added that the World Bank since 1987 has provided $12 billion in loans to Mexico to prepare it to be a more effective partner for its North American neighbors and also has promised $1.8 billion in loans during 1994-96 to support Mexico's environmental protection and cleanup. According to Husain, this policy would effectively create a way station for viable future trade with Mexico and 470 million potential Latin American customers.[17]

So the United States had it right in the first place: Mexico was its springboard to all the Americas.

CHAPTER 12

Free Trade and the
Great U.S. Transformation

From the British occupation of 13 colonies in North America to the 1776 Revolution and an ever-expanding frontier creating regional and sectional interests, the West as a way of structured relations has shaped the economic and political landscape.

Early nineteenth-century relations centered on three expanding modes of regional production and labor: (1) indentured labor and wage workers in Eastern workshops linked to merchant trade with Europe, Africa, the Caribbean, and the expanding southern and western frontiers, (2) southern slave labor producing staples, linked by plantation owners to imports of slaves from Africa and tools, food, and textiles from the northeastern states, the western frontier and Europe, and (3) yeoman farm labor occupying the expanding western frontier, producing subsistence and supplying eastern and southern markets.

From the end of the Civil War to World War I, the eastern system of wage labor for industrial production and mining and salaried workers in office management, commerce, and finance extended its sway to the expanding West and parts of the South. These regions variously deployed the labor of northern European immigrants; Jews and slavs of eastern Europe; Italians, Sicilans and Sarcedotians of southern Europe; and convicts, children, and Chinese chain gangs.

Just as transportation and communication regularized the marketing of goods and services, the brute force of managers and employers' guards—often backed by government troops—kept labor cheap, yet not passive; powerless, yet hopeful for a better life for their children.

After the Civil War, the South slowly returned to rural peonage, sharecropping, and company mill towns. The frontier of farming, ranching, and mining stretched beyond the old Northwest Territories into the Ohio Valley to California, Texas, and New Mexico. Agriculture and the extraction of resources increased under the pressure of an enlarging urban industrial base and labor force and the growing needs for raw materials for manufacturing and food to supply the urban domain.

Subsistence wages, treacherous, often deadly industrial work, and the outlawing of unions by states fueled the rapid accumulation of wealth by the upper classes. And the frontier was beset by constant conflicts and local wars among large investors operating mines, ranchers grazing and running herds, breaching the fences erected by smallholders and sodbusters.

The Great War quickened the pace of industrial expansion and consolidation, and the postwar period extending to 1941 heralded mass production, intensified commerce, and unrelenting unemployment that impacted the nation's impoverished workforce in growing cities. The farm population also began a steady decline, exploited by corporate lenders and speculators, struck down by the depression, forced into near starvation and set afoot on the search for survival in western states. The South meanwhile languished between the old modes of land tenure, the new urban financial centers in Houston and Atlanta, and its own "gold rush" in oil and mineral wealth.

From the bowels of depression, the New Deal programs of the 1930s reframed the conditions essential for production and survival, building an economic and political coalition of desperate farmers, labor, employers, and Democrats representing the populations and minorities of the large cities. Moved by promises of welfare, production, employment, and markets, these forces sought future prosperity, but economic viability was saved only by World War II production and demands.

The second Great War weakened the old regional divisions, strengthening industrial and financial capital nationwide, making urban centers the employment thresholds of manufacturing, commerce, finance, real estate, and professional services. Agriculture fell under the grip of agribusinesses and corporations directing investments for the production and marketing of food. Many workers in basic industries, agriculture, and services were shifted to employment in the government, in the military, and in the latest arsenals of technological production. "Statefare," warfare, and welfare enlarged government bureaucracies, budgets, and deficits. Lobbying for interests by region, social class, industry, and agricultural specialties burgeoned.

These interests became, however, a powerful impediment to unified national action in the political and economic realm. Domestically, they directed the operations of corporations deserting unskilled and semiskilled labor by moving from the old realm of basic industries in the Northeast and

Midwest to the high-tech jobs and dirt-cheap service labor of the Northwest, California, and the South. In agriculture, too, displacement of ranchers large and small loomed as three giant conglomerates took charge of 90 percent of all meat processing, placing production and price restraints on the operations of the 2 to 3 million remaining small cattle farmers. And in fruits, vegetables, sugar, and grains, a dozen giant enterprises dictated national pricing and national policy.

In the ranks of labor, the AFL-CIO bloated its leadership and colluded with an overpaid, overstaffed army of corporate bureaucrats to save wage costs by bargaining away hundreds of thousands of jobs. At the same time, these unions neglected to organize among the lowliest workers and forgot to build solidarity with workers and unions in other nations—the same nations to which the United States exported food, goods, capital, production operations, and jobs.

Together these forces centered Washington trade battles on the narrow struggle of labor unions and minorities against domestic corporations, as well as the unending battle of grain farmers, ranchers, and exporting companies against vulnerable textile manufacturers and other enterprises demanding carte blanche barriers against foreign competitors.

CHANGING THE DOMESTIC FRAMEWORK

By the late 1980s, however, the domestic economic framework had completely changed and led to demands for new foreign policies in the wake of the breakdown of Eurasian communism, and changes in foreign competition based on superior investment ratios, technological breakthroughs, new trade techniques (leading to enlarging, unfavorable U.S. balances), the alteration of domestic production relations, and the extension of new ties with workers abroad.

United States transnationals pondered their counterthrusts, elevated the technical level of machines and trained workers, leading to a rise in labor productivity, and schemed to sell competitively at home and abroad. Fears of imbalance between productive capacity and purchasing power undercut national plans to sustain and retrain the unemployed workforce and to export the surplus output that American workers could produce, but could not sell at home. Government promotion of unrestrained "free trade" amounted to little more than creating custom unions with agreeing nations (EEC, NAFTA, APEC, GATT, etc.). Such a policy might set the framework for transnational corporations to cut costs and the domestic workforce by exporting millions of jobs under the banner of rectifying the balance of trade and at some future date creating the foundation for high-paid, skilled jobs at home.

Basic changes in technology had rehabilitated some old domestic industries by introducing continuous processing that did not require the intervention of any labor—unskilled or semiskilled. As the demand for skilled, technical workers remained limited and new industries did not take up the unemployed that lacked such skills, a flotsam of permanent jobless required both state welfare and retraining. When the latter failed and the former was limited by funding and time, the cumulation of a desperate underclass appeared in both the urban and rural domain from New York to Appalachia, from the rural South to urban California, from the lumber regions of the Northwest back to the small and mid-sized farm communities in the Midwest. In all these regions, the depression bred anger, despair, few alternatives, and desperation to survive by any means.

There was not only a growing body without work or welfare, but also a growing surplus of goods and equipment that could not be sold to those in need, nor to other social groups or classes, nor to industries that hesitated to invest in new rounds of production that could not be sold. As the wages of U.S. workers were meanwhile leveraged down by employers turning to low-wage workers at home and abroad, living standards fell, fears rose, and demands escalated for improvements in wages and working conditions.

High hopes for new technical jobs for those without qualifying education and training hinged on new investments in production and worker training, but these investments were being made abroad to train and employ a foreign pool of unorganized labor. It is hardly surprising that within the United States the conditions for poverty, a growing underground trade in stolen goods and narcotics, and inexplicable personal degradation would prevail for the rest of the twentieth century.

The classic dilemma of too many goods chasing too few buyers not only led to reduced production, employment, and prices, but also to a new political coalition of high-tech workers, transnational corporations, favored agribusinesses, and those small enterprises and subsidized, retrained workers who could be brought in with each round of state expenditures. Recognizing that the flow of incremental wealth now had to come from abroad, the new alliance called for extended markets. Echoed from the highest reach of corporate and public office, market considerations were clearly seen in the plans of the president to do away with the New Deal political coalition and to build a tripartite U.S. sphere for trade and investment in Latin America, Pacific Asia, and Europe.

While Mexico came into the U.S. sphere because the executive office bribed the U.S. Congress and relied on the dictatorship of the 65-year rule of the party of the Mexican oligarchy, the regional economies of Pacific Asia were initially willing only to reduce tariffs and trade barriers product by product, and the members of GATT offered their own restrictions on free and fair trade based on their own autarchic plans.

Wage Funds and the New Relations of Production

Historically, almost all industrialized nations developed funds out of which wages and welfare were paid from total new value produced at home or drawn from others.

Although the allotment for the upper social classes and their supporters increased through usurpation, market forces, and state intervention, the wage fund kept the rest of the population at a given standard of exisence, and many in this group fell below a subsistence level. The condition of those dependent on wages varied with the relative strength of these classes vis-à-vis those who ruled, so the condition of the many changed from place to place and time to time. But whatever reform changed their wage-fund allotment, it was only by a total, revolutionary change that the fund temporarily disappeared and took another form, be it the emancipation of the working population, the direct possession or ownership of the means and instruments of existence, or the taking and reconstruction of state power.

When the revolt of the underclasses could be controlled and legitimacy negotiated, reform guided by the upper classes usually led to the designed structure of a new fund for wages and welfare. The precise attributes of the fund were essential to functionally realign class, group, or caste power. But in every nation vastly different permutations obviously appeared; in the case of the United States and Mexico, these permutations gave rise to a kaleidoscope of temporary balances by race, class, and power. In both nations such reforms were directed by the upper classes at the population's peril during the 1990s.

The general U.S. scheme linked domestic crises with the foreign domain in a way that displaced the old U.S. workforce, which was left on its own to secure lesser positions from a smaller share of the total wage fund. Nor was there any prospect that sufficient state resources would be provided to transform these displaced workers into members of the new, high-skilled workforce that was to be paid at a more elevated tier from total wage allotments. Part of the domestic fund was also transferred abroad by export of the means and relations of production in the name of maximizing profit returns on capital. This transfer involved both wrenching job displacements and lack of new employment at home.[1]

To accomplish its goals, the U.S. government pushed for free-trade blocs, that is to say, unrestricted commerce between members of collective groups of nations that would impose restrictions against outside competitors. After implementing the U.S.-Israeli and Canadian-U.S. bilateral pacts, the U.S. negotiated NAFTA, the first so-called high-wage-nation/low-wage-nation agreement. The next attempt to consolidate an Asian-Pacific free-trade area was destined to be delayed, mainly by China and Japan, because China feared U.S. political impositions might be linked to trade and Japan was keeping the United States as the guardian of Asian security at the same time the commerce and investments Nippon had already secured minimized the U.S. economic role.

In the great contest for markets in Asia, the United States was pitted against both Japan and the European community; in 1992 the E.C. held a greater volume of trade with the Pacific Rim than it held with the United States.

1992 Trade
(In Billions of Dollars)

E.C. & Pacific Rim	E.C. & U.S.	U.S. & Pacific Rim
E.C. Exports $96	E.C. Exports $95	U.S. Exports $128
E.C. Imports $153	E.C. Imports $111	U.S. Imports $215

The polycentered Western trade blocs were all concentrating on East Asia, which was Japan's traditional commercial/investment domain.

Western Europe was casting its net towards both Eastern Europe and East Asia. "Europe is no longer the navel of the universe," the Bonn daily *General Anzeiger* editorialized on 23 November 1993. "The new world order, made fun of so far because nobody knows what it is, is taking shape. It is a world that has more than one center, and it is up to the Europeans not to withdraw but to find their place in it."

Looking to the many centers in Asia, the Asian-Pacific Economic Cooperation (APEC) group had barely defined its goals before U.S. trade representative Mickey Kantor was trying to force GATT negotiations in some cases and threatening to loosen U.S. commercial ties in other cases. "We trust our partners in Geneva will take careful note of this solidarity and unity of purpose of APEC members," he said, stretching believability.

"The thinly veiled U.S. threats about having Asia as an alternative to Europe if world trade talks fail are absurd," chided a French Foreign Ministry official. "It's as if France said it no longer cared about the United States because most of our trade is with other European countries."[2]

GATT AND WTO: FREE TRADE, BUT STILL ON HOLD

The moment of free trade for members of GATT constantly receded as dead-end barriers were encountered and negotiators moved over a switch-back trail of subsidies and tariffs that heralded free trade in a vaguely defined future that saw GATT largely replaced by the World Trade Organization (WTO) in 1995.

The United States set a strategic goal of overall trade advantages, yielding on the questions of the niggling favors sought by French-subsidized farmers, Japanese protectionists, and German revanchists. And the

Big Three in the West, the United States, Britain, and Germany pummeled France to adopt the GATT accord by appeasing French farmers with a compromise that gave France wheat export subsidies worth $700 million.

This strengthening of subsidized French wheat exports was offset by major concessions for indefinite U.S. tariff-free access to Spanish markets for its 2.3 million tons of corn and large E.C. tariff cuts on markets for fruits, vegetables, nuts, almonds, pork, and processed turkey worth several hundred million dollars in U.S. exports. And E.C. tariffs on grains would eventually be lowered to allow U.S. grain to enter at competitive prices.[3]

Then the United States looked to the East.

CHARMING EAST ASIAN TRADERS

As he postured to break into the charmed circle of investing in Asia, President Clinton became Boeing Aircraft's principal salesman.

The largest U.S. exporting corporation, Boeing sold Asia half of all the 747's ever made. China by 1993 bought one of every six of its planes. Although an average of 85 percent of the parts and content of its planes remained U.S.-made, Mitsubishi Heavy Industries in 1993-94 made the fuselages of Boeing's 777 jets in Nagoya as a quid pro quo to get Japan's big airlines to buy the plane. Thus as Boeing announced 28,000 layoffs in Seattle, Mitsubishi was hiring in Nagoya, with a goal of achieving a Japanese input of 20 percent for Boeing planes. The logic of exporting such relations of production was that creating a single high-tech job for a factory worker in Seattle might require creating six jobs abroad.

As such company joint ventures and sharing of production and markets proceeded—hollowing out U.S. industry and switching the locale of production relations—the United States as the remaining, single world superpower had begun to withdraw its military forces from Asia, attempting to place Japan, China, and lesser powers in a strategic position to maintain their own balance of forces. In November 1993, President Clinton told the Asia-Pacific Economic Cooperation forum that the United States' place in the world would "be determined as much by the skills of our workers as by the strength of our weapons, as much by our ability to pull down foreign trade barriers as our ability to breach distant ramparts." But in fact, the United States could no longer afford to help achieve Asian security without drawing on Asian militarized nations as a front line, nor to pierce Asian markets without corporate investment that would to a degree switch the domain of production relations from the United States to Asian economies.

Membership in APEC included most of those nations touching the Pacific Basin: Australia, Brunei, Canada, Chile (1994), China, Hong Kong, Indonesia, Japan, South Korea, Malaysia, Mexico (1993), New Zealand, Papua New Guinea (1993), the Philippines, Singapore, Taiwan,

Thailand, and the United States. Most of the Asian countries were run by authoritarian or one-party regimes and lacked any democratic tradition. To sell to these countries, the United States would have to blink at dictatorial regimes that repressed their people.

Most Asian workers were unable to protest or organize to secure decent wages and conditions of work, but they were already a lode for employment by U.S. transnationals. The sale of a supercomputer to China despite the Tiananmen Square massacre in 1989 was designed to help close the 1993 U.S. trade deficit with China of $19 billion. Secretary of State Christopher insisted that if the United States did not sell the computer, someone else would. Clearly, the United States would not risk losing jobs to protect dissidents in China.[4]

As the United States and other Western nations also sought to block the creation of a powerful East Asian economic group that might become a trade bloc to shut out the Western powers,[5] the Malaysian prime minister, Mahathir Mohamad, boycotted the November 1993 APEC meeting, fearing these Western nations were turning their foreign policies toward Asia "merely in order to have a share of the economic dynamism and the market potential." Although he too encouraged foreign investments and free markets (his near-autocracy limited domestic freedom as it expanded Malaysia's economy more than 8 percent in each of the years from 1988 to 1993), he insisted that the West should focus on Asia "as an important part of the world."[6]

Indeed, the main U.S. concern in APEC talks with Asian leaders at Blake Island in November 1993 was about American trade balances. The United States was eager to provide apples for the Japanese market, and Boeing 747's for any Pacific buyer. China was already purchasing 14 percent of Boeing's output and did business stimulating employment in almost all 50 U.S. states. Potential U.S. trade customers included people like northeast Borneo's sultan of Brunei, whose $35 billion personal fortune made him the world's wealthiest man.[7]

The leaders of APEC thus envisioned a community of Asian-Pacific economies that would work together to promote cooperative solutions to global economic problems, an open international trading system, improved education and training, and advances in telecommunications and transportation among member states.

Asia had little to fear from U.S. traders. Fortress America as an integrated economy stretching from Hudson Bay to Tierra del Fuego was hardly a credible threat to the vastly more important trade and investment ties between North America and the Economic Community. Once approved, GATT (with obligations now replaced by the WTO) promised to add some $270 billion annually to world income by the year 2002 by lowering prices for consumers no longer burdened by tariffs and achieving higher returns on global investments for export-oriented businesses.

Prices might be higher on some exports, of course, and lower on others. With government export subsidies phased out on food, world price levels would rise. With international rules established for what constitutes unfair dumping, prices might also go up; but the lower price of imports might force domestic producers to reduce their prices or go out of business. The cost edge for cheap labor in Third World states might allow them to export to industrialized nations at lower prices, too.[8] But none of this would happen if protection and subsidies continued to secure powerful special interests empowered to shape GATT and the WTO to their own requirements.[9]

The ultimate logic was to reduce everything to its cost of production without state intervention, so that global competitive prices would reflect these costs. Those unable to compete would be driven out of business, the most efficient producers would prevail, and the scale of global commerce would enlarge. The ultimate reality might mean that small industries would be destroyed,[10] the cheap goods pouring in from the Third World would undercut still other enterprises, and millions of workers in weak industries would lose their jobs. In each nation, vulnerable industries and their workers would pressure their political parties and governments for new protection and security against foreign goods, the free-trade pacts would survive more by violation of their provisions than by respect, nationalism and xenophobia would again grow rife, and tight-knit spheres of influence might emerge.

For the 1990s, however, these tendencies might be delayed by attempts to open new markets, sign new regional trade agreements, and concentrate on trading within broad spheres like the WTO. Outreach from Washington would not suffice to create an economic sphere where the United States would become the dominant power in Asia.

NAFTA, U.S. LOCAL INTERESTS, AND CONGRESSIONAL LOBBIES

The historic switch of the U.S. base of industrial production from the Eastern seaboard and the Midwest to replacement plants in the South, new technical production facilities in the West, and labor-intensive *maquiladora* factories at the borderlands found its sequel in opening the door to the entire Mexican economy.

Pressures had built from agriculture interests in the Southeastern states, as well as from technological enterprises, commercial corporations, and financial megaliths in the Eastern, Southern, and Western regions. More than half of all representatives in the House had publicly become agents of enterprise and wealth, abnegating all responsibility to labor organizations, to those lacking skill, and to small and mid-sized businesses and farmers.

As they lobbied for their local and provincial interests, companies, unions, farmers, and laborers demanded politicians do their bidding or lose office. The politicians in turn demanded that NAFTA provisions be changed, and President Clinton promised money for favored projects, trade protection of particular industries, other trade concessions such as lowering Mexican import duties more rapidly and protecting jobs by propping up certain employers. It was not an idealistic enterprise of advocacy, then, but a cheap bazaar in Americana that involved buying votes, logrolling, and pork barrel politics.[11]

In the tristate region of New York, New Jersey, and Connecticut, a revolving door had exited old textile and basic manufacturing industries and offered entrance to fields dominated by banking and finance, law and accounting, publishing and entertainment, telecommunications and high-tech research. The wand of change had swept away semiskilled production, stripping the region of one million jobs between 1988 and 1993. The garment industry with its hundreds of thousands of women, blacks, and Hispanic workers all but disappeared[12]; and a sizeable slice of basic auto manufacturing moved to Mexico under the new trade umbrella, though the highest paying jobs would remain in the United States.[13]

Included in NAFTA were crucial provisions strengthening New York protection for copyrights and other intellectual property. The pact also eliminated restrictions on U.S. ownership of Mexican subsidiaries, enabled banks and Wall Street securities firms to buy majority interests and invest in Mexican businesses, allowed Citibank's five branches opened before Mexico's 1929 restrictions to plan more branch outlets once NAFTA eliminated barriers, encouraged giant accounting and consulting firms to follow their corporate customers, and opened the door to service companies. All these new industries together were expected to employ more than 4.8 million people in the New York area. Publishing would benefit more than any, as its 220,000 New York workers (in 1993) attempted to elevate their position. In second place, chemicals centered in New Jersey would not move to Mexico because of the high cost of switching technological investments, yet would employ 189,000 or more to ship to the Mexican market under the fire of foreign competition.[14]

The tristate region led by New York was only one of many regional lobbies. Affirmative congressional votes on NAFTA thus cascaded by region, reflecting the material pressures exerted by the dominant interests in each.

Representing 88 districts in the Northeast that were replete with dying industries and their remaining unionized workers, 57 of 88 representatives voted no on NAFTA, leaving 31 who supported the latest in corporate technologies and financial agglomeration.

In the Midwestern industrial heartland, the count among the 103 representatives was close—54 against NAFTA, 49 in favor.

Although unionized labor had mobilized more money, rank-and-file troops, and lobbying muscle than it had on any other issue since the 1930s, the forces representing the latest methods and globalization of production had swung in other directions, leaving the union power base covering less than 16 percent of the entire U.S. workforce. Nonetheless, some 122 of the 156 House Democrats who voted against the trade pact had received more campaign funds from unions than from business. And those representatives supporting the agreement were largely Republicans (132 for, 43 against) or among the 102 Democrats representing rural and Southern districts and the new technological industries in the West where unions barely existed, or working class districts in which financial and corporate interests held the upper political hand.

W. Elisha, chairman of Spring Industries, Inc., the largest textile plant in South Carolina, commented on the potential movement of jobs to Mexico: "The absence of a NAFTA gives no assurance that jobs may not disappear anyway. ... Most of new jobs due to the increase of exports would be in South Carolina. Our interest in Mexico is as a market. If we open anything there, it will be a distribution center."[15]

Past expereinces reaffirmed the process. British machine industries had historically driven handicraft out of existence in India, and eastern U.S. textile factories had succumbed to better equipped shops employing cheaper labor in Asia and Latin America from the 1970s. With NAFTA now battering down Mexican tariffs to U.S.-made fabrics, the International Mass Retail Association hoped these goods would replace sources in the Far East and improve competitiveness in both retailing and telecommunications in Canada and Mexico. Telecommunication was the rage, as U.S. manufacturers represented by TIA foresaw NAFTA opportunities for equipment sales, coordinating spectrum usage, broadcasting rights, and approval procedures.[16]

The deeper logic of competition was at play, as rising expectations from Monterrey to Mendoza were electrified by the Spanish-language MTV, CXNN, HBO, and ESPAN, by faxes, satellite messages, electronic mail, and air transport. The culture of the market was being delivered to Latin and Indian peoples. New economic systems were spreading their reach under civilian leaders who imposed austerity. The mountain of Western debt accumulated in the 1980s was being forgiven or paid to the United States and its leading banks, and this reduced the net capital outflows that had imposed a decade of stagnation, declining wages, impoverishment, and the decimation of the middle class.

Although the door for electronics and communications was opening, old U.S. industries were being left behind. Textile magnate Roger Miliken took umbrage, opposing NAFTA as a job sieve. "It is unbelievable to me that

Clinton, and before him, Bush, and all the members of Congress say with an almost unanimous refrain that we have to create jobs. Now they are pushing to pass something that will take jobs away from the U.S."[17]

ROOTS OF THE UNION CRISIS

Rather than concentrate on the shift of technologies, work functions, and production locale to win global labor solidarity, the unions drove their "no" campaign with frightened rank-and-file and nonunion workers linked loosely to the political right (Ross Perot), liberals (Ralph Nader/Sierra Club), and the forces slightly left-of-center (Jesse Jackson). Thus they were left with little political staying power after NAFTA's congressional passage.

Warning that the United States would lose tariff revenues of $2–3 billion over five years, that workers losing jobs would draw on U.S. unemployment and other benefits, that the cost of NAFTA would put the government $40 billion in debt, NAFTA opponents screeched their message with little thought of achieving solidarity if they were outflanked by lobbyists with greater political clout and capital to spend.[18]

After NAFTA's passage, Lane Kirkland, president of the 13.3 million-memember AFL-CIO, bristled that President Clinton had "stiffed" working people, bribed Congress for votes, and ignored the many. "Amid all the [president's promises for] planes, trains and bridges and all the protections for citrus, peanuts, sugar and wheat, there was not one word about the rights of workers on both sides of the border to obtain decent wages and safe working conditions or to defend themselves from gross exploitation."

The nuts and bolts of the transfer of wage funds that once paid for yesterday's blue-collar workers was the wholesale transfer of jobs to Mexico. In casting his vote against NAFTA, Representative William D. Ford, a Democrat from Michigan, reported: "Hattie Smith worked for U.S. Auto Radiator for 12 years, earning $7.60 an hour. As her last duty before she was fired, Hattie was sent to Mexico to train her 65-cents-an-hour replacements—13-year-old girls working without protective gear."

As a lobby, though, unionized labor's focus was slightly skewed because its alternatives were so limited. United States unions could not even organize a significant segment of labor in the United States, let alone organize the workers of Mexico, where an oligarchical state reigned. But the unions assumed the legislators who supported the agreement were the cause of their plight, rather than the nation's shifting industrial sands. "We will not forget those Congressmen," exploded president William H. Bywater of the electronics workers union. "And I guarantee in November, my union and many other unions that feel as I do, we're going to make sure we get even at the polls."[19]

The unions focused through a darkened lens. The crisis of too many without work or with too little in wages to buy the increasing output of technical production had turned the industrial apparatus backward. Exports of both capital and manufactures were seen as some kind of universal solution to achieve sales, but these exports would not immediately employ the jobless at home. NAFTA was the most lobbied issue in a quarter of a century, and U.S. unions had viewed NAFTA and attempts to transform the U.S. and Mexican economies as outright dangerous to their interests.[20]

Estimates of potential job losses or gains swung wildly. One of the most thoughtful calculations was made by the Washington Institution for International Economics, which foresaw 318,000 new jobs by 2010 resulting from exports to Mexico, and 324,000 jobs lost because of Mexican imports, for a net U.S. job loss of 5,000.[21]

HANDING OUT PLUMS

Although the majority of Democrats in the House of Representatives actively opposed a president from their own party and most Republicans supported him, the president bought NAFTA votes with promises of economic plums, forging a narrow but solid majority that included far more Republicans than Democrats.

The Republic was "sold" lock, stock, and barrel in the sense that the split of both parties along the lines of social class led the president to buy support for the treaty through political promises and favors to polluters, agricultural interests, and representatives seeking military contracts, bridges, judgeships, and other tangible prizes. "The only thing free about NAFTA is the amount of money passed around Washington to pass it," insisted Representative James Traficant of suburban Cleveland, eliciting Texas Democrat and Agricultural Committee chairman E. (Kika) de la Garza's coy reply that, through Clinton's promises, "We have taken care of ourselves."[22]

Rather than votes being bought and sold as opponents claimed, Treasury Secretary Lloyd Bentsen called the eleventh hour arrangements "a strengthening of the agreement" that was "very important from the American point of view." This was a clear paradox obfuscating the president's acceptance of trade restrictions as bribes for congressional votes supporting the "free trade" agreement.

To win support from particular representatives, the president struck deals to restrain imports of orange juice, winter vegetables, sugar, peanut butter, and wheat. He promised a development bank to provide seed money for environmental development projects in the United States and Mexico. And whatever the interests of a particular district, both Republican and Democratic representatives largely lined up with their dominant contributors and then were picked up one-by-one by the president's men.

"Are you on the side of the Fortune 500? Or are you on the side of the unfortunate 500,000, who will lose their jobs if NAFTA passes?" asked Representative Bonior, who comes from a Detroit area blue-collar district, as he made a last-ditch speech in the House. "One thing is clear: If NAFTA passes, Henry Kissinger won't be put out of work. The Fortune 500 executives won't lose their stock options. And Lee Iacocca won't lose his job. But 500,000 Americans will. It's not fair to ask American workers to compete against Mexican workers who earn $1 an hour or less."[23]

Beyond the House floor debate, it was all over. The president had both sold Republicans and bought Democrats, double-talking or double-crossing any group or interest to get NAFTA approved. He even gave Greenpeace and NAFTA-supporting environmentalists promises to scuttle the use of the poison methyl bromide by Florida vegetable farmers to kill microscopic soil worms. Yet this promise offended Florida vegetable growers who had just withdrawn their opposition to NAFTA and put their two Republican representatives on the pro-vote line. These brave legislators then refused to again change positions, insisting that they based their support on other administration promises like the one that would reimpose tariffs on Mexican tomatoes if U.S. prices plunged.[24]

Similar vested political interests appeared throughout the United States. Some forces supported a crass, narrow self-interest overriding any sense of national interest or destiny. The lockstep of local interests pursuing provincial prosperity and autarchic production strove to make the U.S. economy a microcosm of separate, sacrosanct territories, microscopic markets, and shuttered interests that demanded protection from outside forces.

Together these forces hoped to put the nation in servitude to regional interests. President Clinton was locked in their baited trap, forced to trade off their special-interest votes for new tariffs and other barriers to protect their Florida frozen orange juice production worth $3.2 billion a year, fresh vegetables production worth $6 billion, and cucumbers worth $275 million.

To obtain votes, U.S. barriers to subsidized Canadian wheat were promised that would protect U.S. production worth $7.6 billion a year. There would also be barrier-free Canadian exports of peanut butter made from U.S. peanuts that undercut U.S. peanut butter production worth $1.3 billion.

Congressional votes were bought carte blanche to appease the wine lobby's insistence on quickly eliminating Mexican tariffs. And for promised votes from House representatives, the amount of federally guaranteed bonds to clean up the polluted U.S.-Mexican border was to be raised by the Clinton administration from $2 billion to $3 billion and would extend to community economic development projects as well.[25]

The farm lobby stretched its muscle, too; farm exports already accounted for 80 percent of U.S. export subsidies, though they made up but 10 percent of all U.S. exports. It was not surprising that the president purchased pro–NAFTA votes from legislators in cattle-raising Oklahoma for promised barriers to Australian and New Zealand beef entering the United States through Mexico. He also bought more votes from Florida by temporarily raising tariffs on Mexican tomatoes and other winter vegetables; all these tariffs together added a penny or two to the grocery bill of 265 million U.S. consumers.[26]

Labor sensed hypocrisy on the make. Robert M. McGlotten, chief lobbyist for the AFL-CIO, complained of "abandonment by Clinton. Why can't we have a deal for workers if deals can be struck for citrus, sugar and plate glass?"[27]

It was, then, a payoff for restricted-trade balloting; the administration bought votes in support of the trade accord by undermining the agreement's central objective. To eliminate taxes on imports from Mexico and Canada, the White House had agreed to reimpose trade barriers for a long list of commodities.

TRANSNATIONAL CAPITAL AND TRADERS

In contrast, transnational U.S. capital and traders held a wider vision—a barrier-free zone for transcontinental and transoceanic operations.[28]

As the off-again, on-again, principal spokesman of these groups, President Clinton provided the rationale for the linkage of open world markets and a global tide of democratic freedoms. Although his historical analogies were skewed, the logic of restricted trade leading to a production and job crisis was meant to rally pro–NAFTA forces to converge on the Congress just in time. In speaking of World War I, President Clinton recalled:

> We neglected during a careless peace what had been so dearly won in a relentless war. We turned our backs on the rest of the world. We ignored new signs of danger. We let our troops and arms fall out of readiness. We neglected opportunities for collective security in our own national interests. We succumbed to the siren song of protectionism and erected walls against peaceful commerce with other nations. Soon, we had a Great Depression and soon that depression led to aggression and then to another world war, one that would claim a half-million American lives. . . .
>
> [Americans must choose] whether we will swell the global tide of freedom by promoting democracy and open world markets or neglect the duty of our leadership, and in the process and in the withdrawal diminish hope and prosperity not only for our own people, but for billions of others throughout the world.[29]

The renewed frontier would not be in the image of Camelot, but instead would be the extension of U.S. economic interests abroad, Mexico being the test run for the latest era of expansionism. "USA-NAFTA," a pro-treaty umbrella coalition of thousands of companies and trade organizations, had spent $5–30 million for publicity, propaganda, lobbying, and Congressional arm-twisting in 1992-93. Yet this coalition had been upstaged for several months after August 1993, as Ross Perot forces, labor unions, and citizen groups had hit every congressional district. Corporate organizers strategized, waiting for the Clinton administration to sign NAFTA's side agreements, hoping to appease labor and environmentalists.

But allaying the fears of environmentalists was unlikely: Mexico was the third largest market of the U.S. chemical industry and the fastest growing one. It exported $3.1 billion worth of its production in 1992, a 20 percent increase from the previous year.[30] Lethal chemicals were used in most *maquiladoras*, active effluents being dumped in rivers or pooled in open ponds, where they seeped through the soil into the water table drawn on by the *colonias* for drinking water and other uses—NAFTA side agreements be damned.

CHAPTER 13

NAFTA: A Divisive Pact

The passage of NAFTA raised obvious questions of bad law and unfair benefits. It meant more tariff walls came down than went up to protect the special agricultural and other interests. As no amendments were allowed in the House vote on legislation to change U.S. law so the agreement could go into effect, however, benefits would be awarded the special interests by modifications that were themselves protectionist corollaries to market restrictions, so there would be free trade in theory, but not so free as it might have been.

Unskilled labor might be the big loser—up to 500,000 jobs lost in five years, opponents warned. Advocates insisted, however, that there would be a gain of 250,000 additional jobs, and economists said there would be almost 5 million more if the economy worked its usual course of leveraged expansion.[1]

Clearly, benefits would be reaped by U.S. exporters of technology and of parts to manufacture for reexport to the United States and by those selling consumer goods. Vice President Al Gore argued that 80 to 90 percent of U.S. exports to Mexico did not return by reexport to the United States. He was backed by President Clinton who said he spoke for general U.S. welfare in supporting Republican incumbents against any Democratic challenger's attack if it was based on the incumbent's vote for NAFTA.

"I'll give it to them in writing," Clinton promised, cracking the frail façade of Democratic party unity. "I'll give it to them in public statements. I do not believe any member of Congress should be defeated for doing what is plainly in the national interest."[2]

Lobbying up on the Hill, Clinton's adversaries held a different vision. The Citizens Trade Campaign, heralding its message through offices in

249

47 states, visited legislators in Washington and at their home offices. It jangled Democratic party stalwarts, insisting that the people at the grass roots had to keep control over their communities to stop the corporate boardrooms from taking charge of their destiny.

Although the group's meager budget of $400,000 spelled weakness, its allies in the unions and among nonunion workers signified their power to oust any Congress member who voted the NAFTA ticket. The AFL-CIO laid out $3.2 million to advertise against the pact to reach the hinterlands of unionists and nonunionists alike, making the NAFTA issue its largest fight ever to protect jobs against the onslaught of corporate and government schemes.

The destruction of jobs that relocated textile industries from the northern and midwestern states to the six southern ones and then moved them to Mexico, with NAFTA to hasten the exodus, meant job losses as high technology hopscotched across the Rio Grande. Smaller industries and workers—union or nonunion—that could not move made alliance from New York and Detroit to Georgia and San Francisco to defeat NAFTA, oust Congressional members who voted for the accord, and (in the memorable words of Pennsylvania Teamster leader John P. Morris) "take up a collection to get that Congressman a ticket on a bus to Mexico."

Teachers too might lose as industries closed, jobs were lost, and public expenditures shrunk. "Our self-interest is very similar," President Albert Shanker of the American Federation of Teachers explained in discussing runaway industries. "When factories close, community tax revenues plunge, so teachers lose wages and jobs."

Jobs lost to Mexico were clearly the issue. After the vote, President Clinton would have the AFL-CIO in his hip pocket again. "We disagree on this single issue, and that's it," the Federation's secretary-treasurer Thomas R. Donahue reported, forgetting the long political shadow that the passage of NAFTA would imprint on work-a-day life.

"Every time a factory departs for Mexico, Clinton is going to get hell," predicted Frank Jackalone, a southern organizer for Ralph Nader's Public Citizen.[3]

Ross Perot zeroed in with the assertion that the Mexican people's wages were so low that they could not afford to buy U.S.-made consumer goods and that U.S. exports involved largely technology and parts:

> People who don't make anything can't buy anything. . . . We're [the U.S.] 85 percent of the combined [potential NAFTA] market. Canada is 11 percent of the buying power. And Mexico is only 4 percent. . . .
>
> Let's just say you have a piece of glass crystal that you spend $100 making in this country, you're going to send it to Mexico to have $10 of additional work done to it, they count it as a $100 export, then they count it as $100 to come into Mexico from the U.S., then they count it as a $110 import back into the United States.

Now then, when you look at how they count, the real export figures to Mexican consumers are tiny. The used factory equipment coming from U.S. factories going into Mexico ... we count that as if Mexican consumers bought it. Nobody bought anything. Old equipment must come to Mexico [for U.S. investment to promote production].[4]

SEEKING THE CHEAPEST LABOR

Stressing twenty-odd years of dislocation of labor and communities in the wake of runaway industries since 1971, grass-roots forces insisted that under NAFTA, labor-intensive operations would move to cheap Mexican labor at a quickened pace.

Corporations that envisioned either an opportunity to move their production operations or to build a market for technical equipment like gas turbines and heavy machinery clearly favored the pact. Others that hoped to escape the overregulated U.S. business milieu also supported the agreement. And still others that expected purchases of consumer goods by Mexican employees of U.S. companies on the border also favored unfettered trade.

While U.S. companies operating nationwide and globally pumped NAFTA, many local companies and workers in branch plants argued that under the treaty production, their jobs would be moved to Mexico. As each Congressional member then had to decide how to vote based on the support and lobbying of companies, workers, and their unions in the district represented, the obvious dilemma on the vote turned on the potential for the mobility of capital, the lack of mobility of labor to follow the job, and the differences in wages, costs, and market access in the United States and Mexico.

The auto companies, Procter and Gamble, and other giant manufacturers backed NAFTA to the hilt. It was much more likely that G.M. would close its plant in Baltimore employing 3,500 people and move to Mexico, for example, than it was that Mexicans would buy the commercial vans assembled in Baltimore. "Mexicans," said Rodney Trump, president of the local Baltimore United Auto Workers, "don't make enough money to buy the headlight of my Chevy Cavalier."[5]

Many U.S. industries were also worried about the effects of NAFTA on their domestic output. United States consumers might desert them for lower-price, Mexican-made goods if the trade pact passed. Proof lay with the garment industry that had already lost hundreds of thousands of jobs to overseas production.[6] One estimate was that U.S. consumers annually spend some $32 billion more on U.S. goods produced by 21 heavily protected industries (with sales of $1 billion or more) than they would if there were no barriers to goods entering the U.S. This estimate suggested that the price of protection amounted to $170,000 a year per job saved and that the net cost (after tariff revenue receipts and reduced unemployment and welfare benefit costs) was $54,000 per job saved.[7]

While consumers might save on prices of Mexican-made goods under NAFTA, workers might face joblessness with limited government compensation.

SWEET TRADING

Flexing their political muscle, the U.S. producers of sugar beets and sugar cane sought to keep domestic prices high by preventing Mexico from exporting any sugar to the U.S. market. Rather, they sought to make Mexico a net importer of U.S. sugar or at least corn sweeteners. They didn't want Mexican imported corn sweeteners to replace Mexican sugar used in domestic production, however, because they feared Mexican sugar might then be in surplus and be exported to the United States.

Senator John B. Breaux, a Democrat from Louisiana, was the leading congressional advocate on sugar matters in 1993. He urged President Salinas to accept a formally agreed clarification that under NAFTA, Mexico could not export sugar to the United States without producing more than it actually uses. It was an easy request for Salinas to grant, as the Mexican sugar mills were antiquated, inefficient, and privatized into the hands of soft-drink bottlers using sugar, rather than high-fructose corn-sweeteners (that undoubtedly would become even less expensive as the Mexican tariff fell under NAFTA). And even Coca-Cola's Latin American Group was prepared to switch from costly refined sugar—not to corn-sweeteners, but to less-expensive, treated raw sugar, which had the same low cost as high-fructose corn syrup.

Although Mexico promised to raise its wholesale sugar prices to U.S. levels—whatever the cost of treated raw sugar or high-fructose corn syrup—if Mexico switched to those alternatives, it could still export surplus sugar beyond its use, flooding the highly protected U.S. sugar market and driving prices down. This the U.S. sugar lobby opposed, striving to block two NAFTA provisions:

1. Mexico's export quota to the United States of 7,258 metric tons of sugar would rise to 25,000 tons six years after implementation of the pact and disappear after 15 years
2. Some seven years after the agreement would take effect, if Mexico could produce more sugar than it consumes for two consecutive years, it could start shipping as much sugar as it wants to the United States.

Thus a last-minute sugar agreement worked its way to President Clinton's desk that counted corn syrup as sugar in determining whether Mexican "sugar" production was exceeded by consumption. Only then would Mexico be allowed to export sugar under NAFTA—which meant that very little, if any, will ever cross the border.

Surely this legal obfuscation was sweet trading. As NAFTA made its way through the legislative strainer, at least 12 members of Congress harking from the northern states that grow sugar beets and southern states that grow sugar cane lined up their ballot counts for NAFTA.[8]

PLUCKING VOTES, NOT CITRUS

Fearing Mexican imports, citrus growers, glass producers, appliance manufacturers, and other U.S. industries threw their weight for or against NAFTA provisions affecting their interests.

The citrus arrangement was made to impose automatic tariffs on frozen concentrated orange juice imported from Mexico if the price fell below a certain specified level for several consecutive days. This effectively prevented Mexican dumping.

The same time table was arranged for Mexican vegetables and meat processing.[9] And U.S. officials promised to monitor closely imports of electrical appliances, automobiles, and brooms.

The strategems were all about picking up NAFTA support votes from specific members of the House of Representatives so that the sugar and citrus concessions might win 18 to 20 votes, mostly from the Florida delegation, thereby building a majority that would approve the pact without amendment.

"I know there are a lot of deals being made by the White House," Michigan Democratic Representative David E. Bonior protested. "They're porking it down and loading it up. They may pick up a couple of votes." The critical matter was the effect on people in the United States, Bonior went on. "This NAFTA is nothing but a job-stealing, tax-raising, community-destroying agreement, and we're going to do everything we can, humanly possible, to defeat it."[10]

Congressmen and senators would nonetheless vote the interests of their dominant constituency in most cases. Potential U.S. export markets for corn in Mexico brought North Dakota farmers to their feet supporting NAFTA's promise to cut the 215 percent Mexican tax on the value of U.S. corn. This would allow them to store more corn during the 20-degrees-below-zero winters that killed insects and push up the price by 6 cents a bushel due to the extra Mexican demand. But North Dakota wheat farmers saw the U.S.-Canada Free Trade Agreement and NAFTA as presenting the danger of subsidized Canadian wheat growers dumping on the U.S. market, cutting prices, and absorbing the profits of the international grain companies milling their wheat in Minneapolis and St. Paul.

In the anti–NAFTA portfolios of the state's two senators and lone representative, corn lost the day to wheat because wheat covered most of North Dakota, while corn and sugar beets were grown only on the moist land near the Red River on the state's eastern border. "Any farmer in North

Dakota who has to put up with the Canada Free Trade agreement can't possibly put up with NAFTA," offered wheat farmer Doug Richman, echoing the agrarian populism of decades past.[11]

Meanwhile, in Washington, Democrats shuddered in the wake of the defeat of their candidates in leading gubernatorial and mayoral elections on 2 October 1993. These already jittery Democratic lawmakers were prompted to vote against NAFTA to avoid further alienating skeptical voters and organized labor.[12]

POLITICAL GUNSLINGERS

It was a scene from the OK Corral. The White House threw down the gauntlet and challenged Ross Perot to a debate with fact-laden Vice President Gore on the North American Free Trade Agreement. Knowing the trade measure was in trouble in Congress, the administration hoped to portray Perot as a mudslinger and demagogue and to identify the opposition.

"As the negotiations progressed today," remarked the *New York Times* "Mr. Clinton and Mr. Perot sounded like two gunslingers blustering in the saloon before a shootout."

"It's the stupidest damn thing the White House can do," maintained former Ross Perot consultant Ed Rollins. Perot "will chew up Al Gore and spit him out. Gore will give intellectual answers, and Perot will hit the emotional buttons and spit out sound bites."[13]

"He's a demagogue that we've got to get rid of," intoned Jim Kolbe, a pro–NAFTA Arizona Republican representative, referring to Perot.

Trying to slay the troublesome dragon, Vice President Gore turned to half-truths, depicting Perot as having a personal financial interest in the defeat of NAFTA to aid his company Alliance Corridor, Inc., a 9,700-acre distribution center near Fort Worth, Texas. Although Alliance had much more to gain from passage of NAFTA than from its defeat, nonetheless the White House effectively played dirty pool for millions of TV viewers to gain the wrong impression. A *USA Today*/CNN/Gallup poll reported that 47 percent of adult viewers believed Perot opposition to NAFTA sprang from "personal interests."[14]

Perot maintained he was protecting U.S. workers by proposing comparable wages for labor on both sides of the border through a U.S.-imposed "social" tariff on Mexican goods that would be phased out as Mexico lifted its wages to U.S. levels.[15]

Even military logistics mattered. The White House sent the former chairman of the Joint Chiefs of Staff, Gen. Colin L. Powell, to its press room to endorse NAFTA in its militant campaign. Republican political consultant William D. McInturff discerned the logic: "The bounds between public policy and political campaigns have become very fuzzy."

"I think it's the wave of the future," agreed Brooklyn Democratic Representative Charles E. Shumer.[16]

AND WHO MIGHT PAY THE PRICE?

Forgotten in the hoopla were the people who might pay the price. For the fact remained that there was no assurance that U.S. workers displaced by jobs moving abroad to Mexico or elsewhere would be retrained with usable skills that would secure them future jobs at comparable pay to the employment lost. Although the U.S. administration under NAFTA was to set aside $90 million to assist workers who might lose their jobs due to trade with Mexico and the Labor Department planned to overhaul federal unemployment assistance and training services for all Americans who had lost their jobs, few unemployed deserted by their employers believed the program would emerge, or if it did, that it would assure them a well-paying job.

"I worked all the way from assembler to technician," Bill Beeman said of his Zenith Corporation job that went abroad for cheaper labor. "I took all the schooling that Zenith offered. But when I left, their certificates were worth nothing. Now here I am trying to better my education [at Ozarks Technical Community College in Springfield, Mo.] and be a more productive human being. Why can't they just say, 'This person is trying. Let's help him.'"[17] Those so situated do not like the prospect of NAFTA at all.

Some joked the tables should be reversed, with the presidents of the United States and Mexico being forced to work for a living in each other's countries until they woke up to the facts of workaday life. What was certain, though, was that the path of NAFTA was beset by special interest groups like corporations, farmers, and labor unions that demanded self-serving legislation in the agreement, however long it might be in effect.

NEW PRODUCTION PATTERNS

NAFTA was an adventure in U.S. investments in production by low-wage Mexican workers using yesterday's U.S. machinery to make goods to export back to the U.S. tariff-free.

That was exactly how other U.S. companies had operated under the *maquilas* and what European and Japanese companies also planned in Mexico if NAFTA emerged as a sphere of U.S. influence centered on the giant U.S. market.[19]

Under the control of the giant auto companies, the center of the Mexican auto industry had shifted to the north to simplify everything from shipping to commuting. Cars were Mexico's largest export after oil, employing 60,000 people directly and more than 300,000 indirectly in parts manufacturing and distribution.

Foreign Car Plants in Mexico, 1992

Company	Location	Date Plant Built	Production	Number Vehicles Exports	Mexican Sales
Ford	Chihuahua	1983	Engine		
Ford	Hermosilla	1986	Assembly		
Ford	Mexico City	1962	Assembly/ Engine		
			Total	135,000+	130,000
Chrysler	Toluca	1964	Assembly/ Engine		
Chrysler	Mexico City	1938	Assembly		
Chrysler	Satillo	1981	Engine		
		1995	Assembly		
			Total	100,000+	137,000
GM	Ramos	1979	Assembly/ Engine		
GM	Mexico City	1964	Assembly		
GM	Toluca	1963	Engine		
			Total	80,000	120,000
Nissan	Aguascalientes	1982	Engine		
		1992	Assembly		
Nissan	Cuernavaca	1966	Assembly/ Engine		
			Total	40,000	140,000
Renault	Gomez	unavailable	Engine		
	Palacio	1985	Engine		
			Total	Unavailable	
Volkswagen	Puebla	1966	Assembly/ Engine		
			Total	43,000	150,000+

These companies built more than a million cars in Mexico in 1992; exports of cars grew by an average of 142 percent a year from 1985 to 1989, continued to grow at a slower pace thereafter, but promised to expand as NAFTA gave these companies leverage over those not situated in North America.

With billions of dollars invested, the Big Three Detroit companies would likely shift small-car production to Mexico from South Korea and other Asian nations and concentrate big-car production in the United States and Canada. The wage differential—$1.55 an hour for Mexican assemblers versus $17.38 in the United States—would not only lever U.S.

auto wages down, but would eventually shift the Big Three's advanced technical production to Mexico for a double savings.[19] Although most parts and systems, as well as styling, design, engineering, testing, and development would be done in the United States, low skilled assembly would take place in Mexico, a division of labor promising to maximize profits.[20]

To get ready to market within the United States under NAFTA, German-owned Volkswagen provided the test-run case implementing the Mexican government's planned transformation of the auto and other industries:

- Volkswagen used a lockout approved by the Salinas administration to split and destroy the workers' union, which was among the most powerful, independent unions in Mexico. Through a 35-hour strike in July 1992, this union had secured a 20 percent wage rise to $15 a day, one of the highest wages in Mexico.
- Volkswagen also imposed a new contract restructuring the labor process using Japanese-style, team-production work rules that the workers had no say in designing. With inadequate retraining, each worker had to perform multiple tasks in record time that caused extreme physical stress.
- In addition, Volkswagen imposed the speed-up at piece-rate wages under the misnomer "productivity." This did away with seniority wages that older workers relied on and made it difficult for them to work fast enough to earn sufficient wages or even keep their jobs on a sped-up production line.
- Volkswagen deployed the combined strength of a government-approved lockout, the company's dismissal of 15,000 union employees, state-declared illegality of the workers' sit-down strike, and state police using shotguns to force the workers back to work, to renounce their "dissident" leaders outside the government-linked official union and to reemploy 13,000 complaint workers.
- Production was restarted using 55 percent of Volkswagen parts coming from the United States and Canada, thereby almost meeting the NAFTA content requirement of 62.5 percent North American parts to comply with the tariff-free U.S. auto market.[21]

A Fail-Safe Pact

The failure of NAFTA, former assistant secretary of state Bernard Aronson concluded, would harm Latin America, as it would "strengthen traditional economic cliques, which have grown rich by manipulating and sometimes corrupting their political system to shut out competition at the expense of ordinary citizens."[22]

Trying to capture the allure and thunder of John F. Kennedy, President Clinton then called for a return to the policies of U.S. security and prosperity tied to reaching out to the rest of the world through trade, exemplified by NAFTA.[23] And with the Mexican government having spent

$25 million for Washington lobbying since 1989 to promote NAFTA, Mexican lobbyists switched in late 1993 to lining up a coalition of U.S. companies called U.S.A. Nafta; its 3,000 members included the top 200 U.S. companies.[24]

President Clinton supported the effort by speaking to a U.S. Chamber of Commerce conference in Washington beamed on TV by satellite to forums organized by business leaders at some one thousand locations around the United States. His message, which was imperial, jingoistic, and trade-mongering, counted potential customers as European colonial powers once did in the nineteenth century and issued a warning about what might happen if Congress rejected the pact:

> If I were Prime Minister of Japan and I had a low growth rate and I had my companies going crazy, I would jump on this like flies on a June bug.
> If Congress votes this down on the 17th of November, I would, if I were the Prime Minister of Japan, have the Finance Minister of the country in to see the President of Mexico on the 18th of November. . . . I'd say, "We've got more money than they do anyway; make the deal with us." And if I were running the economic affairs of the European Community, I would do the same thing.
> If we walk away from this [pact] and Mexico decides to pursue its development strategy, what must it do? It must make this deal with Europe or Japan. And what would that do? That could change the purchasing habits of 90 million Mexicans and hundreds of millions of people in Latin America. It could cut us off from not only economic but political opportunities to promote democracy and freedom and stability in our hemisphere that we can now only imagine.[25]

But such hype was believed by none of those who understood the meaning of infrastructural developments and investment patterns and knew that President Salinas had initially rejected NAFTA and had embraced it only after he had difficulties getting European and Asian investors to enter Mexico.

"Mexico will become truly important to the Japanese and the Asians [as investors in production to export to the U.S.] to the extent that it finally joins the North American economy," said Professor Gabriel Székely, a leading expert on Mexican-Asian economic relations at the University of California, San Diego. "Without NAFTA, that won't happen."

"This has touched a chord in the United States because people are afraid of Japan, but it is not an alternative as such," estimated a pro–NAFTA senior Mexican official. "Japan will be interested in Mexico. The same goes for Europe. But it would be naïve to think that Japan is poised to jump in."

"He's joking, right?" a senior Japanese government politician asked in reference to Clinton's statement, knowing that total Japanese investment in Mexico in 1992 was $60 million, barely 3 percent of what the United States invested. "Japan and Mexico? Does that sound like a big alliance?"

Not quite, anyway. Mexico's 1992 trade with Japan was $3.2 billion, less than 5 percent of Mexico's total. True, with a fall in the value of Mexico's oil sales, its trade deficit with Japan skyrocketed from $542 million in 1991 to $2.2 billion in 1992. But by comparison, 1992 Mexican imports from the United States alone were $24.6 billion (28 percent of its imports), while the United States accounted for $18.7 billion (68 percent) of Mexican exports.

"It is conceivable that in the absence of NAFTA, we would go ahead and negotiate trade agreements with the European Community and Japan," portended Mexico's trade secretary, Jaime Serra Puche. Yet in 1992, Mexican trade with the E.C. nations was only $10.3 billion, accounting for 11.5 percent of Mexico's imports and 7.2 percent of its exports.

Europe and Japan's advantage without the NAFTA would be unfettered investment opportunities in Mexico and no need to worry about NAFTA "rules of origin" discrimination involving content requirements that goods moving freely through the trade zone would have to be made mostly from North American materials. But U.S. and Canadian tariffs would then block such goods made in Mexico. So NAFTA was actually better for Japanese and European investors in Mexican production, as Mexico could offer duty-free entrance of their goods into Canada and the United States, as well as greater economic stability and the improvement of transportation, communications, and other infrastructure.[26]

The Vacuum in Logic

The vacuum in logic affected Ross Perot's hoopla as well. His forecast of the flight of U.S. jobs to Mexico was first 5.9 million, but then took a quantum leap to 85 million, which is the approximate population of Mexico and is nearly the size of the entire U.S. workforce. "Eighty-five million can elect anybody—anybody!" Perot insisted as he defined the politics of the discontented. "Do you hear that, White House?"[27]

On "Meet the Press," President Clinton took the foot-in-mouth tack, declaring that the AFL-CIO was misbehaving as a "real roughshod" rider in their lobbying, but he neglected the fact that all big lobbies ride roughshod in their self-justifying stampede. "I hope," columnist A.M. Rosenthal objected, "he does not turn his support for Nafta into a blunderbuss attack on Americans who exercise their constitutional right to be afraid for their jobs, correctly or not, and have the nerve to say so."[28]

Bringing logic back in focus, Mexican poet Octavio Paz criticized isolated groups in the United States for defending their own interests and prejudices against the nation's general, popular interests, and thus driving the United States into an isolationist posture. As an internationalist, Paz supported NAFTA as the middle course between the big nation-state unable to accommodate the needs of small nations and federations that were too small to solve global problems. "The creation of continental communities," he surmised, "would represent an intermediate solution that would preserve the existence of the nation-state and that of small nations at an equal distance from old-style imperialism and international anarchy. That community would be the beginning of the international order that politicians have promised for so long. . . . Nafta is a step towards the construction of a genuine international order."[29]

ENVIRONMENTAL DEGRADATION

In times past, Mexican industrialization had neglected the needs of the population for clean water and air, adequate urban housing and sewage systems, and adequate transport and communication networks. Every step improving technical production had taken a heavy toll on the conditions essential for survival in the urban domain. This was reflected most harshly in the degradation of the atmosphere; a blanket of smog covers Mexico City's sky most of the year.

It is not surprising that the global outcry for environmental protection was joined by *Mexicanos* in a powerful way that led to the shutdown of oil refining in Mexico City and the elevation of the issue of pollution-free production to the forefront of the nation's politics. Thus the government's proposal to join NAFTA accompanied promises to devote national revenues and foreign loans to creating the essential environmental conditions that would improve the quality of life itself.

Yet NAFTA, by stimulating Mexican industrial concentration, was likely to undermine the nation's biospheric foundations. The logic of Mexican domestic reorganization under the scheduled free-trade bloc with the United States was centered on the emergent market in unhindered movement of resources, goods, services, finance, investments, and eventually labor. Such a market would create a more or less equal competitive field where giant firms and banks from the north would gain maximum advantages at the expense of Mexican capital, labor, and operating milieu. Concentration on the conditions necessary for production might well lead to the neglect, even the destruction, of the conditions essential for health and welfare of the Mexican people.

The proposed side agreements on environmental and labor cooperation claimed otherwise, though it was up to each of the three NAFTA partners to commit itself to so-called environmentally sustainable growth, with each promising not to lower standards to attract investments from their other partners. But standards in Mexico were already far below those in the United States or Canada, neither of which held to more than minimal provisions and both of which lacked adequate annual budgetary allocations. "While the NAFTA sets the stage for economic growth through trade," argued Tom Hockin, the Canadian minister for international trade, "the two additional agreements help to ensure that this growth will not come at the expense of workers' rights or the environment. A competitive advantage gained by a failure to enforce environmental or labor laws is plainly unfair."[30]

In fact, in each of the three countries, the relations of employers, labor, and the medium of the state had established the degree to which labor rights and the environment had been protected in the past; all three partners entered the agreement with far different general wage levels, work conditions, and provisions for protection of the biosphere.

A critical 1993 assessment of the borderlands by two U.S. environmental consultants documented alarming conditions:

> There are approximately 150,000 industrial plants operating in Mexico with some 20 thousand facilities located in the 2,000 mile long inter-border area called the maquiladora zone. About forty-five percent are foreign-owned (40 percent U.S., 4 percent Korean or Japanese, and 1 percent European). This maquiladora zone has rapidly expanding populations with wholly inadequate basic municipal services and infrastructure. Air pollution levels rival those of Los Angeles and Mexico City. Only 15 percent of all industries in Mexico are estimated to have any pretreatment of their waste water discharges.
>
> Approximately 100,000 tons of hazardous waste are generated daily by maquiladoras and industries. To date, there is only one hazardous waste incinerator available for the whole country although several new treatment and disposal facilities are in the planning stages. At the San Antonio Border Infrastructure Conference this year, it was estimated that $6.5 billion is needed over the next ten years for the inter-border area to achieve accepted standards for water supply, sewage treatment, and solid and hazardous waste services.[31]

"Expanded free trade has the potential to break the chain of poverty of millions of people while providing enormous new resources for investment in environmental cleanup and conservation," President Roger Schlickeisen of Defenders of Wildlife announced, putting an idealistic edge on the relationship of open trade, impoverishment, and environmental crisis.[32]

Given Mexico's lack of attention to environmental needs as the border area was industrialized, substantial degradation of air, water, and land resources on both sides of the border would require from $6.5 to $20.5 billion—two thirds of it in Mexico—over ten years to provide water and sewer systems, solid and hazardous waste facilities, and road surfacing. Another $1.4 to $10 billion would be necessary for modern highways connecting major trade centers and for substantial additional investments to upgrade rail, air, and port facilities.

Most of the needed Mexican funds would be government-guaranteed and would be borrowed from the United States or would be dependent on U.S. investments in privately owned infrastructure providing both security and competitive earnings.[33] Such debt structuring and investments might compromise or undermine Mexico's original purposes in upgrading its independent economic structure and well-being.

As the debt escalated, other dangers loomed, for Mexico relied on local communities to be the most ardent protectors of the ecosystems around them. Mexico was already spending one percent of its gross national product on the environment in 1992 and planned to spend in excess of $1 billion per year on water and sewage and $100 million per year on air-pollution control. But Mexico did not produce the equipment or other means to achieve environmental safety.

With global environmental demand for material means and services enlarging to $408 billion by the mid–1990s and the transformation of a technical segment of the U.S. economy to produce these means ensured, there was still no assurance that the new technocracies would not themselves endanger the biosphere.[34] Indeed, the technical aspects of energy production to process the wastes of the industrial world often created their own blight of hydrocarbons and other discharges of affluents inimical to the natural environment.

United States production of these technical means was ready to provide Mexico with a protective shield. Donald L. Connors, president of the Environmental Business Council of the United States, comprised of leading members of the U.S. environmental business industry, government agencies, and environmental and business associations, recognized this potential:

> NAFTA is a window of opportunity for this growing U.S. industry. The passage of NAFTA gives U.S. environmental businesses a relationship advantage, as well as the existing geographic advantage, to service a market that is not only needy but completely opened up to consuming U.S. environmental goods and services for years to come. ... NAFTA gives us leverage in our own hemisphere. It moves our smaller companies into the global marketplace, and trades on our geographic advantage. NAFTA forges a marketplace, and trades on our geographic advantage. NAFTA forges a relationship with Mexico, gateway to Latin America.[35]

These U.S. environmental firms thus hoped to mobilize their own 50,000 companies and expand their 1 million workforce to increase their revenues beyond the 1993 level of $120 billion. "There is an enormous opportunity in Mexico for the distribution of U.S. environmental goods and services whether it is direct sales, consulting, construction or joint ventures with Mexican companies," two U.S. business experts say.[36]

This dovetails with the flexible, legal mechanisms Mexico had already set up in 1993. The head of enforcement for the Secretariat of Social Development, Dr. Santiago Ornate Laborde, ruminated: "I would rather see the CEO's of our companies spend their money productively on pollution prevention and waste minimization than to have them invest their profits in [government-imposed] fines and penalties."[37]

And thus the pollution that foreign and domestic enterprises spread in the Mexican domain could be cleansed by other foreign enterprises selling Mexico the means to clean it up. This process would elevate Mexican imports of added technologies, impact budgetary resources, and enhance the long-run negative balance of trade.

CHAPTER 14

The New Sphere of Influence

Mexico, once largely a rural nation of ten million in 1910, now has a population of nearly 92 million and is lurching towards industrialization to attain its place in the economically developed world.

Rejecting past attempts to return the population to the land, the nation's current leaders are driving their citizens to the urban domain, destroying the old status quo with its antiquated methods of production and establishing a new elite directing the first and second phases of industrialization. They are mobilizing both domestic and foreign capital to bring the nation into the U.S. sphere and, perhaps, the global marketplace.

THE EMERGING STAGE

The emerging stage of U.S.-Mexican relations is something less than a master-servant relationship, something short of a community of equals, and something other than conflict-free regional or hemispheric cooperation.

Mexican industry is now on sale to the highest bidder, foreign banks and concerns are taking over significant positions controlling the nation's finances, agricultural land can now be rented or bought through *presta-nombres* by foreign transnationals, and both peasants and workers are again purloined as dirt-cheap labor. There has been, however, practically no public information, heated political discussion, or protest in Mexico.

Rather, Mexico's elite has sprung these plans on a helpless public that lacks the political venues of influence, while offering them the illusion of ballots to elect politicians who are part of the dominating party that is forwarding these same schemes leading to their impoverishment.

In the maddened quest for industrial progress, this elite has meanwhile closed its eyes to the vulnerability of its own industries to foreign capital

264

and goods, a vulnerability arising because Mexico lacks adequate technology, good railways, highways, and ports to distribute and compete.

Pursuing industrial advance, Mexico acquired 1986 membership in the General Agreement on Tariffs and Trade, and opened its borders to imports, though lower tariffs threatened textile and antiquated factories in Tlaxcala and other regions. Then came NAFTA, which promised to affect half the Mexican population in the short-term, though there was little initial protest that the United States would secure the largest benefits from the pact and make Mexico more dependent on the United States.

Pressure by the PRI government, business chambers, and big labor union coalitions contained dissent as these organizations reiterated their confidence in the long-term wisdom of the pact, saying little about their lack of information about future prospects and ignoring the likely short-term loss of jobs, displacement of industries, and future demographic movements.

Lacking a democratic forum and acting as a rubber stamp for President Salinas, 61 of 64 PRI congressional representatives approved the agreement after the vote in Washington. They seemed immune to the likelihood that Mexico would face the demise of many industries, as well as a significant short-term loss of jobs. Although this possibility led to widespread apprehension and a steady fall in political support from certain industrial and agricultural interests, the only overt protest came from the Indians of Chiapas.

Only then did textile manufacturers, toy makers, leather workers, and grain farmers begin to raise their objections publicly. The small, union-supported Mexican Action Network also tried to raise opposition, though the PRI gave it short shrift and no platform. "There is an ambivalence that is starting to emerge," admitted Trade Secretary Jaime Serra Punche in early November 1993. "In industry and agriculture, people support trade liberalization in general, but not in their own sector. The more protectionist attitudes are gaining weight."[1]

STEAMROLLERS FURTHER NORTH

Ross Perot asserted that U.S. companies had done little but exploit Mexican labor, violate Mexican environmental laws, and move their plants into Mexico, replacing Mexican industries and jeopardizing 85 million U.S. jobs.[2]

President Clinton continued his steamroller, calling on business executives to build a grass-roots response against U.S. unions, a tactic that only denoted his inability to make a rational defense of the pact's dangers to the workforce. The administration attacked the unions' "naked pressure" and circulated a 4 November 1993 letter from Secretary-Treasurer Walter Johnson of the San Francisco Council of the AFL-CIO warning Nancy

Pelosi, California Democratic representative, that her announced support for NAFTA constituted "turncoat action." "Even though you are considered a safe district, we will not forget," Johnson wrote. "Many other Democratic fence-riders do not have your assumed luxury. We intend to take this action against all Democrats who support this dastardly treaty."[3]

In the early 1990s, U.S. NAFTA advocates had concentrated on trade, not on the bedrock of capital movements. This meant the agreement promised to be a bumpy commercial terrain, with bickering over tariffs on this or that item of trade, as well as over controls on the exchange of currency. True, U.S. and Canadian investors in Mexican Hyatt, Westin, Hilton, Holiday Inn, and other hotels and resorts were legally allowed, helping bring 6.7 million visitors to Mexico and generating nearly $4 billion and 150,000 new jobs.[4] Although investment barriers on banks and in other key sectors would temporarily remain, the future would witness the unfettered movement of capital once the peso was battered to a low point.

As NAFTA faced possible defeat in the U.S. Congress in November 1993, the new ratio of 3.30 pesos to the dollar began to fall. Foreign investors withdrew as much as $1 billion a day in the week ending November 10, and Mexico's central bank raised interest rates to try to stem the tide of investors limiting their peso exposure.[5]

Despite short-term capital movements, some saw an empire in the making. In the NAFTA-supporting shorthand of William Safire: "Common sense says that opening new markets enlarges the pie, and what is good for all business is good for all workers. ... Better to give Mexico a bright capitalist future, attracting investment that will pay higher wages and create consumers for U.S. goods."

A competitive U.S. sphere of exclusive trading influence was clearly envisioned, as Secretary of Agriculture Mike Espy foresaw:

> If NAFTA passes, we create the world's largest market with 370 million people and a $6.5 trillion annual economic output. Jobs will be created in the U.S. because our products will be given preferential access to the Mexican market—that is, they will not be subjected to tariff and non-tariff barriers that goods from other countries will continue to face. If NAFTA is defeated, the winners will be the European Community and the countries of the Pacific Rim who recognized years ago the advantages and the necessity of having a special trading relationship with countries nearest their borders and who are aggressively creating new preferential markets for their goods while we choose to rely on our old markets.

The logic of such a competitive U.S. sphere, Espy says, is to use NAFTA to play to Mexico's growing middle class, and to enlarge U.S. agricultural exports to Mexico from $4 billion in 1993 to $6.5 billion, creating 50,000 additional U.S. jobs on the farm and in the food industries by capitalizing on U.S. advantages in large-scale farm productivity and utilizing productive capacity.[6]

DUMPING THE U.S. FARM SURPLUS

As U.S. corporate farms would thereby reach full capacity, they could sell high in the U.S. market, dump at lower prices in Mexico, and, using farm legislation, sell to the U.S. government for dumping elsewhere.

Surplus U.S. farm output was the foundation for such two-tier dumping. "Our ever-increasing productivity eclipses domestic demand, which is basically flat because of limited population growth," notes American Farm Bureau Federation president Dean Kleckner. "We export 25 percent of our production, more than $40 billion annually, and in 1992 ran a trade surplus of more than $18 billion. It was not simply a coincidence that we had both an export slump and a farm crisis in the mid–1980s."[7]

To avoid a repeat of this production catastrophe, farm organizations were looking for new markets and trying to develop new business with established trading partners. Mexico was the fastest growing U.S. market and the third largest U.S. customer by 1993, with farm exports also fostering jobs in processing, packaging, and transport. Preferential U.S. access to the Mexican market was seen as essential.[8]

Lobbying as "AG for NAFTA" and pressuring Congress to approve the trade pact, agribusinesses supporting the American Farm Bureau Federation drew in 150 ranchers and organizations representing large-scale farming that together produced more than 70 percent of the nation's total farm output. "We are confident [U.S.] farm exports will increase because of our competitive advantages in farm production, our highly efficient processing industries and our more advanced infrastructure," AG stated. "Mexico has inherent limitations that will prevent it from becoming a farm superpower that threatens U.S. producers."

NAFTA would secure the Mexican market for U.S. agribusiness output, AG explained, "because NAFTA will provide us with preferential treatment in the Mexican market, giving us a huge competitive advantage over other exporters. NAFTA will eliminate high Mexican tariffs and onerous import licensing requirements that limit our export opportunities in many commodities. Combined with Mexico's growing economy and growing population, there is a tremendous opportunity for U.S. farmers." But, AG continued: "If we reject NAFTA, we will be forfeiting a large and growing market. Mexico's increasing demand for food will instead be filled by Canadian, European and South American farmers."[9]

Arguing in the voice of a collective "we" representing the entire United States was more propaganda than factual, though. The U.S. farm lobby was a very small segment of the U.S. economy that nonetheless represented the farm states and controlled the votes of the two U.S. senators from each of these states for any essential farm bill like NAFTA. Farming per se was carried on by less than 3 percent of the nation's entire population. Yet, the farm lobby was made up of those industries and farm interests that supported export dumping of food worldwide, Mexico being one more potential market. The lobby claimed it supported the interests of 26.5 million working people: the 2.1 million employees operating corporate farms; 1.3 million in food processing; 2.6 million in manufacturing tractors, trucks, and other farm equipment and farm-oriented amenities; 10.8 million in transport, trade, and retail outlets; 4.1 million in ancillary industries; and some of the 5.6 million living on family farms. The latter comprised a bare 2.25 percent of the entire U.S. population.

For the benefit of these interests, Mexican agriculture was put in future jeopardy, with proximity, price, and quality awarding U.S. agribusinesses and trading interests a powerful boost in dealing with Mexico. By 1993, processed foods that combined many nutrient and chemical components, and embodied added labor value, already made up 60 percent of Mexico's food imports from the United States—up from 40 percent of such imports in 1988. Some 81,000 U.S. workers had come to rely on this export of U.S. farm output.

Mexico had meanwhile weakened its resistance by amending Article 27 of its constitution, now allowing land sales and rentals to foreign interests. As well, the traditional *hacendado*–peon system was backward looking and restrained output. Without these and other self-defeating restrictions, sufficient quantities of Mexico's 161 varieties of corn and dozens of strains of beans and rice might have been produced to meet its own needs.

EMERGING COMPETITIVE TRADE BLOCS

Mexico, confident that as a nation it would be the recipient of economic advantages emerging from the promise of NAFTA, was possibly placing itself at the mercy of the interests of its trading partners.

Perhaps the end will be less dire, though, as conservative wordsmith William Safire believes:

> Look to the East: a free-trading bloc is forming there that could knock our made-in-China socks off. Look to the West: the French farmers behind "So Be It" Balladur are leading Europe into an us-against-them Common Market, holding a GATT to the head of world trade. Hey, [U.S.] protectionists: Wouldn't it be nice to have a whole hemisphere with us—370 million strong—to keep the Europeans and Asians from ganging up? (This is not an argument that free-trade purists make, but it's time we gave wider meaning to "America first."[10])

The concept of America first in commercial war and peace was both a nationalist and a manipulative argument used in pressing for NAFTA. NAFTA meant the United States would hold the trump card in calling for GATT enforcement of fair trade, or it would put up its own trading barriers around itself and the NAFTA zone.

"All the GATT countries that oppose the Uruguay Round will consider themselves winners as well if NAFTA is defeated," argued U.S. Agriculture Department's Espy in 1993, "because assuredly our GATT negotiating position would not be nearly as strong without NAFTA as it would be with it."[11]

Scare tactics became official U.S. policy as predictions circulated that if NAFTA failed, Japan would make its own deal with Mexico to flood the United States with goods undercutting U.S. products. "What would we do in America if we turn away from this and they make this sort of arrangement with Japan, or with Europe, and they make the investments there, and then we have to deal with their products coming through the back door from Mexico?" asked President Clinton, appealing to Americans accustomed to seeing Japan as the enemy on trade matters.

"I tell you," Treasury Secretary Lloyd Bentsen told the Senate Committee on Environment and Public Works on 19 October 1993, "the Japanese and the Europeans will be just delighted if we do not approve NAFTA."

It was an absurd, emotive argument that avoided stating that NAFTA would still allow European or Japanese investments in Mexican production to seek tariff-free export markets in the United States.

"Certainly we would expect Mexico and other Latin American countries would be very much disappointed if Nafta does not succeed," Japanese Embassy economic counselor Hadeaki Domichi responded. "They may look to other countries, including Japan. That is a natural reaction. But our relationship with Mexico will go on, regardless of Nafta."[12]

Yet not everyone was satisfied.

"I am all for helping poor nations develop their economies, but not at the expense of workers in Ohio and the rest of the United States," insisted Howard M. Metzenbaum, a well-heeled Ohio Democratic senator, looking over his shoulder at ten million out of work in the United States in October 1992.

Those jobless who stood in wait made politicians carp and sweat over the effects of the North American Free Trade Agreement on their own political futures. For lower U.S. customs duties on imports to enable the free movement of goods was only the end result of the mobility of investment capital, technology, and managerial skills to Mexican factories and facilities. This drain effectively destroyed well-paid U.S. jobs and replaced them, if at all, with lower-paid work.

Others using selected statistics argued that jobs protected by U.S. tariffs tended to be low-paying, while export-related jobs paid 17 percent more than the national average.[13] But if these export-related jobs were eliminated by imports of cheaply manufactured Mexican goods, then the cycle of replacing high-price workers with low-price labor might continue.

THE UNDERLYING MATTER

The underlying issue was the accumulation drives of large enterprises that foresaw opportunities of using variously priced labor at several points of the production, distribution, and marketing compass. They hoped, in effect, to build a hierarchical ladder of poorer and better paid workers, ratcheting wages lower in each location, lowering living standards, and employing some workers at the expense of others. Not only would there be a spatially segmented pool of workers, but they would also be divided along the lines of employment/unemployment, wage levels, living standards, and political rights.

As the previous relation between U.S. employers and workers was being severed at one location, a new relation between these employers and less expensive Mexican workers was being created south of the Rio Grande, and the output of these workers was being distributed in the United States at a price that was not necessarily lower than when the goods were produced in the United States. Politicians offered banalities and trite syllogisms to explain the process but did not account for the probable effects of the reorganization of production and work life throughout North America. Former President Bush said: "Nafta means more exports, and more exports means more American jobs." But this statement at the San Antonio ceremonial signing of the agreement was meant to play well in Texas, which was assumed to be the future source and transit point of much of the increase in the flow of goods to and from Mexico.[14]

The agreement actually threatened Texan agricultural interests, since dirt-cheap Mexican agricultural workers produced fruits and vegetables that would be much cheaper to buy in the United States. United States manufacturing jobs in other parts of the country would also be lost to cheaper Mexican labor. There were estimates of between 150,000 and 500,000 high-paid U.S. jobs to be destroyed over the seven years 1993–2000, and these jobs would not be replaced with new jobs or at best would be replaced by 325,000 low-wage, unskilled service jobs.

President Clinton, too, attempted to line up votes for passage of NAFTA based on near-surrealistic expectations rather than dealing with the known facts. Proposing a formal U.S. review of the agreement after three years — though the agreement already allowed each country to withdraw unilaterally with six months notice — the administration tried to persuade undecided members of Congress to vote for the act, while reminding their constituents that the United States could pull out if job losses were severe. "It could make the difference in five or ten Democratic votes," surmised Bill Richardson, a pro–NAFTA, New Mexico Democratic representative. Yet the crux of the matter lay elsewhere, and as the AFL-CIO secretary-treasurer, Tom Donahue, who opposed NAFTA, insisted: "The greatest damage of this [to labor] would be done in the first five to ten years."[15]

Antilabor forces hurried to President Clinton's camp, as the chief executive predicted worldwide turmoil if the Congress defeated the agreement. Former secretary of state Henry Kissinger, who declared that the House of Representatives vote on 17 November was the most important foreign policy vote lawmakers would cast this decade, urged passage of NAFTA:

> If NAFTA fails, the relationship with Mexico will be damaged for the foreseeable future. .... About once in a generation, this country has an opportunity in foreign policy to do something defining, something that establishes the structure for decades to come. After it is established, people wonder how it could have ever been otherwise, but when one goes through the debate, one is conscious of all the technical objections that are raised. Now we live in a world in which the ideological challenge has disintegrated and a new architecture needs to be created, and NAFTA is the first and crucial step in that direction.[16]

It was great theater, but a little lacking in believability.

PART OF A LARGER PICTURE?

However flawed, the cursory history of the twentieth century posits that outside the Americas, the Caribbean, the Philippines, Hawaii, and China, the United States remained isolationist before and after World War I, that after World War II it became an expansionist force on an economic and geopolitical plane, and that it capped the process in the extended global economy after the end of the cold war.

In terms of comparative power, the United States was indeed a small competitor before World War I, when Britain was the leading empire and was able to keep competitors on the European continent in check. Nonetheless, the United States was the leading political, military, and economic superpower in the Americas, sharing control over the Mexican economy with the lesser forces of Spain, France, and Britain. After World War I, the United States became an economic power in its own right in financing, and then deserting, continental recovery. Each of the great powers, including the United States, scrambled to return to tight-knit empires and/or spheres of exclusive influence.

By World War II, the United States had consolidated its political and economic hegemony in the Americas. After World War II, the United States assumed a front-line role against Communism by financing the Marshall Plan for European reconstruction, building West Germany as the financial hub on the Continent, strengthening NATO, constructing the Japanese-American alliance in Asia, and extending U.S. influence and economic controls worldwide. The end of the cold war again found the United States building its own sphere of influence, seeking advantages in emergent markets and investment zones.

Would U.S. regional integration of its sphere through NAFTA be a lever to promote a broader economic market in the Americas—an American Free Trade Agreement encompassing 800 million people? Would the United States encourage future global economic integration guaranteeing Eastern Europe, the former republics of the Soviet Union, Asian and Pacific nations, including China, access to world markets?

Can the United States win others over to unrestricted trade practices while it promotes restricted regional American markets that third nations can enter only by making investments in production?

This seems an unlikely possibility, but the United States is pursuing NAFTA as its own sphere for investment and trade and is planning to expand this sphere throughout the Americas, and, at the same time, encourage others to follow free-trade practices through GATT and now the WTO.

The U.S. advantages under NAFTA are to be secured by rules of origin of materials manufactured in member nations, so factories within the trade zone can block out European or Japanese or other exports that pass through or are transshipped via Mexico or Canada. That helps U.S. companies operating in Mexico, while harming smaller U.S.-based companies and displacing U.S. workers. It also offers an advantage to Japanese or European companies operating in Mexico, Canada, or the United States, as they too will benefit from barrier-free trade within NAFTA, though their respective nations might continue to maintain tariff and nontariff barriers against U.S. goods. "There is no such thing as free trade—it doesn't exist," admitted U.S. trade representative Mickey Kantor. "You have to have rules of the road."

Posted signs on the commercial highway still read "Tariff Schedule," "Quotas," "No Dumping," "No Transshipping," "Local Content Only," "No Free Access." Rules of origin for materials under NAFTA prevent other countries from taking advantage of lower import taxes between member nations and from importing parts to be assembled in member nations.

Going beyond the usual rules of origin—determining the nationality of a product by the last country in which it underwent a "substantial transformation"—NAFTA added rules that assembly in North America also had to be from materials and parts made in North America. These were political rules meant to appease special manufacturing interests in the U.S. auto industry (cars would be duty-free only if 50 percent of their value in parts and labor was produced in North America; this number would rise to 62.5 percent by the year 2002). Other industries such as the television industry and ball bearing industry also received special treatment.

This was a form of regional protectionism not unlike that practiced by Britain in the old Commonwealth or France *outre mer* in North Africa.

When the Japanese attacked the NAFTA rules of origin as "sneaky protectionism," Mickey Kantor tried to make the United States sound nationalist in order to win NAFTA's passage. "They're complaining because the United States is finally trying to protect the jobs of our workers and the competitiveness of our businesses," he spoke ad hominem for particular U.S. agricultural, industrial, and banking interests that he publicly reformulated as the vague joint interests of workers and businesses of the United States, Canada, and Mexico.

"The real question is not whether it's good for the hemisphere but whether it's good for the United States," argued NAFTA opponent Sander Levin, a Michigan Democratic representative.[17] In part, this is why, if NAFTA succeeds in the future, GATT and the WTO may weaken or fail, contrary to the opinion of Goldman Sachs vice president Robert D. Hormats, who argues: "Our moral authority to persuade other countries to support freer trade would certainly be eroded if NAFTA fails, and therefore our ability to secure expanded markets for our exports would decline."[18]

RUNAWAY FACTORIES, STRANDED LABOR, AND THE WAGE FUND

Once NAFTA passed congressional mustard, the question remained: would U.S. employers act rationally to close domestic plants, desert their traditional labor force, move to Mexico or the rest of Latin America, and establish a "fund" for the payment of low-wage workers that effectively guaranteed predetermined profit margins based on a scheme for global marketing and preset prices in different regions?

Faced with intense foreign competition and diminishing market shares, those U.S. companies establishing joint U.S.-Mexican production facilities in Mexico attempted to maintain their competitive edge by reorganizing the workforce in their combined operations. For the 12 U.S. companies studied by the consulting firm of Arthur D. Little, their combined production of consumer goods and industrial equipment in Mexico created 47,275 jobs, destroying 850 to 1,100 old jobs in the United States, but creating 2,200 to 2,650 new jobs at their home base in the United States, as well as 6,800 to 8,100 additional jobs at U.S.-located suppliers.[19]

A final accounting might read otherwise in the twenty-first century. And such a selection of a few companies in minor industries did not depict the possibilities for mainline industrial relocation to Mexico.

Sounding more like the classical free trader Adam Smith than a U.S. secretary of labor in a global market beset by restricted trading zones, Robert Reich called for a special trade link with Mexico that would allegedly benefit U.S. labor. "NAFTA doesn't so much open the U.S. market to Mexican goods as it opens the Mexican market to American goods," he argued. "Despite the remaining barriers to U.S. goods, the Mexican market is growing so quickly, and American producers are so well positioned to serve it, that we are already selling more to them than they are to us. These exports translate directly into jobs for U.S. workers."

But using time-loaded words like "growing" and "already," Reich was more a trade salesman using hype and guesswork than an analyst in search of fact to link existing and purported future trade. He argued: "Merchandise exports to Mexico today already account for an estimated 600,000 jobs. Jobs created by expanded trade, moreover, typically are the sorts of higher-wage, higher-skill jobs on which the future of America's workforce depends."[20]

"If NAFTA didn't mean more and better American jobs, the President wouldn't support it," special counselor to the president for NAFTA, William M. Daley, offered in one of 1993's most absurd political non sequitors. And using scare tactics to gain support, Daley warned: "If NAFTA is defeated, Germany and Japan will increase their market-share in Mexico and throughout the Western hemisphere."[21]

DETRITUS OF FACTS AND PHRASES

Do all these heated political fulminations have any theoretical foundation?

For United States transnationals operating globally with production operations in many nations, three components of potential profit have been compacted in their cost/price structure:

1. The comparative difference in several locations between production costs, including wages, and the values of the inventory of goods labor created
2. The difference between these values and the market price of goods secured in lower-priced Mexican, Latin American, or other markets
3. The difference between these values and the market price of goods sold in the inflationary U.S., Canadian, or other markets.

The other part of the global assembly line and marketing apparatus is the replication of the large employers' monopoly over various geographic pools of labor that represent labor's employment and legal rights. Each group of workers is awarded a certain level of superior or inferior living standards, and a degree of control over the wage fund is allotted to each of them.

Transnational capital mobilized by great enterprises has taken command of these labor pools, and even labor's own mobility has only shifted workers and wage levels from one transcontinental organization to another. Worldwide in 1994 there were three billion people in very poor countries where living standards were far below those of U.S., Canadian, and even Mexican workers. And workers in Mexico earn less than a tenth of the wages of U.S. workers in almost all lines of labor.

There were also few bars on U.S. enterprises setting up operations in Mexico. In September 1992, congressional legislation barred the nation's main foreign aid agency from bankrolling projects that could result in more

U.S. factories moving abroad, but large enterprises with their own capital did not require such public funding in the search for foreign investment opportunities.

Competitive fears that Mexico would attract U.S. investments under the NAFTA agreement also led other Latin nations to bow to, and copy, the Mexican-U.S. alliance to break their own restrictions on foreign investments. Central American and Caribbean countries had expressed particular alarm that they might be damaged by NAFTA's gradual reduction of trade and investment barriers. But strong Mexican lobbying pressured them to close ranks with Chile, Colombia, Venezuela, and other South American nations that themselves sought to enter the pact under its access clause permitting adherence to the agreement's lower tariffs and other reduced barriers to trade and investments.

President Clinton's 18 October 1993 message to Latin American leaders gathered in Santiago, Chile, promised that U.S. approval of NAFTA would be the first step in achieving free trade throughout the region. The gathered Latin leaders agreed, emphasizing "the transcendence of the treaty for the whole continent."

"When negotiations for the treaty began," President Carlos Salinas de Gortari rationalized, "many people thought Mexico was turning its back on Latin America, and events have shown the opposite to be true. For Latin America, the free trade agreement has come to mean a different policy of the United States towards the region."[22]

UTOPIA AND THE ECONOMIC FRAME OF TRANSNATIONAL CAPITAL

NAFTA has led to high hopes for continental integration on an economic plane. Though a crisis is brewing, the illusion has been created that foreign ownership and management of technical capital will promote benefits beyond the upper social and educational reaches at any location where such transnational organizations operate. Supposedly pan-continental operations will be centered on the wage, skill, and technocratic diversity of the labor force in each location, with careful consideration given to each set of workers' economic and political organizations securing their material, legal, and civil rights.

The problem with this formulation for Mexico is that it is not an accurate depiction of the alignment of social forces or classes. For here modern technology has been largely foreign-owned. Much domestic capital that had been accumulated by raiding the nation's wealth in the past was invested abroad. Workers' skills for modern technology and services are still lacking, and the educational apparatus is dismally out of sync with an industrial society. The Vatican also remains revanchist, making a powerful return to the scene with the theological accoutrement of obedience to scripture, the work ethic, and abnegation of wordly goods by the faithful awaiting the rewards of the hereafter. The rural half of the population has been forced off the land and out of towns and drawn into the cities without the means to live. This migration has required the government to fund either social services to sustain these people or a police apparatus to repress them. Local political opposition has grown in towns and states and can be kept in the fold of electoral politics for only a few years at best. And the PRI has pursued its scheme for enrichment of the elite under pressure of an unregulated, ticking political clock foretelling a social explosion.

CHAPTER 15

Political Boundaries, Unified Economy, and Maquiladoras

Borderlands and political boundaries are inventions of modern times; nomadic societies respected neither in the search for survival and a habitable climate. The American anthropological and historical record reveals population movements through what later became Siberia, Alaska, Canada, the United States, Mexico, and South America. Asian people, migrating across the frozen surface of today's Bering Strait, wended their way throughout all the Americas. And the descendants of spear-wielding Paleo-Indian hunters and food gatherers occupied an area that stretched from present day Wisconsin to Mexico City and beyond.

In modern American history, there were different forces behind population flows and settled political boundaries that defined people's residence and citizenship. The very contours of U.S. geography and its inhabitants were in part inherited from Mexico because during the Mexican-American War of 1846–48, the United States used a volunteer army to supplement small regular units to defeat Mexican forces and annex one-third of Mexico, which was then made into California and Texas. And with later land concessions from war came some 75,000 Mexicans and Indians, two-thirds living in northern New Mexico.[1]

For the rest of the nineteenth century, the Mexican-U.S. boundary remained porous; immigration to the United States was largely unrestricted and surpassed 1,000 for the first time in 1904. The Revolution of 1910 that left nearly a million Mexican people dead also saw millions abandoning their villages, fleeing across the U.S. border.[2]

The pace of Mexican emigration again quickened when the United

States entered World War I, increasing production and employment and drawing Mexican workers, especially to southwestern industrial centers. A high point of 51,000 Mexican immigrants was reached in 1929, but immigration tapered off and then stopped, as the United States expelled Mexicans following the 1929 onset of the Great Depression and massive joblessness.

World War II again reversed the flow as the United States replaced its own workers who had become soldiers with government-contracted Mexican *braceros* consigned under subcontracts sold to private land owners engaged in commercial agriculture. As the farm lobby immediately seized the advantage of cheap labor under the banner "food will win the war!" the large landowners sidestepped the Mexican government declaration of Texas as off limits to *braceros* suffering racial discrimination. Farm representatives in the U.S. Senate continued the *bracero* program for two decades after the war and relinquished the advantage of low cost labor only when mechanization of agricultural machinery lowered costs by replacing some forms of manual labor.[3]

Opposing the powerful agricultural lobby, other U.S. lobbies led by churches, labor unions, and U.S. farm workers successfully pressed Congress to end the government *bracero* system in 1964. Congress failed, however, to create a firm regulatory infrastructure to stop undocumented immigration.

The consequences were disastrous, as the fluid border led to a four-cornered struggle between (1) illegal Mexican workers crossing the border for season harvests, (2) local Caucasian agricultural workers displaced by cheaper Mexican labor and forced to find other jobs to survive year-round, (3) higher price Chicano agricultural workers also displaced from the rural domain, who fled to the cities in the 1960s without the essential skills for industrial work, and (4) unionized, white industrial workers whose jobs were being threatened as their positions were both simplified by the advance of technology and taken by unskilled Chicano and undocumented Mexican workers.[4]

By the mid–1960s, low-wage undocumented workers were driving out the better paid not only in agriculture, but also in manufacturing and services. While the employers and the *coyotes* transporting the *illegales* reaped minimal rewards, union workers lost jobs, the undocumented workers feared deportation if they organized for better pay or objected to their harsh treatment, and there was a general lowering of the wage-scale structure as less than half of all illegal workers earned the federal minimum wage.[5]

During the rest of the 1960s, the 1970s, and 1980s, thousands organized the farm workers, only to face government support for the large corporate growers in the 12-year period, 1980–92 of the Republican administrations of Ronald Reagan and George Bush. By early 1994, migratory Mexican farm workers were again being pushed back to the relative economic position they held when the *bracero* program ended 30 years earlier in 1964.

Crossing the U.S. Border

During these 30 years (1964–94), migratory workers continued to possess little power along the border region, though the movement of populations, goods, and investments intensified many times.

Maquiladora twin-plant industries had been established on both sides of the border, retail trade had flourished, and the flow of commuter workers, immigration, and tourism had intensified. But with Tijuana and other Mexican border cities the transit points for millions of undocumented immigrants into the United States and the return of these migrants back to Mexico, control over and unification of the workforce seemed outside the reach of government.

Then in 1986, the U.S. Congress passed the Immigration Reform and Control Act granting amnesty and resident status to some three million illegal immigrants, including some one million migrant farm workers. Not only those with falsified documents qualified for amnesty, but also their spouses and children who could show they were in the country before the law was enacted.

Congress thought this law would resolve subsequent problems of rounding up and deporting illegal immigrants. By imposing sanctions on employers hiring newly arrived workers lacking proper documents, the lawmakers reasoned they would prevent further illegal immigration, force employers to compete for a more restricted supply of workers with legal-immigrant status, and thereby lead to an improvement in workers' wages and working conditions.

For this end, some 3,200 agents of the Immigration and Naturalization Service were to patrol the 2,000-mile border between the United States and Mexico to halt the flow of illegal immigrants. But over a million were attempting to cross each year, and the slender force of immigration agents was able to apprehend only a fraction of those determined to cross or recross if they were returned to Mexico. Forged Social Security and resident-alien identification cards were also easily purchased in the growing underground industry of counterfeited, plastic-coated replicas of the government's "fraud-resistant" documents, complete with personal data, fingerprints, and picture-profile for future border crossings. Employers asking for such documents were legally protected if the identification appeared authentic.

Immigration agents did not easily apprehend the undocumented either because Congress required the agents to secure search warrants describing the reason for the search, the agricultural field where the specified immigrants would be working at a particular time, and the identity of the landowner. With underlying land ownership and tenancy not always easily determined by the best of lawyers and farm workers often switching fields in the course of a single day, the Immigration Service could not carry out its mandate to apprehend and charge the offenders.

The growing pool of agricultural workers meanwhile undermined enforcement of minimum wage and safety laws. With the confluent supply of those receiving amnesty, their working spouses and children, and the constant flow of illegal immigrants, the pool of labor far exceeded employer demands by 1991-93, keeping down wages and empowering the employers to dictate the conditions of work. This meant that migratory labor faced harsh conditions and low pay. Workers often lived in shacks without running water or sanitary facilities. The 1992-93 federal minimum wage of $4.25 an hour was openly violated, as were federal Department of Labor regulations against child labor.

The undocumented kept coming, too. Workers crossing the border into Texas and California fanned out across the nation, often using Florida as the point for buying forged documents, and then departing for the seasonal picking of fruits and vegetables in the Midwest, primarily in Wisconsin and Michigan. After 1964, rundown labor camps in Wisconsin continued to attract many thousands of undocumented workers. Michigan was one of the nation's leading employers of migratory labor, with some nine hundred labor camps attracting 45,000 migrants, though enforcement of minimum standards was weak at best. The average Michigan migrant family of four earned $7,200 in 1991, about half the $13,924 level the government established as the poverty line. And sanitary facilities often violated both federal and state standards for cleanliness and privacy. Enforcement staff and procedures were meanwhile being undermined by government budgetary cuts at all levels. And here, too, the migrants were thrown back to the status they occupied when the *bracero* program ended three decades earlier.[6]

United States factories were also set up across the border in Mexico to employ inexpensive Mexican workers, with the scale of comparative hourly labor costs being approximately $10 for every U.S. worker, $4.50 for every Puerto Rican, and 50 cents for every Mexican.

U.S. CAPITAL EXPORTS, MAQUILADORAS, AND MEXICAN LABOR

For more than a quarter of a century all along the borderlands a vast pool of cheap Mexican labor had attracted U.S. industrial investors and vice versa.

Rather than Mexican labor moving to be employed by agricultural capital within U.S. borders under the *bracero* program that ended in 1964, the year of 1965 opened an era in which U.S. manufacturing capital moved to employ factory workers in Mexico's northern reach to produce for export to the U.S. market. Looking at comparatively high costs of production in the United States, the American Manufacturers Association and large enterprises had successfully lobbied for new opportunities to employ inexpensive Mexican factory workers. Under such pressures, Congress passed preferential tariffs unlocking new trade opportunities, the U.S. tariff code providing that U.S.-manufactured components assembled in Mexico could be reexported to the United States with a tariff placed only on the value added in wages paid Mexican workers.[7]

Both Mexico and the United States had their own rationale for entering and extending the new relationship. Mexico sought the agreement to meet three immediate needs: to pay service charges on its huge foreign debt by providing factory employment that would stimulate production for export generating hard currency earnings, to create a domestic class of wage-rich consumers to increase Mexican economic growth and service jobs, and to encourage internal migration that would absorb both industrial and rural unemployed who might otherwise protest and search for political alternatives. Seeking social and class peace as a foundation for industrial development, the Mexican government thus attempted to finance an infrastructure to accommodate foreign factories, build modest homes for Mexican workers, and promise minimum costs of rent, utilities, and transportation, thereby attracting foreign investors by the low wage level that would cover the workers' modest living costs.[8]

The Mexican government nonetheless feared U.S. manufactures made in Mexico would be sold there, rather than being exported to generate foreign exchange to finance both the foreign debt and imports. The government also feared that these U.S. manufactures would displace more costly, lower-quality Mexican-made goods seeking export markets, thereby undermining Mexican-owned factory production and employment. Only with the U.S. assurance that these U.S.-plant manufactures would be "exported" to the United States did the Mexican government waive all duties and restrictions on imports of U.S.-made raw materials and parts, as well as on 100 percent foreign ownership of capital investments placed in Mexican *maquiladora*.

This waiver formed an exception to Mexico's own 1973 Law to Regulate Foreign Investment that provided that all new companies had to have majority Mexican ownership, and foreign investors had to meet Mexican capital needs by locating their factories in under-industrialized regions, in fields not competitive with Mexican-owned enterprises, and in operations creating jobs rather than concentrating on those promising higher returns.

Export-oriented investments to earn foreign exchange and improve Mexico's balance of payments were also encouraged by other laws that adjusted restrictions on foreign borrowing and controlling imports. By using foreign investment capital to build a positive trade balance, it was reasoned that Mexico could accumulate foreign exchange and bootstrap its own industrial development.[9]

U.S. Pressure for an Open Door

Mexico was also deeply in debt to U.S. banks, could barely pay interest and other service charges from national earnings and exports, had no capital left for domestic development, and could not pay for its current imports. It was thus forced to grant trade concessions to the United States.

By 1986, Mexico had $100 billion in foreign debt, the value of its oil exports had collapsed, and Senator Bill Bradley proposed default relief for Mexican and Latin American interest service charges on their $380 billion accumulated debt in exchange for trade concessions and economic reforms by debtors.[10]

Pressure on Mexico for an open door thus took the form of a "free-market arrangement" as a condition for International Monetary Fund relief. And IMF financial gymnastics also became the core of new Mexican loans extended by U.S. and other Western commercial banks. Alexander Cockburn was critical of U.S. policy:

> Some of the nostrums being thrust upon Mexico and other debtor countries are familiar—tighter fiscal and monetary policy, higher interest rates, elimination of price controls, cuts in social spending. These are the traditional short-term solutions advocated by international bankers down the years. But there is much more. The major demand of the creditor cartel led by the [Treasury Secretary James] Baker-IMF combine requires that Mexico sell off a majority of its 500 state-owned enterprises and turn toward what some exuberantly call "pro-growth strategies," "streamlining" and other verbal disguises for handing over the economy to private capital.
>
> Mexico is also to open up its domestic market to imports, hack away at government subsidies and actively underwrite foreign investment.
>
> In return for all this, a bailout will follow, a process that in plainer English means that the Western banks that lent Mexico most of its debt will not have to write off their loans. . . . In practice this means turning the target country into a free-fire zone for domestic, and especially international capital, achieved through eliminating state subsidies and public investments, opening domestic markets to free trade, encouraging foreign investment through tax giveaways and pushing interest rates up and wages down.[11]

Mexico did make these concessions, opening the door to further U.S. investments in Mexico to produce goods to export to the United States. Investors foresaw that reasonable transport costs from Mexico to the nearby U.S. market would more than offset the even lower cost of labor found in Asia or elsewhere in the Caribbean.

United States–based manufacturers also favored the agreement, calculating that a guaranteed *maquiladora* market for U.S.-made components and raw materials would stimulate production, employment, and profits on the U.S. side of the border. United States machinery manufacturers wanted to bolster their exports because their sales to Latin America had declined almost $20 billion a year by the beginning of the 1980s, reaching a base total of only $9 billion a year from 1984 to 1986.

The U.S. government hoped that the agreement would reduce illegal immigration of Mexican workers to the U.S. Southwest by employing these workers in U.S. factories south of the Rio Grande. With these lobbies and government influence pursuing like goals, special U.S. tariff regulations were designed to allow U.S.-made components to be "exported" to Mexico and used in products assembled in U.S.-owned, Mexican-based plants; the manufactures were then allowed to be "imported" into the United States without imposing any tariff duty except on the value added by labor.[12]

Sweeping in an era of labor-intensive Mexican assembly operations, U.S. investors immediately began setting up plants on both sides of the border. Their U.S.-based plants made the components that the Mexican-based plants assembled and shipped back to the United States for final processing and sale. As these twin *maquiladora* factories grew in number, employees, and output from 1965 to 1993, many surmounted both recessions and peso devaluations. As the employers' demand for labor increased, however, this demand eventually led to a smaller gap between the wage earnings of workers in the U.S. and Mexican plants. To enable U.S. companies to escape rising wage rates along the border, in 1972 the Mexican government allowed *maquiladoras* to enter the Mexican interior.[13]

Two years later in 1974, there were 550 U.S. assembly operations in Mexico employing 84,500 workers, though the downward vicissitudes of the U.S. economy in 1974-75 momentarily cut demand for *maquiladora* goods and led 55 U.S. assembly plants to close their doors on 26,000 Mexican workers. With the start-up of new plants, though, some 78,405 workers were still employed by the close of 1975. And 1975 devaluation of the peso cut the ratio of Mexican to U.S. wages to a low of 1 to 12, rejuvenating U.S. investments and leading to the employment of 80,891 *maquiladora* workers by year's end.

Six years later in 1982 thousands of young, unmarried women were still the main labor force in over 600 U.S.-owned assembly plants. Ten years later in 1992, there were over 1,200 *maquiladora* plants employing more than 136,000 workers, still 90 percent young, unmarried females of ages 17–24; and by 1995 there were over 8,000 assembly plants, some 3,200 U.S.-owned.[14]

THE LOGIC OF MARKETS AND PRODUCTION LOCALE

United States capital had fled domestic investments because foreign competitors underpriced U.S.-made goods sold in foreign markets.

"Prospects for investment and manufacturing activity in the U.S. are heavily dependent on an improved trade outlook," Federal Reserve Board chairman Paul Volcker stated in 1986. But as the world surplus of commodities and manufactured goods had steadily increased faster than new markets, foreign producers cut costs and profit margins, subsidized exports, and moved production to lower-cost areas to maintain their U.S. market share. Many large U.S. manufacturers defensively responded by closing plants in the United States and setting up operations in low-wage countries, giving special emphasis to the Mexican borderlands.[15]

For U.S. owners, then, the *maquiladora* program not only drew substantial investments, but by the mid–1970s, investments concentrated on high-tech output. The investment in production of electronic and electrical equipment was $35.1 million—far exceeding investment in the traditional assembly of manufactured goods like leather and footwear products ($7.8 million), textiles ($4.3 million), sports goods and toys ($2.1 million), wood products ($1.5 million), food products ($1.1 million), and a miscellany of other goods ($10.7 million).[16]

As technical manufacturing became the mainstay in the Mexican borderland states, more workers were drawn into industry. By 1980, manufacturing industry workers made up a substantial part of the economically active population: 24.61 percent in Nuevo León, 14.43 percent in Coahuila, 13.56 percent in Baja California, 11.93 percent in Tamaulipas, and 9.60 percent in Sonora.[17] Three-quarters of all *maquiladora* output was shipped back to the United States, with the North American market absorbing these low-production cost goods (though not often at a comparable reduction in price). These imports frequently undercut more expensive varieties of similar goods made by U.S. workers.

United States capital was more mobile than Mexican workers, too. As the gap between U.S. and Mexican wages along the border had been narrowed from seven-to-one in 1965 to three-to-one in 1976, some U.S. investors looked elsewhere for cheaper labor, relocating assembly operations to other low-wage nations or to the United States. But the 1976 devaluation of the peso again decreased labor costs, to the advantage of the remaining *maquiladora* plants.

Unlike U.S. investors able to stay or leave at will, Mexican *maquiladora* workers did not have the advantages of quickly moving to new jobs from the border's squalid cities; nor could they afford to continue to cross the border to spend two-thirds of their salaries to buy what became a smaller basket of goods on the U.S. side after peso devaluation.[18]

Once drawn towards the urban domain along the U.S.-Mexican border strip, these workers were largely trapped in the Mexican zone of *municipios* extending southwards along the borderlands. Five of the ten *municipios* with the highest in-migration levels per capita in 1980 were located in Nuevo León, and though the average *municipio* in-migration varied by state—from 2.5 percent in Baja California to 9.9 percent in Chihuahua—all along the border region there was a 1.2 average *municipio* in-migration rate.

People were coming for jobs, with the 1980 migration focused on two major zones. In first place, Baja/Northwest Sonora (including Tijuana, Mexicali, and Tecate in Baja, and six Sonoran *municipios*), received 30,472 more migrants than departed (representing an in-migration rate of 2.25 percent). Ranking second, Nuevo León and parts of Coahuila and Tamaulipas (including 27 *municipios* over the entire urban-to-rural range from the large border cities of Nuevo Laredo to rural areas) received 11,818 more migrants than they lost (representing an in-migration rate of 1.8 percent).[19]

Already urbanized, these workers faced uncertain times as the *maquiladora* program swung through the business and political cycles of the 1980s and 1990s, awaiting more intensive Mexican industrialization under a future North American Free Trade Agreement.

TWIN CITIES, TWIN PLANTS, COMMON PROBLEMS

Along the U.S.-Mexican border, the transnational movement of populations, goods, resources, and investment capital promoting mass production and services had thus concentrated on key "twin cities" and their linkages to zones of conurbation.

As the world's longest border separating high and low income nations, the U.S.-Mexican border extended along the four U.S. states of California, Arizona, New Mexico, and Texas, and the six Mexican states of Baja California, Sonora, Chihuahua, Coahuila, Nuevo León, and Tamaulipas.

With the population in all these borderland states and their major twin cities in flux, by 1980 the growth of twin city megapopulation centers had brought together the largest binational population in the Tijuana/San Diego area (1.3 million, comprising 36 percent of the total twin-city populations), followed by the Ciudad Juarez/El Paso area (with one million, accounting for 27 percent). And with several twin cities located in population regions encompassing several other cities, the multi-*municipio* metropolitan regions were becoming the border heartlands for ever more intensified foreign investment and finance, production and services, employment and trade.[20]

The framework for these ties was set over the 30-year period 1963–

94, as job positions and higher wages offered by *maquiladora* factories sped the influx of workers and their families, making Mexico's border cities both more prosperous than comparable nonborder cities and fostering a growth rate over double the rate of their counterpart U.S. twin cities.[21] Almost midpoint in the three-decade cycle, during 1980, the total population of the Mexican borderlands region was 10,688,000, nearly 66 percent being concentrated in eight *municipio* regions.[22]

On the U.S. side, border cities were generally less prosperous economically than comparable nonborder cities—a situation likely to change once the North American Free Trade Agreement facilitated the unfettered movement of capital, goods, and possibly labor.

DEGRADATION IN THE BORDERLANDS

The borderlands were not only the lodestone for migration and a critical link for binational production and marketing in the United States, but the domain of an effusion of pollutants and problems. Divided by political boundaries, the binational metropolitan areas had rapidly transformed social and labor relations in both Mexico and the United States. Rapid borderland industrialization also brought the kind of social problems experienced by other nations and zones that had gone through the transformation process. Urbanization placed ever greater pressures on resources, water and food supplies, living space and the population's culture, and general conditions of health, safety, and tranquility.[23] The dilemma of technological advances endangering and immiserizating populations was thus already felt on both sides of the border.

As these forces unified the northern economy of Mexico with the southern economy of Texas along the Rio Grande, the movement of capital became fluid, the labor force increasingly indivisible, and pollution and politics one.

Nearly thirty years of unregulated U.S. assembly plants operating in Mexico had spewn out environmental pollutants and contamination. And these *maquiladoras* concentrated a huge population, drawing subsistence farmers from the interior and laborers from other zones to assemble products to be sold in the United States. Rapid population concentrations thus bred *colonias* where tens of thousands of people in both nations lived in makeshift shanties without running water or sewage facilities, constantly in danger of the pollutants suffusing the factories in which they worked, the air and ground water that sustained them, and the communities where they lived.

Degradation, extreme privation, and life in the *colonias* were the lot of millions—almost half a million workers in the El Paso/Juárez region alone by mid–1992. "There are 68,000 people living in *colonias* in El Paso," the city's director of health and environment Dr. Laurance Nickey reported. "In Juárez, there are 400,000 people living in similar or much worse conditions. That poses a potentially serious public health issue."

With electrical power but inadequate sanitation and no running water, residents on the Mexican side near Juárez were forced to buy water for drinking and bathing from private companies that drew it from the El Paso city taps, then trucked it into the *colonias* for sale. The price was $20 to $40 a month in the city and $100 to $150 a month in the countryside.

But this itself proved dangerous because storing the water during extended periods in the region's intense heat dissipated the chlorine used to suppress bacteria, so the water itself became a hothouse for multiplying bacteria. "We did a survey of 224 homes in the *colonias* and found that in 47 percent of the cases, the chlorine had dissipated," Dr. Nickey warned. "And we found plenty of fecal and coliform bacteria."

The merger of putrefied and chlorinated water supplies was almost unavoidable, too. Sewage from Juárez flowed untreated into a massive ditch running parallel to the Rio Grande; the ditch water was then used to irrigate farm fields on the Mexican side. The tens of thousands of *colonias* residents without running water or sewage service either took water from the river or bought and stored tap water from El Paso. Southeast of Juárez a giant toxic waste dump had long since seeped into both the river and the ground water from which El Paso water was also drawn. So there was no such thing as a purified common aquifer. Warning signs—"agua contaminada! no entrada!"—were of necessity ignored.

Hepatitis was endemic, cholera bacteria emerged from Juárez waste water, and to prevent an outbreak of deadly disease, both Mexico and the United States beefed up their promises to deal with environmental and health problems along the 2,000-mile border. In 1992, Mexico pledged more than $450 million for a three-year program that included the building of waste-treatment plants, and the U.S. government earmarked $201 million for border cleanup in 1993.

WHAT WILL HAPPEN UNDER NAFTA?

But even such taxpayer-financed cleanup might prove inadequate in the face of unknown levels of pollution left in the wake of the *maquiladora* era's mass production. Under the proposed North American Free Trade Agreement, however, increased production and commercial activity on the Mexican side of the border would require massive infusions of capital and equipment to create an environmentally safe region.

In El Paso/Juárez, the region's population had already doubled to about two million in the two decades 1972–92. Implementation of the North American Free Trade Agreement promised to accelerate the process as North American manufacturers moved south for inexpensive Mexican labor, Mexican workers moved towards the border for newly offered jobs, and industrial and community pollutants merged. "El Paso is so far from Washington and Juarez is so far from Mexico City that nobody paid any attention to our infrastructure problems," the president of the El Paso Chamber of Commerce, Barbara Perez, lamented. "With the NAFTA treaty, we are finally getting some state and Federal money."[24]

Problems handed down from 30 years of urbanization and pollution would affect millions in the twin cities and *colonias*. And from such exploitation and degradation might issue an awareness that the solutions to their problems resided at a higher political reach, beyond the ken of their daily lives.

FORCES OF IMMIGRATION

The United States has been powerless to solve problems of illegal immigration in the past, and the tidal wave of surplus peoples crossing into the United States will probably continue unabated throughout the 1990s. With 95 percent of all crossings illegal—totaling about 10,000 a week—the Mexican-U.S. border near San Diego has become the new Ellis Island, Los Angeles another New York for over 1 million resident illegal immigrants, and the L.A. City Hospital has become their free health care center, where two-thirds of all births are to illegal aliens.

There is no obvious way to stop the annual illegal influx of one million people either. Despite the failure in 1986 to pass President Reagan's proposed legislation to fine employers who failed to identify illegal workers they employed, the bill later became law, but even then the workers forged identifying documents that allowed employers to claim they had made proper inquiry.

As tax outlays, job competition, welfare costs, school enrollments and other pressures intensified in the United States, vain efforts to seal the border brought political xenophobia to a head. In San Diego, which was already suffering from 1993-94 defense industry cuts, unemployment, and intense job competition at ever-lower wages, anti-immigration feelings ran high. United States workers with mortgages to pay and families to support could not compete with immigrants willing to take $7,500 a year for nine months of hard labor and to live in camps that looked like Mexican barrios. And, though many paid taxes, the immigrants were effectively being government-subsidized.

The net cost of the United States to care for 3.5 to 4.5 million illegal immigrants was between $25 to $42.5 billion a year in the first half of the 1990s. Even the apprehension of 1,000 illegals each night at the San Diego border cost the United States about $40 a day per person to detain, feed, and repatriate them. The cost of sealing the border would be extra billions, and even then the influx would probably continue. The passage of legislation for national identification cards that would be necessary to secure public services in the United States would probably be undercut by card forgers possessed of the latest technologies. Such legislation would increase the costs and risks of border crossing, but would not stop the flow.[25]

CHAPTER 16

In the Domain of Each Nation

Historically, colonialism and spheres of influence were structured by institutional accretion that went beyond the initial bursts of conquest and imposed servitude. The process was rooted in changes in social production relations in the metropole that in turn reached irreconcilable levels and imploded. The maintenance of order and political legitimacy demanded reorganization and restructuring of the means of life that were often leveraged by extension of these relations through the imposition of greater inequalities on peripheral nations from which assorted forms of wealth could be extracted to mollify and pacify the various social classes and communities in the metropole itself.

In the relations between the metropole and the periphery, the dominant nation often imposed differences and inequities in the degrees of social freedom, the levels of remuneration for labor, and the disposition of social surplus coursing through controlled, institutionalized channels. Over time, there were often faint or feigned attempts to narrow the gap between the metropole and periphery for wages, working conditions and rights, output, prices, and a host of administrative social services and benefits. But these too were part of the social relations established and evolved in each domain, so that the pace of change moved with the requirements for social stability, framed by the relative level of wealth extraction in each locale.

Such an imperium moved because of its material essences, not because of the pronouncements of politicians railing for its maintenance and rallying their factions with xenophobic fears, racialist jargon, and dire, untrustworthy predictions.

No Easy Answers

Within this scheme of past metropolitan spheres holding other nations at ransom, what is the future for the relative power balance among a much lesser threesome striving for unhindered commerce—the U.S., Mexico, and Canada as three potential NAFTA traders?

The easy answer is that once free trade has begun, all nations will specialize in what they do best, so all will benefit from freely selling what they make in the widest possible market.

Closer analysis shows, though, that once a sustaining infrastructure is built, U.S. transnationals will probably become overwhelming investors in key industries vis-à-vis their Mexican and Canadian competitors. This will allow heavily capitalized U.S. firms to take over land as the means of life and factories as the means of production, and also to provide technical equipment and infrastructure for transportation, communications, environmental services, and direct conservation efforts.

Modern-day free-trade advocates move on the notion that if nations specialize in the goods and services they best produce, trade, income, and welfare of the people of each nation will be maximized. They view the export of technical equipment for investment as a secondary boost to trade and production by the metropole. In the case of Mexico, the export of U.S. capital is thus viewed as leveraging demand for U.S. exports; in its metropolitan role, the U.S. will produce for export more steel, machinery, heavy trucks, and earth-moving equipment.

With free trade between NAFTA members cutting Mexican trade barriers that average 11 percent on export value, there will in theory be a constant enlargement of U.S.-produced exports to an average of $7 billion annually in the late 1990s and some 170,000 U.S. jobs may be created.

Besides, the free traders argue, much U.S. capital (outside the apparel and light electronic manufacturing sector) will not move to Mexico because the 1992 productivity of U.S. manufacturing workers was 7.9 percent higher than that of Mexican workers, while average U.S. hourly compensation was only 6.9 times higher than in Mexico. Even if Mexican wages were frozen and productivity grew at double-digit rates, the free traders say, appreciation of the peso against the dollar would stymie Mexico's exports to the U.S. and maintain the positive U.S. trade balance.[1]

Though the short-term proved otherwise in 1995, nonetheless the deeper answers reside within the domain of each nation.

Canadian Doublethink

There might be many slips in finalizing the NAFTA agreement.

As the third member of NAFTA, Canada was well on its way to implementing the agreement when antifederalist, regionalist, and autarchic sentiments resurfaced in 1993. The new Liberal party prime minister, Jean

Chrétien, promised to seek a new round of negotiations to win greater protection for Canadian exporters against restrictions by the United States. Given the strong regional parties, the secessionist Bloc Québecois, and the Liberal party's left-wing demands for new NAFTA negotiations, the pressures on the previous nine years of Tory-style (Progressive Conservative party) federalism threatened to alter, even undermine, the free-trade accord.

Compromise held the moment. With the liberal party the biggest party in Parliamant—even if it had been forced to form a minority government dependent on other parties to pass legislation—it was able to seek support issue by issue with the regional protest parties, the Reform party in the prairies, and the Bloc Québecois in Quebec. The latter became the second largest party, making it the official opposition.[2]

Support for any agreement between the parties rested on solutions to the nation's conditions of near-depression. The fact that Canada was beset with joblessness of 11 percent in the early 1990s meant that 1,600,000 were unemployed, hundreds of thousands of its 27 million people were on welfare, and Canadian factories that were seeking low-wage workers in Mexico or were at a competitive disadvantage with the United States were threatening to enlarge the Canadian army of the destitute. Chrétien had won the election among 18.5 million eligible voters by focusing on those who were impoverished, without work, and in need of government-directed employment in public works programs to upgrade roads, sewers, and bridges. The 6 billion Canadian dollars (U.S. $4.5 billion) cost increased the federal budget deficit of $35 billion (U.S. $27 billion) to be covered by taking on more debt that would make interest service payments an even larger share of government expenditures.

As part of the resolution of budget deficits and joblessness, Chrétien had called for new talks with Washington to revise some NAFTA provisions protecting Canadian workers producing the nation's exports. Canada would negotiate from strength, not threats, moreover. Although a Canadian withdrawal from NAFTA would have little economic effect on the United States because the two nations already had a separate trade agreement, if Canada rejected NAFTA it would simply block free trade between Canada and Mexico and keep some Canadian capital from venturing there. As NAFTA could also be amended after it went into force, with its provisions subject to interpretation by three governments, both Canada and Washington sought this path to resolve problems rather than reopening the original pact.

Chrétien was positioned for trade compromise, too. His overall victory margin of 178 seats in the House of Commons meant he was not heavily indebted to support from the left-leaning eight representatives of the New Democratic party, which implacably opposed NAFTA. So Chrétien's support for "open-access trade," something less than "free trade," meant friendly discussions and compromise with the United States over interpretation of the pact were possible.[3] Still, Chrétien would have to deal with protest from the Reformist party that had taken 46 of 58 parliamentary seats in British Columbia and Alberta, tapping into western separatism as a right-wing populist party getting votes from the poor on an anti-immigrant program, receiving money from the rich on an antiwelfare plank, and promising each group protection from the other.[4]

Such separatist traditions arose from the past deluge of American farmers seeking Alberta's free land after 1896 (when homesteading ended in the United States), the anticentrist traditions of their descendants, their alienation from the powerbrokers in Ottawa, Ontario, and Quebec, and the fact that for 24 of the previous 25 years and continuing under Chrétien, a Quebecer had been the prime minister.[5]

The Liberal party platform had judiciously called for a set of rules covering "unfair trade" to prevent what the Canadians considered to be often arbitrary harassment of their exports by U.S. trade enforcement agencies. Earlier Canadian-U.S. efforts to write a bilateral subsidy code had met with failure, both governments looking to a rule book that would be part of GATT's global trade liberalization agreement on which they could build. But as GATT faltered, continuing U.S.-Canadian discussions on a code governing subsidies became essential because Canada thought Washington trade enforcement agencies were making up capricious and arbitrary rules as they went along and hitting Canada unfairly. "The United States is a trade bully," criticized Catherine Swift, senior vice president of the Canadian Federation of Independent Business. "You need to police that giant."[6]

NUMBERS COUNT

Canada was also counting customers. With 40 percent of the total output of the private sector being exported, accounting for about a fifth of Canada's gross national output and one in five Canadian jobs, and with three-quarters of Canadian exports going to the United States, the governing U.S.-Canadian Free Trade Pact, not NAFTA, was at issue.

"The play in Washington [over NAFTA] is entirely of regional issues in the U.S., of local interest, and not whether Canada has one attitude or another," said Trade Minister Roy MacLaren, distancing Canada from the U.S. congressional debate. Provided the United States and Mexico would negotiate on specific improvements, Ottawa would apparently accept NAFTA.[7]

But still water had depths unseen. Canadian accommodations with Washington would be firm, beneficial, and nationalist to hold together the Liberal party working majority of 178 seats in the 295-member lower house of Parliament.[8]

Beyond the bilateral U.S.-Canadian tie, Chrétien immediately went on the offensive, saying NAFTA would not become law until he proclaimed it. He insisted he would press for changes in its provisions to protect

Canadian energy reserves and to define rules concerning Canadian low-price exports based on subsidies given for steel, pork, lumber, and other products—items Canadians viewed as suffering from capricious U.S. barriers based on abritrary standards.[9]

Yet, if Canada increased its tariff security, thus altering NAFTA, a U.S. riposte might demand the end of Canadian protection of its cultural industries in magazines, books, television, films, and other cultural products.[10]

Although such a grandiose recoil might undermine NAFTA, negotiations on a lesser scale might resolve the technical problem of Canadian subsidies to flagging industries like lumber and wheat that allow producers to lower their export prices. Bringing on U.S. charges of "unfair competition," such prices had materially injured U.S. producers and led to demands for countervailing tax duties to block offending imports from the U.S. market.[11]

The issue of "unfair trade" was, however, a political issue based on the fundamental way the state viewed and affected the unequal development of the technologies, resources, and skills in Canada and the United States. With Canada attempting to use the state to rectify its disadvantageous condition by subsidies to inefficient, less-technologized, and labor-costly fields of production, Chrétien could politically move in several directions: renegotiate NAFTA so that general subsidies to Canadian industries in distress or in unfavorable regions would be allowed without U.S. retaliation; negotiate the question of subsidies and countervailing duties industry by industry, either within the U.S.-Canadian trade treaty or within NAFTA; or reject NAFTA outright to appease nationalist, autarchic Canadian interests and political parties.

MEXICO: WITHOUT FREE-TRADE QUALMS

Mexico under President Salinas was without free-trade qualms, remaining a moving shadow tracing out the lurching motions of the U.S. leviathan.

As U.S. transnationals and investors invaded, the phantoms shaping the Mexican Senate had changed laws, economic structures, and institutions. These heralds of the governing party, 61 voters en masse for any measure the president allowed, had on 23 November 1993 been dressed down from the legislature's podium by former president Porfirio Muñoz Ledo, who accused the Salinas administration of having sold out a nation, poor and unready, to enter in the United States' schemes backdated to an elite trilateral commission of financiers and oligarchies.

"That is called being a traitor!" shouted down a government partisan from the gallery of the elect, bringing Muñoz's unhesitating exhortation to "the country, my compatriots, to organize with me a line of national resistance against the country's deliverance to foreign powers."

The Senate was so dominated by the executive branch that laws were written in the president's ministries and de facto foreign investments of the past were approved de jure at the moment's critical juncture. Senate budgets passed nearly unchallenged simply because the president prescribed them. Senators winked when the ruler of the nation was more often found lobbying in Washington than running daily affairs. The people did not know how government represented them, who their congressman might be, why Emilio M. Gonzáles as the deputy head of the nation's largest union, the government-affiliated Mexican Workers' Confederation, was also the Senate majority leader for the PRI, which had ruled for 68 years. It is hardly surprising that in a late-night vote on 23 November 1993, the Senate passed NAFTA 56 to 2, with 6 absent to attend to "personal affairs."

Are not these telltale signs of a future relationship of material subjugation and political subservience—of metropole and periphery locked into the U.S. sphere?

PRI members said those who complained about such procedures were opponents eager to discredit the party in an election year. But they could not explain why two days later, 25 November, President Salinas sent Congress new foreign investment legislation to allow foreign companies to own, with state legal security provided, coastal and border property. This legislation struck down a 20-year-old statute once the bulwark of Mexican economic nationalism, though it had in fact been disregarded since 1989. Now it was formally overturned to simplify the transit through the government maze of regulations and bureaucrats. Palms still greased with lucre, large and small investors were drawn into retailing, tourism, airlines, the merchant marine, mining, and petrochemicals.

Although the new statute avoided industries like oil, banking, and television to protect both government and private Mexican monopolies, the so-called financial-services market would be opened on 1 January 1994, with the government upstaging the NAFTA agreement by already authorizing two new banks, three savings and loan organizations, four montage credit companies, and 200 new credit unions.[12]

On 26 November President Salinas sent the Mexican Congress another bill certain to obtain his Institutional Revolutionary party's approval, quieting those asserting their "national patrimony," also carrying a double message:

- Foreign and private investors were barred from owning outright the country's oil and gas reserves, which, following tradition, were to remain in the hands of the Mexican state
- Foreigners were allowed to invest in minority stakes in Mexican oil-drilling companies and in firms that build oil and gas pipelines "in normal circumstances," but would be allowed higher stakes if approved by regulators.[13]

Given the regulatory apparatus demanding bureaucratic bribes and other conditions for investments rewarding the Mexican elite, such approvals would silently allow foreign oil companies to captivate one company after another. The Salinas government was also considering allowing foreign and private companies to build and operate natural gas pipelines for their own use and even to import their own supplies of natural gas instead of depending on gas from the state oil monopoly Pemex.

With Mexican companies specializing in exports already 35 percent foreign-owned by 1994 and the cost of foreign investment declining one-third with the December 1994 devaluation, the government planned to raise dollar revenues by further opening the door to foreign takeover of hitherto restricted sectors of the Mexican economy to raise an expected $14 billion. Slated for sale were mining and auto parts firms, banks, telecommunications satellites, telephone markets, railroads, electricity-generating stations, ports, and parts of the state monopoly in petrochemical plants and natural gas pipelines.

DESTAPE

More of the same was in store, for party lineage was assured by the ritualistic *destape*; Salinas unveiled his personal choice for the next Institutional Revolutionary party's presidential candidate—Luis Donaldo Colosio Murrieta, the president of the PRI and former member of both houses of Congress.

As no PRI candidate had ever lost the presidential race in 64 years since the victorious general of Mexico's 1910 Revolution established the party, the main opposition candidates, Cuauhtémoc Cárdenas from the left-leaning Democratic Revolutionary party (PRD) and Diego Fernández de Ceballos of the right-wing National Action party (PAN), were assumed by some to be two departments of the loyal opposition of a weak electoral system. Yet such legitimation of PRI control could hardly be described as equitable, and it was this twisted rule that would one day undo the nation.

Public popularity for the handsome, gregarious Colosio seemed assured when President Salinas met in conclave with leaders of business and the national political elite to name him as the PRI presidential candidate. Salinas ignored critics of the government who complained that there was no party congress or open nominating process in the PRI, but only the vanities of party leaders who announced the next presidential candidate and, thereby, the next president.

Such devolution of dictatorship was heralded as Mexico's new democracy, but the reality was otherwise. As secretary of social development, the next designated president had used $2.58 billion for political goals, misappropriating funds designated for housing, environmental, and antipoverty programs to crisscross Mexico in his unceasing political campaign to consolidate support for the PRI government and himself.[14]

Such party direction over social welfare and economic change was a barren cover for the evolving oligarchical centralism that would proudly assert the chasteness of Mexico's political affairs, its inviolability to foreign influence and U.S. political standards. Nationalism thus became the cover-story for strengthening the PRI. "The great battle of Mexico is for sovereignty," said President-to-be Colosio, recognizing that democracy and human rights could suffer as the PRI maintained political and social stability and pursued economic change and free trade under NAFTA.[15]

Colosio's meager liberal outreach nonetheless offended the old conservative PRI guard, and his assassination brought in a Salinas clone who could be relied upon to stay the PRI's traditional course. Whatever future measures might be taken, it was now certain that the United States would become the major source of capital, technical equipment, and other capital-intensive resources for Mexico, and Mexico would supply cheap leabor and inexpensively produced goods for tariff-free export.

A CLASSICAL METROPOLE AND PERIPHERY?

Replacing Veracruz as Mexico's commercial windpipe of the past, San Antonio and Laredo became the U.S. gateways. San Antonio alone passed more than half of all goods exported from anywhere in the United States to Mexico along interstate highways and rail lines leading to Mexico's major cities. Situated as close to the major industrial city of Monterrey in Northern Mexico as to the financial megalopolis of Dallas, San Antonio had 200 companies employing 65,000 workers that conducted major business in Mexico, and served as the location for the U.S. headquarters of 50 Mexican companies. The city was poised to take off as a banking, trading, and shipping hub in NAFTA's new world of trade without barriers.[16]

Laredo, Texas, was meanwhile the terminus of U.S. International Highway 35, the busiest crossing over the Rio Grande. The number of trucks heading south jumped from 185,000 in 1987 to 800,000 in 1992 and promised to increase manyfold because trade was expected to double by the end of the century and double again by 2010.

The privatization of toll roads was also on the agenda on both sides of the border, as well as the building of 11 more border bridges in Texas to add to the existing 20 and two dam crossings and a hand-drawn ferry. Even the hardly used international cargo center in Santa Teresa, New Mexico, might be linked to highways and railroads to Mexico. With borders open, the customs search of trucks and cars slowed and backed up at Mexican checkpoints might be smoothed; goods might not have to be loaded and unloaded from trucks designated as U.S. or as Mexican for transfers across the border.

The 12,000 miles of new superhighways President Salinas promised might be built by private companies that would be guaranteed a percentage of the border tolls. And the $100-million, eight-lane span over the Rio Grande, grandly named the International Solidarity Bridge, might eventually be connected to the main highways as it should have been before building ever started. Billions were obviously needed to make such construction possible, so the future held commercial hope if nothing more.[17]

Major U.S. enterprises were ready, too. Having disaccumulated capital for more than two decades since 1971, the United States had become a failed competitor, a country with ever-fewer blue-collar jobs and declining military industries, a powerful foreign investor, a redoubt for unemployed casting aside 1.7 million jobs (from 1970 to October 1993) in the old technical industries based on the cam-system of inanimate energy delivery, a poverty-driven welfare state unable to reeducate and retrain its workforce to the legerdemain of twenty-first century technologies that displace labor, a bankrupt at all levels of government, a vanishing way of life.

The way out of the U.S. dilemma of too many unemployed workers and too many unsalable goods was to speed the export of investments in the instruments of labor, to cut temporarily domestic production and displace more labor, with the hope that U.S. industry would be reorganized at a higher level of technical output deploying more workers with higher levels of skill.

Two economists, Samuel Bowles and Mehrene Larudee, criticized the use of NAFTA as a lever for such goals:

> The agreement would bind all three countries in the strait jacket of 19th-century free market economics, jeopardizing governmental efforts to promote long-term growth of productivity and better living standards throughout the continent. And it would favor footloose corporations as they bargain with employees over wages and working conditions, with communities over taxes and environmental issues and with local suppliers over prices.
>
> In Mexico, the battering ram that will keep wages down is not the threat [of U.S. corporations] to move but a flood of [U.S.] prairie-grown corn. It will bankrupt high-cost farmers, driving them to the cities in search of work and worsening an already severe labor surplus. Even if half a million new jobs open up in Mexico as U.S. companies move South, the number of displaced farmers will mount to twice and perhaps three times this number over a decade. ... Even Nafta supporters concede that the flow of grain south into Mexico will be matched by an increased northward flow of illegal immigrants in search of work. The Mexican labor surplus thus becomes a North American labor surplus.[18]

"There's a real palpable fear," declared Kentucky Democrat Romano L. Mazzoli, "that NAFTA signifies the beginning or continuation of a profound change—that it'll never be like it was before."[19]

Given this U.S. interregnum with its outcroppings of planned domestic restructuring, its image appeared in corresponding plans to reorient Mexico's economic system of production, commerce, agriculture, and finance. The latter was the most volatile, so much so that as the great debate over NAFTA proceeded in the United States, the Mexican stock exchange, the *Bolsa Mexicana de Valores*, metered its ups and downs by whether the U.S. Congress would approve NAFTA—shooting upwards 81.5 points (4.17 percent) to mark the steepest historical rise to a record level of 2,035 points on the news that Vice President Gore had beat Ross Perot in a TV debate. So volatile were the investment and withdrawal of billions worth of U.S. funds on the flash notice of the moment that on 10 November 1993, the Mexican central bank stopped defending the peso at its long-standing rate of 3,309 pesos to the dollar to allow the exchange rate to reflect the real pressures of the market. "Many investors decided they wanted to go into dollars while they wait out the Nafta vote," advised Jonathan Heath, director general of the consulting firm Macro Asesoriá Economica.[20]

Mexico's financial future rested on Wall Street.

PRO AND CON VOTES DETERMINED BY EXTERNAL MATTERS

The Mexican elite saw NAFTA as a bonanza to extend their accumulated wealth. Some observers depicted this upper reach as an elite of 16 extended families, some as a coterie of 25 conglomerated groups, others as an upper echelon of politicians emerging from the nation's leading social groups.

Mexico's own government statistics switched the focus from accumulated wealth by recording that the richest one-tenth of households held nearly 38 percent of the nation's total household income. That left a middle class with nearly 14 percent of the income and left slightly less than half of the population below the poverty line.

"Thirty-six families own over half the country," Ross Perot polemicized on the CNN "Larry King Live" show, though Trade Representative Mickey Kantor depicted Perot as "chairman of the board at the Mad Hatter's tea party."

Perot also excoriated major U.S. transnationals for spending $60 million "in the largest lobbying effort in the history of the country," and he castigated President Clinton's alleged "criminal" attempt to buy NAFTA votes with taxpayer money. (Clinton had promised one member $1.4 billion in military plane construction in his district that the Pentagon did not need, another a $10 million bridge in his district.)

"Do you want members of Congress who can be bought?" Perot asked a blue-collar crowd in Seattle, Washington. "Don't you think they ought to have a criminal inquiry going for buying votes for NAFTA?"[21]

Did the administration know "the more important debate is going on around assembly lines and kitchen tables?" queried House majority leader Richard A. Gephardt, who said he avoided watching the Perot-Gore debate. Approval of the pact would represent a crushing blow to U.S. workers, said Gephart, agreeing with Representative David E. Bonior of Michigan, the majority whip who insisted the agreement would cut U.S. wages and move another 500,000 U.S. jobs to Mexico for lower wages and looser environmental regulations.[22]

There was little logic, much less truth, and no consistency in the debate. Lost in their charges, both Perot and Gore spoke in riddles, as if Mexico was not entitled to national economic sovereignty and that it was either too poor to buy from the United States. ("People who don't make anything cannot buy anything," Perot said) or rich enough to make Mexico the third largest U.S. export customer.

"The NAFTA debate isn't about Al Gore and Ross Perot," insisted David Bonior. "If NAFTA passes, Al Gore and Ross Perot won't lose their jobs."

The simplicity of such political shibboleths extended to President Clinton's global sketch of NAFTA trade bootstrapping similar trade actions with Germany, Japan, and others. "This is a job-winner for our country, more jobs with Latin America, even more jobs when we have a new world trade agreement."

Persuaded by the team of Gore and Clinton, the Mexican Congress did not hold the qualms Canadian Liberals expressed, but instead, wanted NAFTA to proceed without fully dealing with hesitations expressed by smaller enterprises, organized labor, fearful farmers, and environmentalists either in Mexico or the United States. Seeking a more equitable link with the United States, the Mexican Congress seemed blinded by the short-run opportunities to move the nation from the disaccumulation of wealth to its potential for rapid enhancement, privatization, and centralization.

GROUNDWORK

The groundwork had already been laid in the 1970s, when the government had taken on and directed enterprises under a bureaucratic, centrist elite, and in the 1980s, when the government began to unload these enterprises while maintaining its army of state directors.

True enough, until 1970 the number of state-run businesses had been comparatively small. But with the 1973 Arab oil embargo driving up oil prices and yielding Mexico a revenue windfall, the government took on the operation of hundreds of inefficient, unprofitable businesses to provide jobs, paychecks, and the illusion of a fledgling and viable, consumer-oriented market. The government had accumulated 1,155 such entities by the decade ending 1982, when divestiture (called "disincorporation") began under the presidency of Miguel de la Madrid and lasted until 1988.

Government divestments continued under President Salinas from 1988 to 1993, and state revenues were used to reduce Mexico's debt from more than 70 percent of the gross national product to less than 29 percent. As interest payments on the debt declined in step, the government offset the loss of thousands of jobs in state enterprises with a token national antipoverty program that financed public works projects, awarded grants to small businesses, and refurbished schools and community centers.

This transformation reversed earlier efforts. Mexico had been politically molded in its historic, switch-back trail of using centralized state oversight to award control over land and wealth creation—initially to foreign interests and its domestic oligarchy, only later to the common people. The class or classes that controlled the state set the frame for offering these rewards. After 1982, the logic of denationalization of state industries to emancipate private capitalists and pacify Mexico's millions with token service programs was based on the historic switch from draining the population's labor-energy generating surplus to pay off foreign creditors to increasing that surplus from an enlarged working population drawn off the land and redirecting this wealth to the Mexican oligarchy.

This momentary aggrandizement favoring Mexico's elite was not lost on foreign manufacturers and agribusinesses hoping to sell to an enlarged market of Mexican consumers, nor on foreign investors bridling to reenter the heartland of the Mexican economy, however long the government might delay them in order to maintain its domestic legitimacy.

Meanwhile, there were billions of dollars to be reaped by Mexico's wealthier classes through state denationalization of industries; this process created the illusion that Mexico's foreign debt could thereby be permanently eliminated and the foundation laid for efficient, competitive production. By October 1993, the government had already sold or dissolved more than 80 percent of the 1,155 businesses it once operated, used the $21 billion proceeds to retire part of the national debt, and spent more of its budgetary resources on social programs and economic reform.

Obviously, the smaller government outlays for debt service charges and the perennial operating losses of state enterprises reduced government spending, cut the deficit, lessened state competition with businesses and consumers for goods, and thereby cut inflation from more than 150 percent to less than 10 percent a year. With investor optimism riding high, the government capped its successes by opening the economy to competitors and foreign investment.[23]

Investment acumen, efficiency, and profitability were nonetheless largely unknown during this early stage of government giveaways and budgetary savings. Although most of the 940 businesses the government disposed of were closed to save annual budgetary outlays, the plums of industry were sold by the government, which accepted private bids from wealthy Mexican investors, thereby excluding both public and employee purchases. The tight-knit oligarchy's governing party simply sold the state's most viable assets to the oligarchy itself.

The large enterprises shut down to save state resources or sold off at fire-sale prices included:

- Fundidora Steel Foundry (Monterrey): shut down, with loss of 12,000 jobs; turned into a park and business center in a $350 million state of Nuevo León project
- Altos Hornos Foundry (near Monterrey): sold to one of Mexico's leading industrial consortiums owned by a group of Monterrey investors, cutting employment from 24,000 to 10,400
- Aeroméxico: sold to private investors; owned 55 percent of Mexicana airlines and became part of a consortium owning 70 percent of Aeroperú
- Teléphonos de México (Telmex): $1.76 billion sale of a majority of voting rights and 20.4 percent interest to a consortium led by Grupo Carso operated by Carlos Slim Helu; $3.7 billion sale in shares to the public—the only such public tender in the government privatization program
- Eighteen commercial banks: sold for $11 billion at three to four times their old, underpriced book value.

COMMERCIAL STATISM

Commercial statism was tranforming the nation, emancipating a handful of super-rich oligarchies at the expense of impoverished millions.

"The booty of privatization has made multimillionaires of 13 families, while the rest of the population—some 80 million Mexicans—has been subjected to the same gradual impoverishment as though they had suffered through a war," radical columnist Álvaro Cepeda Neri told his Mexico City readers in *La Jornada* in October 1993.

President Salinas could not agree that his privatization of state companies meant the emergence of giant conglomerates, a new elite, and further impoverishment of the poor. Rather, he asserted that somehow poverty had declined (disputed by many economists), and that the concentration of wealth was only threatened by inflation. (This was doubtful in the light of foreign capital inroads, though his administration had cut inflation from an annualized rate of 51.7 percent in 1988 when he took office to 8 percent in October 1993.) He also maintained that the PRI and the parties in opposition were somehow politically equal and thus should "unite in a committed effort to hold clear, transparent and exemplary elections, to join in a political pact of civility within the framework of the law."

Not only would there be no equity in elections, but the PRI controlled election boards dominated TV advertising on its own government channels, depended on state financing by backdoor methods, and could annually collect up to $650,000 from individual executives and others dependent on government support.[24]

Inefficient government enterprises were meanwhile being sold, and the unloaded properties saved the government from making subsidies and absorbing losses. Private investors began, however, to hesitate to pay the price the government asked for other state-owned assets, including Pemex's secondary petrochemical refineries, the pro–PRI newspaper *El Nacional*, and the San Diego–based shrimp-exporting giant, Ocean Garden Products, Inc. To then make these enterprises marketable, the government moved to upgrade their infrastructure and rectify their inefficiencies.

Even foreign investors had prematurely taken over unproven assets; Norwegian investors who bought the nation's largest shipyard (Astilleros Unidos de Veracruz) in 1991 faced labor disputes and a business slowdown that put the yard near bankruptcy by late 1993.

The future also promised popular opposition to the privatization of the government's remaining domain in oil and energy, which were considered inviolate national assets since the 1938 Cárdenas nationalization of U.S. oil companies.[25]

No doubt, then, Mexican industrialization in the 1980s and early 1990s was built upon a weak foundation that depended on the earlier windfall of oil revenues. Assets were divested by the state to private capital at bargain prices to pay off two-thirds of the national debt; as a result, private individuals and business *grupos* controlling the means of industrial and agrarian employment were left to deal with labor and the dispossessed peasantry.

The political fulminations that had led to Mexican state capitalism, then denationalizations placing enterprise in the oligarchy's hands, would now be unleashed on the very social class that had nothing to offer but its potential to work.

Part VI

Steps to Mexico's Future

Mexico has long been the object of the imperial schemes of other nations; even its formal independence and steps towards self-determined advance have been historically thwarted by greater forces beyond its boundaries.

Nationalist fervor, weighed by the need for foreign manufactures, technology, and capital, has also been compromised and reduced to various degrees of servility. Foreign interests have often gained leverage over the economic lifeline of the nation in step with the influence of alternating *caudillos* holding the presidency. The latter dictated their own schemes, appeased the *coterie* supporting them, and created powerful blocs that were backed by other classes and interests giving life to a continuum of plutocracy, beset by aspiring generals and politicians.

Even the turn towards the democratic forums of state rule has belied the underlying control of major domestic interests, their parties, politics, and dictatorial ways, all confounded by the distant possibility of another revolution in action and thinking.

POLITICAL PARTIES AND A REVOLUTION

Mexico's major political parties do not yet reflect the underlying reconstitution of communities and the reemergence of civil society. Such parties speak to already constituted vested interests that are aware of their position and power on a political plane, while civil society in formation has yet to coalesce on a national plane, assume a political posture, and assert both itself and a potential program.

As the major party today, the PRI has been in power for more than six decades and is strongly backed by foreign financial interests linked to the major Mexican owners of the means of production, communications, and commerce, as well as to traditional *latifundias, haciendas,* and *ranchos.* The PRI has sought to tighten its foreign ties by completing the infrastructural and financial arrangements essential to the North American Free Trade Agreement. Enforcing support from the autocratic leaders of the major unions and farm organizations, the party has attempted to balance union rank-and-file demands for higher living standards against the demands of business and land capitalists seeking security and profits. Drawing on government resources, the PRI has surrounded itself with an ex officio bureaucracy that drains the population of its wealth in order to forward its policies, which are tilted towards the nation's elite.

As the second major party, the National Action party (PAN) is a relatively weak organization supported by the great industrial, commercial, and financial interests of Monterrey, and is tied to their expanding sway in the major cities through conglomerated enterprises and subsidiaries in their *grupos.* PAN seeks domestic economic development, with a primary focus on new investments and profits, both in turn to provide employment to Mexico's millions at traditionally low wages. PAN seeks to empower Mexican interests to cooperate with U.S. enterprises but resist their financial domination.

Cuauhtémoc Cárdenas heads the Democratic Revolutionary party (PRD), a minor reformist party that is largely a political movement supported by dispersed groups of workers, peasants, *ejidatarios,* middle-class segments, and public workers who have no future backing the PRI and its austerity programs that keep their wages and real incomes low and may eventually cost them their jobs.

National and Monterrey financial interests, as well as *hacendados* and *rancheros* fear Cárdenas because he envisions cooperative organizations in control of the major means of life and production at the expense of traditional modes of class ownership and domination. The imperial interests also fear Cárdenas, not for his expressed program of liberal democracy and extension of the Mexican market, but for his nonprogrammatic political path that would deepen class antagonisms and further disorganize the national economy.

While these parties shadowbox in the political ring—the PRI and PAN stealing votes and ballot boxes and using the *rurales* to threaten and corral the franchised into their respective corners—nearly every Cárdenas ballot cast is based on convictions that might provoke some kind of retribution. But Cárdenas was still the populist choice in 1988, even though the vote was taken from him by open PRI fraud.

In 1994, PAN was at first the populist choice because it took on some aspects of the Cárdenas program to lift 40 million Mexicans from abject poverty, stimulate investment, and rebuild the economy and marketplace without foreign domination. There were limits to its populist programs though, and both the PRI and PAN feared Mexico's assorted urban and rural far-left-of-center and revolutionary organizations, which have a limited number of actual members, but persuade a wider audience to support central issues that cut to the quick of exploitation—ownership or control of the means of existence, life, language, communications, and cultural beliefs. These organizations' plan to do away with capitalist ownership of land and industry and to gut the systems of peonage and subsistence wages is the nightmare of the ruling classes.

The foreign interests also fear these groups because they would do away with the Mexican ruling class, the Mexican army, the brutal *rurales*, and the emergent U.S. sphere of influence under NAFTA.

Cárdenas does not fear them at all, but his liberal-democratic electoral program sets him apart from their revolutionary goals, making him unable to join them in building a popular, united movement that seeks state empowerment for meeting the needs of both rural and urban populations. He prefers instead to follow the slow path of legislative maneuvering for reforms.

As these forces confronted one another on an ideological, political, and military terrain in the early 1990s, they reignited the issues of Mexico's past, focusing on traditional community rights and inroads sought and secured by foreign interests at the expense of the nation. As a result, future battle lines were drawn over civil interests against centralized state controls and national interests against foreign ones.

TIME CAPSULE OF IMPERIAL INTERESTS

Mexico's history gives powerful evidence of the brutal strokes of empire on its many people. Mexicans of almost all races, castes, and classes have come to believe that imperial interests do not care for the integrity of the nation's peoples, their geographic boundaries, or the regional and national quest for political self-determination and self-sufficiency.

Without doubt, the Spanish conquest began and ended with visions of extracting ever-more wealth from New Spain's resources and human fiber. Spain's mercantile system was weak, and its carnage and brutalities were overwhelming. Land appropriation, *encomienda*, exploited slaves, and regularized commerce in gold and silver made rulers in both New Spain and Iberia incomparably wealthy.

Liberation from Spain brought renewed exploitation of the many peoples of Mexico, this time through extended subjugation by *compañías deslindadores* that discovered and surveyed land; *beneficiares las minas; hacendados, rancheros, comerciantes,* and *financieros.* For the next century, peonage became the principal mode of labor in the rural domain, slavery continued in the mines, and other degrees of domination over labor beset both villages and towns.

Exploitation reached its apogee under Porfirio Díaz, when the foreign commercial and investment stranglehold was powerfully opposed by Mexico's excluded—*latifundias*, industrialists, commercial interests, aspiring middle classes, and labor of other castes and classes.

As a conflict among these forces ensued, spelling long civil war, the revolution left a wake of ruin—uprooted, dispersed populations and a devastated, disorganized economic realm that surviving leaders battled for three decades to rebuilt and control.

As revolution dissolved land peonage and servitude, it empowered commercial forces in the realm of labor, not to free it, but to extract work for subsistence and wages. And despite protections in the 1917 Constitution and Mexico's control of its resources by asserting the nation's rights, *dominio directo*, in the decade 1910–20 new imperial interests again moved by arms and trade to bring Mexico into their spheres.

Using commerce over the ensuing decades, the foreign interests imposed a new stranglehold over Mexico. Now the nation's value of imported luxuries and manufactures exceeded the value of its exports, with the difference paid by selling silver and oil, forfeiting Mexican land and resources, and heavy borrowing on onerous terms.

All through the bitterly impoverished twenties, thirties, and forties, moreover, the needs of the Mexican people exceeded domestic production, again opening the way for foreign trade to keep the Mexican balance of payments negative, foreign investments positive, and repatriated profits flowing.

To reverse Mexico's immiserization, from 1934 to 1940 Cárdenas attempted to break the headlock of the domestic oligarchy and the U.S. and English land and oil interests. But even his state programs of cooperative labor and nationalization only momentarily stemmed the tide of domestic underproduction, foreign influence, and international indebtedness. He too succumbed to the need for private domestic investments and foreign capital operations to employ the nation's idled millions, to produce the nation's basic requirements, and to hold off political reaction from domestic and foreign interests.

Thereafter came a momentary respite from 1941 to 1945, as Mexico became an important supply depot of wartime raw materials for the United States, and importer of U.S. military and production technologies, and a smaller net debtor than before.

Yet from 1946 until at least 1970, the old debtor relationship to foreigner financiers was reestablished by the Mexican state, this time in a more encumbering form. Now the state excused the domestic bourgeoisie from taxes, offering them subsidies to invest and allowing them to export capital freely.

Meanwhile, one nationalist barrier after another fell, opening the gates to foreign interests to trade with, and invest in, Mexico. This policy followed the classic economic logic that greater investment in production would create more jobs for Mexican workers, who in turn would sustain a more viable domestic market to be extended in new rounds of production and employment.

Not everyone gained from this new euphoria of extended production. Rather, through the mediums of government, the peasantry and workers saw rising prices crush real incomes as regulatory controls froze them in place economically and politically. Experiencing downward mobility while state programs limited and restricted their economic, political, and social options, they were trapped for the two decades 1970–90, and then thrust into a new cycle of landlessness, displacement, unemployment, and relative impoverishment. Today, too, populations and communities remain uneasy about the future.

CIVIL SOCIETY ON THE MOVE

Given these conditions, long-repressed civil society powerfully re-emerged during the 1990s. Delayed ethnic, regional, and cultural identities stirred, at first reasserting themselves quietly, then in unpredictable ways.

The authority of the central dictatorship of executive, Congress, and bureaucrats lost popular credence. Their legitimacy began to crumble, and the state's groveling to the mélange of PRI bosses, functionaries, and business groups was criticized by many.

For fully five decades, open resistance to plutocratic government had remained politically unacceptable, repressed by blindsided *aficionados* steeped in their petty, atavistic ways and arcane procedures, empowered to award riches to the nation's elite and sinecures and profits to themselves.

Their lawless order and imposed quietude did not produce tranquility within the hearts of Mexico's impoverished and repressed, who were hungering for another path. Alone they could not resist central authority, however, because above them stood the *rurales* and army, which were supplied and directed from the higher reach of state. Besides these forces, there were lesser guards inhabiting the catacombs of government minutiae who were further empowered by the bureaucracies of state. They directed force and violence, remaining unmoved and unmovable in the face of popular need, petition, or protest.

Ruthless in the ways of ruling from the haunts of security, these forces kept order in the periphery of the downtrodden. The helpless dared not move openly against bureaucrats or army, but their hearts burst aflame when from the poorest, most exploited state of Chiapas, a tiny group raised the banner of their rights and quest for freedom, fanning the faintest hope into another light.

BARREN IN AUTHORITY

It seemed impossible that the centrist state could collapse because a handful of *Zapatistas* declared with guns that the authority of the nation's rulers was barren.

Mexico's coterie of intellectuals of the Left began predicting that all must participate in the new era of civil society on the move against the plutocracy. Both houses of Congress were already being realigned to appease the opposition in 1994 and keep it loyal to the system of state. Legislative posts would now have to offer equality of representation for states in the elevated Senate and an equitable balance of states and political parties among deputies in the Chamber.

Yet singing praises of Mexico's future marketplace and investment haven and trading legislative invectives and votes would liberate few at the bottom rungs of the social scale. Thus resistance to the centrist state remained unabated, with some populations and whole communities opposing the centrist, dictatorial system of the past.

CHAPTER 17

Democracy Led by
a Few: Government
Frame for the New Order

National priorities in Mexico are a function of politics bred of wealth handed down from generations past. The tiny power elite that has ruled Mexico without interruption since 1929 has accumulated vast resources. It has controlled the distribution of the necessities of life, impoverishing some 40 million comprising half the nation. Through greed, corruption, and secrecy, it has established financial links between the state and the ruling Institutional Revolutionary party (PRI). It has mobilized a small, well-honed police network able to quell any who significantly challenge the system or step outside the bounds of electoral politics and public order. And it has controlled access to the two main TV stations that capture the public's attention and imagination.

Over more than six decades, the PRI has also gained massive support. By the late 1940s, the wealthy upper classes and the clergy had shifted their confidence and support to the PRI's right-wing government, attempting to rally support from prosperous peasants holding land, unionized workers, and those impoverished in the urban domain. Although opposition parties variously appealed to the very wealthy, to urban voters, or to those seeking social change, the PRI largely channeled these groups into electoral activities instead of allowing them to become involved in revolutionary ones.[1] The military remained on call by the PRI to oust any state or local civilian government that might sway from servicing the short-term needs of the wealthy and traditional upper classes, and also to respond to other social class interests in maintaining civil order.

Once established, the PRI consolidated its hold over the government's high level positions and its bureaucracies. PRI patronage went to its members and loyal followers. With unlimited access to government funds, the PRI also controlled how much power opposition parties would be allowed to mobilize and use on a political level. Its appointees packed the Federal Electoral Commission, which was empowered to block approval of applications by radical parties the PRI opposed, as well as to judge election results. The PRI also passed electoral rules that made registration of any new party difficult, requiring that it have at least 65,000 members, whose names, occupations, and addresses had to be furnished, opening the door to blacklisting and other reprisals.

To keep opposition parties within the electoral system, moreover, the PRI also paved a legal road to nominal political success. Under the so-called "party-deputy system," national seats in the Chamber of Deputies were given to opposition parties winning over 1.5 percent in any congressional election; the first 1.5 percent awarded five automatic seats, and each .5 percent increment awarded an additional seat up to a maximum of 25. This system effectively offered token representation for the highest vote winners among the minor parties, though the PRI-controlled Federal Electoral Commission retained power to deny accreditation of the vote by any potential party deputy.[2]

By contrast to the Chamber of Deputies, the Mexican Senate did not have such a token-representation system, and this limited the legislative power of minority parties.

In these ways, the PRI set the frame to make all other electoral parties legitimate, but unable to wield federal political power. PRI-established institutions effectively filter the power of all opposition parties, making them adjuncts of its rule. Any criticism they level concentrates on the government's excessive central controls, its overarching bureaucracy, and its inextricable corruptive influences. Even if these practices were reformed, though, the PRI's legislative control would remain.

So when PRI machinations directing the voting process were altered as President Salinas proposed in 1992, blatant fraud was reduced without jeopardizing the party's hold on national power and its use of state resources.[3]

Dwelling on variations of these issues for a quarter century, the National Action party (PAN) sought to replace PRI officialdom, not to advocate an alternative vision or to change the political system.[4]

PAN was arch-conservative in organization; it railed against Communism and resisted central authority that subsidized production and consumption and imposed price controls. It attacked government corruption, castigated excessive state spending that burdened taxpayers, and saw little ideological merit in a nationalism that would keep out foreign investors or stop the Mexican rich from securing their savings abroad.

It was originally backed by the Catholic church, *hacendados*, mid-sized enterprises, and other middle-class groups that had opposed the radical Cárdenas administration's land reforms and labor legislation. Later, when the PRI government moved sharply to the Right, PAN lost both church and large business backing. But PAN retained the support of the professional, urban middle class as well as some upper-class Mexicans, large landholders with a conservative bent, and those on the extreme Right who left the PRI.[5]

Even in presidential elections, PAN candidates have polled poorly—from under 8 percent in 1952 to less than 14 percent in 1970, 17.5 percent in 1982, and, allowing for PRI frauds, about 20 percent in 1988 and 31 percent in 1994.

With PAN's urban following, its greatest command of congressional seats has been in the Federal District enclosing Mexico City and in the states of Mexico, Puebla, and Jalisco.[6] But splits in PAN in 1976 and 1992 weakened the party's role as a potential counterweight to the PRI. Looking back, it is apparent that the PRI's Political Reform Act of 1977 secured it as the dominant party by making it appear to be the legitimate center, ensuring that all minor parties would remain ancillary, and counterpositioning PAN on the Right against the parties of the Left.

Although the PRI's popular legitimacy and share of total congressional votes steadily declined from 1977 to 1988, the party manipulated its control over the electoral commission either to disallow PAN state and local victories or to shift PAN votes to compliant parties of the Left—the Popular Socialist party (PPS), the Authentic party of the Mexican Revolution (PARM), and the Socialist Workers' party (PST).

The PRI not only resisted democratization on a national level, but locally PRI *caciques* also sought to protect their traditional party patronage by opposing demands for fair and open elections—whether these were made by PAN, compliant leftist parties, or their mutual alliances with business groups in the National Movement for Democracy.[7]

From the Left, meanwhile, the Popular Socialist party (PPS) evolved from being an opposition force against foreign investors in the 1940s and 1950s to being an adjunct of the PRI, running common candidates in some states in the 1970s.[8] So, too, the Authentic party of the Mexican Revolution (PARM), which normally commanded less than 2 percent of congressional elections votes, was in the practice of "selling" its party deputy seats to the highest PRI bidder. It followed the PRI lead in congressional votes, was subject to PRI oversight of appointment or nullification of those elections PARM won, and received subsidies from the PRI government.[9]

Further to the Left, the 1919 Communist party that had worked closely with the 1930s Cárdenas administration changed its strategy of revolutionary transformation in 1973 to seeking an alliance with democrats, progressives, socialists, and Communists for a peaceful transition to socialism. With a frail membership varying from 5,000 to 15,000 in the 1960s, the party was kept within the bounds of order by the Echeverría government, was then brought into parliamentary political campaigns in the mid–1970s, and was in the early 1990s made a powerless icon of the multiparty system by the PRI.

To the left of the Communist party, the Mexican Workers' party organized in 1974 called for an end to exploitation of labor by national or foreign interests, a tax on the rich to finance development, state employment, nationalization of means of industrial production, the food industry, communications, finance, and public services. The government used threats and military and diversionary tactics against the efforts of the Mexican Workers' party to organize locally and thus weaken the party and isolate its leaders.[10]

The student movement also held limited political influence. For almost a decade, it excelled in militancy; demands for political rights, economic justice, and freedom from U.S. imperialism; and confrontation with government-directed soldiers. The most powerful confrontation occurred in 1968, leaving 200 to 325 students dead and fueling the public awakening of revolutionary attitudes. There was another protest on a more localized scale at the National University in Puebla, Sinaloa, and Yucatán during 1973–74 to demand higher education and professional jobs for graduates. Later in 1976 and into the 1980s, the student movement demands were channeled by government agents and *porros* (goons), as well as by the Socialist Workers' party which discredited the students' earlier utopian demands and allowed the government to repress them.

Off and on for 30 years, violent repression against protest and the Left was an option used by the PRI-directed government and public and private paramilitary organizations. Thus there was no viable opposition to the PRI in the 1960s, 1970s, and 1980s, and the PRI remained the major party actively controlling and subsidizing other parties in an effort to make it appear to the public that a potential opposition was possible.

CRISIS, STATE LEGITIMACY, AND PARTY REORGANIZATION

Escalating inflation and falling living standards in the 1970s put the working class at odds with PRI Ministry of Labor policies that refused to recognize newly elected union leaders and with the CTM bureaucracy that isolated militant labor unions and attempted to hold down wage demands. Class realignments in the 1980s then turned on the crisis of too little revenue to sustain the old social order and led to PRI attempts to delay a wider distribution of benefits by future promises of political power-sharing.

Global markets had meanwhile caused Mexican oil prices to fall, leading the government to borrow abroad on condition that living standards be reduced for all social classes. In the early 1980s, Mexico was in arrears on an $80 billion debt to foreign banks, interest was barely being paid, and a new $4 billion IMF loan required $10 billion in new consumer and income taxes and across-the-board cuts in government spending. The upper classes recoiled, seeking to shift the entire burden to the working class, the peasantry, and the already impoverished rural and urban underclasses.

As this scheme was implemented under the hegemonic PRI administration that professed revolution while coopting or suppressing the opposition, the polarity of wealth and poverty widened, leading sections of the middle, working, and lower classes to view the government as illegitimate. These groups were unable, however, to build a mass movement to contest PRI rule or replace the existing power structure in the short or intermediate term.

The educated middle class that worked in the urban domain took umbrage at the fall in salaries and living standards; some sought a political alternative in PAN. Small factory owners and entrepreneurs—once tariff-protected, but now caught in the squeeze of failing markets, loss of their government production subsidies, and escalating labor and operating costs—also looked for economic and political alternatives in pressuring the PRI or backing PAN. Unable to pay in dollars, Mexico slowed the import of technical equipment and materials needed for uninterrupted production in construction and heavy industry; this led to factories going on part-time or temporarily closing as their owners sought to pressure the de la Madrid government to change directions.

Unions locked into PRI connections witnessed their rank and file moving against the government's freeing of prices and its imposed wage freezes that sharply reduced real wages. Labor was also protesting a million jobs lost in industry, construction, and corporatized agriculture in the single year 1982. Workers carried out strikes and mass demonstrations and attempted to oust their PRI-picked leaders. Suffering a decline in real wages, militant workers in the cities had their counterpart in an increasingly impoverished and proletarianized peasantry that either held tiny plots or owned no land, farm equipment, or homes. These peasants organized to oppose PRI withdrawal of farm subsidies, credits, and other assistance that had improved living standards and enhanced output.

As its star of legitimacy fell in the early 1990s, the PRI's renewed plans for political "reorganization" followed similar designs and lines of demarcation: the polarity of wealth and poverty that defined the social frame for elite control and civic political helplessness was scheduled to continue unabated.

The right wing that had once formed the main opposition in the National Action party had now become a cooperative, supportive adjunct of PRI government schemes, and left-wing parties at best held power at local levels of government and were no barrier to the PRI's domestic reorganization.

THE PRI RULES ONWARD

At the apex of government, the PRI's coterie of power brokers continued to rule the nation as if they were a throwback to the philosopher kings anointed by ethereal voices echoing from the caves of Delphi. These leaders remained blind to the needs of 92 million Mexicans, more than 27 million of whom were then living in squalor-ridden Mexico City. Few among this tiny group of leaders were democrats in the classical sense of advocating egalitarian rights exercised by majorities—or minorities. Fewer still represented the population's aspirations for a better life, and practically none held to philosophical precepts of a future, equitable society.

Such politics Mexican style were both secretive and selective, with the path designed *en camera* by a plutocracy of self-styled economists, instead of through any public debate. Their political schematic was more functional than social, more a wooden description of tasks to be performed to upgrade infrastructure and production technology than a calibration for upgrading the condition of the many and designing a climbing ladder for their steady improvement. Although President Carlos Salinas had pointed to the hundreds of state and local offices held by opposition parties, the real power brokers were federal, with the economist kings rotating the presidency among an elite of which they were part. With secretive government thus beginning at the upper reaches of Mexican society, the power brokers distributed positions, perks, and salaries as patronage, designating the rights of passage for those who would participate in ruling the nation.

Within the frame of this system, the post of president remained critical, the principal constitutional restraint being that the president could serve only one six-year term. He held monarchlike powers, including the sole right to name his party's next presidential candidate. The latter would be a shoo-in for the Institutional Revolutionary party that had ruled Mexico for fifty-odd years and refused to make meritorious concessions to opposition forces or to offer equity to the population.

"The others in the ruling group wait their turn for high office," a reporter noted with awe. "Their families have known each other for generations. They are mostly well-to-do or rich, highly educated (half the Cabinet members hold Ph.D.'s from the best U.S. universities), talented and tough. They compare favorably with counterparts in the industrialized world."

Opposition party leaders were convinced this group would never willingly share wealth or relinquish power. From PAN on the political Right, party leader Luis Alvarez called them "despots," while Cuauhtémoc Cárdenas as leader of the left-wing Democratic Revolutionary party (PDR) demanded fundamental reforms and cited his party's inability to gain access to the media to make its program known.[11]

The opposition thus faced an uphill climb to sharing power; Carlos Salinas's narrow victory in 1988 was tainted by the mysterious collapse of official computers, the burning of ballots to hide his election fraud, and the subsequent neglected promise to include voters' photographs on registration cards. The government attempted to delay needed electoral reform in the face of the increasing strength of the leftist and rightist parties that might undermine the political stability foreign investors demanded.

THE ROLE OF PAN

On the Right, PAN also fractured in 1992, one wing advocating support for the PRI government, the other opposition to its programs. Although PAN had governors in three Mexican states, representatives in statehouses, mayors in scores of cities, and ample party revenues in 1992, it had never polled much more than 20 percent support in a national vote. It had taken 53 years for the party to inaugurate its third state governor, and its local political victories had followed PRI government pressures for PAN support of election law reforms.

PAN had also put aside earlier conditions to endorse sweeping reform of Mexico's land-tenure system and government sale of Mexican banks to a renewed financial oligarchy. In addition, PAN leadership had ordered its party legislators to support the burning of ballots from the disputed 1988 presidential election of Carlos Salinas, and PAN had supported passage of the PRI government's other major initiatives.

PAN party president Luis H. Alvarez's notion that dialogue with the government was "something obligatory" was powerfully contested by an influential group of PAN veterans, who left the party after its 1992 gathering. "It has been forgotten that we are opposition and not support," nine important dissidents[12] from the party's traditionalist "Doctrinaire and Democratic Forum" wrote in an open letter distributed to party members and the news media in October 1992, anticipating another party comparable to the right-wing Christian Democratic parties found elsewhere in Latin America.[13]

CAN THE LEFT RISE AGAIN?

The 1970s political opposition from the Left was still weak in the late 1980s and early 1990s, despite the fact that the economy had turned negative.

In the wake of the fall in world oil prices in June 1981, 75 percent of all Mexican export earnings were reduced, as were one-third of the revenues of the PRI government. Recognizing the need to maintain its authority and social welfare programs to diffuse unrest, the government borrowed heavily in foreign markets to satisfy the clamorings of the workforce and peasantry without imposing on upper-class interests.

As de la Madrid took office in 1982, living standards fell, the patronage and spoils system of bribes and kickbacks were as rife as ever, the new president freed the movement of foreign finance and tried to sell off shares to reverse his predecessor's expropriation of the private Mexican banks and greater state direction of almost every sector of the economy. The heart of Mexico imploded.

The guerrilla campaigns that had started in 1964 remained small, terrorist attacks launched primarily against the symbols of hegemonic government and foreign interests, and the government periodically used troops and airborne forces to quiet or destroy them.

Ballot-box politics were thus the main focus in the 1980s. The Unified Mexican Socialist party (PSUM), then the largest left-wing opposition party, and the Democratic Revolutionary party (PDR) sought the equality of conditions of competition for electoral success. But political reforms instituted in 1977 were illusory for the Left, as none of the parties was able to expand substantially its constituency in the face of PRI oversight that included direct PRI controls over most labor unions, PRI state controls over the formal recognition of new unions and new parties, PRI suppression of political organizers, and PRI-directed military police and army repression of left-wing parties and wildcat strikers.

The left-wing parties were also largely irrelevant to foreign capital investors, and unemployed workers snubbed or ignored the vague promises of radical organizers. The left-wing parties and PRI unions and other labor organizations either criticized or ignored their natural allies in the *paros cívicos*, which involved all classes, women, and even children organized in communities, civil groups, and by boycotts to protect living standards.

The alliance of left-wing parties to back presidential candidate Herberto Castillo in 1988 was a breakthrough effort to implement the 1987 election reform law.[14] But the alliance did not last much beyond the election, and, as expected, the PRI won by compromising fairness and by outright fraud.

A WEAKENED OPPOSITION

Thus for fifty-odd years, the ideologically split opposition had no chance of electoral success.

Not only were left- and right-wing opposition parties badly splintered or only temporary allies, but under the guidance of the PRI, election fraud was rife and vast state revenues and other resources continued to be sequestered by the ruling party to build a bureaucracy and spoils system to buffer any political challenge from Left or Right.

Reform was illusory as well. Technical reforms and alterations in the election laws were designed to "tune up" the system's appearance as an operational machine, not to overhaul its political engines. So though the 1977 election law was to be supplemented in the early 1990s by an electoral institute, with new voter rolls compiled, new registration cards distributed, and new clear plastic ballot boxes installed to ensure they were properly filled, reform concentrated on the methods by which votes were cast, collected, and counted. Such frail alterations did not cut at the basis of the PRI's intimidation, wholesale vote-buying, or use of state resources sustaining its power base.

SPLIT IN THE PRI

In 1986 one PRI faction attempted to liberate the party from its archaic procedures for presidential succession and its programs to denationalize all aspects of the economy and open the door to foreign investors.

Former PRI chairman Porfirio Muñoz Ledo and Michoacán's populist ex-governor Cuauhtémoc Cárdenas together formed the Movement of Democratic Renovation. They denounced the secretive methods by which PRI presidential successors were chosen and called for reforms so the rank-and-file in the party could express a presidential preference. Their proposals were soundly defeated at the politically orchestrated March 1987 PRI general assembly, and politically inexperienced technocrat Carlos Salinas de Gortari became the heir apparent to President de la Madrid's austerity government, reassuring investors of antilabor policies and economic stability. The *priista democratizadores*, as the opposition members were called, had, however, broken the façade of PRI hegemony.

True, the PRI responded by ousting Muñoz Ledo and Cárdenas. But this led to the formation of a Cárdenista Front of National Reconstruction made up of the dissident *priistas* and the old, equivocating opposition parties (PARM, PPS, and PST) that had cooperated so long with the PRI but now supported the presidential bid of Cárdenas. Although Cárdenas lost in 1988 due to massive PRI computer fraud, ballot burning, and intimidation of voters, the PRI was clearly wary of the future power of Cárdenas supporters.

The political testing laboratory in the early 1990s was Michoacán. Here vote fraud in 1988 had awarded the PRI illusive victories, and here opposition candidates brought protestors to the street to contest 1992 PRI electoral manipulations. To calm the situation, President Salinas had then forced his party's winners to resign, though in the new campaigns the wealthy candidates again hoped to outspend their rivals.

Wealthy pig-farmer Eduardo Villaseñor had made public his substantial business campaign contributions after his election. But this unprecedented disclosure proved only a fleeting "wave of the future" (as President Salinas's aide preferred to depict it) that fell from its crest when the Movement of Democratic Renovation and the Democratic Revolutionary party leader Cuauhtémoc Cárdenas and his Michoacán candidate Cristóbal Arias insisted weeks before the 12 July vote that "fair competition" was impossible.

They also charged that the PRI had wildly outspent its rivals, controlled newspaper and television coverage, stacked the election boards with PRI election hacks, and, just before the elections, elicited popular support by spending hundreds of billions of pesos on antipoverty programs in the state.

Villaseñor's victory was not credible, nor was it able to offset the Movement of Democratic Renovation and Democratic Revolutionary party demonstrations and preparations to win municipal elections in 31 of the 113 town halls in the coming December 1992 elections.

After six Democratic Revolutionary party members were killed in unexplained circumstances, President Salinas ordered Villaseñor to step down to defuse the escalating tension. This led to a PRI-PRD compromise, not for new elections in Michoacán, but for an agreed future of more equal political competition, limits on campaign financing, independent elections boards, and more equitable access to the news media.[15]

And after months of civil disobedience in the leftist Michoacán stronghold, the agreement produced not a government representative of the population, but only the replacement of one PRI governor with another.

Both Right and Left had now compromised an independent stance on substantive matters in favor of equitable procedures for elections.

GOVERNMENT FRAME FOR THE NEW ORDER

Pluralism of Mexican parties might one day consist of a level playing field in running for office. Yet on this turf, the PRI could still win all national elections by sheer weight of connections, monetary resources, and machine politics.

And what would happen if the hierarchy of the PRI government continued to act as plutocrats, imposing their economic will over the nation in a way that favored the nation's wealthy and foreign interests in the short-term, assuaged the middle classes in the intermediate period, and kept the underclasses under control in the long run?

There were no precise textbook answers as the coterie of PRI economists under President Salinas de Gortari started on an untried course to bootstrap the nation by (1) extending the foreign market through the North American Free Trade Agreement, (2) trying to attract domestic and foreign capital to fuel production, employment, and profits (3) holding the middle class and oppositional parties in place by offering them steadily rising economic benefits and gradual political rights, and (4) working toward the creation of a powerful market of variously paid consumers at home.

But the PRI would not tread lightly to keep the working class and peasantry in its fold while buying off the emerging urban middle sector and controlling the underclasses. In the past the PRI had coopted and incorporated the organized workers and *ejidatarios* by offering them a specified stake in the nation's output. But beset by economic crises cutting government revenues and investment profits and faced by the demands of the new urban professionals and jobless, rural immigrants, the PRI reduced traditional rewards, making its rule questionable in the eyes of organized labor and *campesinos*.

Unable to promote economic growth and fairly distribute wealth, the PRI was then forced to create a pecking order for distributing the nation's shrinking surplus that favored the upper classes, then those in the middle sector, and last and least the working population and peasants. Thereby the PRI sought to win over and align with the middle-class opposition in maintaining stability, holding in abeyance the working class, peasants, and underclasses the PRI feared most and hoping they could be kept in check long enough to transform the economy and foster a mass consumer market.[16]

Theirs was a short-term holding action with a long-term political downside. But in the short and intermediate term, so long as the PRI held overwhelming power to negotiate NAFTA as a first step and entice domestic and foreign investors to stimulate production and employment as a second step, the gradual emergence of a fairly paid workforce as the frame of the domestic market would pacify the population long enough to allow the PRI to liberalize the electoral rules for power sharing with all opposition parties committed to the peaceful road to social transformation.

POWER-SHARING AND THE PEACEFUL ROAD

Transforming Mexico's domestic power balance, the Congress approved the Salinas administration's proposed changes in the congressional election system for the 22 August 1994 election.

The composition of the bicameral legislature was thereby transformed, shattering the traditional roles of the Chamber of Deputies and the Senate as supporting shields for presidential programs:

1. The 500-seat, three-year term Chamber of Deputies was to be elected under a new proportional representation system, that precluded a two-thirds majority for any party and made compromise necessary to secure passage of any legislation by a required two-thirds.

   A two-thirds party majority was unlikely because although 300 of 500 deputies were to be directly elected from popular constituencies, the remaining 200 were to be distributed among parties in proportion to their share of the vote. Factional and vested interests by region, ethnicity, caste, class, and party thus promised an unremitting, contentious balance in the Chamber.

2. The Senate was meanwhile doubled in size to 128 seats—many seats going to opposition forces—with four members each from 31 states and the Federal District.

   Old members were not ousted. But the six-year term senators would all be replaced in the year 2000 election, coinciding with the election to the presidency.

Together, both houses would now barter votes and power, preventing PRI presidents from open and arbitrary alterations of the constitution that would pit future legislatures against the executive branch of government. The PRI could still create an effective two-thirds majority by forming alliances with smaller parties, following the method used after the 1988 presidential elections. But that itself would clearly spell power sharing. Henceforth, then, if no single party won more than 40 percent of the vote, the fractious legislature would demand a coalition government to rule. Refusal would threaten the polarized nation with civil unrest.

"The premise," insists Jorge Castañeda of the center-left collective, San Angel Group, "is that Mexico is ungovernable with a PRI president. You need a coalition government—a real coalition that includes everyone. You have to share power—really share power—and you have to secure an acceptable arrangement on a common program."

Thereby coalitions could work against the president, with the executive unable to pass laws without both Senate and Chamber realigning and balancing their power.

The logic was unassailable, though the locus of power might shift to another domain. For henceforth the six-year, one-term-only senators that arrived with each president would represent the divergent interests of communities as well as different production modes and assorted regional and ethnic mores and beliefs.

The Senate turnover itself would ensure the equal number from each state would not easily be captivated by a PRI president and his policies. And four senators from each state would also ensure an equality that empowered people from less populated rural states to protect their way of life, work, and production.

In addition, the 300 deputies who were directly elected would voice the concerns of their constituencies, while those 200 from political parties would represent divergent ideological viewpoints.

Congress would thus become a playing field for indecision, compromise, and combat, so that president, PRI bosses, and dominant economic interests could no longer use the state as before and would have to employ other means to attain their ends. Civil society through both houses would now appear in combat readiness to mediate the national economy and social relations and to take on foreign interests and implement or impede trade and investment treaties.

Rightly or not, the PRI's economist kings thus judged the political necessities of the 1990s to require domestic compromise that would offer a peaceful road to the future while holding the political opposition in place. They also favored complete negotiations on NAFTA, while encouraging substantial investments in production.

In the hiatus following this plan, the domestic economy was to be reorganized, potentially creating a mass consumer market for the first time in Mexican history.

CHAPTER 18

The War on Civil Society[1]

As a Third World nation with purported First World status, for almost a decade Mexico lived beyond its means on short-term foreign loans that financed excessive importation. But as its reserves of foreign exchange dwindled and lenders' risks for timely repayment rose, in December 1994 the creditors pulled the plug, driving home the message that Mexico was still a Third World nation barely surviving on the brink of bankruptcy.

Old loans remained unpaid; new ones dried up. And the United States forced Mexico to devalue its currency, cutting off further imports that had created the illusion of the emergence of a viable Mexican middle class and the hope of a better life for the nation's impoverished millions. Spurred by rapidly worsening economic conditions in early 1995, Washington moved to liven Mexican exports to pay off its debts and resume future imports under NAFTA, with the U.S. Treasury making conditional loans designed to supervise Mexican economic affairs. Spending billions to pay off government short-term loans to Wall Street and the Mexican oligarchy, more billions to support Mexico's 24 super-rich family groups selling pesos for dollars, and untold millions to prop up Mexico's banks, the United States powerfully sustained the operations of Mexico's one-party, authoritarian system.

Yet Mexico paid dearly for this intervention, for the nation increasingly lost its self-determination in the economic realm and became little more than a political ward of the United States. Rather than the proletarianization of an urbanized nation aspiring to First World prosperity as former President Salinas had promised, under President Zedillo, the population was being degraded, made jobless and impoverished as a backwater of the Third World.

Economic malaise was spreading as well, with the Zedillo government

324

forcing labor and peasantry alike to accept a lower standard of living through allocation of a smaller share of national output. Government-imposed austerities led to less state spending, reduced subsidies for agriculture, failed welfare programs, and drastic cuts in real wages. Consumer prices simultaneously shot up, however, as there were no government enforcement mechanisms to force companies to absorb increased costs of wages, new taxes, rising energy and transportation outlays, or more expensive imported equipment, parts and raw materials. Crushed by higher prices and taxes, the middle and working classes openly complained and turned to mass meetings and street demonstrations.

The population also watched warily as its president, cabinet and Congress were turned into a battering ram for U.S.–imposed austerities. And it was clear that the entire Mexican government was now the bursar to cycle billions in U.S. loans to pay off the Mexican elite and foreign investors holding short-term government bonds, meanwhile surrendering the nation's earnings from oil exports as collateral to pay off U.S. loans in case of default.

Further U.S. loans were issued only with a set of unalterable conditions, in order to put a fresh face of legitimacy on both lenders and Mexico's new, untried president: the gunfight in Chiapas would have to end, and a political cover story would have to be designed to quiet discord surrounding the murders of two leading politicians, one cardinal, one infamous state police chief, several high-placed drug traffickers, and protesting peasants and workers in four states. Conflicts within the government and between it and the two leading opposition parties, the PAN and the PRD, would meanwhile have to be resolved by power-sharing to restore stability in Tabasco, Veracruz, Chiapas and other troubled states. Revolution was ruled out of the question, but no one dared put a cap on Mexican protest, and there were definite limits to foreign-imposed conditions as President Clinton struggled with a dissident Congress trying to cut off future loans to prop up the Mexican oligarchy and guarantee existing U.S. loans would be repaid.

With the United States hammering at Mexico's already modest living standards, millions of Mexicans began accusing their leaders of selling out to "El Norte." And once their short-term loans were repaid, foreign investors fled to safer havens, despite international aid. Their desertion drove the Mexican economy further into penury. Major banks were teetering, too, as indebted Mexican importers, unable to overcome the devaluation of the peso, defaulted on their loans. President Ernesto Zedillo seemed tied to a sinking economy that would take years to recover.

More helpless still were workers who had long awaited better wages from the promised benefits of market reform, but would now wait again beside impoverished peasants who had marched to the cities in search of a better life. More were marching too, as 100 percent rates of interest cut

off loans for seed, fertilizer and tools, while the government's rural subsidies, technical services, and so-called development funds dried up,
squelching the hope for equitable transformation of a countryside that required vast amounts of credit from the government to support a change of
crops—to one day make Mexico self-sufficient as an agrarian nation.

Cosmetic changes in the allocation of political power might at best
offer momentary legitimacy to the one-party state. President Zedillo
brashly calculated that in the short run, despite forcing Mexico through a
brutal recession with massive unemployment, he could balance his failing
popularity with a more open political system—allowing more demonstrations, channeling discontent through balloting at still fraud-laced polling
stations, and generally letting the population blow off steam rather than
blowing off the lid held fast by the nation's economic elite, the PRI's old
guard and the U.S. Treasury.

In the long run, through diffusing power rather than concentrating it
like his predecessors, Zedillo gambled he could ultimately garner more
legitimacy, more central authority and more compliance with austerities
from the corrupt unions and the oligarchy, lifting Mexico out of bankruptcy. Yet such freedoms opened the door for the elite and the PRI's right
wing to strengthen and secure their positions in the face of the weakened
Zedillo presidency. As the archconservative wing of the PRI then pulled the
strings of austerity, Mexico's most powerful business group, *Coparmex*,
opposed the government's plan because it included tax increases that
would further erode domestic markets, jeopardizing their wealth and controls.

Yet even rehabilitation of the domestic market would not resolve the
nation's underlying dilemma. For the devolution of wealth handed down
from Mexico's past saddled the country with the world's fourth largest crop
of billionaires—a mere .0026 percent of the population owning over one-
quarter of all land, machinery and factories. Even with existing debts to the
United States—and then further debts under the 1995 U.S. bailout—the
oligarchy's assets were secured by loan conditions that required protection
for Mexican bank depositors; tight monetary policies insuring that the rate
of interest on bank loans to others exceeded the rate of inflation; accelerated structural reforms in banking, telecommunications and transportation that favored conglomeration and monopolization; and the continued
sale of government-owned businesses and concessions at a fraction of their
values to raise a paltry $12–14 billion to pay off the holders of short-term
government debts, which were in part owned by the Mexican oligarchy
itself.

In this shell game favoring Mexico's oligarchy, the super-rich would
get richer still. And the hold of these plutocrats' great power and wealth,
exploiting a country nearly half of whose population remained mired in

poverty, had again become an explosive political and social issue. The more enlightened among the superwealthy paid lip service to the notion that their own well-being depended on the vibrancy of the wider market they served, and from the lofty heights of the Mexican Businessmen's Council, they expressed their concern for broader social programs for the poor. But the president's plan to discipline the already weakened economy seemed likely to further polarize wealth and poverty, to squeeze the middle classes, and to deepen the misery of Mexico's already desperate millions.

CHAPTER 19

Mexico in the
Twenty-first Century[1]

The Mexican Revolution is not over.

In fact, the Revolution has hardly begun. Clearly its form has dramatically changed from an open, nationwide military challenge to the dictatorship to the present disillusionment with, and grudging accommodation to, its mock democracy and anemic economy. Hope breeds strong, however, for its future transformation into an egalitarian social system. For even now, landlessness, joblessness, illiteracy, extreme privation, and hunger drive the nation to transform itself despite the self-assuring, disingenuous pronouncements by sequential, look-alike government technocrats and politicians depicting the nation's progress.

THE IDIOM OF PROGRESS

The idiom of progress delivered through the newspeak of government, science, economics, and the marketplace is simply incongruous with the condition of Mexico's millions seeking survival. For such progress, elaborated as enlarging gross national output and financial wealth, does not necessarily involve distribution of wealth to the general population. Average income figures, even when increasing, give no indication whether the poor are earning enough to feed their families.

The progress seen by the technocratic mind also does not square with 40 million Mexicans living in grinding poverty, hundreds of thousands of homeless, sick, and uneducated children, and a countryside releasing its idle surplus hands to an overpopulated urban domain that already lacks adequate housing, amenities, jobs, and services.

Progress has remained relative, too, with benefits for one group coming at the loss of welfare of another. Without employers and state offering decent pay for labor, the market remains only partly developed; and without employment of the Mexican people's vast production potential, domestic output of food and goods cannot keep pace with need, let alone supply the narrow circle of those able to buy.

Nor do imports and unfettered markets necessarily constitute progress. When imports inundate the domestic market, wiping out handicrafts and machine-made goods, the resulting unemployment spells hunger, desperation, often crime, sometimes even death.

ENFORCED POLARITY

With Mexico's governing party at the helm of such enforced polarity of accumulation and impoverishment, the plunder taken by the old imperiums is no longer alone to blame for the sorry present. Revolution, independence, land reform, industrializing, government expropriation, and state-induced capital investments—these historic efforts once promised to bootstrap both production and some degree of social equity. Yet Mexico has reaped neither adequate output nor egalitarian relations.

As the nation's millions have experienced desperate misery, unending poverty, and lawless servitude at the base of the social structure, for others it has been the best of times, a moment of security, a period to accumulate wealth amidst the most unsettling economic crises, a time to absorb smaller businesses. A handful of people have dominated the main means of production, controlling middle-class mobility to better jobs. Others have exhibited a blind, relentless striving to consume.

Nonetheless, Mexico's elite still attempt to rise above the flood of international capital entering the nation. With Mexican export goods relatively low priced compared to more sophisticated technical imports, the imbalance has placed the nation in almost perennial debt, offset by foreign investment in its land, resources, and industries. The upgrading of the latter has been falsely, if audaciously, passed off as steps towards domestic industrialization, factory employment, manufacturing output, and independent, indigenous accumulation.

But the truth lies elsewhere. Export earnings from domestic and foreign-owned production are periodically cycled to pay for the import of capital goods essential to reorganize the national economy. The failure of the government to control all foreign exchange earned from such Mexican exports has also allowed its private possessors to import luxuries rather than purchase industrial equipment and essential foreign services, as well as to export annually as much as $20 billion in dollars, sterling, deutsche marks, and yen to be placed in numbered, overseas bank accounts and as private investments.

Such capital exports effectively undercut the Bank of Mexico's control over foreign exchange, forcing it to repeatedly raise domestic interest rates. These higher rates attract needed foreign capital, while undercutting borrowing for investment at home. The increased cost of domestic borrowing both cuts new investments and raises the cost of production, pricing Mexican manufactures out of home and foreign markets at the same time foreign investors replace them in both production and marketing.

The illogic of the system of extensive foreign ownership has also been seen in the trade balance reflecting interest and profit returns due foreigners for their Mexican investments. Indeed, Mexico's overall balance reflects a long-term net outflow of investment capital, interest, and profits over and above the import of new capital; the resulting national disaccumulation foretells long-term disinvestment in production.

Mexico's expropriations of foreign investments in the past have only momentarily changed this outflow favoring foreign interests. And despite new inroads of foreign investors in the mainframe of the economy, Mexico's bourgeoisie has railed against any government restrictions on its right to withhold domestic investments from production, to acquire foreign stocks and bonds, to invest in the export sector and speculative domestic real estate, and to hoard periodically vast quantities of gold and foreign exchange while waiting for the best speculative opportunity.

THE FIBER OF MEXICO

Without a shadow of doubt, the detritus of impoverishment following centuries of empire has hung heavily on the fiber of Mexico's varied peóples, settling harshly in its countryside, imposing wracking poverty within the adobe, brick, and now concrete domain of its aging cities.

The pure Indian blood of its races has long since been fused with that of Spaniards, Africans, other indigenous Americans, and Europeans. Its hundreds of native languages have been obliterated, transmogrified, or exchanged for the conqueror's common tongue. Its forests have been destroyed, its rivers polluted, its countryside seeded with more roads, rail beds, and corporate enterprises than with corn and beans. Its farms have again grown vast, its peasants are landless, its soil and labor are deployed by others to produce for distant markets. Its ancient sugar mills, textile factories, and shops of handmade goods have closed, and have only partly been replaced by foreign-owned megaliths run by armies of technicians who are themselves dutifully put in motion by computers, and corporate directors.

Mexico's cities have grown with pollution and disease, its rural zones have become impoverished and depopulated, a graveyard of forgotten people, ravines, fields, and open mines. The cultural roots of generations past have given way, self-destructed with its aging progenitors, closing the last gateway of retreat from the urban domain. This urban domain is itself enclosed by fusing smog and clouds into an inversion layer hermetically sealing off the life of changing seasons and the cycled wellsprings of purified air and water.

Through the converging putrefactions of the cities, millions march to the cadenced rhythms of grinding industries as dangers, sickness, and death spread. And so senseless seems the present, that only the churches remain as sentinels unchanged, their priests in habits again seeking to proselytize openly on the streets and recruit the young into the blinding light of Catholic liturgy piously passed off as education.

FUTURE TRANSFORMATIONS

Future transformation in Mexico will come in both the economic and social realm. One simply cannot take place without the other if there is to be accumulation with social justice.

Mexico's ruling party has separated the two, however, pursuing accumulation and closing its eyes to the desperation of the overwhelming popular majority.

True to this structured myopia, post–World War II government assurances concentrated on a favorable investment climate, security, and subsidies offered to the wealthy possessed of *haciendas*, large production facilities, substantial commercial enterprises, and financial institutions. At the apogee of government accommodation to these interests during the Salinas presidency, a heavy price was paid by 40 million impoverished workers in industry and agriculture, 20 million unemployed, underemployed, and idle workers, and another 18 million partially active tradespeople at the brink of subsistence.

Caring little for the nation and its charges, giant domestic enterprises, *hacendados*, and banks switched capital from one deployment to another, and favored speculation and unproductive ventures, exporting their dollar holdings at will.

The Bank of Mexico exerted few restrictions, other than the domestic efforts to control and raise interest rates through buying and selling state bonds and discounting commercial paper regulating the money supply. These were inappropriate methods for Mexico, learned in subservience to the U.S. Federal Reserve. As Mexican rates rose under the bank's guidance and the rate of return on capital invested in production fell below interest rates, borrowing for productive investments fell, and capital sought the highest rate of return in government bonds, speculative ventures, and foreign markets.

Rather than nationalizing the bank system as a whole, the government allowed private and corporate banking to extend to the point where there was no government control over the diverse uses of unproductive, speculative capital that employed relatively few workers compared to the millions of surplus rural peasants and peons, the involuntarily unemployed, day-laborers, casual and migratory workers, redundant merchants, microscopic traders, able-bodied beggars, and outcasts.

DOWNWARD MOBILITY AND FEAR OF FUTURE POSITIONING

Even the middle classes with secure and relatively steady incomes suffered downward mobility in the price-inflated market. Fearing for their futures, they became a powerful force sustaining the expanding service sector and battalions of government bureaucracies of apparats lording over clerks, accountants, and assorted scribes, superfluous road, rail, oil, and utility workers, and police, guards, military recruiters, and lowly recruits. These government agencies in turn enlarged their hold over the federal budget without proportionately extending their economic sway into building new homes for the poor, roads, rail-beds, sewers, aqueducts, sanitary wells, irrigation networks, schools, hospitals, agricultural research facilities, crop-improvement centers, and the like.

Rather, government bureaucrats opened the way for inefficiencies, absence, and idleness of their own charges. They created a superordinated hierarchy demanding bribes and payoffs for permission to invest, employ, produce, and sell, but lacked adequate regulations over private capital thrown into unproductive fields. They had no way to guide domestic prices or interest rates to promote sound investments in production, to employ the nation's unemployed and partially idled millions, to balance output with need, and to provide wages to fill that need through the market.

It was, then, clearly a time for change in government and private programs and priorities to place social well-being on an equal plane with, and reaping the rewards of, the uses of capital and government revenues.

SURPLUS PEOPLE AND CAPITALIST CITY-STATES

At the present time, Mexico remains partly tied on the rural scene to the *hacienda* system using peon labor and keeping land in abeyance, as well as to the system of *ejidatarios*, common lands, and inefficient farming.

With the exodus of part of the superfluous and subsistence population from the rural domain, Mexico is increasingly becoming urbanized at a pace that has outrun available housing, fresh water and food supplies, sanitation, health, and educational facilities, and government services. The government's antiquated social security system also leaves over three-fourths of the population completely uncovered.

The slow development of production outside the major cities has, meanwhile, transformed Mexico's major urban zones into city-states that offer privileged access to the world's modern infrastructure for some and unemployment, poverty, and degradation for most. Mexico City is the largest city-state in the world, holding 27 to 28 million in a thrall of concentric factory and business districts, neighborhoods, and *barrios*. But these artifacts of the industrial and cybernetic age count little for the well-being of the urban population.

These city-states remain unable to transform themselves or the rest of Mexico into viable productive entities able to provide for its people. And this failing has been produced by the atavistic hold of the Institutional Revolutionary party on the government and its army of lifeless bureaucrats; by the limited attempt of government policies to promote social welfare; by the structured system of bribes, payoffs, and enforcement police; by the total absence of a viable way to control the national currency, interest rates, or capital exports; by the absence of regulations designed to direct national production and promote full employment; by the inadequate and backward medical and educational system; and by thought controls relayed and amplified by the official media alongside government limits on civil liberties that diminish and repress alternatives.

Thus Mexico's closed city-state cares for neither unregulated capitalism nor popular democracy.

Bound by a feudal mentality of lordlike industrialists, bankers, merchants, and *hacendados* influencing and shaping state bureaucracies regulating social and economic life, the many peoples of the nation's rural and urban domain will remain in relative bondage until they change the party, the government, the bureaucracies, and the outmoded structures that rule their lives.

That they will do so in the long run is a certainty. That they will anguish in the short term is likewise almost a certainty.

Notes

Chapter 1. From Inquisition to Independence

1. See E.H. Lecky, *History of the Rise and Influence of the Spirit of Rationalism in Europe* (New York: George Braziller, 1955), 267 and passim.

2. Irwin St. John Tucker, *A History of Imperialism* (New York: Rand School of Social Science, 1920), 298; Andrew McCall, *The Medieval World* (New York: Barnes & Noble, 1979), 259–84; Lecky, *Spirit of Rationalism*, 116, 119, 263, 265 notes, 267, 268, 270; for dramatization and depiction based on historical evidence, see James A. Michener, *Mexico* (New York: Random House, 1992), 321–22; and "Holy Office," 12th Annual Jewish Film Festival, Berkeley, California, U.A. Theater, 30 July 1992.

3. Lecky, *Spirit of Rationalism*, 270.

4. Adam Smith, *An Inquiry into the Nature and Causes of the Wealth of Nations* (New York: Modern Library, 1937), 850–51; see also Immanuel Wallerstein, *The Modern World-System: Capitalist Agriculture and the Origins of the European World-Economy in the Sixteenth Century* (New York: Academic Press, 1974), 191.

5. See Lewis Hanke, *Aristotle and the American Indian: A Study of Race Prejudice in the Modern World* (London: Hollis and Carter, 1959), 8–9; Richard Krooth, *Empire: A Bicentennial Appraisal* (Santa Barbara: Harvest, 1976).

6. Wallerstein, *Modern World-System*, 165, 187.

7. Gaci-Ardóñez de Montalvo, *La cergas de esplendian* (Sevilla, 1510); Oakland Museum exhibit: "The Spanish in California," Oakland, California, 1992; museum exhibit, Drake's Bay, Inverness, California, February 1993; Adam Smith, *Wealth of Nations*, 204, notes 137, 207, 209.

8. Lecky, *Spirit of Rationalism*, 314–17.

9. Hanke, *Aristotle and the American Indian*, 9.

10. Ibid., 10–11.

11. Ray Allen Billington, *American History Before 1877* (Paterson, N.J.: Littlefield, Adams, 1960), 4; Peter Farb, *Man's Rise to Civilization as Shown by the Indians of North America from Primeval Times to the Coming of the Industrial State* (New York: Dutton, 1968), 243.

12. Lewis Hanke, "The New Laws—Another Analysis," in *Indian Labor in the Spanish Indies*, ed. John Francis Bannon (Boston: D.C. Heath, 1966), 56.

13. Billington, *American History*, 4.

14. Billington, *American History*, 4; Wallerstein, *Modern World*, 187.

15. Hanke, *Aristotle and the American Indian*, 19.

16. Ibid., 8.

17. Raul Alcides Reissner, *El indio en los diccionarios: exegesis léxica de un estereotipo*, Serie de Antropología Social, Collección Número 67 (México, D.F.: Instituto Nacional Indigenista, n.d.), 18–19.

18. Ibid., 21.

19. G.C. Lewis, *On the Government of Dependencies* (Oxford: Clarendon, 1841); Krooth, *Empire*, 3; Wallerstein, *Modern World-System*, 187 n. 109, 191 n. 127, 192 n. 133.

20. See Reissner, *El Indio*, 15–23; Lewis, *Government of Dependencies*, passim; Smith, *Wealth of Nations*, 203.

21. Smith, *Wealth of Nations*, 758.

22. Lecky, *Spirit of Rationalism*, 319–20.

23. See Lecky, *Spirit of Rationalism*, 318–19; Krooth, *Empire*, 1–3.

24. Krooth, *Empire*, 1–2.

25. Lecky, *Spirit of Rationalism*, 313.

26. Maurice Collins, *Cortés and Montezuma* (New York: Avon Books, 1978), 151.

27. Krooth, *Empire*, 2; Lewis, *Government of Dependencies*, passim.

28. Jan Bazant, *A Concise History of Mexico from Hidalgo to Cárdenas, 1804–1940* (London: Cambridge University Press, 1977), 5–8.

29. John M. Tutino, "Provincial Spaniards, Indian Towns, and Haciendas: Interrelated Agrarian Sectors in the Valleys of Mexico and Toluca, 1750–1810," in *Provinces of Early Mexico: Variants of Spanish American Regional Evolution* (Los Angeles: UCLA Latin American Center Publications, 1976), 192–93.

30. Irwin St. John Tucker, *A History of Imperialism*, 295–304.

31. Bazant, *Concise History of Mexico*, 5–8.

32. Edwin Emerson, Jr., *A History of the Nineteenth Century Year by Year*, vol. 1 (New York: P.F. Collier and Son, 1900), 370–76.

33. Daniel Fogel, *Junípero Serra, the Vatican, and Enslavement Theology* (San Francisco: Ism Press, 1988), 28–29.

34. Lucas Alamán, *Historia de Méjico*, 5 vols. (Mexico, 1849–52), 2:25–26. Quotation translated by Richard Krooth.

35. Bazant, *Concise History of Mexico*, 18.

36. Alamán, *Historia de Méjico*, 1:425–33, 2:25–26; Fogel, *Junípero Serra*, 29–32; Bazant, *Concise History of Mexico*, 14–19.

37. Tucker, *History of Imperialism*, 302.

38. Lewis, *Government of Dependencies*, passim; Wallerstein, *Modern World-System*, 192 n. 133.

39. Edward Boorstein, *Allende's Chile: An Inside View* (New York: International Publishers, 1977), 18.

40. Daniel A. del Rio, *Simon Bolivar* (Clinton, Mass.: Colonial Press, 1965), passim.

41. The plot ran deep, too, for France held revanchist plans on North America. Aaron Burr planned the destruction of the United States by soliciting Fouché's help in an effort to use Louisiana as a monarchical stronghold for the French Bourbons to ally with French troops attacking from Canada. But both the British ministry and Napoleon dismissed the scheme. Napoleon also dismissed Fouché, exiling him to Italy as governor of Rome. Emerson, *History of the Nineteenth Century*, 1:370–76.

42. Ernest Ludlow Bogart, *The Economic History of the United States* (New York: Longmans, Green, 1907), 27.

43. The Social Economic Union of Cuba, *Commercial Relations Between Cuba and the United States of America* (Havana: SEUC, 1936), 22–26.

44. International Commission of Jurists, *Cuba and the Rule of Law* (Geneva: ICJ, 1962), 1.

45. International Commission of Jurists, *Cuba and the Rule of Law*, 1.

46. The Social Economic Union of Cuba, *Commercial Relations*, 23.

47. Ibid.

48. Ibid.

49. Henry Steele Commager, *Documents of American History*, 7th ed. (New York: Meredith, 1963), 234–37.

50. Bazant, *Concise History of Mexico*, 26–27.

51. Lorenzo de Zavala, *Ensayo histórico de los revoluciones de México*, 2 vols. (México, 1918), 1:69–79; Emerson, *History of the Nineteenth Century*, 2:670, 688.

52. Emerson, *History of the Nineteenth Century*, 2:702.

Chapter 2. From Empire to the War of Reform

1. Jan Bazant, *A Concise History of Mexico from Hidalgo to Cárdenas, 1804–1940* (London: Cambridge University Press, 1977), 40–42; Edwin Emerson, Jr., *A History of the Nineteenth Century Year by Year* (New York: P.F. Collier and Son, 1900), 2:711.

2. Emerson, *History of the Nineteenth Century*, 2:861.

3. Ibid., 2:870.

4. Ibid., 2:880.

5. Ibid., 2:915, 965.

6. Ibid., 2:895.

7. Ibid., 2:899.

8. Ibid., 2:915, 938.

9. Emerson, *History of the Nineteenth Century*, 2:965; Bazant, *Concise History of Mexico*, 55–56.

10. Emerson, *History of the Nineteenth Century*, 2:1003–6.

11. Ibid., 2:1006–9.

12. Ibid., 2:1027–33.

13. Emerson, *History of the Nineteenth Century*, 2:1041–42; Bogart, *Economic History*, 27, 257.

14. Emerson, *History of the Nineteenth Century*, 2:1178.

15. Justo Sierra, *Obras completas, I, Juárez, su obra y su tiempo* (México, 1948), 87–92.

16. Emerson, *History of the Nineteenth Century*, 2:1214–16.

17. Justo Sierra, *Obras completas*, vol. 1, *Juárez, su obra y su tiempo* 92–113; Emerson, *History of the Nineteenth Century*, 2:1219–20.

18. Emerson, *History of the Nineteenth Century*, 3:1265.

19. Ibid., 3:1292.

20. Ibid., 3:1336–37.

21. Ibid., 3:1343–45, 1380–81.

22. Ibid., 3:1381.

23. Ibid., 3:1410–13.
24. Ibid., 3:1414–15.
25. Ibid., 3:1446–49.

Chapter 3. Revolution, Independence, and Imperial Impositions

1. Even today along the Tuxpan beaches on the Gulf of Mexico there are vast state-owned Pemex oil drilling and refining facilities that pollute air and sea next to the shacks and tiny homes of the oil company workers. To substitute nuclear power for oil, Pemex has begun to turn to nuclear plant generators on the Gulf near Tecoluta and is fouling the sea with radioactive debris. Richard Krooth, travels in Tuxpan, Mexico, December 1993–January 1994.

2. U.S. Senate, 66th Cong., 2d sess., "Investigation of Mexican Affairs," *Senate Document* v. 9, 209–14.

3. Frank Tannenbaum, *Peace by Revolution: An Interpretation of Mexico* (New York: Columbia University Press, 1933), 228–30.

4. Ibid., 230–31.

5. Benjamin Franklin Library, collected manuscripts, 1890–1910, Mexico, D.F.

6. Tannenbaum, *Peace by Revolution*, 226–27.

7. Charles Curtis Cumberland, *Mexican Revolution: Genesis Under Madero* (New York: Greenwood, 1969), 208–11.

8. Bazant, *Concise History of Mexico*, 126–27.

9. S. Jeffrey K. Wilkerson, *National Geographic Research and Exploration* (New York: National Geographic Society, Spring 1994).

10. Bazant, *Concise History of Mexico*, 126–29.

11. Ibid., 129–30.

12. Ibid., 140.

13. Ibid., 141.

14. Ibid., 140, 144–45.

15. Ibid., 141–42.

16. Ibid., 143–44.

17. Cumberland, *Mexican Revolution*, 212–14.

18. Cumberland, *Mexican Revolution*, 214–17.

19. Robert Labarge, oral account of a retiree, U.S. Cavalry, as told to the author, Chicago, December 1950.

20. Hector Galan, "The American Experience: Looking at Pancho Villa's 1916 Raid on New Mexico and U.S. Efforts to Track Him Down," PBS, Boston, Galan Production, 3 November 1993.

21. Bazant, *Concise History of Mexico*, 144–45.

22. Ibid., 145–47.

23. Galan, "The American Experience."

24. Bazant, *Concise History of Mexico*, 148–50.

25. James A. Waterworth, "The Conflict Historically Considered," in Richard Krooth, ed., *The Great Social Struggle*, vol. 2 (Santa Barbara: Harvest, 1979), 51–85.

26. Tannenbaum, *Peace by Revolution*, 193–95.

27. Ibid., 202–3.

28. Ibid., 204–6.

29. Ibid., 202–3.

30. Ibid., 215.

31. Ibid., 215–17.

32. Ibid., 219–24.

33. Ibid., 217–18.

34. Ibid., 217–18, 223–24.

35. Ibid., 192–93.

36. Ibid., 192.

37. Richard Krooth, *Arms and Empire: Imperial Patterns Before World War II* (Santa Barbara: Harvest, 1980), chapters 1–3.

38. Fray Bernardino de Sahagún, *Historia general de las cosas de Nueva Espagna* (México: 1830), 3:63.

39. In 1883 the Mexican Constitution was amended to authorize the federal Congress to enact a republic-wide mining code. The first code was promulgated in 1884 under the administration of president Manuel Gonzales; Article 10 declared substances such as coal and petroleum to be the "exclusive property" or the "exclusive ownership" (*propiedad exclusiva*) of the landowner.

In 1892 this code was superseded by a new law that reaffirmed under Article 4 that the owner of the soil could exploit mineral fuels "freely and without the need of special concession in any instance." This meant they could not be denounced by a nonlandowner, according to the prevailing opinion of Academy of Jurisprudence in Mexico City in 1905, when coal and petroleum had become substances of considerable importance in Mexico.

The mining code of 1892 was superseded by that of 1909. Article 1 declared that certain substances were the *dominio directo* of the nation, and Article 2 reaffirmed that other substances, including the deposits of mineral fuels and bituminous materials, were the "exclusive property" or the "exclusive ownership" of the landowner.

With a twist of ownership rights, the Mining Law of 1909 later became the basis of Article 27 of the postrevolutionary constitution of 31 January 1917.

40. Anton Mohr, *The Oil War* (New York: Ph.D. diss., Columbia University, 1932).

41. Burton J. Henrick, *The Life and Letters of Walter P. Page* (Boston: Houghton Mifflin, 1922), 1:203.

42. United States Senate, 66th Cong., 2d sess., *Senate Document*, vol. 10, 3121.

43. United States, 66th Cong., 2d sess., *Senate Document*, vol. 9, 266.

44. United States, 66th Cong., 2d sess., *Senate Document*, vol. 9, 267.

45. Captain Francis McCullagh, *Red Mexico: a Reign of Terror in America* (New York: Louis Carrier, 1928), 376, 378.

46. Ibid., 364.

47. Guy Stevens, *Current Controversies with Mexico: Addresses and Writings* (New York: Foreign Policy Association, 1926), 334–35.

48. McCullagh, *Red Mexico*, 368.

49. Stevens, *Current Controversies*, 346–47.

50. Ibid., 252–55.

51. Ibid., 349, 352, 353.

52. William English Walling, *The Mexican Question* (New York: Walling, 1927), 13.

53. McCullagh, *Red Mexico*, 364.
54. Ibid., 78–79.
55. Ibid., 364–65.
56. Ibid., 83.
57. Krooth, *Arms and Empire*, 117.

Chapter 4. Nationalism, Development, and Foreign Influence in the Late 1920s and the 1930s

1. Jan Bazant, *A Concise History of Mexico from Hidalgo to Cárdenas, 1804–1940* (London: Cambridge University Press, 1977), 176–77.
2. Ibid., 176.
3. Betty Kirk, *Covering the Mexican Front* (Norman: University of Oklahoma Press, 1942), 157, quoted by William Cameron Townsend, *Lázaro Cárdenas, Mexican Democrat* (Ann Arbor, Mich.: George Wahr, 1952).
4. Townsend, *Lázaro Cárdenas*, 365.
5. Nelson Reed, *The Caste War of Yucatán* (Stanford: Stanford University Press, 1964), 153–56.
6. Bazant, *Concise History of Mexico*, 136–38; see Chapter 1.
7. Ibid., 166.
8. Nathaniel Weyl and Sylvia Weyl, *The Reconquest of Mexico: The Years of Lázaro Cárdenas* (London: Oxford University Press, 1939), 148–50.
9. Ibid., 151–52.
10. Ibid., 152–58.
11. Ibid., 158.
12. Ibid., 158–59.
13. Ibid., 160.
14. Ibid., 161–62.
15. Ibid., 164–66.
16. Ibid., 166–67.
17. Ibid., 167–70.
18. Bazant, *Concise History of Mexico*, 175–77; Richard Krooth, *Arms and Empire: Imperial Patterns Before World War I* (Santa Barbara: Harvest, 1981), Chapter 3.
19. Weyl, *Reconquest of Mexico*, 129.
20. Ibid., 130.
21. Bazant, *Concise History of Mexico*, 179–80.
22. Blanche B. De Vore, *Land and Liberty: A History of the Mexican Revolution* (New York: Pageant, 1966), 271.
23. Weyl, *Reconquest of Mexico*, 190–91.
24. De Vore, *Land and Liberty*, 272–74.
25. Bazant, *Concise History of Mexico*, 179–80.
26. De Vore, *Land and Liberty*, 274.
27. Weyl, *Reconquest of Mexico*, 191.
28. Ibid., 191–92.
29. Bazant, *Concise History of Mexico*, 183–84.
30. Ibid., 184.
31. Weyl, *Reconquest of Mexico*, 192–93.

32. Ibid., 194n.
33. Ibid., 194.
34. Ibid., 194–95.
35. De Vore, *Land and Liberty*, 275–76.
36. Weyl, *Reconquest of Mexico*, 196.
37. Bazant, *Concise History of Mexico*, 184–85.
38. Townsend, *Lázaro Cárdenas*, 165–76.
39. Bazant, *Concise History of Mexico*, 185.
40. Ibid.
41. Weyl, *Reconquest of Mexico*, 177.
42. Tim Golden, "Salinas's Chosen Path: Peace and Progress Too," *The New York Times*, 4 March 1994; John Ross, *Rebellion from the Roots: Indian Uprising in Chiapas* (Monroe, Maine: Common Courage Press, 1995); General Command of the Zapatista National Liberation Army, *El despertador mexicano* (Lacandona Jungle, 31 December 1993), photocopy of "Declaration of War."
43. Weyl, *Reconquest of Mexico*, 180–86.
44. Ibid., 173–76.
45. Ibid., 177–78.
46. Ibid., 178–79.
47. Ibid., 220.
48. Bazant, *Concise History of Mexico*, 185–86.
49. Weyl, *Reconquest of Mexico*, 176.
50. Ibid., 176–77.
51. Ibid., 180, 186.

Chapter 5. Nationalism and Industrial Reform in the 1930s

1. Nathaniel and Sylvia Weyl, *The Reconquest of Mexico: The Years of Lázaro Cárdenas* (London: Oxford University Press, 1939), 176; Jan Bazant, *A Concise History of Mexico from Hidalgo to Cárdenas, 1804–1940* (London: Cambridge University Press, 1977), 187–88.
2. Weyl, *Reconquest of Mexico*, 228–29.
3. Weyl, *Reconquest of Mexico*, 230; James B. Pick, Edgar W. Butler, and Elizabeth L. Lanzer, *Atlas of Mexico* (Boulder, Colo.: Westview, 1989), 14, Table 2.1A. The total population figure is for 1930.
4. Weyl, *Reconquest of Mexico*, 238–43.
5. Ibid., 254.
6. Ibid., 256.
7. Ibid., 257.
8. Ibid., 346.
9. Bazant, *Concise History of Mexico*, 186.
10. Weyl, *Reconquest of Mexico*, 233–34.
11. Ibid., 230–32.
12. Ibid., 244.
13. Ibid.
14. Ibid., 244–47.

Chapter 6. Nationalization and Imperial Oil

1. Production had skyrocketed from 10,000 barrels in 1901 to 193,398 barrels in 1921 and had then fallen to 33,039 barrels during the crisis year 1931. Jan Bazant, *A Concise History of Mexico from Hidalgo to Cárdenas, 1804–1940* (London: Cambridge University Press, 1977), 195, Table 13.

2. Blanche B. De Vore, *Land and Liberty: A History of the Mexican Revolution* (New York: Pageant, 1966), 283.

3. Nathaniel Weyl and Sylvia Weyl, *The Reconquest of Mexico: The Years of Lázaro Cárdenas* (London: Oxford University Press, 1939), 282.

4. Ibid., 298–99.

5. De Vore, *Land and Liberty*, 282–83.

6. Ibid., 283.

7. Bazant, *Concise History of Mexico*, 195, Table 12.

8. Ibid., 186–87.

9. Weyl, *Reconquest of Mexico*, 301–2.

10. Ibid., 296.

11. Ibid., 302.

12. De Vore, *Land and Liberty*, 283–84.

13. Weyl, *Reconquest of Mexico*, 303.

14. De Vore, *Land and Liberty*, 283–84.

15. William Cameron Townsend, *Lázaro Cárdenas, Mexican Democrat* (Ann Arbor, Mich.: George Wahr, 1952), 263–72.

16. Weyl, *Reconquest of Mexico*, 303–4.

17. Townsend, *Lázaro Cárdenas*, 275–80.

18. Weyl, *Reconquest of Mexico*, 305.

19. Ibid., 306.

20. Ibid., 306–7.

21. Ibid., 312–14.

22. De Vore, *Land and Liberty*, 286; Weyl, *Reconquest of Mexico*, 383–84.

23. De Vore, *Land and Liberty*, 289–90.

Chapter 7. A Historic Breakthrough

1. William Cameron Townsend, *Lázaro Cárdenas, Mexican Democrat* (Ann Arbor, Mich.: George Wahr, 1952), 285.

2. Ibid., 346.

3. Ibid., 336–37.

4. Nathaniel Weyl and Sylvia Weyl, *The Reconquest of Mexico: The Years of Lázaro Cárdenas* (London: Oxford University Press, 1939), 251.

5. Cárdenas's theory was not lost on future progressive politicians anointing his philosopher's stone, from Latin America to Africa. "You still have this question of populism—'Let the workers strike!'" noted President Nelson Mandela of South Africa. "They say, 'We want only investors who will invest at all costs.' I'm trying to warn against that type of thinking. That is irresponsible. We must move from the position of a resistance movement to one of builders." Bill Keller, "A Day in the Life of Mandela: Charm, Control, a Bit of Acid," *New York Times*, 12 September 1994.

6. Townsend, *Lázaro Cárdenas*, 306, quoting a letter Townsend received from Cárdenas, April 1946. Such a formulation could not be negotiated on a state level in April 1946 because the U.S. had lost interest in manipulating Mexico after World War II. Cárdenas was out of power, and the U.S. was not about to create industrial or agricultural competitors in the face of the collapse of postwar government markets for manufactured goods and grain.

7. Townsend, *Lázaro Cárdenas*, 307.

8. Jan Bazant, *A Concise History of Mexico from Hidalgo to Cárdenas, 1804– 1940* (London: Cambridge University Press, 1977), 192, Table 4.

9. Ibid., 193, Table 9.

10. Ibid., 193, Table 8.

11. Ibid., 190, Table 1; James B. Pick, Edgar W. Butler, and Elizabeth L. Lanzer, *Atlas of Mexico* (Boulder, Colo.: Westview, 1989), 14, Table 2.1A.

12. Bazant, *Concise History of Mexico*, 196, Table 14.

13. Ibid., 196, Table 15.

14. Ibid., 194, Table 11.

15. Ibid., 196, Table 14.

16. Ibid., 193, Table 7.

17. Ibid., 192, Table 6.

18. Ibid., 192, Table 5.

19. Townsend, *Lázaro Cárdenas*, 319–29.

20. Ibid., 307–17, 323–25.

21. Ibid., 283–89.

22. Ibid., 164.

Part IV. From the Status Quo Ante to the Policy of Progress

1. Nathaniel Weyl and Sylvia Weyl, *The Reconquest of Mexico: The Years of Lázaro Cárdenas* (London: Oxford University Press, 1939), 247–49.

2. William Cameron Townsend, *Lázaro Cárdenas, Mexican Democrat* (Ann Arbor, Mich.: George Wahr, 1952), 342–47. In the economic realm, for example, Cárdenas focused particularly on the complete takeover of the nation's oil resources from Standard Oil and British Dutch Shell. See chapters 6 and 7.

3. Blanche B. De Vore, *Land and Liberty: A History of the Mexican Revolution* (New York: Pageant, 1966), 292–93.

4. Ibid., 293–95.

5. Ibid., 296–98.

6. See Chapter 1.

7. De Vore, *Land and Liberty*, 295–96.

Chapter 8. Mexico's Historic Transformation

1. United States, *Foreign Relations of the United States* (Washington, D.C.: State Department, U.S. Government Printing Office, 1914), 444.

2. Col. Willis M. Smsyer, *The Evolution of U.S. Foreign Policy*, Document AD 241-578, unclassified (Arlington, Va.: Armed Services Technical Information Agency, 1960); Karl E. Meyer, "Editorial Notebook: The Doctrine Nobody Can Define," *New York Times*, 14 August 1994.

3. Policy Research Committee, Committee for Economic Development, *Defense Against Inflation: Policies for Price Stability in a Growing Economy* (New York: CED, July 1958), 63–64.

4. Mario Ramón Beteta, "Government Policy Towards Foreign Investors, Mexico: A Statist Survey," *The Statist* (London), 8 January 1965, 21–23.

5. Refugio Bautista Zane (coordinator), *Los días sin tregua 1876–1970* (Carretera, México: Centuria de Lucha Populares, University Autónoma Chapingo, Dirección de Difusion Cultural, 1991), 225.

6. Margarita A. Nolasco, comp., *Aspectos sociales de la migración en Mexico*, vol. 2 (México: Instituto National de Antropología e Historia, Departmento de Proyectos Especiales de Investigación, 1979), 52.

7. José López Portillo, "State of the Nation Address," 1 September 1982 (México: Poder Ejecutivo Federal, 1982).

8. Robert A. Pastor, "NAFTA as Center of Integration Process," in *North American Free Trade: Assessing the Impact*, ed. Nora Lustig, Barry P. Bosworth, and Robert Z. Lawrence (Washington, D.C.: Brookings Institution, 1992), 181–82, 283.

9. Pastor, "NAFTA," 182.

10. Said El Mansour Cherkaqoui, "A Mexican Perspective on the North American Free Trade Agreement: An Interview with Cuauhtémoc Cárdenas in Mexico City," *The GateWay* (San Francisco: Golden Gate University, July 1993), 6; compare Professor Michael W. Gordon, "The Contemporary Mexican Approach to Growth with Foreign Investment: Controlled but Participatory Independence," 10 *California Western Law Review* 1 (1973); with professors N. Ogarrio and Pereznieto Castro, "Mexico–United States Relations: Economic Integration and Foreign Investment," 12 *Houston Journal of International Law* 223 (1990).

11. Richard Krooth, interviews in Mexico, July 1992, December 1993–January 1994; also see "Interview: Mexico's hottest industry: Human rights work grows as the Mexican economy liberalizes," *Dollars & Sense* (January/February 1993): 16–17.

12. These paragraphs are based on the author's extensive interviews with common people, government officials, and opposition forces in Mexico during July 1992 and December 1993–January 1994; see also Cristina Pacheco, "Aquí y ahora" (Here and Now), Mexico City: Radio, 1990–; "Aquí nos tocó vivir" (We Happen to Live Here), Mexico City: TV show, 1990–; *Para vivir quí*, 1985; *Zona de desastres*, 1987. Interviewed government officials either equivocate in expressing their conclusions or demand strict anonymity for forthright statements, saying they fear PRI harassment, loss of their jobs, or even strong-arm consequences. See also U.S. Senate, Banking Committee Hearings, Chairman Alfonse M. D'Amato, "Opening Statement," and Javier Livas, "Testimony," 24 May 1995 (Washington, D.C.: Government Printing Office, 1995).

13. Krooth, interviews in Mexico, July 1992, December 1993–January 1994; also see Cherkaqoui, "Mexican Perspective," 6; *Dollars & Sense*, "Mexico's hottest industry," 16–17.

14. Raul Alcides Reissner, *El indio en los diccionarios, exegeis léxica de un estereotipo*, Serie de Antropología Social, Colección Número 67 (México, D.F.: Instituto Nacional Indigenista, n.d.), 23. See also Chapter 1.

15. See Dip. Hugo Andres Araujo, Secretario General, *La reforma campesina* (México: Confederación Nacional Campesina, December 1992); Gustavo Gordillo de Anda, *Dilemas de la nueva reforma agraria*, Berkeley, Calif.: Conference on the Transformation of Mexican Agricultural Opportunities, December 3–4, 1992.

16. Display plaque, Manuel Suárez y Suárez, *Polyforum cultural siqueiros*, México, El Hotel de México y el Polyforum Cultural Siqueiros, Ciudad de México, 1992. The "bourgeois-democratic" Revolution was a commercial venture. Mexico's cultural/ethnic domain has suffered under its onslaught of foreign interests. Attempting to secure itself in 1975, the "Law of Interventions and Trademarks of Mexico" (30 Dec. 1975, *Diario oficial*, 10 Feb. 1976) provided in articles 127 and 128 for the reduction of the influence of *foreign trademarks* in the Mexican market by requiring that both the foreign-mark of origin be placed on goods produced in Mexico *and* a Mexican mark be placed representing the property of the Mexican licensee of the foreign enterprise.

Coca-Cola went into action to block the law. First, it registered its new trademark "Moctezuma" in Mexico. Then it lobbied with the Mexican National Registry of the Transfer of Technology to gain an exception, so Coca-Cola's green bottles with its logo molded in glass would *not* have to be changed at a cost in recognition (goodwill) and millions of discarded bottles. And Coca-Cola won: the law has *never* been used since. Coca-Cola culture rules the Mexican market.

17. Cherkaqoui, "Mexican Perspective," 6; see also Lawrence A. Herzog, ed. *Planning the International Border Metropolis* (La Jolla, Calif.: University of California at San Diego, Center for U.S.-Mexican Studies, 1986).

Chapter 9. The Policy of Progress

1. Joel Brinkley, "A Success at the Border Earned Only a Shrug," *New York Times*, 14 September 1994; for background see also Wayne A. Cornelius and Jorge A. Bustamente, eds., *Mexican Migration to the United States: Origins, Consequences, and Policy Options*, vol. 3 of *Dimensions of U.S.-Mexican Relations*. (La Jolla, California: University of California at San Diego, Center for U.S.-Mexican Studies, 1989).

2. Even to take the "good" year 1981, for example, exports of $9.7 billion to the U.S. were outstripped by its import of $12.1 billion of U.S. goods.

3. Economist Intelligence Unit, *Country Profiles: Mexico*, 1981/82 (London: EIU, 1981).

4. Barry P. Bosworth, Robert Lawrence, and Nora Lustig, eds., Introduction to *North American Free Trade* (Washington, D.C.: Brookings Institution, 1992), 5.

5. Economist Intelligence Unit, *Country Profiles: Mexico*, 1981/82, et seq.

6. *Nacional financiera*, Internal Office Memorandum, Mexico, D.F., 1951 et seq.; see also Professor Michael W. Gordon, "The Contemporary Mexican Approach to Growth with Foreign Investment: Controlled but Participatory Independence," 10 *California Western Law Review* 1 (1973).

7. International Monetary Fund, *Financial Statistics*, 1961–1983 (New York: IMF); Economist Intelligence Unit, *Country Profiles: Mexico*, 1981/82, et seq.

8. International Monetary Fund, *Financial Statistics*, 1961–1983 (New York: IMF); Economist Intelligence Unit, *Country Profiles: Mexico*, 1981/82, et seq.

9. James B. Pick, Edgar W. Butler, and Elizabeth L. Lanzer, *Atlas of Mexico* (Boulder, Colo.: Westview, 1989), 246, Table 7.17.

10. See chapters 16 and 17 for a detailed discussion.

11. Richard Krooth, interviews in Mexico, January 1994. See also Chapter 17.

12. *The Transformation of Rural Mexico Series*: SARH-CEPAL, *Productores del*

sector social rural en Mexico, 1990; Cynthia Hewitt de Alcántara, ed., *Economic Restructuring and Rural Subsistence in Mexico: Corn and the Crisis of the 1980s*, 1994; Neil Harvey, *Rebellion in Chiapas: Rural Reforms, Campesino Radicalism, and the Limits to Salinismo*, 1995. (La Jolla, Calif.: University of California at San Diego, Center for U.S.-Mexican Studies, 1991–95).

13. Pick, *Atlas of Mexico*, 291–95, Tables 87.11, 8.12, Maps 8.4A, 8.4B.

14. Richard Krooth, analysis of Mexican census figures for 1980 and 1990 and the preliminary 1993 figures. See also Chapter 17.

15. Economist Intelligence Unit, *Country Profiles: Mexico*, 1993/94, 24; for legal authorization facilitating foreign investments, see also "Law to Promote Mexican Investment and to Regulate Foreign Investment," 7 February 1973, *Diario oficial*, 9 March 1973; and "Regulations of the Law to Promote Mexican Investment and Regulate Foreign Investment," *Diario oficial*, 16 May 1989.

16. Ibid.

17. Organo de Difusión del Instituto Nacional Indigenista, "Mapa de grupos indígenas de México," *México indígena, INI 30 años despues revisión critica* (México, D.F.: December 1978), 388.

18. "Mensaje del presidente e la república," *México indígena*, 5–6.

19. Pick, *Atlas*, 271–72 and Map 8.2F.

20. Pick, *Atlas*, 212–13, Figures 7.2A, 7.2B; Economist Intelligence Unit, *Country Profiles: Mexico*, 1993/94, 21.

21. Economist Intelligence Unit, *Country Profiles: Mexico*, 1993/94, 21.

22. Pick, *Atlas*, 157.

23. Ibid., 161, Table 6.5.

24. Mexico, *1990 Mexican Census.*

25. *1990 Mexican Census*; Richard Krooth, travels in Veracruz, January 1994.

Chapter 10. The Policy of Progress

1. James B. Pick, Edgar W. Butler, and Elizabeth L. Lanzer, *Atlas of Mexico* (Boulder, Colo.: Westview, 1989), 228–29.

2. Carlos Montañez and Horacio Aburto, *Maíz: Política institucional y crisis agricola* (México, D.F.: Nueva Imagen, 1979).

3. Alain de Janvry, "Agriculture in Crisis," *Society* 17:6 (September-October, 1980), 130.

4. Montañez and Aburto, *Maíz*, 1979, 37.

5. DGEA, "Consomos aparentes de productos agrícolas 1925–1980," *Econotecnia agricola* 5, no. 9 (1981).

6. DGEA, "Consomos aparentes," 1981.

7. David Barkin and Blanca Suárez, *El fin de la autosufficencia alimentaria* (México, D.F.: Nueva Imgen, 1982), 58.

8. Steven E. Sanderson, *The Receding Frontier: Aspects of the Internationalization of U.S.-Mexican Agriculture and Their Implications for Bilateral Relations in the 1980s* (La Jolla, Calif.: University of California at San Diego, Center for U.S.-Mexican Studies, 1981); see also Ruth Rama and Raúl Vigorito, *El complejo de frutas y legumbres en México* (México, D.F.: Nueva Imagen, 1879); Ruth Rama and Fernando Rello, "La internacionalización de la agricultura," unpublished manuscript, 1986.

9. Barkin and Suárez, 37.

10. Pick, *Atlas*, 279–80, Table 8.7.

11. Economist Intelligence Unit, *Country Profiles: Mexico*, 1993/94 (London: EIU, 18.

12. Ibid.

13. Economist Intelligence Unit, *Country Profiles: Mexico*, 1993/94, 19, citing Banco de México; INEGI.

14. Ibid.

15. Pick, *Atlas*, 200.

16. Montañez and Aburto, *Maíz*, 1979; Rama and Rello, "*La internacionalización*," 1980, 86–87.

17. For watermelons, exports rose from a 62,800 ton average in 1970–74 to 77,800 tons in 1975–79. So too for cantaloupes, where export volume rose from an average of 87,300 tons in 1970–74 to 96,500 tons in 1975–79. DGEA, "Consumos aparentes de productos agrícolas 1925–1980," *Econotecnia agrícola* 5, no. 9 (1981).

18. Oficina de Asesores del C. Presidente, *Reports* (Mexico, D.F.: OSP, March 1980, May 1980, December 1980); for background see also Michael Redclift, "Agrarian Populism in Mexico—the 'Via Campesina,'" *Journal of Peasant Studies* 7, no. 4 (July 1980).

19. SINE-SAM, "Sistema alimentario méxicano: Evaluación 1981 y 1982" (México, D.F., SINE-SAM, 1982).

20. See Donald L. Wyman, *Mexico's Economic Crisis: Challenges and Opportunities* (La Jolla, Calif.: University of California at San Diego, Center for U.S.-Mexican Studies, 1983).

21. Economist Intelligence Unit, *Country Profiles: Mexico*, 1993/94, 19.

22. José López Portillo, "State of the Nation Address, 1 September 1982" (México, D.F.: Poder Ejecutivo Federal, 1982), 60.

23. Economist Intelligence Unit, *Country Profiles: Mexico*, 1993/94, 19.

24. Ibid.

25. Sanderson, *Receding Frontier*, 1981, passim; David Mares, *The Evolution of U.S. Mexican Agricultural Relations: The Changing Roles of the Mexican State and Mexican Agricultural Producers* (La Jolla: University of California at San Diego, Center for U.S.-Mexican Studies, 1981), passim.

26. Richard Krooth, "Interviews in Mexico," January 1994. To compare earlier daily meat consumption figures, see statistics issued by the Mexican Secretaría de Agricultura y Granadería (1970–75) and the Secretaría de Programación y Presupuesto (1975–85).

27. Sylvia Nasar, "Third World Embracing Reforms to Encourage Economic Growth," *New York Times*, 8 July 1990.

28. See chapters 16, 17, 18, and 19; Introduction.

Part V. From the Old Status Quo to a New Order

1. Adam Smith, *The Wealth of Nations* (New York: Everyman's Library, 1937).

2. See Kenichi Ohmae, *The Borderless World: Power and Strategy in the Interlinked Economy* (New York: Harper Business, 1990); Robert J.S. Ross and Kent C. Trachte, *Global Capitalism: The New Leviathan* (New York: State University of

New York Press, 1990); Robert Reich, *The Work of Nations* (New York: Knopf, 1991); Robin Broad and John Cavanagh, "No More NIC's," *Foreign Policy* (Fall 1988).

3. See Jacob Viner, *The Customs Unions Issue* (New York: MacMillan, 1950); Richard Krooth, *Arms and Empire: Imperial Patterns Before World War I* (Santa Barbara: Harvest, 1981); Raghavan Chakravarthi, *Recolonization: GATT, the Uruguay Round and the Third World* (Penang, Malaysia: Third World Network, 1990).

4. Krooth, *Arms and Empire*, chapters 3–5.

5. See Viner, *Customs Unions Issue*; John Kenneth Galbraith, *A Short History of Financial Euphoria* (New York: Viking, 1993); C. Fred Bergsten, Thomas Horst, and Theodore H. Moran, *American Multinationals and American Interests* (Washington, D.C.: Brookings Institute, 1978).

6. Kenneth A. Oye, *Economic Discrimination and Political Exchange: World Political Economy in the 1930's and 1980's* (Princeton: Princeton University Press, 1992), passim.

7. Krooth, *Arms and Empire*, chapters 3, 4.

8. Sanford J. Ungar, *Estrangement: America and the World* (Oxford: Oxford University Press, 1985); Walter Wriston, *Twilight of Sovereignty* (New York: Macmillan, 1992); the World Trade Organization (WTO) established by GATT is designed to regulate the agriculture, services and textiles trade on a global plane. Banking, aeronautics, shipping and telecommunications will probably be brought into the fold. See Seth Goldschlager and Dominique Jacomet, "Business, Be Wary of New Trade Group," *New York Times*, 29 January 1995.

9. Sandra Masur, "The North American Free Trade Agreement: Why It's in the Interest of U.S. Business," *Columbia Journal of World Business* (Summer 1991).

10. Bela Balassa, *The Theory of Economic Integration* (London: Allen and Unwin, 1962).

11. Paul Robson, *The Economics of International Integration*, 2d ed. (London: Allen and Unwin, 1984).

12. Contrast Walt W. Rostow, "The Stages of Economic Growth," *Economic History Review* (August 1958); Paul Kennedy, *Preparing for the Twenty-First Century* (New York: Random House, 1993); Viner, *Customs Unions Issue*; Oye, *Economic Discrimination*; Krooth, *Arms & Empire*.

13. For the material frame, see Harley Shaiken, "Transfering High Tech Production to Mexico," *Columbia Journal of World Business* (Summer 1991); William R. Johnston, "Global Work Force 2000: The New World Labor Market," *Harvard Business Review* (March/April 1991).

14. John E. Carroll, "Environment, Free Trade, and Canadian-U.S. Relations," in *The Canada-U.S. Relationship: The Politics of Energy and Environmental Coordination*, ed. Jonathan Lemco (Westport, Conn., London: Praeger, 1992), 89.

15. Carroll, "Environment," 81–92.

Chapter 11. Domestic Reorganization and the Emergent Zone of Influence

1. Peter Passell, "Economic Scene," *New York Times*, 18 November 1993.

2. José Luis Reyna and Richard S. Weinert, eds., *Authoritarianism in Mexico* (Philadelphia: Institute for the Study of Human Issues, 1977).

3. Fernando Henrique Cardoso, "On the Characterization of Authoritarian Regimes in Latin America," in *The New Authoritarianism in Latin America*, ed. David Collier (Princeton: Princeton University Press, 1979), 33–57.

4. Daniel Levy and Gabriel Székely, *Mexico: Paradoxes of Stability and Change*, 2d. ed. (Boulder, Colo.: Westview, 1987), 163–64.

5. "McNeil/Lehrer NewsHour," PBS, 8 November 1993.

6. Tim Golden, "Back of the New Mall, Age-Old Ritual Slaughter," *New York Times*, 1 November 1993.

7. Richard Krooth, travels in Mexico, 1991–94.

8. Trejo Delarbre, "El movimiento obrero: Situación y perspectivas," in *Mexico Hoy*, ed. Pablo Gonzáles Casanova and Enrique Flotescano (México, D.F.: Siglo Vientiuno Editores, 1979), 139–40.

9. See Arnaldo Córdova, "Mass Politics and the Future of the Left in Mexico," *Latin American Perspectives* 9, no. 1 (Winter 1982): 84; Peter Baird and Ed McCaughan, "Labor and Imperialism in Mexico's Electrical Industry," *NACLA Report on the America* 11, no. 6 (September–October 1977): 35–38.

10. Krooth, interviews in Mexico, 1993–94; for historic contexts see Eric Van Young, ed., *Mexico's Regions: Comparative History and Development* (La Jolla, Calif.: University of California at San Diego, Center for U.S.-Mexican Studies, 1992); and Mercedes Gonzáles de la Rocha and Agustín Escobar Latapi, eds., *Social Responses to Mexico's Economic Crisis of the 1980s* (La Jolla, Calif.: University of California at San Diego, Center for U.S.-Mexican Studies, 1991).

11. Ibid.

12. S. Shahid Husain, "Getting the NAFTA Debate Back on Track," cited in NAFTA advertisement, *New York Times*, 19 October 1993, C12.

13. Ralph Nader, "Open Letter to President Clinton," fax, Washington, D.C., 3 November 1993.

14. Douglas Jehl, "Clinton Seeks to Direct His Campaign for Trade Accord at Working People," *New York Times*, 10 November 1993.

15. Keith Bradsher, "Commerce Dept. in '91 Urged Move to Caribbean for Low Wages," *New York Times*, 10 November 1993.

16. Bob Herbert, "Nafta and the Elite," Op-Ed, *New York Times*, 10 November 1993.

17. Husain, "Getting the NAFTA Debate Back on Track."

Chapter 12. Free Trade and the Great U.S. Transformation

1. United States, Commerce Department, Bureau of Economics analysis, July 1994; see Robert Reich, *The Work of Nations*, (New York: Knopf, 1991).

2. Roger Cohen, "Like U.S., West Europe Steps Up Its Asia Trade," *New York Times*, 24 November 1993.

3. Roger Cohen, "U.S. Seeks to Bring France into Trade Pact's Fold," *New York Times*, 4 December 1993.

4. See R.W. Apple, Jr., "Godfather to Pacific Era?" *New York Times*, 21 November 1993; David E. Sanger, "Salesman in Chief," *New York Times*, 21 November 1993.

5. See Richard Krooth and Hiroshi Fukurai, *Common Destiny: Japan and the United States in the Global Age* (Jefferson, N.C.: McFarland, 1990); Taggart R.

Murphy, "Power Without Purpose: The Crisis of Japan's Global Financial Dominance," *Harvard Business Review*, March/April 1989.

6. Philip Shenon, "Boycott in Order, Malaysian Says," *New York Times*, 21 November 1993.

7. Timothy Egan, "The Pacific Summit," *New York Times*, 21 November 1993.

8. Indonesia's main trading partners were Japan and the United States. Of total Indonesian exports, Japan took 41.32 percent in 1986 and 36.9 percent in 1991; the U.S. absorbed 21.6 percent in 1986, but 12 percent in 1991. During these five years, other industrialized nation's shares rose: South Korea from 5.1 percent to 6.7 percent; China from 1 to 4.1 percent; Taiwan from zero to 3.6 percent; Germany from 1.8 to 3.1 percent; the Netherlands from 2.5 to 2.9 percent; Hong Kong from 2 to 2.4 percent; and Britain from 1.2 to 2.2 percent. Indonesia, Central Bureau of Statistics, *Indikator Ekonomi*, 1992–93.

9. Peter Passell, "Economic Scene," *New York Times*, 2 December 1993.

10. In second industrial revolution industries, the U.S. advantage over Mexico was obvious. The U.S. steel industry produced nine times more than the Mexican, was more technologically advanced, concentrated on superior specialty steels versus Mexican semifinished varieties, and 1992 U.S. exports to Mexico exceeded imports from Mexico by $243 million. "NAFTA Sets Stage for Steel Success," *American Metal Market*, 8 June 1993, 14.

11. Michael Wines, "A 'Bazaar' Method of Dealing for Votes," *New York Times*, 11 November 1993.

12. "25 Years of Industrial Textiles," *Textile World* (September 1993): 79.

13. "NAFTA Math," *Automotive Industries* (March 1993): 19.

14. Thomas J. Lueck, "Businesses Say Most Jobs Now Exist in Industries Trade Pact Would Help," *New York Times*, 18 November 1993.

15. See "Springs Industry Says It Will Add 900 Jobs If NAFTA Is Enacted," *Daily News Record*, 7 May 1993, 3; "Concern for U.S. Jobs Key to NAFTA Battle," *Women's Wear Daily*, 11 August 1993, 22; "Prospects for U.S. Corn and Sorghum Under NAFTA," *Research Studies USDA-ERS-Feed* (May 1993): 24.

16. "Why NAFTA Will Benefit U.S. Telecommunications Equipment Manufacturers," *Telecommunications*, North American Edition (February 1993): 17.

17. "FACE OFF: Roger Miliken: NAFTA," *Women's Wear Daily*, 1 September 1993, 23.

18. "IMRA Mobilizes Support for Floundering NAFTA; Organized Labor Against Treaty; Congress to Decide," *Discount Store News*, 16 August 1993, 13; "TDA Votes Its Opposition to NAFTA, But Is Planning to Take No Action," *Women's Wear Daily*, 1 May 1993, 16; "The Pain and Gain of Trade," *U.S. News and World Report*, 28 September 1992, 62.

19. Peter T. Kilborn, "Pledging Retribution to Those Who Voted for Pact," *New York Times*, 19 November 1993.

20. "Trade Pact Job Gain Discounted," *New York Times*, 22 February 1993, C1.

21. Ibid.

22. Michael Wines, "Off Stage, Trade Pact Lobby Had a Star's Dressing Room," *New York Times*, 18 November 1993.

23. David E. Rosenbaum, "Clinton Musters a Majority for Trade Pact in the House After a Long Hunt for Votes," *New York Times*, 18 November 1993.

24. For background on chemical industry competitive pressures and lobbying promoting NAFTA, see "The Three Major Trade Areas—Key Figures for Total Industry and Chemicals and Pharmaceuticals 1991," *European Chemical News*, 12 October 1992, 14; "Without Borders," *Chemical Marketing Reporter*, 14 June 1993, SR24; "Mr. Clark Goes to Washington," *Chemical Week*, 1 August 1993, 6; "NAFTA: Proponents Find Unexpected Allies," *Chemical Week*, 22 September 1993, 16; "U.S.-Chemicals Nafta-Gewinner," *Nachrichten-für-Aussenhandel*, 13 October 1993, 1; "The Dealing: Worm-Killing Chemical Threatened Pact," *New York Times*, 18 November 1993.

25. "What the President Has Promised So Far," *New York Times*, 17 November 1993.

26. Keith Bradsher, "Clinton's Shopping List for Votes Has Ring of Grocery Buyer's List," *New York Times*, 17 November 1993.

27. Douglas Jehl, "Clinton Succeeds in Luring Some to Switch," *New York Times*, 17 November 1993.

28. Robert J.S. Ross and Kent C. Trachte, *Global Capitalism: The New Leviathan* (New York: State University of New York Press, 1990); "Opening the Borders," *Midrange Systems*, 9 February 1993, 17.

29. Douglas Jehl, "Mindful of Trade Pact, Clinton Recalls Peril of Isolationism After Great War," *New York Times*, 12 November 1993.

30. *Chemical Marketing Reporter*, 14 June 1993, SR 24.

Chapter 13. NAFTA: A Divisive Pact

1. R.W. Apple, Jr., "A High-Stakes Gamble That Paid Off," *New York Times*, 18 November 1993.

2. Gwen Ifill, "Clinton Would Protect Republicans Who Vote for Trade Pact," *New York Times*, 13 November 1993.

3. Peter T. Kilborn, "Little Voices Roar in the Chorus of Trade-Pact Foes," *New York Times*, 13 November 1993.

4. "Larry King Live," CNN, 10 November 1993.

5. David Rosenbaum, "Politics of the Trade Pact: A Lawmaker Who Is Torn," *New York Times*, 30 October 1993.

6. See "25 Years of Textile," *Textile World* (September 1993): 79; "Concern for U.S. Jobs Key to NAFTA Battle," *Women's Wear Daily*, 11 August 1993, 22.

7. Sylvia Nasar, "The High Cost of Protectionism," *New York Times*, 12 November 1993.

8. Tim Golden, "Trade Pact Approval May Hinge on Mexican Sugar," *New York Times*, 29 October 1993; Richard Krooth, assessment of the sugar lobbyists, Washington, D.C., December 1993; see also background data by Tim Josling, "NAFTA and Agriculture: A Review of the Economic Impacts," a paper presented at the Conferencia Universidad de California–Berkeley, 10 December 1992, and Food Research Institute, Stanford University, May 1992.

9. "Meat and Potatoes of NAFTA," *Meat Processing* (August 1993): 32.

10. David E. Rosenbaum, "Clinton Sweetens Trade Agreement," *New York Times*, 4 November 1993.

11. See "Prospects for U.S. Corn and Sorghum Under NAFTA," *Research*

Studies, USDA-ERS-Feed (May 1993): 24; Keith Bradsher, "Farmers and Trade Pact: Wheat vs. Corn," _New York Times_, 5 November 1993; see also Josling, "NAFTA and Agriculture," 10 December 1992.

12. Thomas L. Friedman, "Gore and Perot Are Set to Debate Trade Accord," _New York Times_, 5 November 1993.

13. David E. Rosenbaum, "White House Wants to Debate Perot on Trade," _New York Times_, 6 November 1993.

14. See Keith Bradsher, "Perot Stake Under Pact Is Not Clear," _New York Times_, 11 November 1993; "The Nafta Debate That Wasn't," editorial, _New York Times_, 11 November 1993.

15. Ibid.

16. David E. Rosenbaum, "White House Wants to Debate Perot on Trade," _New York Times_, 6 November 1993.

17. Peter T. Kilborn, "After a Town's Jobs Went South: A Program to Retrain Has Pitfalls," _New York Times_, 6 November 1993.

18. See "Broader Horizons for Free Trade," _Nation's Business_ (December 1993): 18; "NAFTA Backers Cite Rise of U.S. Exports to Mexico," _Nation's Business_ (October 1993): 8; "Why NAFTA Just Might Squeak Through," _Business Week_, industrial edition, 30 August 1993, 36; "NAFTA to Create Up to 170,000 U.S. Jobs," _PRS Automotive Service_, 28 July 1993; "NAFTA Should Oil Oilseed Industries," _International News on Fats, Oils and Related Materials_ (April 1993): 418; for background see Mary Burfisher, Sherman Robinson, and Karen Thierfelder, _Agricultural and Food Policies in a U.S.-Mexico Free Trade Area_, draft manuscript, 1992.

19. Anthony DePalma, "An Auto Sea Change in Mexico," _New York Times_, 16 November 1993; Richard Krooth, Interviews with Volkswagen auto workers in Puebla, January 1994.

20. _PRS Automotive Service_, 28 July 1993.

21. Anthony DePalma, "Painful Lessons for Mexican Labor," _New York Times_, 13 November 1993.

22. Quoted by Anthony Lewis, "If Nafta Loses," _New York Times_, 5 November 1993.

23. Gwen Ifill, "Evoking Kennedy, Clinton Pushes Trade Pact," _New York Times_, 31 October 1993.

24. "U.S. Companies Go to Bat for the Trade Agreement," _New York Times_, 2 November 1993.

25. Thomas L. Friedman, "Clinton Steps Up Campaign for Trade Accord," _New York Times_, 2 November 1993.

26. Tim Golden, "Mexican Trade Accord: Japanese Role Is Doubted," _New York Times_, 4 November 1993.

27. "The 'Great Debate' Over Nafta," editorial, _New York Times_, 9 November 1993.

28. A.M. Rosenthal, "Grovel and Pander," Op-Ed, _New York Times_, 9 November 1993.

29. Octavio Paz, "Why Incite Demagogy?" Op-Ed, _New York Times_, 9 November 1993.

30. Tom Hockin, "Side Agreements Keep Vital Interests in the Forefront," NAFTA advertisement, _New York Times_, 19 October 1993, C16.

31. John R. Funderburk and Jane Ginn, "Major Envirotech Market Awaits U.S. Investment," NAFTA advertisement, _New York Times_, 19 October 1993, C18.

32. Roger Schlickeisen, NAFTA advertisement, *New York Times*, 19 October 1993, C15.

33. Peggy L. Cuciti and Marshall Kaplan, "Getting Infrastructure Change Under Way," NAFTA advertisement, *New York Times*, 19 October 1993, C17.

34. Donald L. Connors, "What NAFTA Means to U.S. Environmental Firms," NAFTA advertisement, *New York Times*, 19 October 1993, C10; Francisco Javier Alejo Lopez, "The North American Environment Thrives on a Free Interchange of Peoples and Goods," NAFTA advertisement, *New York Times*, 19 October 1993, C17.

35. Connors, "What NAFTA Means," C10.

36. Funderburk and Ginn, "Major Envirotech Market," C18.

37. Dr. Santiago Ornate Laborde, "NAFTA and Pollution Controls," *New York Times* 19 October 1993, C18.

Chapter 14. The New Sphere of Influence

1. Tim Golden, "As U.S. Vote on Trade Pact Nears, Mexicans Are Expressing Doubts," *New York Times*, 8 November 1993; for background on Mexican sectoral interests see Dip. Hugo Andres Araujo, Secretario General, Confederación Campesina, *La reforma campesina* (Mexico: Unios Campesinos de America, December 1992).

2. B. Drummond Ayres, Jr., "Perot Ridicules Gore As Stand-in in Trade Debate," *New York Times*, 8 November 1993.

3. Gwen Ifill, "Clinton Is Critical of Labor on Trade," *New York Times*, 8 November 1993.

4. Francisco Javier Alejo Lopez, "The North American Environment Thrives on a Free Interchange of People and Goods," NAFTA advertisement, *New York Times*, 19 October 1993, C17.

5. "Fears on Nafta Lower Peso," *New York Times*, 10 November 1993. From January to mid–September 1994, the peso had depreciated about 10 percent against the dollar, without the political fallout of a big one-time devaluation. Anthony DePalma, "World Markets: Waiting for the Other Peso to Drop," *New York Times*, 18 September 1994; the peso plummeted in the closing 10 days in December. Richard Krooth, "Mexico in Crisis and the Twenty-first Century," manuscript, 1995.

6. Mike Espy, "Exports Are Key to Our Farmers' Future," NAFTA advertisement, *New York Times*, 19 October 1993, C16.

7. Dean Kleckner, "U.S. Farmers Serve Up Their Bounty," NAFTA advertisement, *New York Times*, 19 October 1993, C18.

8. See chapters 10 and 12; see also "NAFTA Should Oil Oilseed Industries," *International News on Fats, Oils and Related Materials* (April 1993): 418; "Meat and Potatoes of NAFTA," *Meat Processing* (August 1993): 32; "Prospects for U.S. Corn and Sorghum Under NAFTA," *Research Studies, USDA-ERS-Feed* (May 1993) 24; for background see Tim Josling, "NAFTA and Agriculture," 10 December 1992.

9. Dean Kleckner, "U.S. Farmers Serve Up Their Bounty," NAFTA advertisement, *New York Times*, 19 October 1993, C18.

10. William Safire, "Laughter After Nafta," *New York Times*, 21 October 1993.

11. Mike Espy, "Exports Are Key," C16.

12. Gwen Ifill, "Clinton Uses Japan to Sell Mexico Pact," *New York Times*, 21 October 1993.

13. Office of U.S. trade representative, Carla A. Hills, Provisional Staff Report, September 1992. Fax.

14. Andrew Rosenthal, "Bush Seeks a Lift from Trade Pact," *New York Times*, 8 October 1992.

15. Keith Bradsher, "Clinton and Congress Discuss 3-Year Test of Trade Pact," *New York Times*, 23 October 1993.

16. Gwen Ifill, "Turning Up Heat in Trade Campaign," *New York Times*, 3 November 1993.

17. Keith Bradsher, "Trade Pact Sale Relies on a Twist," *New York Times*, 7 November 1993.

18. Thomas L. Friedman, "Clinton Maintains U.S. Standing Rides on Trade Accord," *New York Times*, 7 November 1993; Hormat's statement is based on the sections of GATT that relate to subsidies [articles VI, XVI and XXII (1979)]; dumping [Article VI (1979)]; the Government Procurement Agreement (1979); Technical Barriers [GATT Standards Code (1979)]; and Customs Valuation [Article VII (1979)].

19. NAFTA advertisement, *New York Times*, 19 October 1993, C10.

20. Robert Reich, "Agreement to Be a Boon for U.S. Workers," The McLeod Group, NAFTA advertisement, *New York Times*, 19 October 1993, C10.

21. William M. Daley, "U.S. Jobs: Swept Away by the Competition or Saved with a Strategy," The McLeod Group, NAFTA advertisement, *New York Times*, 19 October 1993, C10.

22. Tim Golden, "Mexican Chief Calls Nafta a Test of U.S. Relations with the Region," *New York Times*, 19 October 1993; for past investment relations between the U.S. and Mexico compare NAFTA proposals with "Regulations of the Law to Promote Mexican Investment and Regulate Foreign Investment," *Diario oficial*, 16 May 1989.

Chapter 15. Political Boundaries, Unified Economy, and Maquiladoras

1. Exhibits, Museo Nacional de Antropología, Parque de Chapultepec, México, D.F.; Exhibits, Wisconsin Historical Society, Madison, Wisconsin, 1991-92; Nancy D. Sachse, *A Thousand Ages* (Madison: University of Wisconsin, 1965, 1–3; Krooth, *Arms and Empire*, 24; *International Labour Review* (November 1975): 352–53.

2. See chapters 1, 2; José E. Iturriaga, *La estructura social y cultural de México* (México, D.F.: Fondo de Cultura Económica, 1951), 33 et passim.

3. See *International Labor Review* (November 1975): 353; Harvey A. Levenstein, *Labor Organizations in the United States and Mexico* (Westport, Conn.: Greenwood, 1971), 204; *Aztlan* (Summer 1975, Summer 1981); Richard Krooth, *La raza tiene causa* (Madison, Wisc.: CAREP/Wisconsin Historical Society, 1965).

4. Richard Krooth, interviews, California, 1971–94; for background covering the pressures on the Mexican labor force, see Arturo Warman, "El destino del campesinado mexicano," paper presented at a conference, University of California-

Berkeley, 3-4 December 1992; Félix Vélez, "Los desafíos que enfrenta el campo en México," conference, University of California–Berkeley, California, 3-4 December 1992.

5. *Southwest Economy and Society* (Oct.-Nov. 1976): 11; Richard Krooth, *La raza*, 1–20; *International Labour Review* (November 1975): 357–62; *Hanson's Latin America Letter*, 31 July 1976, 1.

6. Krooth, interviews, Wisconsin and Michigan 1965–94; also compare Krooth, *La raza*; Peter T. Kilborn, "Tide of Migrant Labor Tells of a Law's Failure," *New York Times*, 4 November 1992.

7. The provision that the U.S. import duty on Mexican-based manufactures would only cover the "value added" by cheap Mexican workers to U.S. parts entering Mexico duty-free is: "Law to Promote Mexican Investment and to Regulate Foreign Investment," Chapter 1, Article 5(d), *Diario oficial*, 9 March 1973. Manufacturing in the periphery for export to the metropolis in part reversed traditional mercantile and colonial relations of production and trade. Dominant nations traditionally prohibited any manufacturing in the subjugated territories, limiting them to agriculture and mining for exports to the dominant nation. See Sir G.C. Lewis, *On the Government of Dependencies* (Oxford: Clarendon, 1841); Earl of Cromer (aka Lord Baring), *Ancient and Modern Imperialism* (New York: Longmans, Green, 1910).

8. Krooth, interviews, California, 1972–94. By government purpose or happenstance, this followed the classical British, German, and U.S. design of company towns that were designed to lower the price of labor by regulating labor's cost of living. See Richard Krooth, *The Great Homestead Strike* (Ph.D. diss., University of California at Santa Barbara, 1981).

9. See Jorge Eduardo Navarete, ed., *La política económica para 1972* (México, D.F.: Banco Nacional de Comercio Exterior [Mexico City], 1972), 127–28; Richard S. Weinert, "The State and Foreign Capital," in *Authoritarianism in Mexico*, eds. José Luis Reyna and Richard S. Weinert (Philadelphia: Institute for the Study of Human Issues, 1977), 120–22; see "Regulations of the Law...," *Diario oficial*, 16 May 1989.

10. Pedro-Pablo Kuczynski, "Real Relief for World Debt," *New York Times*, 24 August 1986.

11. Alexander Cockburn, "If Latin Nations Default, the Heavens Won't Fall," *Wall Street Journal*, 31 July 1986.

12. See Pedro-Pablo Kuczynski, "Real Relief for World Debt"; U.S. Tariff Regulation, items 806.30 and 807.00; see Trade Act of 1974, Public Law 93-618, approved 3 January 1975, U.S.C., paras. 2101–2487, 88 stat. 1978. For the historic context, see Richard Krooth, *Empire: A Bicentennial Appraisal* (Santa Barbara: Harvest, 1976); C. Daniel Dillman, "Assembly Industries in Mexico: Contexts of Development," *Journal of Interamerican Studies and World Affairs* 25 (February 1983): 38–42.

13. See *Excélsior*, 8 March 1975; *Comercio Exterior 1977*, 41; *Wall Street Journal*, 21 November 1975; *Business Latin America*, 1976, 62.

14. See *Wall Street Journal*, 21 November 1975; Donald W. Baerresen, "Unemployment and Mexico's Border Industrialization Program," *Inter-American Economic Affairs* 29, no. 2 (Autumn 1975): 81–82; *Comercio Exterior 1977*, 41; North American Congress on Latin America, "Hit and Run: U.S. Runaway Shops on the Mexican Border," *NACLA Report* 9, no. 5 (July/August 1975): 7; see chapters 16 17, 18 and Leslie Sklair, "The Maquila Industry and the Creation of a Transnational

Capitalist Class in the United States–Mexican Border Region," chapter in *Changing Boundaries in the Americas: New Perspectives on the U.S.-Mexican, Central American and South American Borders*, ed. Lawrence A. Herzog (La Jolla, California: University of California at San Diego, Center for the U.S.-Mexican Studies, 1992).

15. Richard Krooth, *The Dynamics of Enterprise in the American Milieu*, vol. 1, *History and Contemporary Patterns* (Berkeley, Calif.: CIM, 1986), 144.

16. *Mexican-American Review* (March 1975): 65.

17. James B. Pick, Edgar W. Butler, and Elizabeth L. Lanzer, *Atlas of Mexico* (Boulder, Colo.: Westview, 1989), 208, Table 7.4.

18. See Jorge Bustamente, *Maquiladoras: A New Face of International Capitalism in Mexico's Northern Frontier*, a paper presented at the Sixth National Meeting of the Latin American Studies Associated, Atlanta, Georgia, March 1976, 10–20; C. Daniel Dillman, *Mexico's Border Industrialization Program: Current Patterns and Alternative Futures*, a paper presented at the Sixth National Meeting of the Latin American Studies Association, Atlanta, Georgia, March 1976.

19. Pick, et al., 114, 115, Map 4.4.

20. Rebecca Morales and Jesús Tamayo, "Urbanization and Development of the United States–Mexican Border," chapter in *Changing Boundaries in the Americas*, 1992; Professor Robert H. Girling, oral account of trips to the borderlands, as told to Richard Krooth, 1993–94.

21. Pick, *Atlas*, 47.

22. Monterrey, together with seven other *municipios*, was the largest zone, with 2,279,980 people making up 21.3 percent of the borderland population. These cities were followed by the four *municipios* of Tijuana, Mexicali Enseñada, San Luis, and Río Grande in the Baja region in Northwest Sonora with 1,240,136, together making up 11.6 percent of the borderland population. Ranging below them were the *municipios* of Hermosilla, with 5 others, 927,362 (8.7 percent), Reynosa, with 5 others, 627,460 (5.9 percent), Torreón, with 3 others, 576,578 (5.4 percent), Juárez 567,360 (5.3 percent); Chihuahua 406,830 (3.8 percent); and Tampico and Ciudad Madero 400,401 (3.7 percent). Pick, *Atlas*, 50, Table 2.9.

23. Simcha Ronen, *Comparative and Multinational Management* (New York: John Wiley and Sons, 1986), Chapters 1–2.

24. John Holusha, "Trade Pact May Intensify Problems at Border," *New York Times*, 20 August 1992.

25. "Go Back to Mexico," *Frontline*, 14 June 1994.

Chapter 16. In the Domain of Each Nation

1. Gary Hufbauer, "Nafta: Friend or Foe?" *New York Times*, 15 November 1993.

2. Clyde H. Farnsworth, "Canada Votes in Election Today," *New York Times*, 25 October 1993.

3. Keith Bradsher, "U.S. Says Chrétien Will Not Undo Nafta," *New York Times*, 27 October 1993.

4. Timothy Egan, "New Canada Party Surges in Election," *New York Times*, 28 October 1993.

5. Clyde Farnsworth, "Canada Joins the World in Dumping Incumbent Leaders," *New York Times*, 31 October 1993.

6. Clyde H. Farnsworth, "Canada Links Trade Pact to an Accord on Subsidies," *New York Times*, 9 November 1993.

7. Clyde H. Farnsworth, "Canada's Cabinet to Be Pro-Trade," *New York Times*, 5 November 1993.

8. Clyde H. Farnsworth, "Governing Tories in Canada Ousted by Liberal Party," *New York Times*, 26 October 1993; Keith Bradsher, "U.S. Says Chrétien Will Not Undo Nafta," *New York Times*, 27 October 1993.

9. Clyde H. Farnsworth, "Chrétien Says He Will Insist on Changes in Trade Pact," *New York Times*, 28 October 1993; the *United States–Canada Free Trade Agreement Implementation Act of 1988* (Act Sept. 28, 1988, P.L. 100-49, 102 Stat. 1851, 19 U.S.C. 2112 note) gave United States law (both Federal and State) power of nullification of the agreement itself (Title I, Article 102). To secure its national interests, the *Investment Canada Act*, 30 June 1985 (Bill C-15, 1984) as amended by Bill C-2, 1988, encouraged foreign investments and resulting economic growth, but provided for review of significant investments in Canada by non–Canadians (Part IX), particularly those "related to Canada's cultural heritage or national identity. . . ." (Part IV 15). Any trade pact that opened the door to violate Canadian controls and oversight was politically vulnerable.

10. Clyde H. Farnsworth, "Effects on Trade Accord Are Seen from Canadian Voting Tomorrow," *New York Times*, 24 October 1993.

11. "Canada's Quarrel with Nafta," editorial, *New York Times*, 30 October 1993.

12. Tim Golden, "Mexico Planning to Loosen Foreign Investment Rules," *New York Times*, 26 November 1993.

13. Reuters (Ciudad de Mexico), 26 November 1993; Richard Krooth, "Mexico in Crisis and the Twenty-first Century," manuscript, 1995.

14. Tim Golden, "Mexican President Backs a Successor," *New York Times*, 29 November 1993.

15. Tim Golden, "U.S. and Mexico Wrestling Over Limits of Intervention," *New York Times*, 1 December 1993.

16. Sam Howe Verhovek, "San Antonio's Wild About Free Trade," *New York Times*, 15 November 1993.

17. Sam Howe Verhovek, "Trade Pact with Mexico Won't Ease a Crossing," *New York Times*, 30 November 1993.

18. Samuel Bowles and Mehrene Larudee, "A Low-Wage Game Plan," *New York Times*, 15 November 1993.

19. David E. Rosenbaum, "Beyond a Trade Pact," *New York Times*, 11 November 1993.

20. Anthony DePalma, "Mexican Stocks Soar After Nafta Debate," *New York Times*, 11 November 1993.

21. B. Drummond Ayres, Jr., "Perot Accuses Clinton of 'Buying' Trade Pact Votes," *New York Times*, 15 November 1993.

22. David E. Rosenbaum, "Both Sides Emphasize Stakes of the Trade Vote," *New York Times*, 15 November 1993.

23. Anthony DePalma, "Mexico Unloads State Companies, Pocketing Billions, but Hits Snags," *New York Times*, 27 October 1993.

24. Tim Golden, "Salinas Defends Government and Pledges Civility in Presidential Election Next Year," *New York Times*, 2 November 1993.

25. Anthony DePalma, "Mexico Unloads State Companies, Pocketing Billions, but Hits Snags."

Chapter 17. Democracy Led by a Few:
Government Frame for the New Order

1. Cosío Villegas, *El sistema político mexicano* (México: Joaquín Moritz, 1972), 70; Philip Agee, *Inside the Company: CIA Diary* (Harmondsworth, Middlesex: Penguin, 1975), 518.

2. Jorge Carrión, "Retablo de la política 'a la mexicana,'" in *El milagro mexicano*, 3d. ed. (México: Nuestro Tiempo, 1973), 206; Vincente Fuentes Díaz, *Los partidos políticos en México* (México: Editorial Altiplano, 1972), 386.

3. Tim Golden, "Mexico's Leader Cautiously Backs Some Big Changes," *New York Times*, 2 November 1992.

4. Rafael Segovia, "La reforma política," in *La vida política en México 1970–1973* (México: El Colegio de México, 1974), 57; Raymond Vernon, *The Dilemma of Mexico's Development* (Cambridge: Harvard University Press, 1963), 132–33.

5. Bo Anderson and James D. Cockcroft, "Control and Co-optation in Mexican Politics," in *Dependence and Underdevelopment* (Garden City: Anchor/Doubleday, 1972), 70; Cosío Villegas, *El sistema*, 1972, 70; Fuentes Díaz, *Los partidos*, 283; *Social Science Quarterly* (December 1975): 506.

6. Segovia, *La reforma*, 1974, 60–65.

7. Daniel Levy and Gabriel Székely, *Mexico: Paradoxes of Stability and Change*, 2d. ed. (Boulder, Colo.: Westview, 1987), 67–68, 258ff; Silvia Gómez Tagle, "Democracy and Power in Mexico: The Meaning of Conflict in the 1979, 1982 and 1985 Elections," in *Mexican Politics in Transition*, 161–70; Martin Needler, "The Significance of Recent Events for the Mexican Political System," in *Mexican Politics in Transition*, 208–11.

8. Fuentes Díaz, *Los partidos*, 346; *Excélsior*, 6 April 1976.

9. Soledad Loaeza, "El partido acción nacional: La oposición leal en México," in *La vida política en México 1970–1973* (México: Colegio de México, 1974), 108; *Siempre*, 29 April 1972; *Proceso*, 1 January 1977.

10. Agee, *CIA Diary*, passim; *Excélsior*, 21 March 1974, 20 September 1974, 25 March 1976; *Insurgencia popular* (November 1974): 19; (October 1975): 34–35.

11. Leslie H. Gelb, "Mexico's Economist Kings," *New York Times*, 4 October 1992.

12. These dissidents included Pablo Emilio Madero, the party's presidential candidate in 1982; Bernardo Bátiz, a former party secretary general; and Jesús González Schmal, a former secretary of the party leadership.

13. See *Excélsior*, 11–13 October 1992; Golden, "Mexican Opposition Party Split."

14. Barry Carr, "The Mexican Left, the Popular Movements and the Politics of Austerity 1982–1985," in *The Mexican Left, the Popular Movements, and the Politics of Austerity*, ed. by Barry Carr and Ricardo Anzaldúa Montoya (San Diego: Center for U.S.-Mexican Studies, 1986), 5–18.

15. *Excélsior*, 8–12 October 1992; Tim Golden, "A Real Political Pluralism in Mexico?" *New York Times*, 10 October 1992.

16. Cristina Pacheco, "Aquí y ahora" (México: Radio México), 1991–92; Cristina Pacheco, "Aquí nos tocó vivir" (México: TV México), 1991–92; see Levy and Székely, *Paradoxes*, 124; Needler, *Significance of Recent Events*, 202–3; Joseph L. Klesner, "Changing Patterns of Electoral Participation and Official Party Support in Mexico," in *Mexican Politics in Transition*, 97.

Chapter 18. The War on Civil Society

1. Based on Richard Krooth, "Mexico in Crisis and the Twenty-first Century," manuscript, 1995.

Chapter 19. Mexico in the Twenty-first Century

1. Based on Richard Krooth, "Mexico in Crisis and the Twenty-first Century," manuscript, 1995.

Bibliography

Agee, Philip. "Inside the Company: CIA Diary." Harmondsworth, Middlesex: Penguin, 1975.

Alamán, Lucas. *Historia de Méjico.* 5 vols. México: 1849–52.

American Metal Market (8 June 1993): 14.

Anderson, Bo, and James D. Cockcroft. "Control and Co-optation in Mexican Politics." *Dependence and Underdevelopment.* Garden City, N.Y.: Doubleday, 1972.

Apple, R.W., Jr. "Godfather to Pacific Era?" *New York Times,* 21 November 1993.

———. "A High-Stakes Gamble That Paid Off." *New York Times,* 18 November 1993.

Araujo, Dip. Hugo Andres, Secretario General. *La reforma campesina.* México: Confederación Nacional Campesina, December 1992.

Asensio, Luis Mendez. "Everyone Is Sure That Was a Plot." *World Press Review* (June 1994): 10.

Ayres, B. Drummond, Jr. "Perot Accuses Clinton of 'Buying' Trade Pact Votes." *New York Times,* 15 November 1993.

———. "Perot Ridicules Gore as Stand-in in Trade Debate." *New York Times,* 8 November 1993.

Azatlan (Summer 1975, Summer 1981).

Baerresen, Donald W. "Unemployment and Mexico's Border Industrialization Program." *Inter-American Economic Affairs* 29, no. 2 (Autumn 1975): 81–82.

Baird, Peter, and Ed McCaughan. "Labor and Imperialism in Mexico's Electrical Industry." *NACLA Report on the Americas* 11, no. 6 (September-October 1977): 35–38.

Baker, Russell. "Easy on That Cucumber." *New York Times,* 20 November 1993.

Balassa, Bela. *The Theory of Economic Integration.* London: Allen and Unwin, 1962.

Barkin, David. *Distorted Development: Mexico in the World Economy.* Boulder, Colo.: Westview, 1990.

———. *El uso de la tierra agricola en Mexico.* Center for U.S.-Mexican Studies. La Jolla: University of California at San Diego, 1981.

———, and Blanca Suárez. *El fin de la autosufficencia alimentaria.* México, D.F.: Nueva Imgen, 1982.

Bazant, Jan. *A Concise History of Mexico from Hidalgo to Cárdenas, 1804–1940.* London: Cambridge University Press, 1977.

Bergsten, C. Fred, Thomas Horst, and Theodore H. Moran. *American Multinationals and American Interests.* Washington, D.C.: Brookings Institute, 1978.

Beteta, Mario Rámon. "Government Policy Towards Foreign Investors, Mexico: A Statist Survey." *The Statist* (London), 8 January 1965.

Billington, Ray Allen. *American History Before 1877.* Paterson, N.J.: Littlefield, Adams, 1960.

Bogart, Ernest Ludlow. *The Economic History of the United States.* New York: Longmans Green, 1907.

Boorstein, Edward. *Allende's Chile: An Inside View.* New York: International, 1977.

Bosworth, Barry P., Robert Lawrence, and Nora Lustig, eds. *North American Free Trade.* Washington, D.C.: Brookings Institution, 1992.

Bowles, Sam, and Mehrene Larudee. "A Low-Wage Game Plan." Op-Ed, *New York Times,* 15 November 1993.

Bradsher, Keith. "Clinton and Congress Discuss 3-Year Test of Trade Pact." *New York Times,* 23 October 1993.

_____. "Clinton's Shopping List for Votes Has Ring of Grocery Buyer's List." *New York Times,* 17 November 1993.

_____. "Commerce Department in '91 Urged Move to Caribbean for Low Wages." *New York Times,* 10 November 1993.

_____. "Farmers and Trade Pact: Wheat vs. Corn." *New York Times,* 5 November 1993.

_____. "Perot Stake Under Pact Is Not Clear." *New York Times,* 11 November 1993.

_____. "Trade Pact Sale Relies on a Twist." *New York Times,* 7 November 1993.

_____. "U.S. Says Chrétien Will Not Undo Nafta." *New York Times,* 27 October 1993.

Brinkley, Joel. "A Success at the Border Earned Only a Shrug." *New York Times,* 14 September 1994.

Broad, Robin, and John Cavanagh. "No More NIC's." *Foreign Policy* (Fall 1988).

"Broader Horizons for Free Trade." *Nation's Business* (December 1992): 18.

Brotman, Stuart N. "Markets See Opportunity in NAFTA." *National Law Journal,* 7 March 1994, 31–34.

Burfisher, Mary, Sherman Robinson, and Karen Thierfelder. "Agricultural and Food Policies in a U.S.–Mexico Free Trade Area." Draft manuscript, 1992.

Business Latin America (1976): 62.

Bustamente, Jorge. "Maquiladoras: A New Face of International Capitalism in Mexico's Northern Frontier." Paper presented at the Sixth National Meeting of the Latin American Studies Association, Atlanta, Georgia, March 1976.

Campa, Homero. "Mexico's Guerrillas Shake the Nation." *World Press Review* (March 1994): 17.

"Canada's Quarrel with Nafta." Editorial, *New York Times,* 30 October 1993.

Carr, Barry. "The Mexican Left, the Popular Movements, and the Politics of Austerity 1982–1985." In *The Mexican Left, the Popular Movements, and the Politics of Austerity,* eds. Barry Carr and Ricardi Anzaldúa Montoya, 5–18. San Diego: Center for U.S.-Mexican Studies, 1986.

Carrión, Jorge. "Retablo de la política à la mexicana." In *El milagro mexicano.* 3d ed. Mexico City: Nuestro Tiempo, 1973.

Carroll, John E. "Environment, Free Trade, and Canadian-U.S. Relations." In *The Canadian-U.S. Relationship: The Politics of Energy and Environmental Coordination,* ed. Jonathan Lemco. Westport, Conn., and London: Praeger, 1992.

Chakravarthi, Raghavan. *Recolonization: GATT, the Uruguay Round and the Third World*. Penang, Malaysia: Third World Network, 1990.

Chemical Marketing Reporter, 14 June 1993, SR 24.

Chemical Week, 4 August 1992, 6.

Cherkaqoui, Said El Mansour. "A Mexican Perspective on the North American Free Trade Agreement: An Interview with Cuauhtémoc Cárdenas in Mexico City." *The Gateway*, San Francisco: Golden Gate University (July 1993).

Cockburn, Alexander. "If Latin Nations Default, the Heavens Won't Fall." *Wall Street Journal*, 31 July 1986.

Cohen, Roger. "Like U.S., West Europe Steps Up Its Asia Trade." *New York Times*, 24 November 1993.

————. "U.S. Seeks to Bring France into Trade Pact's Fold." *New York Times*, 4 December 1993.

Collins, Maurice. *Cortés and Montezuma*. New York: Avon Books, 1978.

Comercio Exterior (Mexico, D.F.), 1977, 41.

Commager, Henry Steele. *Documents of American History*, 7th ed. New York: Meredith, 1963.

"Concern for U.S. Jobs Key to NAFTA Battle." *Women's Wear Daily*, 11 August 1993, 22.

Connors, Donald L. "What NAFTA Means to U.S. Environmental Firms." NAFTA advertisement, *New York Times*, 19 October 1993.

Córdova, Arnaldo. "Mass Politics and the Future of the Left in Mexico." *Latin American Perspectives* 9, no. 1 (Winter 1982): 84.

Córdova, Carlos Acosta. "Bargaining on Our Knees." *World Press Review* (January 1994): 16.

Cornelius, Wayne A., and Jorge A. Bustamente, eds. *Mexican Migration to the United States: Origins, Consequences, and Policy Options*. Vol. 3 of *Dimensions of U.S.-Mexican Relations*. La Jolla, Calif.: University of California at San Diego, Center for U.S.-Mexican Studies, 1989.

Cuciti, Peggy L., and Marshall Kaplan. "Getting Infrastructure Change Under Way." NAFTA advertisement, *New York Times*, 19 October 1993.

Cumberland, Charles Curtis. *The Mexican Revolution: Genesis Under Madero*. New York: Greenwood Press, 1969.

————. *Mexico: The Struggle for Modernity*. New York: Oxford University Press, 1968.

Daily News Record, 4 May 1993, 4.

de Alcántara, Cynthia Hewitt, ed. *Economic Restructuring and Rural Subsistence in Mexico: Corn and the Crisis of the 1980s*. La Jolla, Calif.: University of California at San Diego, Center for U.S.-Mexican Studies, 1994.

"The Dealing: Worm-Killing Chemical Threatened Pact." *New York Times*, 18 November 1993.

de Anda, Gustavo Gordillo. "Dilemas de la Nueva Reforma Agraria." Conference on the Transformation of Mexican Agricultural Opportunities, Berkeley, Calif., 3–4 December 1992.

Delarbre, Trejo. "El movimiento obrero: Situación y perspectivas." In *México Hoy*, ed. Pablo Gonzáles Casanova and Enrique Flotescano. México, D.F.: Siglo Vientiuno Editores, 1979.

de la Rocha, Mercedes Gonzáles, and Agustín Escobar Latapí, eds. *Social*

Responses to Mexico's Economic Crisis of the 1980s. La Jolla, Calif.: University of California at San Diego, Center for U.S.-Mexican Studies, 1991.

del Rio, Daniel A. *Simón Bolívar*. Clinton, Mass.: Colonial Press, 1965.

DePalma, Anthony. "For Mexico's Indians, Promises Not Kept." *New York Times*, 15 June 1994.

————. "Mexican Stocks Soar After Nafta Debate." *New York Times*, 11 November 1993.

————. "Mexico Unloads State Companies, Pocketing Billions, but Hits Snags." *New York Times*, 27 October 1993.

————. "Painful Lessons for Mexican Labor." *New York Times*, 13 November 1993.

de Sahagún, Fray Bernardino. *Historia general de las cosas Nueva Espagna*. Vol. 3. México, 1830.

De Vore, Blanche B. *Land and Liberty: A History of the Mexican Revolution*. New York: Pageant, 1966.

de Zavala, Lorenzo. *Ensayo histórico de los revoluciones de México*. 2 vols. México, 1918.

DGEA. "Consomos aparentes de productos agrícolas 1925–1980." *Econotecnia agrícola* 5, no. 9 (1981): passim.

Díaz, Vincente Fuentes. "Los partidos políticos en México." México, D.F.: Editorial Altiplano, 1972.

Dillman, C. Daniel. "Assembly Industries in Mexico: Contexts of Development." *Journal of Interamerican Studies and World Affairs*, 25 February 1983, 38–42.

————. "Mexico's Border Industrialization Program: Current Patterns and Alternative Futures." Paper presented at the Sixth National Meeting of the Latin American Studies Association, Atlanta, Georgia, March 1976.

Earl of Cromer (a.k.a. Francis Baring). *Ancient and Modern Imperialism*. New York: Longmans, Green, 1910.

Economist Intelligence Unit. *Country Profiles: Mexico, 1981/82*, et seq. London: EIU, 1981–94.

Egan, Timothy. "New Canada Party Surges in Election." *New York Times*, 28 October 1993.

————. "The Pacific Summit." *New York Times*, 21 November 1993.

Emerson, Edwin, Jr. *A History of the Nineteenth Century Year by Year*. 3 vols. New York: P.F. Collier and Son, 1900.

"Energiesbranche setzt auf NAFTA." *Nachrichten-für-Aussenhandel*, 5 October 1993, 1.

Espy, Mike. "Exports Are Key to Our Farmers' Future." NAFTA advertisement, *New York Times*, 19 October 1993.

Estados Unidos Mexicanos, Poder Ejecutivo Federal. *Plan nacional de desarrollos 1989–1994*. Primera edición. México: Secretaría de Programación y Presupuesto, May 1989.

European Chemical News, 12 October 1992, 14.

Excélsior, 21 March 1974; 20 September 1974; 8 March 1975; 25 March 1976; 6 April 1976; 8–13 October 1992.

"FACE OFF: Roger Milliken: NAFTA." *Women's Wear Daily*, 1 September 1993, 23.

Farb, Peter. *Man's Rise to Civilization as Shown by the Indians of North America from Primeval Times to the Coming of the Industrial State*. New York: E.P. Dutton, 1968.

Farnsworth, Clyde H. "Canada Joins the World in Dumping Incumbent Leaders." *New York Times*, 31 October 1993.

————. "Canada Links Trade Pact to an Accord on Subsidies." *New York Times*, 9 November 1993.

_____. "Canada Votes in Election Today." *New York Times*, 25 October 1993.

_____. "Canada's Cabinet to Be Pro-Trade." *New York Times*, 5 November 1993.

_____. "Chrétien Says He Will Insist on Changes in Trade Pact." *New York Times*, 28 October 1993.

_____. "Effects on Trade Accord Are Seen from Canadian Voting Tomorrow." *New York Times*, 24 October 1993.

_____. "Governing Tories in Canada Ousted by Liberal Party." *New York Times*, 26 October 1993.

"Fears on Nafta Lower Peso." *New York Times*, 10 November 1993.

Fogel, Daniel. *Junípero Serra, the Vatican and Enslavement Theology.* San Francisco: Ism Press, 1988.

Fraser, Damian. "Mexico's Crisis Campaign." *Financial Times* (June 1994): 9.

Friedland, William H. *The New Globalization: The Case of Fresh Produce.* Santa Cruz: University of California at Santa Cruz, June 1991.

Friedman, Thomas L. "Clinton Maintains U.S. Standing Rides on Trade Accord." *New York Times*, 7 November 1993.

_____. "Clinton Steps Up Campaign for Trade Accord." *New York Times*, 2 November 1993.

_____. "Gore and Perot Are Set to Debate Trade Accord." *New York Times*, 5 November 1993.

Fuentes, Carlos. *La jornada*, 20 August 1994.

Funderburk, John R., and Jane Ginn. "Major Envirotech Market Awaits U.S. Investment." NAFTA advertisement, *New York Times*, 19 October 1993.

Galan, Hector. *The American Experience: Looking at Pancho Villa's 1916 Raid on New Mexico and U.S. Efforts to Track Him Down.* PBS (KQED), Boston, Galan Production, GDH, 3 November 1993.

Galbraith, John Kenneth. *A Short History of Financial Euphoria.* New York: Viking, 1993.

Gelb, Leslie. "Mexico's Economist Kings." *New York Times*, 4 October 1993.

General Agreement on Tariffs and Trade (GATT). Articles VI, VII, XVI, XXII (1979); Government Procurement Agreement (1979); Standards Code (1979).

"Go Back to Mexico." *Frontline*. PBS, San Francisco, 14 June 1994.

Golden, Tim. "As U.S. Vote on Trade Pact Nears, Mexicans Are Expressing Doubts." *New York Times*, 8 November 1993.

_____. "Back of the New Mall—Old Ritual Slaughter." *New York Times*, 1 November 1993.

_____. "Mexican Chief Calls Nafta a Test of U.S. Relations with the Region." *New York Times*, 19 October 1993.

_____. "Mexican Opposition Party Split by Identity Crisis and Altered Role." *New York Times*, 11 October 1992.

_____. "Mexican President Backs a Successor." *New York Times*, 29 November 1993.

_____. "Mexican Trade Accords: Japanese Role Is Doubted." *New York Times*, 4 November 1993.

_____. "Mexico Planning to Loosen Foreign Investment Rules." *New York Times*, 26 November 1993.

_____. "Mexico's Leader Cautiously Backs Some Big Changes." *New York Times*, 2 November 1992.

_____. "A Real Political Plurism in Mexico?" *New York Times*, 10 October 1992.

_____. "Salinas Defends Government and Pledges Civility in Presidential Election Next Year." *New York Times*, 2 November 1993.

_____. "Salinas's Chosen Path: Peace and Progress Too." *New York Times*, 4 March 1994.

_____. "Trade Pact Approval May Hinge on Mexican Sugar." *New York Times*, 29 October 1993.

_____. "U.S. and Mexico Wrestling Over Limits of Intervention." *New York Times*, 1 December 1993.

Goldschlager, Seth, and Dominique Jacomet. "Business Be Wary of New Trade Group." *New York Times*, 29 January 1995.

Gordon, Michael W. "The Contemporary Mexican Approach to Growth with Foreign Investment: Controlled but Participatory Independence," 10 *California Western Law Review* 1 (1973).

Great Britain, House of Commons. Parliamentary Debates, 23 March 1938, vol. 333.

"The 'Great Debate' Over Nafta." Editorial, *New York Times*, 9 November 1993.

Hanke, Lewis. *Aristotle and the American Indian: A Study of Race Prejudice in the Modern World.* London: Hollis and Carter, 1959.

_____. "The New Laws—Another Analysis." In *Indian Labor in the Spanish Indies*, ed. John Francis Bannon. Boston: D.C. Heath, 1966.

Hansen's Latin American Letter. 31 July 1976, 1–2.

Harvey, Neil. *Rebellion in Chiapas: Rural Reforms, Campesino Radicalism, and the Limits to Salinismo.* La Jolla, Calif.: University of California at San Diego, Center for U.S.-Mexican Studies, 1995.

Henrick, Burton J. *The Life and Letters of Walter P. Page.* Vol. 1. Boston: Houghton Mifflin, 1922.

Herbert, Bob. "Nafta and the Elite." Op-Ed, *New York Times*, 10 November 1993.

Herzog, Lawrence A., ed. *Planning the International Border Metropolis.* La Jolla, Calif.: University of California at San Diego, Center for U.S.-Mexican Studies, 1986.

Hockin, Tom. "Side Agreements Keep Vital Interests in the Forefront." NAFTA advertisement, *New York Times*, 19 October 1993.

Holusha, John. "Trade Pact May Intensify Problems at Border." *New York Times*, 20 August 1992.

"Holy Office." 12th Annual Jewish Film Festival. Berkeley, Calif.: U.A. Theater, 30 July 1992.

Hufbauer, Gary. "Nafta: Friend or Foe?" Op-Ed, *New York Times*, 15 November 1993.

Husain, S. Shahid. "Getting the NAFTA Debate Back on Track." NAFTA advertisement, *New York Times*, 19 October 1993.

Ifill, Gwen. "Clinton Is Critical of Labor on Trade." *New York Times*, 8 November 1993.

_____. "Clinton Uses Japan to Sell Mexico Pact." *New York Times*, 21 October 1993.

_____. "Clinton Would Protect Republicans Who Vote for Trade Pact." *New York Times*, 13 November 1993.

_____. "Evoking Kennedy, Clinton Pushes Trade Pact." *New York Times*, 31 October 1993.

_____. "Turning Up Heat in Trade Campaign." *New York Times*, 3 November 1993.

"IMRA Mobilizes Support for Floundering NAFTA: Organized Labor Against Treaty: Congress to Decide." *Discount Store News*, 16 August 1993, 13.

Insurgencia popular (November 1974): 19; (October 1975): 34–35.

International Commission of Jurists. *Cuba and the Rule of Law*. Geneva: International Commission of Jurists, 1962.

International Labour Review (November 1975): 352–62.

International Monetary Fund. *Monthly Statistics*. New York: IMF, 1961–94.

"Interview: Mexico's hottest industry: Human rights work grows as the Mexican economy liberalizes." *Dollars & Sense* (January/February 1993): 16–17.

Iturriaga, José E. *La estructura social y cultural de México*. México, D.F.: Fondo de Cultura Económica, 1951.

Jehl, Douglas. "Clinton Seeks to Direct His Campaign for Trade Accord at Working People." *New York Times*, 10 November 1993.

————. "Mindful of Trade Pact, Clinton Recalls Peril of Isolationism After Great War." *New York Times*, 12 November 1993.

Johnston, William R. "Global Work Force 2000: The New World Labor Market." *Harvard Business Review* (March/April 1991).

Josling, Tim. "NAFTA and Agriculture: A Review of the Economic Impacts." Conference on the Transformation of Mexican Agricultural Opportunities, Berkeley, Calif., 3-4 December 1992; and Food Research Institute, Stanford University, May 1992.

Kennedy, Paul. *Preparing for the Twenty-First Century*. New York: Random House, 1993.

Kilborn, Peter T. "After a Town's Jobs Went South: A Program to Retrain Has Pitfalls." *New York Times*, 6 November 1993.

————. "Little Voices Roar in the Chorus of Trade-Pact Foes." *New York Times*, 13 November 1993.

————. "Pledging Retribution to Those Who Voted for the Pact." *New York Times*, 19 November 1993.

————. "Tide of Migrant Labor Tells of a Law's Failure." *New York Times*, 4 November 1992.

Kirk, Betty. *Covering the Mexican Front*. Norman: University of Oklahoma Press, 1942.

Kleckner, Dean. "U.S. Farmers Serve Up Their Bounty." NAFTA advertisement, *New York Times*, 19 October 1993.

Klesner, Joseph L. "Changing Patterns of Electoral Participation and Official Party Support in Mexico." In *Mexico in Transition*, ed., Judith Gettleman. Boulder, Colo.: Westview, 1987.

Krebs, A.V. *The Corporate Reapers: The Book of Agribusiness*. Washington, D.C.: Essential Books, 1992.

Krooth, Richard. "Analysis of Mexican Census Figures for 1980 and 1990, and Preliminary Data 1993." Berkeley, Calif.: Unpublished manuscript, 1994.

————. *Arms and Empire: Imperial Patterns Before World War I*. Santa Barbara: Harvest, 1981.

————, ed. *The Dynamics of Enterprise in the American Milieu*. Vol. 1, *History and Contemporary Patterns*. Berkeley, Calif.: CIM, 1986.

————. *Empire: A Bicentennial Appraisal*. Santa Barbara: Harvest, 1976.

————. "The Great Homestead Strike: A Classic Industrial Conflict." Ph.D. diss., University of California at Santa Barbara, 1981.

_____. Interviews in Mexico, July 1992, December 1993–January 1994.

_____. Interviews with Volkswagen Auto Workers in Puebla, January 1994.

_____. Journals: travels in Tuxpan, Mexico, December 1993–January 1994.

_____. "Mexico in Crisis and the Twenty-first Century." Manuscript, 1995.

_____. *La raza tiene causa.* Madison, Wisc.: CAREP/Wisconsin Historical Society, 1965.

_____. Travels in Mexico, 1985, 1987, 1990, 1992, 1993, 1994.

_____. Travels in the North Central Gulf Region of Mexico, December 1993–January 1994.

_____, and Hiroshi Fukurai. *Common Destiny: Japan and the United States in the Global Age.* Jefferson, N.C.: McFarland, 1990.

Kuczynski, Pedro-Pablo. "Real Relief for World Debt." *New York Times,* 24 August 1986.

Laborde, Dr. Santiago Ornate. "NAFTA and Pollution Controls." Cited in NAFTA advertisement, *New York Times,* 19 October 1993, C18.

"Larry King Live." CNN, 10 November 1993.

Lecky, E.H. *History of the Rise and Influence of the Spirit of Rationalism in Europe.* New York: George Braziller, 1955.

Levenstein, Harvey A. *Labor Organizations in the United States and Mexico.* Westport, Conn.: Greenwood, 1971.

Levitt, Theodore. "The Globalization of Markets." *Harvard Business Review* (May 1983).

Levy, Daniel, and Gabriel Székeley. *Mexico: Paradoxes of Stability and Change.* 2d ed. Boulder, Colo.: Westview, 1987.

Lewis, Anthony. "If Nafta Loses." *New York Times,* 5 November 1993.

Lewis, G.C. *On the Government of Dependencies,* ed. C.P. Lucas. Oxford, England: Clarendon, 1841.

Loaeza, Soledad. "El Partido Acción Nacional: La oposición legal en México." In *La vida política en México 1970–1973.* México, D.F.: Colegio de México, 1974.

Lopez, Francisco Javier Alejo. "The North American Environment Thrives on a Free Interchange of People and Goods." NAFTA advertisement, *New York Times,* 19 October 1993.

Lueck, Thomas J. "Businesses Say Most Jobs Now Exist in Industries Trade Pact Would Help." *New York Times,* 18 November 1993.

Lustig, Nora. *Mexico: The Remaking of an Economy.* Washington, D.C.: Brookings Institution, 1992.

McCall, Andrew. *The Medieval World.* New York: Barnes & Noble, 1979.

McCullagh, Captain Francis. *Red Mexico: A Reign of Terror in America.* New York: Louis Carrier, 1928.

"McNeil/Lehrer NewsHour." PBS, 8 November 1993.

"Mapa de grupos indígenas de México." In *México indígena, INI 30 años despues revisión crítica,* Organo de Difusión del Instituto Nacional Indigenista. México, D.F., December 1978.

Mares, David. *The Evolution of U.S. Mexican Agricultural Relations: The Changing Roles of the Mexican State and Mexican Agricultural Producers.* La Jolla: University of California at San Diego, Center for U.S.-Mexican Studies, 1981.

Masur, Sandra. "The North American Free Trade Agreement: Why It's in the Interest of U.S. Business." *Columbia Journal of World Business* (Summer 1991).

"Meat and Potatoes of NAFTA." *Meat Processing* (August 1993): 32.

"Mensaje del presidente de la república." In *México indígena, INI 30 años despues revisión crítica*, Organo de Difusión del Instituto Nacional Indigenista. Mexico, D.F.: December 1978.

Mexican-American Review (March 1975): 65.

Mexico. *Constitución de México*. México, D.F.: 5 February 1919.

Mexico. *Law to Promote Mexican Investment and to Regulate Foreign Investment*, 7 February 1973. *Diario oficial*, 9 March 1973.

Mexico. *Mexican Census, 1990*. Mexico, D.F.: 1993.

Mexico. *Regulations of the Law to Promote Mexican Investment and Regulate Foreign Investment. Diario Oficial*, 16 May 1989.

Mexico. Secretaría de Agricultura y Granadería. Statistics on daily meat consumption, 1970–75.

Mexico. Secretaría de Programación y Presupuesto. Statistics on meat consumption, 1975–85.

Mexico, Nacional Financiera. Internal Office Memorandum, 1951 et seq.

"Mexico's Choice." Editorial, *New York Times*, 23 August 1994.

Meyer, Lorenzo. "A New Chapter in Mexican Politics?" *World Press Review* (January 1994): 14–15.

Michener, James A. *Mexico*. New York: Random House, 1992.

Millman, Joel. "Craig McCaw del sur." *Forbes*, 11 April 1994, 56–57.

"Mr. Clark Goes to Washington." *Chemical Week*, 1 August 1993, 6.

Mohr, Anton. "The Oil War." Diss., Columbia University, 1932.

Montañez, Carlos, and Horacio Aburto. *Maíz: Política institucional y crisis agrícola*. México: D. F. Nueva Imagen, 1979.

Morales, Rebecca, and Jesús Tamayo. "Urbanization and Development of the United States–Mexican Border." In *Changing Boundaries in the Americas: New Perspectives on the U.S.-Mexican, Central American, and South American Borders*. Lawrence A. Herzog, ed. La Jolla, Calif.: University of California at San Diego, Center for U.S.-Mexican Studies, 1992.

Muggah, Mary Gates, and Paul H. Raihle. "Early History [re: Azatlan]." In *Forty-Seven Wisconsin Stories*. Chippew Falls, Wisc.: Chippew Falls Book Agency, 1944.

Murphy, R. Taggart. "Power Without Purpose: The Crisis of Japan's Global Financial Dominance." *Harvard Business Review* (March/April 1989).

Museo Nacional de Antropología. México, D.F., Parque de Chapultepec: 1992.

"Nafta: Proponents Find Unexpected Allies." *Chemical Week* (22 September 1993): 16.

"Nafta Backers Cite Rise of U.S. Exports to Mexico." *Nation's Business* (October 1993): 8.

"The Nafta Debate That Wasn't." Editorial, *New York Times*, 11 November 1993.

"Nafta Math." *Automotive Industries* (March 1993): 19.

"Nafta Sets Stage for Steel Success." *American Metal Market* (8 June 1993): 14.

"Nafta Should Oil Oilseed Industries." *International News on Fats, Oils and Related Materials* (April 1993): 418.

"Nafta to Create Up to 170,000 U.S. Jobs." *PRS Automotive Service* (28 July 1993).

Nasar, Sylvia. "The High Cost of Protectionism." *New York Times*, 12 November 1993.

————. "Third World Embracing Reforms to Encourage Economic Growth." *New York Times*, 8 July 1990.

Navarete, Jorge Eduardo, ed. *La política económica para 1972*. México, D.F.: Banco Nacional de Comercio Exterior, 1972.

Needler, Martin. "The Significance of Recent Events for the Mexican Political System." In *Mexican Politics in Transition*, ed. Judith Gettleman. Boulder, Colo.: Westview, 1987.

Nolasco, Margarita A., comp. *Aspectos sociales de la migración en México*. Vol. 2. México: Instituto National de Antropología e Historia, Departmento de Proyectos Especiales de Investigación, 1979.

North American Congress on Latin America. Assorted publications (1978–94).

_____. "Hit and Run: U.S. Runaway Shops on the Mexican Border." *NACLA Report* 9, no. 5 (July/August 1975): 7.

Oakland Museum. "Exhibit: The Spanish in California." Oakland, Calif., 1992-94.

O'Brien, Richard. *Global Financial Integration: The End of Geography*. New York: Council on Foreign Relations Press, 1992.

Oficina de Asesores del Presidente. Reports. México, D.F.: OSP, March 1980, May 1980, December 1980.

Ogarrio, N., and Pereznieto Castro. "Mexico–United States Relations: Economic Integration and Foreign Investment." 12 *Houston Journal of International Law* 223 (1990).

Ohmae, Kenichi. *The Borderless World: Power and Strategy in the Interlinked Economy*. New York: Harper Business, 1990.

"Opening the Borders." *Midrange Systems* (9 February 1993): 17.

Orme, William A., Jr. "The NAFTA Debate, Myths Versus Fact." *Foreign Affairs* (November/December 1993): 2–3.

Oye, Kenneth A. *Economic Discrimination and Political Exchange: World Political Economy in the 1930's and 1980's*. Princeton: Princeton University Press, 1992.

Pacheco, Cristina. "Aquí nos tocó vivir" (We Happen to Live Here). TV Mexico, 1990–94.

_____. "Aquí y ahora" (Here and Now). Radio México, 1990–94.

_____. *Para vivir aquí*. México, D.F.: Colección Divulgación, 1985.

_____. *Zona de desastres*. México, D.F.: Colección Divulgación, 1987.

"The Pain and Gain of Trade." *U.S. News and World Report*, 28 September 1992, 62.

Passell, Peter. "Economic Scene." *New York Times*, 18 November 1993.

_____. "Economic Scene." *New York Times*, 2 December 1993.

Pastor, Robert A. "NAFTA As Center of Integration Process." In *North American Free Trade*, eds. Nora Lustig, Barry P. Bosworth, and Robert Z. Lawrence. Washington, D.C.: Brookings Institution, 1992.

Paz, Octavio. "Why Incite Demagogy?" Op-Ed, *New York Times*, 9 November 1993.

Perot, Ross. "Larry King Live." CNN, 10 November 1993.

Pick, James B., Edgar W. Butler, and Elizabeth L. Lanzer. *Atlas of Mexico*. Boulder, Colo.: Westview, 1989.

Policy Research Committee, Committee for Economic Development. *Defense Against Inflation: Policies for Price Stability in a Growing Economy*. New York: CED, July 1958.

Porter, Michael E. *The Competitive Advantage of Nations*. New York: Free Press, 1990.

Portillo, José López. "State of the Nation Address, 1 September 1982." México, D.F.: Poder Ejecutivo Federal, 1982.

Proceso (México, D.F.), 1 January 1977.

"Prospects for U.S. Corn and Sorghum Under NAFTA." *Research Studies, USDA-ERS-Feed* (May 1993): 24.

Rama, Ruth and Raúl Vigorito. *El complejo y frutas y legumbres en México.* México, D.F.: Nueva Imagen, 1979.

_____, and Fernando Rello. "La internacionalización de la agricultura." Unpublished manuscript, 1980.

Redclift. "Agrarian Populism in Mexico—The 'Via Campesina.'" *Journal of Peasant Studies* 7, No. 4 (July 1980).

Reed, Nelson. *The Caste War of Yucatán.* Stanford, Calif.: Stanford University Press, 1964.

Reich, Robert. "Agreement to Be a Boon for U.S. Workers." The McLeod Group, NAFTA advertisement, *New York Times*, 19 October 1993.

_____. *The Work of Nations.* New York: Knopf, 1991.

Reissner, Raul Alcides. *El indio en los diccionarios: Exegesis léxica de un estereotipo.* Serie de Antropologá, Social Colección Número 67. México, D.F.: Instituto Nacional Indigenista, n.d.

Reuters (Ciudad de México). *Wire Service.* 26 November 1993.

Ronen, Simcha. *Comparative and Multinational Management.* New York: John Wiley and Sons, 1986.

Ronson, Paul. *The Economics of International Integration.* 2d ed. London: Allen and Unwin, 1984.

Rosenbaum, David E. "Beyond a Trade Pact." *New York Times,* 11 November 1993.

_____. "Both Sides Emphasize Stakes of the Trade Vote." *New York Times,* 15 November 1993.

_____. "Clinton Musters a Majority for Trade Pact in the House After a Long Hunt for Votes." *New York Times,* 18 November 1993.

_____. "Clinton Sweetens Trade Agreement." *New York Times,* 4 November 1993.

_____. "Politics of the Trade Pact: A Lawmaker Who Is Torn." *New York Times,* 30 October 1993.

_____. "White House Wants to Debate Perot on Trade." *New York Times,* 6 November 1993.

Rosenthal, A.M. "Grovel and Pander." Op-Ed, *New York Times,* 9 November 1993.

Rosenthal, Andrew. "Bush Seeks a Lift from Trade Pact." *New York Times,* 8 October 1992.

Ross, John. *Rebellion from the Roots: Indian Uprising in Chiapas.* Monroe, Maine: Common Courage Press, 1995.

Ross, Robert J.S., and Kent C. Trachte. *Global Capitalism: The New Leviathan.* New York: State University of New York Press, 1990.

Rostow, Walt W. "The Stages of Economic Growth." *Economic History Review* (August 1959).

Rydell, Robert W. *All the World's a Fair.* Chicago: University of Chicago Press, 1984.

Safire, William. "Laughter After Nafta." Op-Ed, *New York Times,* 21 October 1993.

Salinas de Gortari, President Carlos. *State of the Union Address.* 1 November 1992.

Sallot, Jeff. "A Man for Some Seasons: Ernesto Zedillo." *World Press Review* (June 1994): 10.

Sanderson, Steven E. *The Receding Frontier: Aspects of the Internationalization of U.S.-Mexican Agriculture and Their Implications for Bilateral Relations in the 1980s.* La Jolla, Calif.: University of California at San Diego, Center for U.S.-Mexican Studies, 1981.

_____. *Trade Aspects of the Internationalization of Mexican Agriculture: Consequences for Mexico's Food Crisis*. La Jolla, Calif.: University of California at San Diego, Center for U.S.-Mexican Studies, 1981.

Sanger, David E. "Salesman in Chief." *New York Times*, 21 November 1993.

SARH-CEPAL. *Productores del sector social rural en Mexico*. La Jolla, Calif.: University of California at San Diego, Center for U.S.-Mexican Studies, 1990-91.

Scott, David Clark. "Mexican Domestic Events Slow NAFTA's Start-Up." *Christian Science Monitor*, 20 April 1994.

Segovia, Rafael. "La reforma política." *La vida política en méxico 1970–1973*. México, D.F.: El Colegio de México, 1974.

Shaiken, Harley. "Transferring High Tech Production to Mexico." *Columbia Journal of World Business* (Summer 1991).

_____. *Work Transformed: Automation and Labor in the Computer Age*. New York: Holt, Rinehart & Winston, 1985.

Shenon, Philip. "Boycott in Order, Malaysia Says." *New York Times*, 21 November 1993.

Siempre, 29 April 1972.

Sierra, Justo. *Obras completas*, vol. 1, *Juárez, su obra y su tiempo*. México: 1948.

SINE-SAM. *Sistema alimentario mexicana: Evaluación 1981 and 1982*. México, D.F.: SINE-SAM, 1982.

Sklair, Leslie. "The Maquila Industry and the Creation of a Transnational Capitalist Class in the United States–Mexican Border Region." In *Changing Boundaries in the Americas: New Perspectives on the U.S.-Mexican, Central American, and South American Borders*. Lawrence A. Herzog, ed. La Jolla, Calif.: University of California at San Diego, Center for U.S.-Mexican Studies, 1992.

Smith, Adam. *An Inquiry into the Nature and Causes of the Wealth of Nations*. New York: Modern Library, 1937.

Smsyer, Col. Willis M. *The Evolution of U.S. Foreign Policy* (Document AD 241-578, unclassified). Arlington, Va.: Armed Services Technical Information Agency, 1960.

The Social Economic Union of Cuba. *Commercial Relations Between Cuba and the United States of America*. Havana: SEUC, 1936.

Social Science Quarterly (December 1975).

Southwest Economy and Society (October-November 1976): 11.

Stevens, Guy. *Current Controversies with Mexico: Addresses and Writings*. New York: Foreign Policy Association, 1926.

Suárez, Luis. *Echeverría en el sexenio de López Portillo: El caso de un expresidente ante el sucesor*. 3d ed. México: Política Mexicana, 1983.

Suárez y Suárez, Manuel. *Polyforum cultural siqueiros*. México, D.F.: El Hotel de México y el Polyforum Cultural Siqueiros, Ciudad de México, 1992.

Tagle, Silvia Gómez. "Democracy and Power in Mexico: The Meaning of Conflict in the 1979, 1982 and 1985 Elections." *Mexican Politics in Transition*, ed. Judith Gettleman. Boulder, Colo.: Westview, 1987.

Tannenbaum, Frank. *Peace by Revolution: An Interpretation of Mexico*. New York: Columbia University Press, 1933.

"TDA Votes Its Opposition to NAFTA, but Is Planning to Take No Action." *Women's Wear Daily*, 1 May 1993, 16.

"The three major trade areas—key figures for total industry and chemicals and pharmaceuticals 1991." *European Chemical News* (12 October 1992): 14.

Townsend, William Careron. *Lázaro Cárdenas, Mexican Democrat.* Ann Arbor, Mich.: George Wahr, 1952.

Tucker, Irwin St. John. *A History of Imperialism.* New York: Rand School of Social Science, 1920.

Tutino, John M. "Provincial Spaniards, Indian Towns, and Haciendas: Inter-related Agrarian Sectors in the Valleys of Mexico and Toluca, 1750–1810." In *Provinces of Early Mexico: Variants of Spanish American Regional Evolution.* Los Angeles: UCLA Latin American Center Publications, 1976.

"Twenty-Five Years of Industrial Textiles." *Textile World* (September 1993): 79.

Ungar, Stanford J. *Estrangement: America and the World.* Oxford: Oxford University Press, 1985.

United States. Congress. Senate. Banking Committee. *Hearings,* 24 May 1995. Washington, D.C.: U.S. Government Printing Office, 1995.

_____. _____. _____. *Senate Document,* vols. 9, 10. 66th Congress, 2d Session. Washington, D.C.: U.S. Government Printing Office, 1916.

_____. Office of U.S. Trade Representative Carla A. Hill. *Provisional Staff Report.* Fax. Washington, D.C.: September 1992.

_____. State Department. *Foreign Relations of the United States.* Washington, D.C.: U.S. Government Printing Office, 1914.

_____. _____. *Foreign Relations of the United States.* Washington, D.C.: U.S. Government Printing Office, 1944.

_____. *Tariff Regulation. Items 806.30, 807.00.* Washington, D.C.: U.S. Government Printing Office, 1965 et seq.

"U.S. Companies Go to Bat for the Trade Agreement." *New York Times,* 2 November 1993.

U.S. *Trade Act of 1974.* Public law 93-618, approved 3 January 1975, U.S.C., paras. 2101–2487, 88 stat. 1978.

"US-chemia als Nafta-Gewinner." *Nachrichten-für-Aussenhandel,* 13 October 1993, 1.

Vélez, Félix. "Los desafios que enfrenta el campo en México." Conference on the Transformation of Mexican Agricultural Opportunities, Berkeley, Calif., 3-4 December 1992.

Verhovek, Sam Howe. "San Antonio Wild About Free Trade." *New York Times,* 15 November 1993.

_____. "Trade Pact with Mexico Won't Ease a Crossing." *New York Times,* 30 November 1993.

Vernon, Raymond. *The Dilemma of Mexico's Development.* Cambridge: Harvard University Press, 1963.

Villegas, Cosío. *El sistema político mexicano.* México, D.F.: Joaquín Moritz, 1972.

Viner, Jacob. *The Customs Unions Issue.* New York: Macmillan, 1950.

Wallerstein, Immanuel. *The Modern World-System: Capitalist Agriculture and the Origins of the European World-Economy of the Sixteenth Century.* New York: Academic Press, 1974.

Walling, William English. *The Mexican Question.* New York: Macmillan, 1927.

Warman, Arturo. "El destino del campesinado mexicano." Conference on the Transformation of Mexican Agricultural Opportunities, Berkeley, Calif., 3-4 December 1992.

Waterworth, James A. "The Conflict Historically Considered." In *The Great Social Struggle,* vol. 2, ed. Richard Krooth. Santa Barbara, Calif.: Harvest, 1982.

Weinert, Richard S. "The State and Foreign Capital." In *Authoritarianism in Mexico*, eds. José Luis Reyna and Richard S. Weinert, 120–22. Philadelphia: Institute for the Study of Human Issues, 1977.

Weyl, Nathaniel, and Sylvia Weyl. *The Reconquest of Mexico: The Years of Lázaro Cárdenas*. London: Oxford University Press, 1939.

"What Is NAFTA?" *Wall Street Journal*, 15 September 1993, A17.

"What the President Has Promised So Far." *New York Times*, 17 November 1993.

"Why NAFTA Just Might Squeak Through." *Business Week* (Industrial Edition), 30 August 1993, 36.

"Why NAFTA Will Benefit U.S. Telecommunications Equipment Manufacturers." *Telecommunications* (North American Edition) (February 1993): 17.

Wilkerson, S. Jeffrey K. *National Geographic Research and Exploration*. New York: National Geographic Society, Spring 1994.

Wines, Michael. "A 'Bazaar' Method of Dealing for Votes." *New York Times*, 11 November 1993.

———. "Off Stage, Trade Pact Lobby Had a Star's Dressing Room." *New York Times*, 18 November 1993.

Wisconsin Historical Society. "Exhibits: Frontiers." Madison, Wisconsin, 1991–92.

"Without Borders." *Chemical Marketing Reporter*, 14 June 1993, SR 24.

Women's Wear Daily, 1 September 1993, 23.

Wriston, Walter. *Twilight of Sovereignty*. New York: Macmillan, 1992.

Wyman, Donald L. *Mexico's Economic Crisis: Challenges and Opportunities*. La Jolla, Calif.: University of California at San Diego, Center for U.S.-Mexican Studies, 1983.

Young, Eric Van, ed. *Mexico's Regions: Comparative History and Development*. La Jolla, Calif.: University of California at San Diego, Center for U.S.-Mexican Studies, 1992.

Zane, Refugio Bautista (coordinator). *Los días sin tregua 1876–1970*. Carretera, México: Centuria de Lucha Populares, University Autónoma Chapingo, Dirección de Difusión Cultural, 1991.

Zapatista National Liberation Army. *El despertador mexicano*. Lacandona Jungle, 31 December 1993. Photocopy of Declaration of War.

Index

FRANKLIN PIERCE COLLEGE LIBRARY

00092836

DATE DUE

	NOV 13 '97		
MAR 15 '98			
APR 06 '99			
APR 16 2001			
NOV 02 2004			
GAYLORD			PRINTED IN U.S.A.